REVOLUTIONS IN MEXICAN CATHOLICISM

REVOLUTIONS
IN

MEXICAN CATHOLICISM

REFORM AND REVELATION IN OAXACA, 1887–1934

Edward Wright-Rios

DUKE UNIVERSITY PRESS *Durham & London 2009*

Printed in the United States of America on acid-free paper ∞
Designed by Jennifer Hill
Typeset in Adobe Warnock Pro by Keystone Typesetting, Inc.

Library of Congress Cataloging-in-Publication Data
appear on the last printed page of this book.

Duke University Press gratefully acknowledges the support of Vanderbilt University,
which provided funds towards the production of this book.

Earlier versions of portions of this book appeared in "Envisioning Mexico's Catholic
Resurgence: The Virgin of Solitude and the Talking Christ of Tlacoxcalco, 1908–1924,"
Past and Present 195 (May 2007): 197–239; "A Revolution in Local Catholicism? Oaxaca, 1928–1934," in *Faith and Impiety in Revolutionary Mexico, 1910–1940*, edited by
Matthew Butler, New York: Palgrave Macmillan, 2007; and "Visions of Women: Revelation, Gender, and Catholic Resurgence," in *Religious Culture in Modern Mexico*, edited by Martin Austin Nesvig, Boulder: Rowman and Littlefield, 2007.

FOR GINI, ELITO, AND SARITA

ILLUSTRATIONS

ILLUSTRATIONS

ACKNOWLEDGMENTS

While working on this project, I have counted on a cast of mentors, colleagues, family, friends, and institutions. Much of the research took place while I was at the University of California, San Diego (UCSD), working under the guidance of Eric Van Young. His counsel, support, and countless close readings of papers, articles, and chapter drafts have been invaluable. Now that I teach graduate students and realize how much time and energy this takes, I am doubly grateful. Other scholars at UCSD who generously shared their time and expertise with me were Dain Borges, Michael Monteón, and David Jordan. In addition, I must extend a special thank you to Paul Vanderwood. His books have been a key source of inspiration for this project, and he has been exceptionally kind in sharing his insights on Mexican devotionalism and writing.

Perhaps research at shrines and contact with many devotees of miraculous images has brought me especially good luck, because after leaving UCSD I joined the faculty at Vanderbilt University. I am very grateful for the collegial culture of the Vanderbilt history department and the university's wider circle of scholars. Friends and students from the departments of history, anthropology, Spanish and Portuguese, political science, art, and sociology have kept me on my toes and helped me sharpen my analysis.

This study would not have been possible without generous institutional and financial support. Backing from the UCSD's Department of History, the Center for Iberian and Latin American Studies at UCSD, the Tinker Foundation, and UCSD's Center for U.S.-Mexican Studies supported different stages of this project. The Fulbright Foundation and the University of California Institute for Mexico and the United States (UC-MEXUS) also supported my research in Mexico. In Oaxaca I also enjoyed the support of the Centro de Investigación y Estudios Superiores en Antropología Social (CIESAS). Here at Vanderbilt I must thank the College of Arts and Sciences and the office of the provost for their generous support of this research and the subvention of this publication. Thank you also to Valerie Millholland, Miriam Angress, and Tim Elfenbein at Duke University Press, and to Tracy Ellen Smith of Creative Design Resources for making the maps that accompany this book.

Over the years the input and advice of a large group of *colegas* helped me design the original project, reshape it while immersed in the archives, and rethink it yet again while writing. Among them are the stalwarts of the Oaxaca Summer Seminar: Bill Beezley, Bill French, and Alan Knight. I owe a special debt of gratitude to Daniela Traffano. She was among the leaders of a group of scholars who organized Oaxaca's archdiocesan archive a few years before I began my research. She also very generously shared her understanding of its holdings and put me in contact with the community of Oaxacan scholars who, in turn, offered insights and helped me access other collections. These include Francisco José Ruíz Cervantes, Rosalba Montíel, Carlos Sánchez Silva, Miguel Bartolomé, Alicia Barabas, and Jorge Hernández-Díaz. Berenice Ibarra, who was the secretary (or, should I say, de facto director) of the archdiocesan archive at the time, was very friendly and helpful during the long hours I spent at the little desk looking out on Avenida Independencia. I also would like to acknowledge don Juan I. Bustamante and don Luis Castañeda Guzmán, the long-standing guardians of the Fundación Bustamante Vasconcelos (FBV) and the Fondo Luís Castañeda Guzmán, respectively. These gentlemen allowed me to consult their private collections and took the time to discuss their lives and the state's past with me. I regret that both of them have passed on before I could finish this book. I must also thank Chelito, Nancy, and Frida at the FBV for their help in finding books and such, as well as their unwavering cheerfulness. They kindly allowed

ACKNOWLEDGMENTS

me to drag a table out of the reading room and into the lovely court-yard on many pleasant afternoons. Other fellow scholars who lent a hand at various stages include Alison Lee, Mark Overmyer-Velásquez, Francie Chassen-López, Matthew Butler, and Ben Smith. Ben and his wife, Noemi, even joined me on a road trip/pilgrimage to Juquila, Cuixtla, and Ixpantepec. As we learned, the trek to Nicha's grotto is not for the faint of heart. I would also like to thank William Taylor and Terry Rugeley for their incisive readings of the entire manuscript. Your comments and suggestions have been inestimable.

In Juquila and Ixpantepec I must thank all the individuals that agreed to discuss the region's past with me, although some of them preferred I not publish their names. I am particularly indebted to Felipe Neri Cuevas, who befriended me in front of his souvenir stall next to the shrine and not only entertained me with stories drawn from local history, but also directed me to other individuals whose recollections could be helpful. Justina Vásquez kindly shared her family's history and photographs with me. Aurelio Sánchez Lima, Pablo Cervantes Bolaños, and other members of the brotherhood of the Señor de las Llagas (Lord of the Wounds) in Tlacoxcalco were also very kind in sharing their memories. Mr. Sánchez and his family have been especially friendly and hospitable.

I have also counted on collaborators close to home. In particular, I have benefited from innumerable readings and analytical strategy sessions with my sister and colleague Elizabeth Wright. In addition, my father, Richard N. Wright, gamely agreed to do several rounds of proofreading. Finally my wife, Virginia Pupo-Walker, and my children, Elías and Sara, have been excellent company throughout the process. Best of all, they have been a constant source of joy and helped me keep academic life in perspective.

≋ Moving the Faithful

When Matilde Narváez, a fervent Catholic in the southern Mexican state of Oaxaca, wrote to her prelate on February 8, 1934, she had reached the point of despair:

> I beg you one more time to give me permission to go with the girl that talks to the Sacred Virgin at the Holy Grotto of Ixpantepec to see if we can communicate with his Majesty. I will tell him of our situation. In this region there is sickness, and we are threatened by earthquakes and other calamities; for these reasons I would like to go with the girl that talks to her so that she can tell us what to do. . . . Since I have faith in the Queen of Heaven that has come down there, forgive me for bothering you with this matter. . The calamities are approaching, and what greater grace than if the Divine Mother calms our situation?[1]

Since the late nineteenth century, devout local women had looked to Narváez for leadership, and people throughout her community knew her as the Catholic school principal, a tireless church activist, and the confidant of priests. By the 1930s, however, her reputation, profession, and strong ties to the clergy lay in tatters. Her anguish is palpable in her fretful quest for miraculous help, and it appears magnified in her missive by her tremulous handwriting. When she put pen to paper in February 1934, Narváez, or doña Matildita as she was known, faced strict ecclesiastical sanctions, and considerable local criticism. Under accusations of fomenting doctrinal error and misusing church funds, she found herself banned from taking the sacraments, which—according to Catholic teaching—jeopardized her salvation. Some fellow townspeople wondered if she had been duped by the devil or had simply gone insane. As her plea hints, the clergy had expressly banned consultations with "the girl that talks to the Sacred Virgin." Despite these pressures, Narváez clung to her beliefs. What was going on in doña Matildita's rural Oaxaca amidst sickness, earthquakes, catastrophes, and appearances of the Queen of Heaven?

It is a complicated story, but for the moment it will suffice it to say that Narváez's life spanned a vibrant and at times difficult period for dutiful Mexican Catholics. First, she took part in the church's late-nineteenth-century international resurgence, which was built, in large part, on the public labor and energetic activism of thousands of likeminded women. Second, she lived amidst the ongoing sociopolitical and religious ferment stoked by Mexico's modernization and enflamed by revolutionary anticlericalism in the early twentieth century. Finally, in 1928 Narváez found herself in the thick of a local conflict among Catholics due to alleged Marian apparitions in her parish. The seer, a Chatino Indian[2] girl, possessed an uncanny knack for predicting destructive earthquakes. Furthermore, the visionary's admonitions and troubling recent events appeared to echo legendary prophecies that foretold of religious persecutions, violent unrest, and the Catholic Church's definitive triumph in Mexico thanks to pious female action.

When news of the Virgin's appearance reached doña Matildita, she made a fateful and valiant decision. She not only embraced the girl's visions and prophetic pronouncements as true divine miracles, but she seized a key leadership role in the developing apparition movement. Not long after rushing to observe the seer in action, she emerged as her spokeswoman, writing letters and even traveling for four days on foot to the state capital to present the case to ecclesiastical authorities. Closer to home, she took up the role of docent/teacher for the subsequent crush of pilgrims who yearned to behold the newly proclaimed Virgin of Ixpantepec. Perhaps motivated by a sense that a decisive juncture in the divine plan was at hand, this dedicated foot soldier of Catholic action and trusted partner of priests stepped out from behind her pastor and church to lead in her own right. She hoped to convince the clergy to join her, but they initially responded with reluctance and eventually with a campaign to suppress her crusade. Nevertheless, she remained convinced that the Virgin Mary was reaching out to the faithful in her community.

This book is not just about Matilde Narváez; her struggles, rather, provide an entrée into crucial issues in Mexican history and push us to consider a spectrum of religious historical actors. On the broadest level, this woman's apparitionist gambit encourages us to reexamine our notions of Catholicism's complex and dynamic role in Mexican society, from the level of prelates to the most humble of pilgrims. Her life can teach us a great deal about religious women as intellectuals and leaders in public life, and offers us a rare glimpse into the emergence of a new Catholic devotion. In addition, Narváez leads us to ponder the Chatino Indian visionary's sociocultural milieu and gauge the interactions of indigenous Catholics and the broader church. Furthermore, understanding her predicament necessitates an examination of the village clergy in action. Doña Matildita's pastor—for decades her close ally, but ultimately a bitter opponent—emerged from Oaxaca's reformed seminary amidst the surge of Catholic activism in the 1890s and ministered effectively for nearly forty years in the region's indigenous hinterlands. He provides considerable insight into Mexico's Catholic resurgence, the clergy's approach to the native population, and grassroots efforts to sustain the church amidst social, political, and economic upheaval. Finally, Narváez, and nearly all of the actors discussed in this book, reveal a cross-section of Mexicans deploying their religious beliefs and reworking Catholicism amidst the unique challenges and opportunities of this historical period.

I had come to Oaxaca to examine the rich and accessible collection of the Archivo Histórico de la Arquidiócesis de Oaxaca (AHAO) and gain insights on Catholic activists' efforts, in the late nineteenth and early twentieth century, to implement the church's newly elaborated social mission (frequently referred to as social Catholicism) among the region's parishes. I also expected to glimpse how Oaxacan communities responded to these endeavors and the often-discussed Catholic resurgence of the period. Anticipating that priests and laypersons inspired by revivalist rhetoric would have sought more intimate contact with common Catholics, I envisioned tracking the agents of modern Catholicism into Oaxaca's predominantly indigenous villages. I hoped that the documents generated by these actors would provide detailed evidence about the evolution of religious practices and popular ideologies during a period that witnessed Oaxaca's belated, patchwork implementation of liberal reforms, the expansion of commercial agriculture, the Mexican Revolution, and revolutionary state building.

I was not disappointed, but as is often the case, the motivations and actions of historical actors diverge from what we imagine them to be in preliminary research. As I pondered letters and reports concerning apparitions, shrines, and sacred images, I began to understand that the ground upon which the agents of the resurgent church and ordinary Mexicans met was their common interest in the founding, fueling, and managing devotions. If archdiocesan documents are any guide, outside of Oaxaca City the pet topics of the period's Catholic intellectuals—such as just wages, workers' circles, cross-class Christian harmony, and the shortcomings of liberal capitalist development—inspired minimal local debate. Neither newly minted priests steeped in the era's revivalism and the Catholic analysis of the "social question" nor the region's peasants and townspeople seemed preoccupied with these issues. Instead, in one pueblo after another, and from village priests to the prelate, the dynamics of cooperation and conflict often played out around the marshalling people and resources beneath the banner of sacred figures and their cults. The devotions that sparked the most impassioned activity were those enjoying either long-standing or recently acquired reputations for miraculous intercession. Almost exclusively linked to representations of the Virgin Mary or Christ, the perceived powers of these images stirred individuals from beyond the communities that "cared" for them to journey to their shrines. Thus I abandoned the effort to locate social Catholic firebrands in the field and instead tracked three unique programs/movements from the 1880s to the 1930s, which sought to spiritually and physically move *la feligresía* (the faithful).

From the center of the archdiocese, I examine the policies of Archbishop Eulogio Gillow's pastorate (1887–1922). I focus on his efforts to survey his flock's religious traditions through frequent pastoral visits, correspondence with priests, and an ambitious all-parish questionnaire, as well as his attempts to reform popular religiosity. This energetic prelate targeted practice more than belief. Above all, he sought to change the rhythm, feel, and structure of Oaxacan religiosity, from a primarily community-based festival system to an archdiocesan-centered network of devotional associations that emphasized frequent sacramental observance, devotions closely associated with Rome, and periodic pilgrimage to select images under clerical control. Gillow envisioned a recovery of the church's central role in public life and a generalizing of new European modes of pious expression. In Oaxaca City he facilitated the establishment of institutions associated with social Catholicism—such as the Círculo Católico de Trabajadores (Catholic Workers' Circle), various international lay associations, and a combative Catholic newspaper—but he did not approach the majority of the faithful with the church's new social ideology. Instead, he sought to bind Oaxacans to the church by cultivating the social and emotional bonds that emerged from group spiritual exercises, coordinated pilgrimages, and the cult of miraculous images. The archbishop and his priests adopted a practical approach to their ministry, selecting certain devotional traditions that already functioned with minimal clerical oversight, instead of attempting jarring changes that were sure to face resistance. In essence, they grafted their reform program on to local religious practices that at times clashed with their centralizing goals, hoping that they could simultaneously stimulate and harness the region's pious energies, and ultimately lead local Catholics in directions more to their liking. Gillow chose to raise the coronation of a particular Oaxacan image as the standard of his religious reform campaign.

As Matilde Narváez demonstrates, Oaxaca's clergymen were not the only social actors seeking to mobilize individuals and groups with miraculous devotions. Two powerful, but heretofore unstudied, female-led indigenous apparition movements emerged from opposite fringes of the archdiocese: one during the heyday of Gillow's religious modernization program in 1911, and the other amidst the echoes of his endeavors and the difficult tenure of his successor in the late 1920s. These movements not only attracted scores of devotees and exposed the glaring limitations of the church's efforts to shape popular piety; they also reveal the crucial roles played by religious women and locally inspired devotions in the refashioning of Catholicism in modern Mexico. The first of these movements took shape around the revelations of a Nahua woman who reputedly communicated with an image of Christ in Tlacoxcalco, Puebla (a village which at the time was within the Oaxacan archdiocese). It endures to this day as one of many regional Lenten pilgrimage festivals celebrating various images of Christ. The latter, centered on Narváez's Virgin of Ixpantepec, emerged from Oaxaca's Chatino Indian heartland in the mountains above the Pacific Coast. In both cases, the female leaders and their supporters clashed with the clergy but refused to relinquish their claims to legitimately interpret and lead their respective devotions. Likewise, they insisted that their spiritual experiences constituted authentic miracles worthy of the church's recognition. It is from their writings, priestly correspondence, the commentary of eyewitnesses, and oral history that these events emerge from the shadows of historical inquiry.

This coming together of high churchmen, village priests, and devout lay persons around Oaxacan devotionalism provides the foundations of this regional history of Mexican Catholicism. In a recent symposium addressing the legacy of Catholic social thought in Mexico, José Andrés-Gallego urged scholars to seize the opportunity to "remake the history of Mexican Catholicism itself (as a complex organization and as a way of life), divorcing it once and for all from the fetters that still reduce it to a history of relations between the Church and state."[3] Despite the fact that the analysis presented here has been greatly influenced by works on church-state conflict, it is in this spirit of transition that the present study emerges. This book is also born of the recent turn in Mexican history focusing our attention on the complex historical processes of sociocultural change that incorporated participants from across the social and ethno-cultural spectrum.

The trick to conveying the multifaceted nature of religion in any society is delineating and shifting back and forth between different horizons of abstraction while tracing the articulations between various spheres of action. In this case, the challenge is to bring together the international, national, and provincial arenas of institutional agency and the intimate local settings of religious practice and transformation. Thus, although I break from the previous emphasis on large-scale institutional conflict, I nevertheless keep those struggles in the picture while elucidating the actions and understandings of individuals far from centers of power. The goal is to place events in Oaxacan localities within the context of events in Mexico and the Catholic world where they belong.

Scholars of various disciplines have pondered the history of relations between nation-states and populations, as well as the processes of culture change, conflict, and negotiation that accompany state formation. Insightful studies have schooled us in the way subalterns think, and the way that states "see."[4] This study contemplates a different relationship—the relationship between the Catholic Church and communities of believers. Like a state, ecclesiastical authorities tirelessly voice their dogmas and dictates, but assume a more flexible stance when faced with specific issues in communities. The church, however, concerns itself with the intricate rhythms of religious practice and intimate feelings associated with religious faith and personal devotion. This study, then, ponders this institution's role as a body relentlessly seeking to define cultural meanings, identities, beliefs, and even the cadence of life. It also traces how Catholicism endures in Mexico without centralized funding, with a relatively small number of clerics, and amidst a diversity of indigenous cultures. In a sense, I knit together the worlds of Archbishop Gillow with those of the devotees of Ixpantepec's Virgin and Tlacoxcalco's Christ.

This approach may unsettle some scholars of Mesoamerican native peoples, but the writing of a more comprehensive Mexican cultural history requires the inclusion of postconquest indigenous religious cultures as part of Mexican Catholicism. Clerics may have qualified their Indian parishioners as superstitious, stubborn, and ignorant, but they never denied that they remained Catholic. Indian groups may have challenged ecclesiastical authority and maintained religious beliefs and practices without much concern for their orthodoxy or origins, but they repeatedly proclaimed themselves subjects of "Our Holy Mother Church." The evidence cited here does not support the notion that popular religion in the Archdiocese of Oaxaca exists in a perpetual standoff with the institutional church or flares up as a straightforward expression of protest by marginal groups. Instead, it reveals ongoing processes of interaction and negotiation *within* the church.

Aside from addressing the complex issues of religion in Mexico's cultural history, this book examines events that took place before, during, and after the Mexican Revolution. Undoubtedly, some readers will feel that this important political upheaval receives short shrift. Indeed, this book deliberately implies a gentle revisionism of the "revolutionary period," placing the famous conflict in the background while emphasizing the religious events and ideas that preoccupied the historical actors at the center of this study. Doing so, of course, suggests that the political struggles were not the foremost concern of many Oaxacans or, presumably, other Mexicans. It is nothing new to suggest that that there was no uniform Mexican experience of this period or to question the allegedly transformative nature of the famous conflict. This is not to say that national politics did not impact individual lives in Oaxaca; to the extent that they did, however, they tended to arrive filtered through regional factionalism and local contingency. The objective here is to privilege the concerns and actions of religious actors. I invoke "the revolution" to draw attention to other "revolutions" which, until now, have not inspired significant scholarly attention. This book explores revolutions *in Mexican Catholicism* in the hope that understanding the efforts of indigenous seers, lay organizers, and activist clergymen to infuse their lives with spiritual significance and invigorate Catholicism will allow us to color in some of the grey areas of Mexican experience.

FROM LOURDES TO TLACOXCALCO

The protracted nineteenth century (1789–1914 or even 1770–1930) proved a challenging and transformative period throughout Catholic Europe and Latin America. In many countries, the ascendancy of nationalism, liberal democracy, secularism, and industrial capitalism reshaped societies and social identities and thus shifted the foundations undergirding the church. Peasants moved to cities and other centers of expanding capitalist production and became wage laborers, middle-class populations expanded and gained political clout, and a new entrepreneurial class became fantastically wealthy. Advances in science undermined doctrine, while population growth and the inequities of rapid capitalist development fueled squalor, providing propitious conditions for innovative social ideologies that questioned the value of religious institutions. In some cases they raised the banner of unabashed atheism. The uneven nature of change also produced marked regional disparities; some areas boomed and went through extensive, swift transformation, whereas others experienced marginalization. Naturally, the distribution of power within increasingly centralized nation-states often matched these discrepancies. Amidst these mounting tensions, notions of nationality and class threatened to undo longstanding Catholic identities, lay deference, and devout commitment. Moreover, as secularist governments gained confidence, the church faced emboldened reformers pursuing religious toleration, expropriations of ecclesiastical wealth, and complete church-state separation. By the mid-nineteenth century, the Catholic Church—long the partner of monarchical regimes—found its dogmas doubted, its finances destabilized, and its political flank exposed. The clergy's influence among political and economic elites had steadily eroded, and some feared that even popular groups would abandon the church in the wake of expanding anticlerical social movements.[5]

Predictions of religion's inexorable decline never materialized, but the Catholic priesthood and its supporters experienced the period as a troubling, sinister time. It was not uncommon for clergymen to frame the complex difficulties besetting the church and traditional social structures as a diabolical plot. At times the confrontations between Catholics and anticlerical secularists became violent and deadly. What proved remarkable was the array of strategies that Catholics deployed to sustain their faith and, by the late nineteenth century, regain their footing. These responses included reactionary intransigence, thorough institutional reform, novel engagements of secular culture, and a reemphasis on miraculous experience. In actuality, many individuals and groups employed all of these approaches to some degree. Pope Pius IX's 1864 *Syllabus of Errors* and his declaration of papal infallibility at the First Vatican Council (1869–70) represent the vocal refusal to make any accommodation to sociopolitical and cultural change. The pope based his stance on assertions of the church's divine, incorruptible character, and a strident critique of efforts to alter the celestially ordained social order. However, despite shrill proclamations of inflexibility, these extensive ecclesiastical reforms, new currents of social thought, and a rethinking of the devout individual's role in society amounted to a creative adjustment to the new state of affairs. The church's simultaneous celebration of new apparitions, visionaries, and prophecies was not simply a desperate reactionary ploy. As new social movements engaged popular socioeconomic discontent, the church spoke to abiding notions of divine agency in human affairs and hopeful expectations of miraculous assistance.

Together, these processes, and the concomitant surge in grassroots Catholic action, constituted a fight-fire-with-fire reaction to the challenge of modernity. The extent and breadth of reform was astounding.

Addressing concerns about priestly moral failings and basic competence, Rome pushed to improve clerical education, professionalize the priesthood, rationalize ecclesiastical administration, and instill hierarchical discipline. Responding to fears of apostasy, the Vatican promoted the reorganization of the laity in priest-led, centrally controlled organizations. In the public sphere, the church exploited social tensions engendered by liberal development. Catholic leaders spoke to conservative elites' fears of ascendant socialism and in so doing found new sources of patronage. Among middle sectors and the up-and-coming skilled working class, it raised the banner of Christian social justice and responsibility —or as they called it, "Catholic action"—inspiring a great number of laypersons to dedicate themselves to church-sponsored charities, mutual aid, and education. A whole new array of Catholic schools, religious orders committed to social work, and lay associations emerged to coordinate these efforts. In many ways, they served as a religious counterpoint to evolving networks of modern secular organizations. Furthermore, Catholic intellectuals denounced expanding socioeconomic disparities, entrepreneurial greed, conspicuous consumption, and elite contempt for the poor. Leo XIII enshrined this critique in his famous encyclical *Rerum novarum* (1891), addressing the right of workers to seek fair wages and gain a voice in politics. In addition, the pontiff laid the blame for rising social unrest at the feet of liberal governance and unrestrained capitalism.[6] The church then broadcast this message through a recently created network of Catholic newspapers. Thus the church—through its new focus on social welfare, the establishment of institutions for lay social action, and its opening to popular piety—reached out to groups marginalized by modern development.

According to the historian David Blackbourn, the church's nineteenth-century transformation must be understood as a "thoroughly modern success story."[7] The institutional church became a more efficient, organized body and effectively took up the evolving game of mass politics. Throngs of Catholics took part in shaping a modernized religious culture: they embraced various strains of Catholic nationalism, they responded to new campaigns to market shrines, they filled chartered pilgrimage trains and fueled a booming religious tourism industry, they supplied a surging demand for mass-produced religious images, and they internalized increasingly individualistic notions of pious self-actualization.[8] Catholic

MOVING THE FAITHFUL

activists went to great lengths to coordinate public religious expression, with considerable success. In their great numbers and orderly fervor, the energized laity demonstrated resurgent Catholic sociopolitical power to all observers. Apparition movements in such disparate places as Lourdes and Ixpantepec, however, revealed that Catholicism's modern renovation also enshrined important dissonances—namely, enchantment remained.

CATHOLICISM IN MEXICO

Although Catholics on both sides of the Atlantic faced some similar struggles, we should not overstate the congruence between Western Europe and postcolonial Mexico. Europe has no parallel for the religious complexities that emerged from Mexico's twin legacies of Mesoamerican indigenous civilization and colonial domination. Efforts to describe indigenous beliefs and practices and evaluate missionary methods began with the writings of the sixteenth-century mendicant orders seeking to effect Christian cultural transformation. Since then, generations of scholars have scrutinized these works and scoured archives in hopes of reconstructing the mechanics of evangelization. Three currents of interpretation mark the study of religious change in Mexico: Christian transformation, "pagan" resistance, and syncretism.[9] The first school embraces the claims of missionary chroniclers, who asserted that Mexico's Indians underwent a true religious conversion.[10] The essentially Eurocentric depiction of a successful subjugation of the indigenous soul on the heels of military conquest has invited repeated critique over the years. The antithesis of Christian transformation resides in the pagan resistance school. Rooted in the nationalist indigenista glory days of the 1920s and 1930s, this interpretation holds that Mexico's Indians preserved their core religious traditions while affecting the outward expression of Christianity.[11] A third way alleging syncretism maintains that indigenous responses to Catholic evangelization resulted in a blended religion. Emerging in its classic form in anthropological studies from the late 1950s and early 1960s, this model of religious change proposed that a stable synthesis of religious traditions was achieved by the mid-seventeenth century.[12] Currently, most scholars agree that a combination of beliefs and practices epitomized the colonial period; however, they chafe at syncretism's imprecise application.[13]

Map 1 Mexico, Oaxaca, Ixpantepec, and Tlacoxcalco

Many prefer the concept of "hybridity." The shift in terminology suggests creative, ongoing processes of culture change and mixture resulting in new, internally coherent ideologies rather than a gelled jumble of traits from distinct cultural stockpiles. It is not, however, a congenial phenomenon. Hybridity, its adherents argue, emerges when customs and beliefs are brought together in ways that undermine previous understandings. In a place like colonial Mexico, the practices and objects associated with the European and Mesoamerican cultures took on new meanings in charged colonial contexts. The individuals making their way in these societies altered the signification of various practices, or reworked them altogether, while coping with oppressive conditions. What we perceive as hybrid cultures at a given historical juncture, then, represent uneasy, conditional mixes fraught by the establishment and perpetuation of colonial hegemony.[14] In sum, for proponents of hybridity, mixing does not just happen. Processes of domination and resistance stir the cauldron of mixture and supply the "heat" beneath colonial culture change.

MOVING THE FAITHFUL

Recent literature on religious change often revolves around a matrix-type debate. Scholars generally shun the notion that Christianity replaced preconquest traditions, and they doubt that indigenous religions endured unsullied by European ideas. Still open to debate, however, is the degree to which religious beliefs during various periods, and among particular groups, evince Christian or indigenous ideological formations.[15] A fortuitous outgrowth of this debate has been the careful examination of how indigenous historical actors practiced religion.[16] This trend has given us a sensitive picture of how Mesoamerican native peoples grew to consider themselves Christians, but often preserved independent cultural conceptions of how humans approached the divine.[17]

For most scholars, neither resistance nor conversion accurately describes the gradual process of interaction and transculturation. Incrementally increasing contact between Spanish, mestizo, and indigenous individuals over the intervening centuries served as the motor of transformation. Quite simply, the number of Hispanized individuals in close contact with the Mesoamerican native population probably determined the breadth and depth of culture change. Although there are considerable regional variations, the first few decades after the conquest reveal only slight alterations in indigenous thought and culture, followed by approximately a century of considerable change within enduring indigenous social, cultural, and political structures. From the eighteenth century to the present, the increasing percentage of Spanish speakers relative to monolingual Indians, along with expanding bilingualism, provided the foundations for much more profound changes.[18]

The intertwining of spiritual, economic, and political concerns in colonial administration has allowed historians to craft rich studies of religious culture. To date we have been less successful in our examinations of the same issues in the nineteenth and twentieth centuries, in large part because the period's political conflicts permeated and clouded analysis, although scholars are busily filling the gaps. Mexico's postindependence church-state conflict has dominated two centuries of historical analysis and produced oppositional lines of interpretation maintained by generations of scholars.[19] Asserting that Hispanic Catholicism forms the eternal bulwark of Mexico's cultural and social stability, conservative scholars rejected secularization and liberalism as destabilizing foreign ideologies forced upon the Mexican people. They underscored the importance of maintaining the structures of order and authority inherited from Spain, and interpreted nineteenth-century unrest as the inevitable by-product of their arriviste opponents' foolhardy undermining of the nation's core traditions. Liberal scholars portrayed Catholicism as a colonial holdover retarding Mexico's advancement. The clergy and their conservative allies, they argued, simply sought to perpetuate their privileged colonial status and repeatedly acted with disregard for the nation's welfare. In short, liberal scholars tarred the church as antinational and framed liberalism in terms of eradicating the vestiges of foreign domination.[20] Mexican realities, of course, were much more complex than either side cared to admit.

The kernel of debate resides in Mexico's heritage of corporatism, in which the Spanish crown took pains to control and protect the most influential corporate entity—the Catholic Church. It was an extraordinarily complex enterprise, maintaining infrastructure, naming candidates to religious posts, overseeing educational and charitable institutions, supervising revenue collection, policing priestly discipline, and reviewing internal affairs. Naturally, the state also excluded other religions from the Americas. Of course, the degree of effective control and oversight was at times questionable, but in law and public discourse the crown's authority remained paramount, and the clergy's complete loyalty anticipated. Colonial church-state relations could be quite acrimonious, particularly when eighteenth-century functionaries moved to curtail the wealth and influence of religious orders, and late-colonial penury drove crown administrators to requisition church assets. Despite grumblings, however, few Spaniards or colonial subjects questioned the premise of state patronage.[21]

Independence in 1821, however, opened the door to deliberation, although the presumption of essentially corporatist relations proved remarkably stable. In the early republican period, deliberations centered on whether the new government inherited the crown's authority over the church or political independence freed the church from state control. Those supporting the latter position argued that patronage rights could only be gained by a new papal decree. Most politicians advocated some degree of compromise, but some states, citing federalist principals, asserted patronage rights within their jurisdictions. By refusing to recognize Mexican sovereignty until the late 1830s, the Vatican exacerbated disputes. For the most part, though, Catholicism's stature as the nation's officially established, exclusive religion remained uncontroversial.

Staunchly secular liberalism took root very gradually in Mexico, evolving from moderate Spanish antecedents and drawing on North American and English models.[22] Church wealth proved to be among the most contentious issues. Over time, liberals pushed for limiting the Catholic financial resources, claiming that the extensive land holdings of religious corporations blocked broader property ownership (and by extension democratic values) and thus stifled modern development. They criticized collective asset holding in general, including indigenous village landownership, because it theoretically kept factors of production out of market circulation. Liberals also maintained that church lending practices— religious institutions functioned as the de facto colonial banking sector— served only to sustain bloated clerical institutions and excessive ceremonial pomp. They also complained about high clerical fees, tithing, and what they viewed as the wasteful, disorderly ethos of popular piety. In addition, in the name of universal equality they advocated abolishing corporate legal privileges and reducing the influence of the clergy in general.

Mexican liberalism, however, took shape as a highly heterogeneous movement. Radicals, or "*puros*" (i.e., pure liberals), as they were called, sought to alter society by uprooting colonial social, cultural, and economic traditions. Moderate liberals developed a measured constitutionalist approach, arguing that progressive legislation could bring about the transition to a more modern society over time. Many moderates from the 1820s through the 1840s sought compromise and served in conservative regimes; hence, they became tainted collaborators in the estimation of the *puros*. Mexican liberalism developed popular variants as well. Rooted in the quest for local self-governance, and thus drawn to representative democracy and liberal egalitarianism, some communities and rural areas emerged as key nodes of liberal support. During some of the most intense periods of civil war they became safe havens for liberal armies, and the militias formed in these regions proved indispensable in national struggles. But in general, they fought for municipal-level autonomy and control of local resources. Often, they had little interest in attacking the church. Many popular liberals, needless to say, were observant Catholics.

For some of them, sustaining local religious practice was part of self-government.[23] Toward the end of the nineteenth century, another group would lay claim to the mantle of liberalism with yet another perspective—the capitalist elite. In some ways the mirror image of popular liberals, Mexico's emerging entrepreneurial class embraced notions of free-market modernization and supported a strong, essentially undemocratic, state to maintain order and attract investment. This group ultimately incorporated many conservatives and proved more amenable to the church. Perhaps nothing characterizes the heterodoxy of Mexican liberalism more than the fact that the nation's economic elite of the 1890s began to refer to themselves as "liberal-conservatives."

That stance would have been unthinkable in the 1850s and 1860s. Before mid-century, *puros* provided inflammatory criticism of conservatives and the church, but never held power long enough to implement lasting reform. Over time, however, foreign intervention and incessant uprisings led to increasing polarization. By the 1850s, a new generation of committed radical liberals came to the fore, and the colonial compact, which ensconced the state's right to control, and its duty to protect, the church, disintegrated. Amidst civil war and conservative collusion with French imperialists, the debate devolved into a struggle to exert absolute control over the nation and the church. Issues of patronage fell by the wayside.[24] Liberals now asserted that the church had to be definitively humbled, lest it continue to compromise national sovereignty and bankroll conservative insurrection.

Reformers took their first strong steps following the Ayutla Revolt (1854–55). Over the next few years, the new liberal government passed a series of laws collectively known as the "reform laws" and promulgated the 1857 constitution. In concert they abolished corporate legal privileges and decreed the forced sale of all ecclesiastical properties (although the church was allowed to keep the proceeds). Although the new constitution mentioned religious tolerance, it also made vague statements about the protected status of Catholicism. Still leaning on colonial precedent, however, it stipulated that the federal government enjoyed oversight in matters of religious practice and clerical discipline, in addition to the right to make church appointments. Thus although the document fell short of complete radical reform, it made it abundantly clear that the state demanded supremacy over the church. The clergy, and many Mexicans, however, found it too extreme, and The War of the Reform (1858–61) ensued. Amidst the brutal rancor of hostilities, liberal leaders turned to more radical measures. First they decreed the outright expropriation of all church property, a ban on future property transfers to ecclesiastical institutions, and the suppression of male religious orders. Subsequently they declared marriage a strictly civil contract and assumed responsibility for the official registry of births, marriages, and deaths. New regulations also reduced the number of religious holidays, barred civil authorities from taking part in religious ceremonies, and sanctioned priests for wearing clerical garb in public. Ultimately, legislation prohibited public religious services without special civil dispensation and suppressed female religious orders.

Liberals emerged victorious, but the conflict proved especially destructive and set the stage for foreign invasion. Mexico's resultant poverty and suspension of loan payments provided Napoleon III a pretext for invading and setting up a puppet monarchy. Tragically, imperialism gave civil war new life, but by 1867 the liberals had gained definitive victory. Not surprisingly, liberal triumph gave birth to a historiography. A few decades afterward, liberal historian Justo Sierra christened the Reform the "second emancipation": the first, La Independencia, achieved national sovereignty, while La Reforma, he declared, belatedly established Mexico's cultural autonomy.[25] Liberalism's leading figures and its laws also conquered the pantheon of Mexican nationalism, and for a century historical analysis often seemed a prisoner of liberal patriotism.

It was not until the 1960s and 1970s that social historians brought forth a more objective interpretation of the Catholic Church and the liberal-conservative conflict.[26] They revealed that the church had not been as wealthy as liberals claimed, and generally managed its assets well while providing easy credit. In addition, the chaotic privatization of church properties failed to improve state finances significantly or produce a nation of small property holders. Liberal and conservative armies consumed the lion's share of ecclesiastical wealth, while speculators were the chief beneficiaries of expropriation. Furthermore, the cycles of implementation, repeal, and reimplementation of anticlerical reform that accompanied back-and-forth regime changes caused decades of legal chaos with respect to property rights. This scholarship also shows that radical liberals proved doctrinaire and impractical. In essence, they dismantled colonial intuitions without considering the impact on society. Their critique of the church's role in the economy assumed the emergence of an alternative modern financial system, yet the foundations for this simply did not exist. They also suppressed religious charities, orphanages, and hospitals without contemplating their replacement. In sum, liberal reform achieved state supremacy over the church, but the nation was arguably more battered than bettered.

It is one thing to write laws, and it is an entirely different proposition to alter societies' long-established rhythms and lifeways. To the outsider it still appears bewildering: deeply Catholic Mexico adopted a secularist magna carta. Smoothing over the disjuncture between the modern nation on paper and traditional forms of authority proved to be the central genius of Porfirio Díaz after he seized power in 1876. Díaz dominated the nation for twenty-five years, manipulating politics from atop a pyramid of regional strongmen and a new class of entrepreneurs. The system worked for two main reasons: first, sustained international economic expansion resulting in abundant foreign credit buoyed the regime; second, Díaz allowed elites to run their respective regions as long as they maintained stability, embraced the regime's export-driven development model, and expressed an unequivocal allegiance to Díaz. Compliance with the constitution was of lesser importance. Likewise, the president made an unofficial pact with the church hierarchy. Essentially, Díaz and key prelates fashioned a church-state modus vivendi. Church leaders quietly supported the president and refrained from criticizing the government or openly engaging in politics. In turn, the administration largely ignored federal-level enforcement of the constitution's anticlerical provisions. The laws remained on the books, but by and large Díaz granted Catholics enough space to restore church finances and institutional foundations, and gradually reassert themselves in public discourse.[27]

This overview of church-state relations in nineteenth-century Mexico has thus far remained at the level of national politics, but scholars rarely tire of stressing the idiosyncratic regional experience of the nation's past. This is especially true in church-related issues, since each ecclesiastical province negotiated their relations with a variety of state-level institutions and officials. In addition, as Oaxacan evidence demonstrates, each village clergymen had to engage in local micro-diplomacy, and priest-parishioner interaction represents the locus of most individuals' interface with *la Iglesia.* Nonetheless, President Díaz, a native of Oaxaca, paid close attention to his home state, and Archbishop Eulogio Gillow emerged as one of his important prelate collaborators. The president and key prelates modeled the stand-down in tensions, rather than codifying it. Doctrinaire liberals fumed, but in many states such as Oaxaca, extreme anticlerical-ism and measures to dampen public religiosity enjoyed only limited support. Rapprochement at the top signaled to locals that they could overlook certain statutes. The arrangements varied. In some communities, public school teachers still taught Catholic doctrine in league with the priests, and public officials openly took part in religious events. In others, officials enforced laws limiting public piety. The restrictions on religious expression often occasioned intense acrimony. For many Mexicans, celebrating feasts like Holy Week without public ceremonies, such as re-enactments of the Passion, proved unacceptable. In localities where officials deemed these traditions a threat to their authority, many Catholics preferred to suffer sanctions, usually fines, rather than desist. Again, the key was often the exercise of tact and flexibility among priests, prominent Catholics, and civil authorities. Good personal relationships between these figures often smoothed tensions in many communities. By the end of the Porfirian period, nevertheless, large public religious festivals had become quite common again in many cities and towns.[28] This was clearly the case for Oaxaca City and villages like Tlacoxcalco and Ixpantepec.

The Mexican Revolution, particularly after 1915, brought a rekindling of church-state hostility. The insecure revolutionary state, which proclaimed its ties to radical liberalism, bristled at the church's perceived disrespect for civil authority. It did not help that members of the high clergy collaborated with the counterrevolutionary Huerta regime in 1913 and 1914. Inspired by its 1857 predecessor, the 1917 constitution's framers reaffirmed reform-era prohibitions and infused the new charter with a still-more punitive spirit. New provisions gave civil authorities the right to determine the number of clergymen working in their jurisdiction, stipulated that all priests be Mexican and abstain from political speech (public or private), and declared the political disenfranchisement of all clerics. Furthermore, the new constitution deprived the church of a distinct juridical identity, and therefore it had no official standing from which to lodge appeals or contest acts of enforcement and unofficial harassment.[29]

Needless to say, the 1917 constitution angered Catholics, but again regional and local arrangements varied considerably. Neither the Carranza administration (1917–20) nor the Obregón government (1920–24), emphasized strict enforcement of the contentious provisions. Where revolutionary governors sought to implement laws fully, tensions mounted and Catholics complained of persecution. In some states, like Jalisco, well-organized Catholics employed protest tactics to force officials to back down.[30] In the mid-1920s, however, President Plutarco Elías Calles (1924–28) moved to fully enforce the constitution's anticlerical provisions, and sparked a full-blown peasant rebellion in the nation's center-west. Oaxaca, as we will see, never experienced this level of hostilities, but local Catholics worked to dull the impact of the offending laws. The religious overtones of the conflict gave unrest its intense rancor, but more was at stake. Calles's offensive against the church coincided with the revolutionary government's energetic effort to create a rural political clientele and thus extend its effective reach in regions distant from the capital, through state-directed agrarian and educational transformation.[31]

Essentially, the president pressed a bundle of aggressive top-down reforms that simultaneously threatened to erode local power arrangements and cultural traditions in certain regions. This struck many Mexicans as an outrageous imposition of state power. For his part, Calles judged the population backward and fanatically superstitious, and expressed a determination to root out these ills and the institutions that harbored them. In protest, the church suspended public religious worship throughout the nation on July 31, 1926, but avoided endorsing the incipient rebellion. The government, deploying federal troops and local auxiliaries, launched a fierce military campaign against insurgent communities. The peasant rebels achieved a stalemate of sorts, controlling some remote areas but never seriously destabilizing the revolutionary state. The Cristero Revolt, as it became known, festered until 1929, when the ecclesiastical hierarchy agreed to lift the suspension of religious services, and the government relented on the enforcement of the most offensive laws. In many locales, however, an unofficial dirty war endured, and a second wave of risings erupted briefly in the mid-1930s. It was not until the 1940s, when President Manuel Ávila Camacho signaled his determination to abandon state anticlericalism, that the conflict over Catholicism in public life began to lose intensity.

MOVING THE FAITHFUL

For the last decade or so, religious culture in Mexico has increasingly drawn scholarly attention. We have long assumed the great influence of the church during the colonial period, but recent scholarship has opened our eyes to the complexity of priest-parishioner relations and popular religious ideologies as well. For the postindependence period, efforts to explain the Cristero Revolt represent the field's most significant attempt to plumb these issues. Scholars describe a web of factors in this revolt, including internal ecclesiastical and revolutionary politics, urban Catholic mobilization, rural religiosity, regional power struggles, variable experiences of state formation, preexisting agrarian structure, and the expansion of capitalism.[32] Other episodes of popular rebellion have also inspired important reexaminations of religion's role in Mexican history, particularly in the Wars of Independence (1810–21) and the Tomochic Rebellion (1891–92).[33] Several recent books explore the diverse impact of Catholic discourse and important religious figures throughout the nineteenth and twentieth centuries.[34] In addition, historians have shed considerable light on the intellectuals and prelates who shaped the Mexican interpretation of social Catholicism and Catholic political resurgence.[35] These studies chronicle the mostly urban and elite struggle to reestablish a Catholic social and political voice, and to fashion a coherent mission tailored to Mexico's modernizing, postcolonial society. Still, how nonelite communities of believers navigated the era's challenges and opportunities remains poorly understood, particularly in the case of the nation's native peoples.[36]

The religious culture of indigenous Mexicans has long been the domain of anthropological scholarship. In a way, Mesoamerica became a mid-twentieth century case study for scholars interested in peasantries and "folk" societies.[37] Ethnographers debated the nature of indigenous social organization at length. The field, however, is still getting over its tendency to suppress cultural diversity in pursuit of broad explanatory models.[38] Of late, scholars have critiqued previous oversimplifications of the relationship between culture and social structure and the exaggeration of indigenous isolation and communal cohesion. Instead, they emphasize various levels of economic and sociocultural openness, as well as much more complex relationships between kin groups, households, and the community at large. They also underscore complex histories of internal social differentiation.[39]

In these debates, the role of religion within the Mesoamerican indigenous community held a distinct prominence. For the most part, early studies focus on the function of civil-religious institutions (the *cargo* system), or explore cosmology and belief systems. For obvious reasons, both approaches are important here. Forging religious collectivities and organizing public ritual was a key arena of action among Oaxaca's reformist clergy and indigenous laity. Among the things that shaped the divergent fates of the apparition movements in Ixpantepec and Tlacoxcalco was the former's failure to institutionalize their devotion, and the latter's fashioning of a novel brotherhood that carved out a niche amidst older devotional sodalities. The *cargo* system in its classic conception is two ladders of ranked civil and religious offices/obligations (i.e. *cargos*). Civil *cargos* include positions like municipal president or constable; religious *cargos* are usually called *mayordomías*, due to the steward-like *mayordomo* role of individuals in charge of specific devotions and their feasts. Young men begin their public lives serving in the low-level posts and over time assume more important positions. Officeholding is unpaid, and individuals meet all the expenses of their post. Some men move through the entire hierarchy of offices and achieve the status of elder.[40] On the surface, the *cargo* system's functions appear clear—individuals take turns organizing religious practice and administering communal affairs. In addition, it bolsters an age-graded, patriarchal social order. Scholars have debated whether it serves primarily to redistribute wealth and limit internal conflict, legitimate preexisting status differences, leach community assets, or sustain an ethos of reciprocity through nonmarket exchange.[41]

These issues continue to reverberate in the field, but changing conceptual standards have sidelined them. First, the rejection of functionalist treatments of religion has made the debate sound off-key. Second, historians have shown that earlier works erred in assuming that the system represented a colonial adaptation sustained by present-day communities without taking into account the dynamic nature of devotional institutions. Finally, the *cargo* system's importance has diminished as indigenous groups have become more integrated into regional and national society.[42] The current consensus is that the development of ladder-like, rotational structures and individual funding responsibilities emerged as a response to nineteenth-century reforms threatening collective assets and the coordination of religious ritual. As a result, scholars now view indigenous institutions as much more responsive to prevailing conditions. Indeed, Oaxacan evidence indicates that many communities' religious collectivities were in a state of creative flux, and that individual agency in specific localities proved crucial. Villages sometimes formed new sodalities, abandoned traditions, and appropriated new devotions emerging from Europe. At times they even rearranged hierarchies of devotional collectivities.[43]

Since our understanding of indigenous culture has been tied to our attempts to characterize social organization, it follows that as models of the Mesoamerican community proved unsatisfactory, we have modified our approach to religion. The field evolved from the emphasis on identifiable behaviors and beliefs within specific groups, to Marxist-inspired critical theory emphasizing relationships of production and power inequalities. More recently researchers analyze Mesoamerican social organization in terms of cultural constructions with primarily symbolic boundaries and characteristics.[44] One of the more enlightening currents in Oaxacan ethnography stresses how people create and maintain relationships in order to accomplish goals; this analytical approach frames these processes as an outgrowth of communal engagement with the divine.[45] In essence, social actors within communities often understand the marshalling of resources and human energies as products of interactions with supernatural forces.[46] In some cases, ritual and religious innovation serve as means to manage tensions between more-egalitarian notions of communal identity and reciprocity on one level, and individualism and more-capitalist mores at the other. Among some groups apparitions are quite common, and individuals openly discuss them in utilitarian terms. Revelation, therefore, can be a resource for initiating change, creating contexts of collective endeavor, and reshaping identities to meet perceived needs. In social groups that embrace instrumental notions of the miraculous, the entire dynamic is part of a longstanding, yet fluid, covenantal relationship between human society and the sacred.[47]

VISIONS OF MODERN CATHOLICISM

This study pivots on the conviction that indigenous apparition movements and reformism among the Oaxacan clergy represent engagements of modernity amidst Catholicism's nineteenth- and early-twentieth-century transformation. Drawing on the scholarship of sociologist Jorge Larraín and literary scholar Carlos Alonso, I view these movements as part of broader Latin American processes that more or less metabolized the modern, incorporating some aspects of reigning European and North American models while keeping others at bay.[48] When we think of modernity we invariably focus on the touchstones of Enlightenment philosophy: reason, science, freedom, and progress. Furthermore, we stress the opposition of these tenets to religion, miraculous thinking, and traditional forms of authority. At issue is the notion of the individual as an autonomous economic, intellectual, ethical, and political actor. Although these ideas and the associated discursive culture emerged from Europe, modernity's globalizing tendencies have led to its adaptation to different social realities and thus produced various configurations/trajectories in diverse societies. In other words, modernity meant different things in different places and times, while sharing certain commonalities. Some scholars, particularly those exploring these issues in postcolonial settings, argue that these disparities represent the construction of distinct "alternative modernities."[49] Larraín's contention, however, that various routes to modernity emerged remains more convincing. In essence, Latin Americans developed specific ways of being modern, although they were never completely disconnected from standard notions of modernity. They forged these conceptions with a keen, even obsessive, awareness of the incongruities between Latin American realities and metropolitan models.

In Mexico, the social and cultural tensions coinciding with the Bourbon reforms of the eighteenth century served as the calling card of emergent modernity. Key among these was the rationalizing of political administration, the expansion of wage-based capitalist production, and the greater integration in North Atlantic markets. These developments caused significant tensions, but it was the sociocultural trends that proved particularly controversial, such as Bourbon efforts to discipline popular culture.[50] Perhaps even more significant for the present study was the role of Bourbon-era reformers who sought to dampen the effusive public piety characteristic of baroque religiosity and replace it with an austere, orderly, personal religiosity emphasizing the individual's relationship with God. This intellectual and spiritual movement, and its application in efforts to alter long-standing cultural practices, paved the way for the advent of

Mexican liberalism and modern notions of citizenship, despite considerable resistance and limited success at the time.[51]

Most Mexicans began to feel the presence of modernity, in a broader sense, during the nineteenth century. Here I am referring to the array of modern modes of social life and organization that first emerged in Europe and, as they spread, imbued the period with a sense of an ever-quickening pace of change toward a new way of being. They include nationalism, mass political participation, secularization, public education, urbanization, bureaucratization, and notions of the interior psychological self. The complex sociopolitical reverberations of these trends were very much in evidence in Oaxaca's state capital and rural indigenous villages. This does not mean that a standard recipe for modern politics arrived in southern Mexico and needed only to be "served up." Oaxacans shaped the local meanings and functions of new modes of organization, participation, rights-based discourses, and political identity formation. Thus, they sketched the outlines and experiences of this transformation.[52]

Documenting these processes in the historical arena of politics proves more straightforward than charting their evolution in daily life. This is due to the fact that the discourse of modernity as expressed in the projects and yearnings of modernizing agents tends to outpace its realization in social practice. Would-be modernizers, often liberal elites, balked at the loosening of social controls that modernity implies: hence their continuing efforts to restrict the rights of women, workers, and nonwhite groups. Indeed, throughout nineteenth-century Latin America, dominant political actors embraced certain political and economic liberalizations while blocking efforts to transform the colonial social order. Clientalism and authoritarianism remained hallmarks of political and social interactions. The final decades of the nineteenth century and the early twentieth century, however, brought crisis to the region's essentially oligarchic modernity, as export-led development failed to broadly distribute the gains of economic growth and popular groups began to agitate for a voice in governance and society.[53] In the parlance of the time, Latin America's modernity appeared flawed, in light of the "social question," and the Catholic Church emerged as a key voice questioning economic development.

Too often scholars characterize Mexican Catholic movements, popular and otherwise, as antimodern. This is due to the history of church-state conflict, a general identification of religious belief and practice as "traditional," and an acceptance of oversimplified linkages of modernity and secularization. As Latin America's sociopolitical history demonstrates, modernizing elites did not assimilate modernity without reservations or modifications. Religious social actors were no different. Despite their reluctance to embrace the irreverent, human-centered challenge that modernity posed to theocratic conceptions of society, they made their way in cultures where other aspects of modernity increasingly shaped identities. For example, Mexican Catholics had to take up nationalism, and the notions of modernization and advancement imbedded in it, in order to be taken seriously in the public sphere. Catholic nationalism, of course, was distinct from its liberal counterpart. Its spokespersons deployed different constructions of tradition and history to ground visions of an idealized Christian nation, but the notions of order, progress, and plenty bandied about by Catholic thinkers echoed their secular rivals.[54] In short, there was simply no escape from modernity; however, people could, and did, mold local experiences to a considerable degree.

In this regard, the term *engagement* is particularly apt since it allows for the complexities of accommodation, ambivalence, and even outright rejection. Indeed, among the more interesting aspects of the movements analyzed here are the unique ways in which they reveal amalgamations of the old and the new: intransigence and innovation, as well as rejection and appropriation. Ixpantepec's new Virgin and Tlacoxcalco's talking Christ embody more than backward-looking mobilizations propelled by periods of collective anomie. They were like homemade *moles* of meanings and actions: native flavors, colonial condiments, local innovations, and the zest of newly appropriated ideas commingled in a sauce of sociopolitical and religious concerns occasionally piquant with millenarian anticipation. This may appear a mismatch of ingredients to outsiders, but among many people at the time it proved quite palatable. In addition, although never expressly articulated, the apparition movements implied a democratization of the Catholic miraculous and the expansion of female agency in the public sphere and religious leadership.

In essence, then, modernity served as something of a pantry of ideas and organizational modes ready for recombination and adaptation to preexisting, less-than-modern customs and social mores. Carlos Alonso's analysis of Spanish American cultural discourse has been particularly influential in fashioning this approach.[55] Alonso's focus, however, is the fundamental rhetorical ambivalence toward modernity embedded in Spanish American literature of the nineteenth and twentieth centuries. He argues that authors labored to master the codes of modernity, in part, out of a sincere desire to become truly modern and avail themselves of the discursive authority they imparted at the time. But they also developed strategies for deviating from European norms and protecting what they identified as authentically Latin American. Thus the intertwined dedication to modernity and its disavowal embedded in Spanish American writing, Alonso argues, is an integral facet of the region's postcolonial nation building rather than an indication of ignorance or incoherence. Oaxacan Catholics' approach-avoidance attitudes toward modernity were not identical to that of contemporary authors, but to a degree they echo these efforts to appropriate aspects of modernity while rejecting its wholesale application. Like Latin American writers, they sought to communicate in a world where modern discourse, organizational modes, and notions of progress were increasingly the norm, but they lived in societies where these clashed with observable reality.

MIRACLES AND MOVEMENTS

Among the most fertile areas of scholarly research related to the present study are efforts to understand historical episodes of religion-fueled political unrest and Catholic apparitionism in the nineteenth and twentieth centuries. In the former, we are still emerging from the debates centered on conceptions of religious rebellion and millenarianism as "primitive politics" (i.e., the idea that religious belief serves as a proxy for full political consciousness in preindustrial social movements) and opposing contentions that acute cultural crises generate anomie and openness to charismatic figures promising miraculous restorations of order and meaning.[56] Naturally, scholars of Mexico have taken part in these discussions when analyzing historical uprisings among indigenous groups.[57]

Both schools remained rooted in the Marxist linkage of ideology and social conditions, and the historiographical tradition chronicling the destructive impact of capitalism in "traditional" societies. More recently, scholars emphasize the crafting of syncretic ideologies of resistance in popular religious movements.[58] The enduring focus on politics and social conditions has invited critique. According to James Holston, scholars too often reduce innovative doctrine, practice, and social modes to function —a psycho-social reaction caused by marginalization at the periphery of modern society.[59] He suggests instead that religious social movements often forge novel ideological structures and devise new ritual cultures that provide them with a sense of mastery over surrounding ideas and social mores. These movements are not necessarily trying to subvert political hierarchies or contest believers' position within the prevailing social order, but rather fashioning their own systems of meaning and merit. Holston sees them as innovative strategies through which groups create discourses, institutions, hierarchies, and specialized knowledge of their own. In the case of the nineteenth- and twentieth-century religious movements he is addressing, Holston suggests they represent alternative modernities. They may have broader social implications, but subversive syncretism and resistance is not the point. Thus Holston underscores the importance of religious engagements with modern discourse and downplays the importance of socioeconomic structures and political events. In essence, he argues that new religious cultures emerge on their own in multiple contexts. Political and social crises are common in most societies and thus are often part of the milieu surrounding religious movements. In fact, scholars tend to overlook movements that emerge in less conspicuously conflictive environments. Therefore, Holston argues that we must guard against the over reliance on economic and political explanations of religious unrest. Social context, nonetheless, is still important. The issue is resonance: prevailing conditions do not necessarily inspire new religions, but they influence the construction of meanings ascribed to events and experiences, and thus sometimes impact popular acceptance of new religious ideas.

It is important to question assumptions of resistance, to preserve the close attention to social environment, and at the same time to rescue religious social movements from notions that they are somehow aberrant. Recent scholarship takes us in this direction, emphasizing the commonplace nature of millenarian ideologies and miraculous thinking. Viewing millenarians as prepolitical rational actors obscures the crucial differences between preparing for the Kingdom of Christ and postrevolutionary state building. Likewise, studies alleging that cultural collapse sparks the emergence of innovative religions assume a link between new beliefs and practices, mental clarity, and cultural coherence. To avoid these pitfalls, it is paramount to scrutinize the local articulation of the ordinary and the extraordinary aspects of religious thinking.[60] In religious social environments there is nothing odd about belief in salvation, miraculous transformation, or supernatural beings. It is also common that political and sacred ideologies remain intricately intertwined. Among believers, there is often little distinction between "expressive" actions, like baptisms, and "instrumental" political actions.[61] The point is that in many religious cultures—particularly those steeped in Christianity—millenarianism and its antecedents, such as calls for regeneration, remain embedded at the deepest levels of religious belief systems, textual traditions, and popular lore. In these environments, believers often deploy these ideas with or without crisis or external threat. Recent historical works on popular ideology and religious movements in Mexico point to the permeation of latent millenarianism in many communities.[62]

Religious movements can incorporate hegemonic, mediating, and resistant ideologies simultaneously, and thus assume an ambiguous stance with respect to the prevailing social order.[63] Jamaican Pentecostalism, for example, reveals that new ideas and transnational institutions can address historical issues and inequalities in a postcolonial cultural milieu, challenging prevailing social mores without framing a program of sociopolitical transformation. In this case, religious innovation allows believers who have suffered socioeconomic, gender, and racial discrimination to undercut prevailing stereotypes; however, the term *resistance* fails to accurately describe the process. The issue is tracking the negotiation of meanings and values without reducing belief to interest-group affiliation or characterizing religious practice as a straightforward political act.[64] Understanding this is also crucial in the context of apparitionism in Mexico, where interactions of race, social status, gender, and religious innovation can lead to social postures that in some ways appear revolutionary and in others seem quite reactionary.

The attention to the agency of individuals contemplating their ideological options represents one of most compelling aspects of these approaches. Recent work on Catholic apparitionism shares this focus in its effort to trace the connections between individual seers, communities, local institutions and officials, and regional and national issues. According to William Christian, the power of apparitions in the Catholic tradition emerges from two sources. For the individual, it emanates from yearnings to establish contact with the divine in hopes of resolving uncertainties about deceased loved ones, personal transgressions, priestly mediation, and the community or larger society as a moral entity. Addressing these anxieties has shaped church history, and its vitality depends upon creating a sense of vigorous hope through the periodic emergence of new holy places and persons. For example, the church's foundational corporations (orders, brotherhoods, and so on) typically represent their mission through the life histories of individuals touched by God in order to inspire lay enthusiasm and commitment. As a result, miraculous expectation pervades church teachings and popular Catholic ideology. This dynamic, however, is fraught with tension. The clergy claims that seers must pass its exclusive judgment of inherent sanctity. In addition, by monopolizing documentation and dominating miracle-lore dissemination, the church domesticates miracle-inspired fervor. But gate-keeping breeds conflict when it censors believers who feel that divine grace is momentarily within reach.[65]

Catholic apparitionism remains tied to the practice of pilgrimage and shrine making. Visions invariably mark a location that is henceforth assumed to merit ritual visitation. In their classic study of Catholic image-centered devotion and peregrination, Victor and Edith Turner defined four types of pilgrimage devotions: *prototypical*, traditions centered on a founding figure or saint; *archaic*, devotions associated with earlier religions; *medieval*, pilgrimages rooted in European apparitions after the loss of the Holy Lands; and *modern*, newer devotions shaped by the church's nineteenth- and twentieth-century reaction to secularization and characterized by their strong female character, the use of technology and mass media, and antimodern rhetoric.[66] The pilgrimages emerging from the visionary experiences of Mexican women chronicled here seem to resist categorization, since they draw on more than one of these traditions. But keeping in mind Latin America's ambivalent approach to modernity, we can say they belong amongst the pilgrimage traditions deemed "modern" by the Turners.

A new spirit of church reform and emotional devotionalism developed alongside the modern idiom of apparitionism and pilgrimage. In this regard, the Archdiocese of Oaxaca sought to follow the European Catholic reform movement toward centralization (increased clerical control of the laity and enhanced episcopal power over the clergy) and initiatives designed to stimulate and discipline popular devotion. The effort to reform religious practice developed as a two-part program drawing directly on European developments. First, the archdiocese stressed more regular personal sacramental practice: monthly, weekly, or daily Mass attendance and frequent confession and communion. This had not been the norm in the past, when collective observance of the main liturgical feasts and confession and communion once a year, usually during Lent, sufficed. Second, clergymen sought to expand emotionally engaging devotions that had proven successful in Europe, particularly the Sacred Heart of Jesus and quasi-martial advocations of Mary Immaculate. In theory, these devotions bolstered the emphasis on regular personal practice, but added the crucial elements of heightened collective public display (usually coordinated pilgrimages and processions) and combative politics. The former centered on notions of the emotional and moral person of Christ, his boundless love of humankind, and his acute personal suffering caused by society's iniquities. Images of the savior's blazing, sword-impaled heart helped dramatize Christ's anguish and engage the laity emotionally. The church encouraged devotees to ponder the gulf between Christ's perfect heart and humanity's moral failures, and frequently take the sacraments together. During the late nineteenth and early twentieth centuries, the church, in coordination with various conservative governments, staged elaborate consecrations of regions and entire nations to the Sacred Heart.

The new Marianism emerged from a surge of European apparitions, most famously La Salette (1846), Lourdes (1858), and Fatima (1917). It had essentially two facets: one was the Immaculate Mother of Christ imploring humanity to repent; the other depicted Mary as God's field marshal leading the battle against modern error. She traversed the boundary separating the divine and mundane to bring miraculous aid to the stubbornly devout who were willing to stand against the irreligious tide of the times. The famous official apparitions became models for subsequent visionaries and Catholics everywhere seeking to fuel popular participation and garner support for the church's sociopolitical positions. In sum, reeling from the erosion of its role in public life, the church in Europe retargeted its message toward abiding popular sensibilities.[67] This strategy served the church well, but it was not without risks. Rome and national ecclesiastical hierarchies opened the door of official recognition to popular revelation, but they struggled to control groups seeking entry. A few apparition movements and seers gained canonical approval and fame, but they inspired an explosion of unapproved apparitions, dubious seers, freelance commercialization, and uninhibited miraculous faith. These trends often embarrassed clergymen seeking orderly, coordinated fervor. They also inspired secular derision and accusations of priestly manipulation. Theologically, the church considers visions to be a grace bestowed upon the seer to fuel the faith without altering doctrine, but they had to meet ecclesiastical criteria for validity in the entire church. According to Victor and Edith Turner, "Where there is too great a disparity—bordering on the grotesque, ridiculous, or improbable—between the alleged vision and the deposit of the faith, the Church . . . rejects the vision as not of God, and nips the devotion in the bud."[68] This issue of clerically determined universal legitimacy marks the history of indigenous apparitions in the Archdiocese of Oaxaca. But gardening is never simple in what churchmen have long conceived as the vineyard of the faithful. "Nipping devotion in the bud" is rarely as easy as it sounds.

In both Catholic Europe and Mexico, church-state tensions in the nineteenth and twentieth centuries formed the backdrop of the period's visionary movements. Previously, scholars tended to depict the apparitions as part of a large-scale conflict pitting advancing modernization against desperate rear-guard action. Recently, historians have developed more complex portraits of states and the Catholic Church, revealing internal heterogeneity, regional variations, and intricate relationships with other sectors of society.[69] Researchers now emphasize the social circles surrounding seers, situating visionary narratives in village life and charting their articulation with regional and national issues. Usually the groups who sparked these devotional movements enjoyed considerable autonomy. In other words, church hierarchies and conservative sectors of society often deployed the new apparitionist culture without really controlling its genesis or interpretation among the populace.[70] Scholars agree that the broad surge in apparition movements during the period bore the marks of popular discontent within modern society. At the same time, however, such movements—while freighted with notions of a just Christian society in an idealized past—provided individuals with ways to adjust to social change instead of shutting it out.

Allowing that many apparitions never made an impression in the his-

MOVING THE FAITHFUL

torical record, the episodes of Marian visionary fervor that generated mass followings in nations like France, Germany, and Spain shared core characteristics. The mid-nineteenth century French visions, particularly Lourdes, established the template from which the others evolved. In fact, apparition movements commonly deploy their own interpretations of previous visionary episodes.[71] The new breed of seer tended to emerge from groups that perceived their way of life, socioeconomic and religious, under attack. Modern means of communication and transportation often strengthened movements, allowing them to bridge the social world of visionaries and larger spheres of identity. The new apparition idiom also expanded upon the medieval visionary repertoire. Frequently invoking Christ's determination to punish impious modern society, seers claimed that the Virgin Mary appeared because she could no longer restrain her son in the absence of broad repentance. According to Thomas Kselman, the famous French visions placed current events in an eschatological framework and thus framed popular conceptions of sociopolitical trans-formations in religious symbolism. As such, notions of France's past re-ligious and imperial glory, along with waves of miracles and prophecies accompanying political crises, gave rise to a quasimillenarian nationalism among French Catholics. The intense episodes of church-state conflict and harsh antireligious state actions, such as Germany's *Kulturekampf* in the 1870s, often bolstered belief in visionary events.[72] Among the devout, revelations, no matter how derivative, seemed timely—the Virgin came down to earth to defend her church from attack and reconquer the "na-tional soul" imperiled by expanding indifference and apostasy.

The feminization of the Catholic Church and religious practice during the eighteenth and nineteenth centuries, moreover, also characterized the apparition movements of this period. As the "Age of Revolution" weakened national church hierarchies, Rome's ability to influence doc-trine and practice expanded. The papacy increasingly promoted more emotional forms of piety. Pius IX fueled this process with his declaration of the dogma of the Immaculate Conception in 1854 and his emphasis on militant Marianism. In the late nineteenth century, this pope's ecclesiasti-cal appointees sustained the climate of superheated Marian piety, main-tained the more open posture toward popular revelation, and integrated the newly combative cult of Mary into the liturgy. This coincided with nineteenth-century conceptions of religion as an increasingly female social sphere. Militant devotion often centered on the manipulation of visual imagery, the contemplation of the Immaculate Mother's sorrows, and the rejection of error. Churchmen and laywomen frequently gendered modern error as male. It proved especially attractive to women and children. Not coincidentally, the period also featured the church's efforts to standardize and greatly expand the religious education of children.[73] On one level, then, having lost ground among nineteenth-century men, the church retargeted its message toward the population still attending Mass. On another level, however, women and children gravitated toward newer devotions that resonated with their life experience and provided them with unique, attractive social identities. It was their broad, energetic response, more than the clergy's actions, that gave the new piety its strength and innovative verve. Priests, of course, quickly perceived the new piety's enthusiastic acceptance and stoked it further.

Why was the church's call to action so attractive to women? In part, women found secular institutions and social action largely closed to them, but they also embraced what the church described as a holy mission to re-Christianize society and thus save humanity. Just as the failure of liberal nation-states to deliver socioeconomic stability and individual freedoms fueled discontent in modernizing societies, women generally weathered the period's social dislocations without securing greater power in secular life. They also lacked significant secular opportunities for personal and economic advancement. The church, meanwhile, offered education, alternatives to marriage, meaningful careers, and structured female spaces. At the same time, women far outnumbered men in religious orders, at shrines, and in the pews. Many women gained prominent posts in Catholic institutions. Other devout women and girls seized the limelight periodically as seers and promoters of new visionary movements. In essence, the church provided women a socially acceptable, inexhaustible outlet for their pious and social energies, as well as opportunities for public distinction unavailable elsewhere. Catholicism, we might say, spoke *to* women at a time when secular elites at best talked about how to control them.

Personal motivations also fomented female pious action. That is, humble female visionaries experienced dramatic, although often only temporary, social elevation as their accounts of apparitions attracted attentive journalists, politicians, and clerics.[74] Priests generally lauded the energetic commitment of Catholic women, but female-dominated piety also

MOVING THE FAITHFUL

troubled them. They feared the church's marginalization as societies increasingly associated Catholic commitment with women. This impelled them to bolster the appearance of male participation whenever possible and to shape the new miracle narratives in ways that targeted lapsed men. Acknowledging society's tendency to disbelieve women, they sometimes deliberately overrepresented male visionary testimonies, even though many more women had actually witnessed the alleged miracles.[75]

Analyzing social movements fired by allegedly miraculous events poses a significant challenge for scholars trained in the Enlightenment tradition. Again, miraculous thinking represents the norm in many religious social environments, and the potential for, and expectation of, new visionary experiences permeates Mexican Catholicism. Mesoamerican indigenous groups have elaborate apparitionist traditions that predate the conquest, although contact and culture change deeply influenced their visionary content. Colonial clergymen often praised indigenous religiosity but criticized the common propensity to assert personal miraculous experience.[76] In Oaxaca, apparitions were (and continue to be) quite common.[77] Akin to what William Christian describes in Spain, a continual visionary static endures in Mexico: that is, a constant background noise of miraculous claims surrounds religious life. Only intermittently, however, do apparitions coincide with local circumstances so as to inspire broad public credibility.[78]

A set of commonalities usually undergirds apparition narratives that strike a religious and sociopolitical chord far beyond their communities of origin. These include widely shared idioms of human-divine interaction; deep traditions of miracle-centered piety; a climate of religious urgency; the supportive, or at least ambivalent, initial response of priests; and a critical mass of local believers. Several contributing factors engendered a broader openness to revelation: church-state conflict, external efforts to shape or dampen religiosity, and shifting conceptions of the relationship of the self to the state and the supernatural. The economic opportunities of shrine development and regional rivalries also influenced apparition movements. In addition, nationalism often played an important role. On one hand, the regions that gave birth to apparition movements frequently felt isolated from the centers of national power and chafed at their marginalization. On the other hand, in Spain, Germany, and Brazil, believers' claims that God sought to grace their respective nations with their own Lady of Lourdes proved very attractive to broad cross-sections of believers. Embedded in this hunger for miracles of national import was the conception of the nation as a moral entity, a sense that national problems stemmed from celestial sanction, and notions that apparitions signaled a need to repair the collective relationship with God.[79]

In Mexico, conceptions of the nation as indelibly Catholic remained strong well into the twentieth century, but early on the nation already had its great apparition legend enveloped in various strains of nationalism—the Virgin of Guadalupe.[80] In this regard, *guadalupanismo* in Mexico forms a bulwark against new apparition movements with nationalist overtones. As we will see, in Ixpantepec no one claimed that the Chatino seer was Mexico's Bernadette. Instead, they hailed her the "Second Juan Diego," as if the Virgin sought to reconnect with her Mexican indigenous flock after nearly four hundred years.[81] This is especially significant, since the Guadalupe tradition remained overtly racialized, and the nation's predominantly Hispanic clergy found local Catholic visionary culture embarrassingly indigenous. In Europe, the beleaguered nineteenth-century church turned to the masses, but Mexican clergymen could not embrace popular revelation to the same degree. The church in Mexico sought to achieve the same effects as their counterparts in Europe with elaborate official coronations of colonial-era Marian images, such as the Guadalupe coronation in Mexico City (1895), and the Soledad coronation in Oaxaca (1909). They also attempted to fashion quasidevotions to the act of crowning these images by promoting new pilgrimages on their anniversaries. Not surprisingly, this transparently top-down effort to harness popular fervor through what were essentially add-on feasts for old devotions proved less inspiring than new apparitions. Mexico's coronation boom lacked precisely what has been so crucial in fueling Catholic devotional energies throughout history—a sense of divine action in the immediate present, and the emergence of new human models of visionary grace and personal sanctity.

There are two key phases in an apparition's transformation from an experience reported by a seer, or seers, to its emergence as a foundational event for a larger movement.[82] The first is the response of the immediate social circle to the visionary's initial claims. At this level, individuals close to the events digest news of the vision and have an almost immediate impact on emerging narratives. They may embrace the seer's assertions, dampen belief, or remain ambivalent. Some individuals may ask pointed questions, suggest meanings, and even fill in details. In some cases, people close to the seer or alternative visionaries simplify and edit what are often elaborate and conflicting claims. In the process, they construct more-coherent, usually singular, narratives of what happened.[83] They may also sketch lines of inquiry for future miraculous encounters and enjoin visionaries to reexamine past experiences for portents that have specific contemporary interpretations. This inner circle, in some instances, also imputes political implications to the visions. Furthermore, they often become spokespersons for the seer, and initiate the next phase—notifying a priest.

Crucial to the growth of historical apparition movements is their ability to spread beyond their immediate origins. Their acceptance among individuals of recognized authority is often critical. Clergymen represent a potential conduit between lower-class, often female, revelation and larger society. If the local priest acts decisively to stifle belief in the presumptive miracle, it may effectively stall a budding devotion. Often maintaining contacts beyond the immediate area, and as the local representatives of orthodoxy, priests can serve as an apparition's springboard to regional prominence. In Europe, clergymen experiencing the local impact of church-state tensions were often linked to conservative political factions; thus, they were among the actors most likely to see miracles as expressions of celestial opinion. Priestly support often sparked a wider dissemination of apparition narratives and attracted pilgrims, members of the religious press, and incipient commercial activities around emerging shrine sites. Ambivalence can be important too. In both Ixpantepec and Tlacoxcalco, pastoral indecision allowed new apparition movements to gain steam of their own accord.

A movement's expansion often depends on the transmission of news regarding miraculous cures and intercession across gender and class lines. The broader dissemination of these claims represents the public presentation of "proof." Such communications broadcast the universal aims of the allegedly divine will manifested in the miracles. Often it was local intellectuals who, deploying their own cultural capital and creativity, masterminded the shaping and spreading of certain interpretations. Among the most interesting figures in religious movements, these inter-

mediaries (they were often teachers, professionals, or small-town politicians) acted as filters/translators between the urban, elite, religious
world and the humbler, usually rural, environs of visionaries. In some instances, they overshadowed the seers.[84] Only after a visionary movement
had surpassed communal isolation and found its regional interpreters/
champions do we see the characteristic debates that serve as the documentary history of apparition movements: public divisions over issues of
validity, tensions between devotees and church leaders, skirmishes in the
press, and state action in the guise of safeguarding law and order.

The preceding pages sketch an eclectic approach to religious social
movements, Catholicism in Mexico, religion among Mesoamerican indigenous groups, and Catholic apparitionism. It should be evident that I
have not come to the analysis of religion in Oaxaca with the intention of
applying a rigid theoretical schema to idiosyncratic, grassroots movements subject to myriad contingencies and individual actions. Theory is
relevant, but I seek to privilege the historical evidence and employ various theoretical concepts when they help provide clarity. Making sense of
historical apparition movements and appreciating the endeavors of those
who supported them requires a close examination of the complex interactions between the institutional church, individual clergymen, and lay
practitioners. Indeed, I strive, in the seven chapters that follow, to expand
our understanding of the work-in-progress nature and multileveled conflicts and accommodations that took place as Mexicans made use of their
faith in everyday life.

In order to bring these issues into sharper focus, I will begin at the top
of the institutional pyramid and work my way to a detailed discussion of
the visionary movements in Tlacoxcalco and Ixpantepec. Thus, chapter 1
charts the personal career of Archbishop Eulogio Gillow and his pivotal
role as a modernizing prelate, interpreter of history, and an exemplar of
fervent piety. Chapter 2 traces this archbishop's efforts to showcase the
new idiom of revivalist Catholic religiosity and perform his vision of
Christian social order by staging the elaborate coronation of Oaxaca's
Virgin of Solitude. Chapter 3 explores the history of archdiocesan efforts
to rebuild the church's social foundations in Oaxacan communities and
reform popular religious practice through the construction of a network
of new, canonically structured associations alongside preexisting religious lay institutions. Chapters 4 and 5 examine an apparition move-

MOVING THE FAITHFUL

ment that took shape around a Nahua seer named Bartola Bolaños in Tlacoxcalco, paying close attention to priest-parishioner relations and the innovative institutionalization of this upstart devotion. Finally, chapters 6 and 7 take up the history of Matilde Narváez, a young visionary girl known as Nicha, and the Virgin of Ixpantepec, scrutinizing divergent local interpretations of the miracles and the gendered dynamics of rural Catholicism amidst Oaxaca's mosaic of Hispanic and indigenous cultures.

PART I

Reform

The Clergy and Catholic Resurgence

ONE

≈ An Enterprising Archbishop

Catholic clergymen have long been crucial sources for historians of Latin American. For the entire colonial period and well into the nineteenth century, friars and priests served as society's educated elite and fancied themselves its moral compass. Diverse postings and the cleric's role as the eyes, ears, voice, and scribe of religious institutions, and sometimes even the state, made them irreplaceable historical witnesses for present-day scholars. Here was a sector of society that nurtured a culture of investigation, commentary, and documentation.

For the most part, the priests who engaged local practitioners of Catholicism in Oaxaca in the late nineteenth and early twentieth centuries emerged from the region's newly reformed archdiocesan seminary. This institution owed its expansion and restored reputation to the efforts of one of the most important figures in the Mexican Catholic hierarchy during this period, Oaxaca's Archbishop Eulogio Gillow y Zavalza. Indeed, this man, and his supporters, sought to recast the experience of Oaxacan Catholicism in a broad, ambitious program that would mark the Mexican church well into the mid-twentieth century. His impact is still very much in evidence on the region's historical landmarks. Hence, it is fitting that this energetic modernizer, devotee of Indian

Ilmo. y Rmo. Sr. Dr. D. Eulogio G. Gillow,
Arzobispo de Antequera.

1 Archbishop Eulogio Gillow (1841–1922). Portrait of the prelate published in 1910 picture book commemorating the coronation of 1909. It was probably taken much earlier, since he would have been nearly 70 at the time of publication (*Álbum de la Santísima Virgen de la Soledad*, used by permission of the AHAO).

martyrs, and polemical point man of Mexico's Catholic resurgence attract our scrutiny.

Gillow presided over the Oaxacan archdiocese from 1887 until 1922, although from 1914 until 1921 he lived in exile in the United States. Before his seven-year hiatus, he forwarded a reform program that sought to bring order to Oaxacan Catholicism while infusing it with the sensibilities and ideological themes in vogue in late-nineteenth- and early-twentieth-century Rome. He endeavored to transplant modernized European Catholicism in Oaxaca, and by his own estimation, he succeeded. Gaining a proper perspective on Oaxacan religious practice during this period requires a flashback to over two decades of concerted reform that began with Gillow's consecration in 1887. As the next three chapters demonstrate, the prelate and his lieutenants revamped urban piety and Catholic institutional culture within Oaxaca City, bringing it in line with prevailing European modes of practice and organizational structure. They experienced only mixed results, though, in their efforts to extend the model throughout the archdiocese. This prelate-conceived vision of Catholic religiosity and social order appeared in its most complete public expression during the 1909 coronation of Oaxaca's Marian patroness, La

REFORM

Virgen de la Soledad. As with all climactic events, a history of personal experiences and coeval projects offers the key to decoding the deeper levels of significance in what appears, at a century's remove, as merely an extravagant, well-attended festival. A close analysis of the Gillow program requires an examination of the man, the hierarch, and his mission.

As symbolically rendered on the souvenirs distributed at the coronation, it is impossible to separate the celebration of the Virgin of Solitude from Gillow's remarkable career. One such keepsake, an approximately five-by-seven-inch card, partners a portrait of Oaxaca's archbishop with a bejeweled but forlorn depiction of the Virgin Mother. On the most basic level, this document speaks of patronage, declaring Gillow the force behind the international recognition bestowed upon a cherished local devotion. But the imposing close-up of the resolute prelate, staring at the viewer, in the robes and ornate pectoral cross of his office, stands in stark contrast to the distant sacred image of a Virgin who appears frail and lost beneath her pearl-encrusted vestments and outsized crown. Of course, doctrine holds that Mary's potency as an intercessor before God is second to none, but this memento depicts Gillow as a formidable, flesh-and-blood image of earthly ecclesiastical power, status, and competence. In short, the archbishop's picture represents the local patriarchal countenance of the newly resurgent Catholic Church.

The pairing of the prelate and the Virgin also reveals a Oaxacan expression of the two faces of modern Catholicism during this period. Gillow's stern likeness represents the church's zealous, masculine clergy, who appropriated modernity's cachet and authority in depicting themselves as a disciplined hierarchy of professionals armed with a revitalized social mission and rigorous methods governed by faith. Soledad symbolizes the feminine refusal to accept Christianity's alienation from public life and embrace of the church's adamant assertion that miraculous intercession in human affairs remained crucial if Christian civilization was to be salvaged from the modern era's fundamental rebellion against God. Here we can perceive the emotive, rationality-be-damned style of Marian piety in the nineteenth and early twentieth centuries. The faithful did not see the presentation of these different Catholic modalities as conflictive. Dogma and faith bound them together, and among believers their twinning made sense: Christians should employ the latest means in working for the common good, but bear witness to God's enduring power to shape

NTRA. SRA. DE LA SOLEDAD
que se venera en Oaxaca.

ILLMO. Y RMO. SR.
Dr. D. Eulogio G. Gillow
Dgmo. Arzobispo de Oaxaca, bajo cuyo pontificado
la Sta Sede concedió la Coronación de la
Sma. Virgen de la Soledad.

2 Gillow and the Virgin of Solitude. A souvenir card from the coronation (Fondo Luis
Castañeda Guzmán, Oaxaca, used by permission of the Castañeda Guzmán family).

human destiny. The Virgin stood for unshakable devotion, doctrinal purity, and submission to divine authority. She also served as the object
of intimate supplication. Men like Gillow served as models of an informed, coordinated Catholic action and pious fortitude in the face of
faith-threatening adversity. Nonetheless, in the context of the times, it is
significant that the church, both in Europe and Mexico, communicated in
two registers: one measured, intellectual, nearly rationalist, and gendered
male; the other effusive, usually gendered female, and fused to the era's
allegedly miraculous apparitions.

Gillow's career encapsulates the Mexican church's efforts to convey
this message to its heterogeneous flock. It also gives us a platform from
which to comment on how emergent social Catholicism, and the performative modes of European practice emulated in Mexico by Romanizing
clergymen, influenced local religion. Both the church's retooled social
ideology and new pious style had roots in Catholic tradition. In fact, the
local clergy did not attempt to uproot existing Catholic practices so much
as to graft new meanings and institutions on existing religious customs.
Gillow, the Oaxacan Curia, and their supporters sought to implement

practical programs rooted in new teachings, as well as to heighten and harness popular devotion. To put it another way, they attempted to redirect local practices, rather than radically alter them. Borrowing the vinicultural metaphors that these men were fond of invoking, they viewed themselves as caretakers of God's Oaxacan grapes, entrusted with their maintenance and fruitful production. As such, they had to undertake the determined extirpation of weeds and the careful pruning of wayward sprouts, without damaging rootstocks, the mother vine, or shoots deserving of nurtured growth.

Archdiocesan efforts to reform belief and practice centered on the promotion of an idealized hierarchical network of new lay institutions and devotions. Theoretically, these organizations would incorporate the entire population in fervent, orderly aggregations under the direct supervision of the parish clergy, who in turn, answered to the archdiocesan Curia following Vatican directives. The new *asociaciones canónicamente erguidas* (canonically structured associations) stood at the center of their plan. Ideally composed of committed individuals of impeccably pious reputations, and segregated by class and gender, these groups discouraged the time-honored, frenetic celebration of titular feasts. Instead they emphasized scheduled group spiritual exercises, frequent sacramental practice, and special liturgies purged of profane revelries and uninhibited fiesta piety. These new institutions were branches of established international Catholic associations governed by charters written by European hierarchs, administered by prelate-appointed regional directors, and always under the guidance of parish priests. But the plan was more ambitious than simply turning Oaxacans into diligent congregants at daily or weekly Mass and select feasts. These new organizations cultivated fervent dedication to devotions imbued with conservative religious and political positions associated with the primacy of Rome. They were also designed to function as the church's agents in every community, organizing locals to support ecclesiastical initiatives, countering adversaries, and setting an example of proper social and religious conduct. Furthermore, they were to be the devout masses at demonstrations of Catholic political identity when called upon to gather for events showcasing the depth and intensity of popular support for the church. In sum, they represented the imagined grassroots of a modern, conservative Catholic mass politics and the new social foundations of the beleaguered church.

This system also served as both chain of command and watershed of devotion. Vatican directives could be transmitted and implemented at the distinct levels of Catholic society, from the Archdiocese of Mexico and its elite and working-class associations, to the outlying ecclesiastical provinces and their local associations, and from hence to Oaxaca's rural parishes. Priests hypothetically manned each node to ensure that content and meaning remained unadulterated. Conversely, loyalty and devotion, as symbolically enacted in coordinated pilgrimages, flowed in the opposite direction. For example, in Oaxaca during this period, parishes led by their priests began to travel to the archdiocesan seat on a prescribed rotating schedule to "prostrate themselves" before the Virgin of Solitude in Oaxaca City and experience the full sounds and splendors of urban ritual. In turn, from the mid-1890s, representatives of the archdiocese and the local Curia took their place in nationally organized pilgrimages to Mexico City's Virgin of Guadalupe, and groups of Mexicans of sufficient means joined pilgrimages to Rome and Europe's famous shrines.

It was relatively easy to invoke this vision of corporatist social engineering, but entirely another matter to bring it into being. Catholicism has a history of lofty plans abridged by practical accommodation. Gillow's career provides a crucial component of the larger argument in this study: that is, modern, militant revivalism promoted by the Oaxacan Curia influenced popular apparition movements by modeling certain organizational structures, forms of expression, and modes of devotion. In addition, this movement also shaped the ideological foundations of the priests engaging local Catholicism during the period. The evidence presented here suggests that new devotions and modern forms of pious expression had a broader impact than the ideas and programs published by Catholic intellectuals contemplating Mexico's "social question" and "Indian problem." Gillow's biography and the institutional history of the Oaxacan church provide a road map of sorts, but a straightforward narration of top-down reform is not my intention. The point is to rescue the prelate's legacy from both triumphant portrayals of him as a great patriarch and negative interpretations of his career as a cautionary tale of reactionary ecclesiastical power. Gillow and his lieutenants were the interpreters and promoters of a particular conception of Catholicism, and they were key participants in Oaxacan reworkings of the faith.

Historical analysis of Archbishop Gillow's life and career began before the ambitious churchman set his sights on Oaxaca's vacant see in the late 1880s. A biographical text composed for Gillow's ill-fated candidacy for the Diocese of Puebla in 1877 argued that Gillow was a uniquely qualified confidant of Vatican hierarchs.[1] On the very day of his consecration as Bishop of Oaxaca, July 31, 1887, this first official history was published in the form of a poster affixed to the walls of churches throughout the state capital.

Signed simply "Various Catholics" and asserting that its mission was to introduce Oaxacans to their new prelate, this document enumerated a carefully framed set of qualifications: aristocratic Mexican lineage, European Jesuit training, profound vocation and personal piety, facility with the languages and high cultures of western Europe, a sterling reputation in Rome, business acumen, and a network of personal relationships spanning Vatican luminaries, President Porfirio Díaz, and Mexico's economic elite. This initial salvo in the Gillow historiography depicts its subject as a new Catholic renaissance man, combining the finest upbringing, education, and bedrock religious conviction with intimate knowledge of the modern world and mastery within the halls of power. Conspicuously absent from this glowing portrayal of Oaxaca's new bishop was any mention of pastoral experience. Indeed, Gillow had none.

Two years later Gillow authored *Apuntes históricos* (1889).[2] On the surface, this text is a hagiography of two Zapotec Indians who died defending the faith in 1700. It also represents the inauguration of a lengthy canonization campaign. But at a deeper level, this book reveals Gillow's efforts to shape the historical backdrop and define the themes of his episcopal career far from the papal court where it began. In *Apuntes* Gillow frames the coming-of-age of a heathen mission province, emerging first from the hell of paganism thanks to the heroic Dominican missionaries, and second from demonically inspired idolatrous backsliding, thanks to the unshakable faith of select Indian Catholics. Finally, under a new bishop's zealous guidance, Oaxaca sat poised to attain its rightful glorious place in Christendom as Gillow unearthed the physical remains and history of native martyrs. This text also allowed Gillow to depict his posting to a remote Mexican province in the best possible light. Prelates in the Vatican and within Mexico viewed indigenous practice with suspicion, and *Apuntes* addressed this unease. It ratified fears of crypto-paganism in the Oaxacan countryside, but defended church claims that colonial missionaries implanted the foundations of pristine belief and practice, and proclaimed that a core of devout natives embraced the faith wholeheartedly, despite idolatrous social pressures. Gillow thus preempted notions that he was the titular head of a pagan province and depicted his pastoral mission as one of protecting and nurturing a simple orthodoxy implanted in colonial times and still unsullied by modern error.

As his career progressed, Archbishop Gillow elaborated on this liberation-from-darkness narrative with an interpretation of local history in three basic phases: colonial evangelical glory, characterized by a successful missionary campaign; nineteenth-century, state-sponsored persecution, occasioning a cooling of religiosity and the near collapse of church infrastructure; and finally, a late-nineteenth- and early-twentieth-century return to grandeur and fervor thanks to Gillow's pastoral wisdom and inspired reforms. This triumphant narrative pervades many articles and editorials in the region's Catholic press of the period, but it appears in its most distilled fashion in a serialized history of Gillow's tenure in the *Boletín Oficial y Revista Ecclesiástica de Antequera*, and in the prelate's official biography, *Reminicencias*, written during his exile in the United States (1914–21).[3] These texts remain the foundation of scholarly analyses of Gillow's legacy.

They also are the source of assertions that he enjoyed a close friendship with President Porfirio Díaz. As a result, historians rank him among the architects of Mexico's unofficial church-state conciliation. Getting to the bottom of the Díaz-era rapprochement is difficult, because it was shaped through the personal contacts and commitments. Gillow's biography is one of the few sources that elaborates on unofficial president-prelate social ties. This text's claims would be less problematic if the biography were not so unabashedly self-aggrandizing.[4] Both prochurch interpretations of history and recent critics of the church's role in Oaxaca acknowledge this cozy relationship. The former camp interprets church-state conciliation as a product of Gillow's Vatican-honed diplomatic arts; the latter views it as evidence of a Faustian pact between the autocratic dictator and the aristocratic archbishop. For the Oaxacan church, Gillow remains a great leader who used all the tools at his disposal, among them wealth, social position, and political influence, to revitalize Catholicism.[5]

Oaxacan historian Manuel Esparza, Gillow's most prominent present-day critic, argues that the archbishop's role as a landowner and his developmentalist political leanings overshadowed his pastoral duties and created an irreconcilable conflict of interest.[6] His treatment of the prelate is a blistering commentary on the Gillow-sponsored texts and the prelate's diaries of his pastoral visits, underscoring the archbishop's elitist and, in contemporary estimation, racist approach to his primarily indigenous flock. Perhaps even more offensive to Gillow's defenders, Esparza mocks the prelate's personal belief in the miraculous powers of relics, saints, and the Virgin Mary asserting, "They approach the limit of the most naive, uneducated faith or unvarnished magical thinking."[7] The bile directed at the long-dead archbishop, and the class interests he represents, stems from a larger discussion within Oaxacan studies related to the region's complex response to the revolution. At issue are questions about Oaxaca's reactionary reputation in revolutionary-period scholarship and the region's national significance as Benito Juárez's and Porfirio Díaz's homeland. Esparza argues that the archbishop colluded with President Díaz and capitalist interests to smother or co-opt nascent dissent and independent social organizing. In this interpretation, Gillow was a powerful agent of false consciousness, wielding paternalism and Catholic pageantry but offering little of real value to Oaxacans beyond the restoration of colonial monuments.[8]

This debate about the legacy of a prelate and the Oaxacan church in many ways stands as a regional recapitulation of disputes concerning the church's role in Mexican history. Of particular import for the present study is Oaxaca's experience of liberal reform, especially considering that Gillow's depiction of the Reform served a central purpose in his interpretation of history. For Gillow, exaggerating liberal persecution bolstered his claims of dramatic renewal under his stewardship. Again, the prelate sketched a barbell-like trajectory for the church in Oaxaca: late-colonial expansion and zenith of piety, Reform-era deprivation and near collapse of religious zeal, and a Porfirian institutional resurrection and rekindling of fervor. Of course, there is considerable truth in claims that the institutional church and the clergy suffered decline during the mid-nineteenth century; however, Gillow's claim that Oaxacans became less religious as a result of liberal reform remains doubtful. Too often, historians accept this interpretation without comment. In addition, as with much elite commentary in Oaxaca, there is a tendency in Gillow's texts to conflate the state of affairs in Oaxaca City and surrounding Central District with the entire ecclesiastical province and state.

THE OAXACAN CHURCH BEFORE GILLOW

In many ways, recession and political instability—chronic problems throughout nineteenth-century Mexico—aided the archbishop's historical arguments. The eighteenth century was indeed good for Oaxacan elites, most of whom lived in or near Oaxaca City, as well as for the church. The city had become a bustling provincial commercial hub at the center of a large indigenous hinterland and was a key point along trade routes linking Mexico City to points south. Oaxaca produced textiles, tallow, hides, and indigo, but above all cochineal, the insect-based, scarlet dyestuff. Wealth in the region was a matter of dominating trade, rather than controlling land or production and exerting direct political dominion over the rugged countryside.[9] Through the colonial administrative apparatus, Oaxacan elites made their fortunes by marketing the production of Indian communities remitted to regional officials and merchants. This was especially true of the dye-producing insects that thrive on local cacti, which pre-Colombian Mesoamericans had long collected to produce red and orange tinctures. As a result of this arrangement, many Indian pueblos in the region preserved a considerable degree of cultural and political autonomy. Spaniards and their institutions, such as the church, remained concentrated in Oaxaca City and the adjoining central valleys, and they showed limited concern for the administration of indigenous communities as long as trade kept flowing. The Oaxaca cochineal trade boomed in the late eighteenth century. As in other parts of Mexico, the church grew with the expanding commercial economy. Religious orders and other institutions owned considerable urban real estate, and their rural properties produced grains, livestock, and commodities such as sugar. Endowments supported priestly benefices, and the seminary produced plenty of new clergymen. The Oaxacan church also served as an important source of credit for local entrepreneurs. Not surprisingly, the clergy and elite benefactors also directed considerable sums to the construction and decoration of the city's convents and churches. Urban ritual and pomp flourished, and the city's social life seemed regulated by the liturgical calendar, devotional obligations, and the city's many church bells.[10]

The late colonial political and economic turmoil preceding independence weakened Oaxacan elites and inaugurated the local church's decline. Enduring instability after 1821 exacerbated these trends, as stifling economic depression became the general state of affairs. In Oaxaca's case, the increased competition from new producers, and ultimately the European invention of chemical dyes, undercut the cochineal market and hamstrung the local economy for decades. Of course, political violence made matters much worse. The Oaxacan clergy suffered a serious blow with the Spanish expulsion decrees of the late 1820s, but they weakened themselves in internal factional conflicts as well. In their parishes, clergymen also faced increasing complaints concerning parish fees and priestly greed. In the 1840s, the diocesan seminary still drew many students, such as the young Porfirio Díaz, but it increasingly faced competition from the state-funded Instituto de Ciensias y Artes de Oaxaca (ICA, The Oaxacan Institute of Arts and Sciences), which opened in 1826. Many of its early directors, in fact, emerged from the progressive clergy, and thus it initially represented an extension of clerical influence in public education. In the 1840s, however, the ICA gradually evolved into perhaps the most important liberal educational institution in the nation, despite often austere conditions. In a pattern most galling for church educators, men like Benito Juárez inaugurated their education at the seminary only to finish at the ICA and embrace liberalism. Soon priests rechristened this institution the "House of Heretics." Distinguished churchmen contemplating Oaxaca during this period lamented the fading allegiance of the new generation of influential men and the degeneration of Oaxaca's once-exemplary piety. They spoke in terms of contagion: impious books and ideologies corrupted the hearts of men, leading them to Masonry and irreligious philosophies. "Obedience to the Church," complained Father José Mariano Galíndez, "is left to children and pious old women."[11]

Galíndez was referring to Oaxaca City and religiosity among elites. He probably gave little thought to how rural, indigenous faith and practice had evolved since independence, despite the fact that more than 80 percent of the population lived beyond the city and its surrounding towns.

Map 2 The State of Oaxaca

Altitude Key
(above sea level)

200 meters
1,000 meters
2,000 meters
3,000 meters

100 kms.

Gulf of Mexico

VERA CRUZ

Gulf of Tehuantepec

Juchitán

Salina Cruz

Santo Domingo Tehuantepec

Santa Cruz Huatulco

Villa Alta
San Francisco Cajonos
San Pablo Mitla
Tlacolula
Ixtlán
San Jerónimo Taviche
Tlalixtac
Octolán
Oaxaca
Ejutla
Zaachila
Zimatlán
San Pablo Huixtepec
Santa María Lachixío
Sola de Vega

San Andres Miahuatán
San Sebastián Río Hondo
Santa María Ozolotepec

San Pedro Pochutla

Puerto Angel

OAXACA

Mexico Southern Railroad

San Pablo Etla

Santa Catarina Cuixtla
San Francisco Ixpantepec
Santa Catarina Juquila

Tuxtepec
Ojitlán

Teotitlán del Camino
San José Miahuatlán
Tehuacán
Tlacoxcalco
Santiago Miltepec
Coixtlahuaca
Nochixtlán

Huajuapan
Tamazulapan
San Pedro Teposcolula

Tlaxiaco
Putla

Santo Domingo Teojomulco

San Pedro Tututepec
Santiago Jamiltepec

San Pedro Amuzgos
San Juan Cacahuatepec
Pinotepa Nacional

Puerto Escondido

PUEBLA

Charles Berry estimates that during the mid-nineteenth century almost one-third of the priesthood (about 108 of 330 priests in 1858) lived in or near the provincial capital. He suggests there was perhaps 1 priest for every 2,200 inhabitants spread throughout Oaxaca's rugged countryside. Of the famed missionary orders, only the Dominicans ministered to rural Catholics; others had declined to such a state that their cloisters were nearly empty and teetered in disrepair. According to Berry, most pastors in the countryside preferred to remain in their curacies, and neglected the population in outlying villages. These figures seem plausible, although a single priest could have ministered to two thousand souls effectively, depending on terrain and population density. Lamentably, beyond providing statistics on priestly staffing, Berry does not describe rural religious life in any detail.

The conflicts of the Reform era began to heat up in Oaxaca, as they did in much of Mexico, after 1854. Benito Juárez returned to his native state as governor in 1856 and implemented liberal reform. Oaxacans approached the 1856 law stipulating the disamortization of corporately held properties cautiously, but a significant number benefited from forced sales. The state government also promulgated new regulations regarding parish fees, promising their waiver for the poor and threatening to fine priests assessing them. The bishop at the time spoke out against the new laws and warned that religious tolerance would lead to the region's relapse into idolatry. He also instructed priests to resist the constitutional oath, and, furthermore, he directed them to withhold absolution from officeholders who took the pledge. Nonetheless, despite the stir these exhortations caused, few public figures resigned rather than risk rupture with the church. Many priests, though, vigorously attacked liberal reform from the pulpit. The government countered with threats of suspension for antigovernment agitation. In general, however, Oaxacan conservatives and the clergy vented their frustrations but did not rise up against the state government. However, as civil war engulfed Mexico in 1857 and 1858, Oaxaca City became an important battleground thanks to its strategic location and reputation as a center of liberal ferment.

In fact, Oaxaca served as the setting for considerable violence until the mid-1870s. Time and again, armies squared off in the city and nearby towns. On some occasions the intense fighting unfolded within the state capital. Monasteries and churches served as forts, and opposing forces fortified homes and dug trenches in the city streets. Looters targeted residences and businesses. But liberal triumph in 1867 did not end Oaxaca's woes. As internal divisions among the victors mushroomed and national power was in the balance, the fact that two of the main contenders, Juárez and Díaz, were *oaxaqueños* with local followings guaranteed more violence. After the former's death, *juaristas* shifted their allegiance to Sebastián Lerdo de Tejada, another Díaz opponent. Thus, Oaxaca's Central District experienced considerable bloodshed and weathered sustained war damage and economic contraction from the late 1850s until the Tuxtepec Rebellion established Díaz's preeminence in 1876.

The clergy and the rest of Oaxacan society suffered through this period together. The fighting damaged churches and private homes, and recession hampered renovation. The church, however, bore the brunt of punitive legislation. The state carried out the suppression of religious orders and expropriation of religious landmarks. In some cases they desecrated Oaxaca's gilded sacred spaces. For example, Oaxaca City's grand Dominican monastery became the barracks of the Mexican cavalry, who turned its baroque chapel into their stables. The Santa Catalina de Siena convent became a prison, and the ICA took over the building that had housed the seminary. The church's extensive urban property holdings were privatized, too, but Oaxaca's economic morass, particularly its depressed property markets, dampened the frenzy of speculation that emerged in other parts of Mexico. Nonetheless, the city's small middle class and some artisan families benefited from the opportunity to gain properties. Although most of the church's agricultural properties were close to the state capital, they attracted less interest from urbanites with limited assets; some rural agriculturalists, however, gained parcels. In the end, Oaxaca did not experience a rapid transformation as a result of Reform legislation. It lacked domestic or foreign elites with enough capital to fuel extensive land speculation and concentration. In other regions, liberal legislation sometimes led to the broad alienation of Indian communal landholdings. In Oaxaca's countryside, however, the strength of indigenous municipalities, the weak state's reluctance to provoke communities, and a dearth of exportable commodities slowed the privatization. Oaxacan land was simply not worth much, and the region's isolation made it unattractive even to outsiders.[12] It would not be until the late nineteenth century that economic stability, railroad development, new cash crops, and outside investment fueled land alienation in Oaxaca. Thus, under more propitious conditions decades after their promulgation, the Reform Laws proved useful to entrepreneurs coveting village lands.[13]

The Reform's initial impact on Oaxacan Catholicism at the parish level varied, but for the most part it shifted the foundations of local religion without greatly altering belief and practice. On July 27, 1868, the diocese published a circular requiring pastors to report on the state of their parishes after liberal victory. For the next few years, responses trickled in to the ecclesiastical authorities in Oaxaca City.[14] Usually they included a *cuadrante de costumbres* (description of feasts and fees). These hybrid documents often appear to be a combination of table-like fee schedules, liturgical calendars, bureaucratic reports, and narrative commentary. From the broadest perspective, they are a testament to William Christian's notion that all religion is "local" and place-centered.[15] They document distinct rhythms of practice among Oaxaca's diverse communities, as each parish emphasized different feasts and interactions with the clergy in accordance with local precedent. Priests appear as outsiders who learned local customs from their predecessors or by trial and error. Often, the focus of priestly concern centered on parish economics, although clerics frequently equated a community's religiosity with its generosity. In these matters, the Reform Laws had an immediate impact. Essentially, they opened the logistics of local religion to renegotiation, and the upshot was often a decline in priestly income.[16]

For some parishes the change was drastic. A few suffered the depredations of war, such as the burning of curacies and the destruction or looting of churches.[17] But mostly, what comes through in these documents is a sense of transitional uncertainty spiced with indignation. Parish priests often listed the preexisting customary fees associated with sacraments and important feasts, only to complain toward the end of their report that the new laws and attitudes made them increasingly irrelevant. Among the most detailed descriptions came from the pastor in Villa Alta, Father José Manuel (his surname is illegible). First, the establishment of the civil registry in 1862 ended fee collection for burials and marriages. Second, in 1867 the *jefe político* (district prefect) disbanded the parish's brotherhoods, absolved their members of their commitments, and transferred all church and sodality savings to the town's general fund. It was not that religious ritual in Villa Alta ceased, however; it was just that sponsoring the feasts became optional. In addition, only wealthy parishioners compensated priestly services and continued to make periodic offerings. Unnamed ill-intentioned individuals, claimed Father José, advised the parish's Indians that all means of compulsion had been removed, and that fees were either abolished or voluntary. For this priest, civil enforcement was absolutely crucial to making the indigenous population pay even small customary contributions of agricultural produce to sustain ritual: "The *cuadrante*, well, it is a dead letter."[18]

The Reform, then, undercut the church's ability to compel parishes to sustain levels of preexisting liturgical patronage, individual contributions, and fee payment. When local civil officials were no longer responsible for holding the feasts, collecting contributions, and turning them over to the pastor, or enforcing payment levels for funerals, baptisms, and marriages, there was little a parish priest could do. Some of them demanded payment in advance for all services, but holding up rituals could be risky. Refusals to bury the dead or perform baptisms were not likely to improve a priest's local standing.[19] In a way that the Reform's framers probably did not imagine, the laws shifted a degree of power to the laity. Quite simply, it allowed parishioners greater leverage in their dealings with Catholic ministers. Although it had not been unheard of in the past for a village to skip celebrating some feasts during a particular year, it was now more prevalent. Some communities abandoned specific celebrations outright. In short, the laity had more say concerning the number, elaborateness, and ultimate cost of celebrations during a given year, as well as the remuneration for priestly services. Indeed, what galled some pastors most was insubordination, not impiety. As one priest complained, "But today emboldened by the laws of the reform, they do as they please."[20]

Nonetheless, just as it was impolitic for a priest to be inflexible, most parishioners did not alienate the clergy without cause. As frequent petitions reveal, most sizable communities, both before and after the Reform, wanted to have their own pastor and valued priest-mediated ritual and the sacraments.[21] Ecclesiastical authorities occasionally removed priests from localities deemed antagonistic. They could leave the post vacant for some time or even move the parish seat to a friendlier town. Of course, in some communities the new laws' impact on local religion was imperceptible. In San Francisco Cajonos, the priest and his parishioners were in agreement on feasts and fees. The pastor in 1868 was clearly well compensated, particularly in foodstuffs, and civil officials still took charge of sponsoring fiestas. According to San Francisco's pastor, his flock freely agreed to the list of celebrations and their cost, although they occasionally failed to mark some feasts and always owed him fees for past ceremonies.[22] Further evidence of continuity during this period emerges in the receipts and reports from the region's pilgrimage devotions, such as Our Lady of Juquila, San Andrés Miahuatlán's Lord of Cuixtla, and Etla's Lord of Las Peñas. These documents reveal that Oaxacans kept traveling to shrines, fulfilling devout vows, purchasing sacred images, and paying priests to celebrate special shrine Masses.[23] There is also evidence that many smaller shrine brotherhoods endured and remained committed to sponsoring rituals, despite changes.[24]

Pondering this evidence, historian Daniela Traffano argues that amidst deteriorating local church-government cooperation, and facing precarious finances, one of the few advantages the church retained was the enduring faith of the populace.[25] Counting on these sentiments, the Oaxacan church took steps to adjust to the new realities, and played a weak hand well. The altered sociopolitical landscape forced the church to retreat from its traditional emphasis on communal Catholic identity rooted in collectively managed religious corporations, like colonial-era brotherhoods. In the face of less-cooperative communal authorities, the church began promoting new institutions comprised of individual Catholics that were, at least in theory, independent of civil oversight and under clerical control (i.e., canonically structured associations). This represented a transition from the communal organization of Catholic practice to observance anchored in subgroups, or even cliques. In short, adjusting to creeping secularization, the Oaxacan church started emphasizing the individual Catholic and his or her salvation through the church. As part of this trend, both before and during the Gillow period, the clergy threatened individuals with excommunication if they collaborated with state anticlericalism. The church did its best to resist expropriations of assets that supported ritual, as well as attempts to extricate local politics from clerical influence. Sometimes priests refused to administer sacraments to individuals who acquired church properties or participated in governance. Individuals who sought to repair their relationship with the church had to publish retractions of their oath to the national constitution, plead for forgiveness, and profess their fealty to Catholic teachings and hierarchs.

In instances where they acquired church property, they also had to negotiate with the ecclesiastical government concerning restitution. The public humiliations and fears of damnation occasioned by this process engendered a hatred of liberal legislation, and thus helped blunt the impact of the Reform.

As we have seen, despite liberal legislation, some Oaxacan communities elaborated civil-religious arrangements that contravened the spirit, if not the letter, of the Reform. Villages invented myriad ingenious means of circumventing laws, disguising collective landownership, and sustaining local religion and maintaining its links to local governance. The elaboration of the *cargo* system is a classic example. Priests, however, often found themselves on the sidelines while these strategies took shape. For the most part, the adjustments and innovations were lay responses to state intrusions in local culture. The Reform, therefore, often did more to limit clerical oversight than diminish religiosity. In subsequent years, the number of clergymen shrank sharply in Oaxaca, due in large part to the church's institutional problems following the Reform, and this lessened priestly supervision of local practice still further. Reversing both of these trends would emerge as key pastoral projects when Eulogio Gillow arrived in 1887. This prelate, however, forged his views in the Catholic world beyond Oaxaca.

A MODEL CHURCH AND MODELING PERSONAL PIETY

After the ostensible defeat of Mexican conservatism in 1867, Catholic activists and clerics spent two decades quietly rebuilding the church's finances, pious organizations, and educational institutions. Many prelates experienced exile in Rome, where they internalized the Vatican's abiding concerns about expanding socialism and disintegrating traditional authority. From this perspective, returning bishops initiated a Mexican debate over the "social question" inspired by their European counterparts. They also goaded the nation's Catholics to defend their faith against the advance of error. In essence, the Reform-era high clergy and Catholic intelligentsia regrouped and passed on their refusal to accept the progressive de-Christianization of public life.[26] As the twentieth century approached, new Catholic ideologues voiced the accusation that liberalism's ascendancy had destabilized the social edifice. In a Catholic nutshell, liberalism loosed a host of human passions previously restrained by the church and traditional authority. Lest the world revert to an imagined pre-Christian era of brutal anarchy, it was imperative to restore time-honored social controls or fashion new means to rein in the egotism at the root of modern sociopolitical turbulence.

The fear of expanding socialism had been the motor of debate among Catholic thinkers between 1871 and 1891, as they shaped a new social platform that engaged the social realities of the modern world. The culmination of this process was *Rerum Novarum* (1891). Although Leo XIII's famous encyclical may seem tame today, it shocked many Catholics at the time, who perceived it as radical and crypto-socialist. At the most basic level, it stressed that modern societies had produced an acute social polarization with explosive potential, and proposed that the church and secular states work together to solve these root problems with the cooperation of working-class organizations. Catholics did not leap into this mission en masse, but after 1891, dedicated activists inspired by *Rerum Novarum* and subsequent encyclicals envisioned themselves as a vanguard seeking to Christianize civil society and representative democracy by targeting and mobilizing popular groups.[27] In Mexico, the Catholic Church faced a unique set of social and historical issues that colored the impact of these trends.

Eulogio Gillow represents a pivotal intergenerational and well-connected cosmopolitan figure during this period. To understand Gillow's personal faith and the policies he championed, we must consider his upbringing and education. The future prelate was born in Puebla on March 11, 1841, and raised in an elite family that maintained close ties to the church. Gillow's mother inculcated in her only child her personal devotion to Tlaxcala's Virgin of Ocotlán. When he was ten years old, his English father, Thomas Gillow, arranged for Eulogio to attend Jesuit schools in Europe. After receiving tutoring in English, he studied at Stonyhurst and Preston. Later he continued his education at a Jesuit boarding school in Belgium. The Society of Jesus was among the key organizations shaping the emotive new piety that gained wide acceptance in the nineteenth century and which Gillow would model years later in Oaxaca.

Aside from his formation in Jesuit schools, his time in Europe coincided with the surging confrontational Marianism of Pius IX. He must have experienced the transformations occasioned by the pope's declaration of the dogma of the Immaculate Conception in 1854, the Lourdes apparition in 1858, and the potent melding of the Vatican's hierarchical message with the emergent modern idiom of militant apparitionism and piety. Gillow's first visit to Rome in 1862 coincided with the initial construction phase of the massive shrine at Lourdes, and his ordination took place on the cusp of the shrine's inauguration in 1866.[28] According to his official biography, the Vatican pageantry surrounding the canonization of Mexico's colonial martyr Felipe de Jesús and the aura of Pius IX mesmerized Gillow.[29] There he gained the Pope's support to continue his clerical training at Italy's Ecclesiastical Academy for Nobles. In 1865 he returned to Mexico to be ordained in his native Puebla and say his first Mass at the shrine of the Virgin of Ocotlán, but he departed promptly for Rome to serve in the papal court and continue his studies. Gillow completed a doctorate in canon law at the Gregorian University in 1869.

During this period Gillow established a network of Vatican contacts and relationships that served him throughout his career. Simultaneously, the Mexican church was weathering its greatest hour of crisis amidst the triumph of anticlerical liberalism and the implementation of the Reform. An ocean away, it would seem that the ambitious twenty-eight-year-old clergyman's career was unfolding propitiously, but in a turn of events that neither he nor subsequent scholars have clearly explained, Gillow returned to Mexico in 1870 with the vague title of *prelado doméstico* (domestic prelate). This title freed him from the oversight of Mexico's bishops and gave him a nuncio-like aura, but for seventeen years he lacked a defined role in either the Mexican church or the Vatican's diplomatic corps. For much of this time he managed his aging father's economic enterprises, experimenting with agricultural mechanization and occasionally participating in Mexico City's upper-class pious associations. Gillow later claimed that he distinguished himself as a benevolent, moralizing manager of the family's hacienda, which was located strategically between Mexico City and Puebla.[30]

While treading water as a domestic prelate, Gillow augmented his personal network of Vatican connections, cultivating relationships with influential churchmen, entrepreneurs, and politicians in Mexico. He was particularly careful to develop close ties to Mexico City's Archbishop Labastida y Dávalos. After an auspicious meeting at an agricultural exposition in Puebla in 1877, he also began his oft-cited acquaintance with

President Díaz. His church duties were minimal at this time, although Labastida tried to secure for him the bishopric of Puebla in 1877.[31] Labastida succeeded, with Díaz's help, in consecrating him as Bishop of Oaxaca in 1887.

If the period from 1870 to 1887 represents an interruption in Gillow's career, he made the most of his opportunities when he gained the Oaxacan see. As we have seen, he wasted no time in shaping his legacy. He showed himself to be an energetic prelate in other matters as well. His ties to Archbishop Labastida earned him the designation as Mexico's chief representative at the Vatican's Mexican provincial reform debates in the early 1890s. The immediate outcome of these reforms was Oaxaca's elevation to archdiocese and Gillow's concomitant ascension to archbishop, charged with the oversight of most of southern Mexico's dioceses in 1891 (Yucatán, Chiapas, Tabasco, and Tehuantepec). Ever careful to position himself as a trendsetter, Gillow organized a Oaxacan church reform council in late 1892 and early 1893, and then traveled to Rome again in 1899 for the Latin American Plenary Council that established the official norms of doctrine throughout the region. In his subsequent edicts, instructions, and pastoral letters, Gillow cited these councils as the touchstones of his directives on such things as faith and practice, the Catholic press, religious education, and seminary reform.[32]

According to Gillow's commissioned histories, when he arrived in Oaxaca he found the church in complete disarray. The first dozen years of his tenure entailed gauging problems throughout the archdiocese and building the foundations of the church's local restoration. Gillow had to win over Oaxaca's urban elite and the clergy before he could reform the province's diverse rural flock. The Oaxacan church had to be righted and placed on course, and its redirection took time. Gillow's first steps involved reforming the local clergy, cultivating a circle of loyalists within the province's ecclesiastical government, and also inaugurating a campaign to restore urban religious infrastructure. His pastoral visit diaries during the first decade or so of his tenure reveal his survey of the rural church.[33] In the almost daily entries, he repeatedly noted the lack of priests, lax clerical discipline, the miserable aspect of temples and ritual, and the primitive or nonexistent doctrinal understanding of the faithful. Following Catholic doctrine on the clergy's relationship to the laity, he chose to address issues directly related to the clergy, under the preconception that a reformed priesthood could guide the transformation of the region's predominantly indigenous laity. In keeping with long-standing Hispanic tradition, the city, its churches, and urban practice became the laboratory of Gillow's reformed Catholicism.

His program in many ways represented new ways to accomplish traditional goals, both social and religious. The prelate's blue-blood pedigree and European education made him an attractive figure within Oaxaca's upper-class society, which was anxious to emphasize its own European heritage. Gillow also shared this group's deep social conservativism. For Hispanic elites in Oaxaca, the synergy of their enduring fears of the state's vast indigenous population, the cachet associated with all things European, and militant Catholicism's ideological functionality as a bulwark of status and deference traditions made these ideas enticing. But, characterizing the archbishop's legacy as simply an agglomeration of religion, social conservatism, and Porfirian capitalism robs it of its deeper, dynamic, and more widespread significance. Gillow's detractors have accused him of stifling the emergence of an authentic urban labor movement through his sponsorship of the Catholic Workers Circle of Oaxaca, implying that militant labor mobilization would have emerged in his absence. But this seems doubtful, given the tendency of Mexican organized labor to exploit its position within an agrarian economy for wage concessions rather than pursue fundamental political change.[34]

Gillow's religious message was appealing to both elite and popular sectors of society. Just as he wore his personal piety on the sleeve of his prelate's robes, so too did he support a performative communal religiosity with deep roots in urban and rural Oaxaca. But he sought to tame these traditions. The archbishop trumpeted his own commitment to holy figures and specific images, as well as his belief that he had been the beneficiary of miraculous intercession. He also asserted with dogmatic certainty that if Catholics beseeched God and his saints with the proper intensity and openhearted devotion, Divine Providence would change hearts to bring about the ultimate triumph of Catholic society and Christian justice.[35] Individuals may have quibbled with Gillow's vision of how this utopian society might look, or how justice should be administered, but they did not resent his expression of these aspirations, the beliefs that supported them, or his histrionic manner of airing them in public.

Gillow's spiritual outlook remained rooted in the mid-nineteenth century, but he shrewdly associated himself with the late-nineteenth-century reformism. It is important to remember that Gillow left Rome just as European Catholic thinkers began articulating the themes and analyses that later became known as social Catholicism. Scholars list him as a supporter of this movement in Mexico, and he counted among his acquaintances pivotal members of Leo XIII's administration, but Gillow's formative experiences took place during the deeply conservative tenure of Pius IX. His professions of belief and sense of the church's role in society remained rooted in the spirit of Pius's pontificate. Nonetheless, after he became bishop of Oaxaca, he demonstrated a clear understanding of Vatican politics. Rome in the late nineteenth century sought simultaneously to achieve a Catholic restoration in the Americas and to assert its authority over what it viewed as overly independent national hierarchies. In addition, the Vatican considered the American provincial clergy and laity lax in both doctrine and discipline, and thus in need of rigorous top-down reform.[36] Gillow never evinced a deep intellectual commitment to the social Catholic project, but he enthusiastically supported Vatican initiatives. As the Archbishop of Oaxaca, he structured his career around Rome's program of revitalization and centralization. He tirelessly portrayed himself as the Vatican's man in Mexico. Again, Gillow was neither a member of the Reform-era Catholic old guard nor the new wave of activist priests who set their sights on the return of open Catholic political participation and a Catholic resolution of Mexico's "social question." Gillow was primarily a conduit of modernizing currents. He was not so much the source of new ideas and practices as he was a facilitator of their penetration within his archdiocese and the Mexican church as a whole.

Among his more far-reaching legacies related to this process was his championing of graduates of Rome's Colegio Pío Latinoamericano (CPL, Latin American Pious College).[37] Established in 1858 to cultivate a pool of loyal, Vatican-trained high clergymen in the Americas, its graduates faced varying degrees of resistance from locally trained clerics, for obvious career-related reasons. Many Latin American prelates sent chosen individuals to this exclusive institution, but Gillow distinguished himself in his efforts to secure bishoprics for CPL graduates. Over the course of his tenure, he placed them in all the dioceses within his jurisdiction, facilitated their appointments throughout Mexico, and backed their subsequent promotion to more prestigious posts. His initiative in this regard had a lasting impact on the church, since many of Mexico's most prestigious prelates, well into the twentieth century, had been beneficiaries of his ecclesiastical politicking.[38]

Oaxaca's native sons educated at the CPL proved to be crucial agents of Gillow's policies within the archdiocese and important conduits of the latest currents of European Catholic thought and practice. The vocabulary and themes of social Catholicism became increasingly prevalent in Gillow's writings after the mid-1890s, but he appears less comfortable with these ideas than he did holding forth on the Immaculate Conception. In fact, the local articulation of social Catholic ideas and institutions during his tenure should be attributed to José Othón Núñez y Zárate, a Gillow protégé. Gillow's personal initiatives reveal that he preferred traditional projects, such as the renovation of historic churches, seminary reform, clerical recruitment, and energetic pastoral visitation. In contrast, he assumed a benefactor-like stance toward the establishment of the Catholic press, schools, and later, the Catholic Worker's Circle. This did not entail a relinquishing of episcopal powers, but rather the delegation of authority to a group of young deputies.

Soon after his arrival in Oaxaca, Gillow purged the entrenched hierarchy and undertook an overhaul of the seminary.[39] In a classic reorganization strategy, Gillow sidelined individuals and factions with histories of antagonism and opened avenues of advancement to young priests free of longstanding internal conflicts and loyal primarily to him. For the most part, natives of Oaxaca City and products of its parochial schools, they worked in Gillow's shadow for decades. Núñez was chief among them until the archbishop helped him secure the bishopric of Zamora in 1909.[40]

Men like Núñez thus served as the interpreters of new social ideas in Mexico, but Gillow did more than simply remove obstacles to their advancement. He protected them, provided financial support, and gave them space within his archdiocese to experiment at a time when many other Mexican prelates viewed novelties such as Catholic workers' syndicates and Christian democracy as dangerous hybrids of religion and socialism.[41] Born in Oaxaca City to an influential family, Núñez belonged to the generation that came of age in the 1890s and gradually took over the reins of the Mexican church and Catholic sociopolitical activism. He studied at the CPL between 1890 and 1893, precisely the years surrounding the emergence of *Rerum Novarum*. He returned to the arch-diocese as one of the era's "new" priests, willing to "abandon the sacristy," as advocated in activist writings, and minister to the faithful from the new pulpit of print media and in the workplace. It was under Núñez's guidance that Oaxaca's Catholic newspaper, *La Voz de la Verdad* (hereafter *La Voz*), and the archdiocese's official organ, the *Boletín Oficial y Revista Eclesiástica de Antequera* (herafter *Boletín Oficial*), emerged in 1896 and 1901, respectively. He wrote for both publications and remained the un-official director of the former and the chief administrator of the latter until his episcopal consecration. In addition to his role as a modern journalist-priest, Núñez sprinted up the Oaxacan hierarchy. He became the vice-rector of the seminary upon his return from Rome in 1893, and one year later became rector. In 1895 he became archdean of the cathe-dral chapter, and in 1899, at the age of 32, Gillow named him provisor of the archdiocese. In the first decade of the twentieth century, he also served as Oaxaca's representative at the National Catholic Congresses organized primarily by CPL alumni and the nation's social Catholic intel-lectuals. In addition to these accolades, he distinguished himself as a Catholic labor organizer, founding Oaxaca's Catholic Worker's Circle in 1906 and directing it until 1909. Subsequently, he championed the Cath-olic worker movement in Michoacán.[42] Even after his consecration, he continued to cultivate his relationship with Oaxacan workers and sought to guide their activities, making sure to visit them during vacations in his hometown.[43]

Gillow was more of a pietistic social conservative than a progressive Christian democrat, but his genius lay in remaining committed to his intransigent roots while supporting the evolution of a new Catholic social voice in Mexico. As an ambitious and able prelate, he proved sensitive to trends emerging from the Vatican, domestic civil and ecclesiastical poli-tics, and his Oaxacan flock. His success stemmed, in large part, from his ability to embody in his career and public persona the two-sided model of the modern militant clergyman. On the one hand, he was the consum-mate rational reformer and a professionalizing manager of an expanding bureaucracy—that is, a captain of modernization. In this capacity, tradi-tion still had its place. Gillow excelled in navigating the church's "prin-ciple of hierarchy," cultivating his superiors and exerting authority over his subordinates. Among the laity, he assumed a customary patriarchal image, while also distinguishing himself as the benefactor of the new lay associations promoted by the Vatican as the building blocks of a restored Christian society. But on the other hand, Gillow embraced the church's image of the new man/priest, who while well versed in science, economics, and sociology (as taught in Catholic institutions), proclaimed his insignificance and ignorance before the thaumaturgical power of the Almighty. In this aspect, he publicized his personal devotionalism and attested that a benevolent divine hand in his personal life had reduced him to pious tears and humble gratitude.

Gillow's institutional reforms have been well documented by scholars, but they merit further comment. Following his consecration, he moved immediately to restore the city's churches, and to reorganize the Oaxacan seminary. Within a few short years, Oaxaca produced a bumper crop of new priests, and the urban laity began attending services in refurbished churches. In 1889 an astounding thirty-one seminarians petitioned to become presbyters during customary December ordinations. In subsequent years, Gillow usually conferred this honor on seven to fifteen young men, but this one-time surge of ordinations must have been inspired by the prelate's immediate efforts to increase his staff and to begin shaping a circle of loyal followers. This particular class produced several influential clerics, including Carlos Gracida and José Othón Núñez.[44] Such was Gillow's zeal in this regard that Archbishop Labastida joked (or issued a coded warning) in 1890 that Gillow intended to fill the entire nation's clerical vacancies.[45] Two decades later, the Oaxacan prelate's propagandists crowed that he brought about the clergy's expansion from 123 priests, 8 Dominicans, and 1 Franciscan in 1887, to 199 secular clerics, 3 Jesuits, 2 Marists, and 7 Pauline priests in 1907. In other words, within two decades, the number of clergymen working within the archdiocese increased by approximately 60 percent.[46] Mirroring the process of ecclesiastical reform taking place across Mexico at the time, Gillow also moved to rationalize rural parish boundaries, as well as to create new parishes in keeping with the latest population statistics and his estimation of local conditions, pastoral needs, and communal merit.[47]

The themes of his first two official pastoral instructions demonstrate the administrative thrust of the early Gillow period in Oaxaca. Indeed, between them they encapsulate his initiatives during the first dozen years of his tenure. In 1888, he issued directives related to priestly comportment,

3 Newly minted graduates of Gillow's reformed seminary. The young Carlos Gracida is
marked with an X, and the cleric third from the right appears to be future archbishop
José Othón Núñez (AHAO, Fotografías, used by permission of the AHAO).

the priesthood's role and image in society, and the particulars of Catholic
ritual. In this document, he promulgated new regulations and standards
on the appearance of curacies and churches, priestly dress, liturgy, the
administration of the sacraments, the personal spiritual life of priests, and
discipline. The second pastoral instruction (1897) addressed the financial
foundations of the church, with an emphasis on parish revenue collection. Within this text, Gillow discussed the particulars of fee schedules,
mandatory contributions to the seminary and remittances to the ecclesiastical government, the reinstitution of tithe obligations, and the standardization of accounting practices.[48] Revealing that his fiscal reform
program was well underway prior to the publication of this 1897 text, the
archdiocesan archive is full of detailed accounts of parish finances between 1894 and 1896. Many priests provided itemizations of fees, expenses, and remittances each month. In some instances, priests recorded
their daily provision of ministerial services and fee collections.[49] Although Gillow and his priests failed to convince a significant number of
Oaxacans to tithe voluntarily, his ability to fund his expanding revitalization campaign attests to increased revenue collection in the archdiocese.

It should be stressed, however, that until 1907, Gillow's tenure coincided with an extended period of economic growth in the region. Local wealth played a pivotal role in these projects, such as the construction of new churches, the creation of new parishes, the establishment of Catholic newspapers, and the amplified and more frequent displays of public devotion often noted during the Gillow era. Neither his postindependence predecessors nor twentieth-century successors enjoyed the pastoral opportunities afforded by good economic times.

Gillow's third pastoral instruction (1911) reveals that a new set of interests and projects had come to occupy the Oaxacan clergy's energies during the latter portion of his tenure—the cultivation of a broad network of lay associations to sponsor Catholic ritual, enact church social policies, promote the Catholic press, and expand religious education.[50] The prelate's present-day critics cite this document's coincidence with revolutionary insurrection in the nation as evidence of Gillow's inability to recognize the futility of his position in the new national political landscape.[51] Rooted in scholarly hindsight, this contention is flawed on two counts. First, it suggests that in Oaxaca, or in the rest of Mexico, the outcome of the revolution was somehow clear in April 1911. In fact, from a Catholic perspective, it seemed that their chance to reassert themselves in the political arena had finally arrived. Oaxaca's Catholic press telegraphed the sense of political opportunity and excitement in their coverage of the national and local emergence of the Partido Católico Nacional (PCN, National Catholic Party) in 1911 and 1912.[52] The party's early success attests to the fact that Gillow was not alone in proposing Catholic solutions to the era's problems.

Second, the view that Gillow was ideologically out of touch fundamentally misreads the way Oaxaca's archdiocese functioned during this period. Like the second pastoral before it, the third discussed, and attempted to codify and frame, a process already well underway. The Oaxacan clergy and activist laity's efforts on these fronts had been gathering steam since the mid-1890s. The archbishop was not just belatedly raising the *Rerum Novarum* banner in the face of advancing agrarian rebels. Gillow's third pastoral instruction must be understood as part of the prelate's historiographical agenda. This document and its predecessors represent more than straightforward decrees and pronouncements of new policy initiatives. In fact, they functioned as symbolic markers, historical claims, and publicity statements of Gillow's tenure, despite being phrased as directives to be implemented. The first (1888) celebrated his arrival in Oaxaca and promised a restoration of the clergy. The second (1897) commemorated a decade of his leadership and trumpeted a rationalization of parish administration. The third (1911) invoked the upcoming silver anniversary of Gillow's tenure, lauded the two previous pastoral instructions, and proclaimed, "Both participants and observers recognize the improvement that has been achieved in the state of the diocesan clergy, parish buildings, ritual, and in a word, in all that concerns us most."[53] In sum, Gillow declared the Oaxacan church's house in order and its rituals refined, and then turned his attention to broader society.[54] But in reality, the archbishop made this transition more than a decade before his final pastoral instruction. We know now that the revolution short-circuited this project when Constitutionalist ascendancy in 1914 forced Gillow into exile and led to the cessation of his more ambitious socio-political initiatives. In Gillow's absence, his circle of lieutenants struggled to safeguard the church's local gains and infrastructure, but they could do little more than damage control. Gillow returned to Oaxaca in March 1921 and enjoyed a triumphant procession from the train station to the cathedral, but he was unable to pick up where he left off before his death in 1922.[55]

What makes Archbishop Gillow's biography so important is the manner in which he modeled militant personal devotionalism, linked his public image to local sacred figures, and sought to heighten public piety within his see while implementing modernizing reforms. His personal engagement in these processes makes it impossible to separate the institutional policies from the prelate's persona and career history. Beyond his role as an architect of church-state conciliation in Porfirian Mexico, or any impact he may have had in smothering popular dissent and mobilization against the Díaz regime, Gillow should be understood first and foremost as an important conduit and facilitator of militant modern Catholicism in Mexico. Moreover, he sponsored and publicized an interpretation of local history in which he placed himself and the church center stage. This narrative continues to reverberate in Oaxaca.

Upon close examination, Archbishop Gillow's policies were neither particularly imaginative nor original. A cursory glance at the published conclusions of the Vatican's 1899 Latin American Plenary Council reveals that he simply followed Rome's blueprint for Catholic revitalization.[56] If he fails to impress us as the author of grand schemes, Gillow nonetheless distinguished himself as an implementer of plans sketched elsewhere. His Catholic restoration program took shape in two stages: first, internal institutional reform; and second, a broad outreach effort through the creation of a network of church-affiliated, priest-led institutions. The symbolic hallmarks of these two overlapping phases were the lavish restoration and retrofitting of Oaxaca City's colonial churches and convents inaugurated during the first phase, and the promotion of increasingly grandiose manifestations of Catholic piety and political identity during the second.

In fact, the Archbishop's architectural restoration program and religious revitalization crusade reveal the same principles at work. Not surprisingly, Gillow seized upon the city's colonial monuments as symbols of the church's institutional vitality. Just as liberals demonstrated their mastery over their ecclesiastical opponents by plundering the physical evidence of church wealth and power, Gillow's expenditures of personal and political capital to regain, reornament, and reconsecrate these spaces trumpeted Catholicism's sociopolitical renaissance. The prelate, however, was not interested in straightforward restorations. He commissioned new facades and art. In short, Gillow introduced new artistic and architectural expressions that communicated Catholic notions of divinity and social order in an innovative modern fashion. Thus, the beautiful baroque altarpiece in the eighteenth-century church of San Felipe Neri now shares space with art nouveau frescos. But despite his introduction of novel artistic idioms, Gillow cleaved to styles that evoked tradition, such as neobaroque and neo-*mudéjar*.[57] His policies targeting religious practice proved very similar. They spoke of pious tradition, an unsullied forefather's faith, and hierarchical order, but expressed these ideas in a manner that seemed new. The Oaxacan Curia saw all of this as part of the same project. Architectural structures and religious art served as the stage, backdrop, and template of pious practice. The local patroness's official crowning brought it all together, and marked the apex of Gillow's prelacy. As Gillow stated in the 1908 pastoral letter announcing Soledad's coronation, the faithful should exert themselves both in public expression and private preparation. Thus they would manifest, through the pomp and splendor of the festivities, the "internal acts" of their eternal souls.[58]

TWO

≋ Crowning Images

During the first weeks of 1909, Oaxaca braced for a deluge of the devout, as the carefully planned coronation of the Virgen de la Soledad and the city's hosting of the Fourth National Catholic Congress came to fruition. Since the early seventeenth century, Soledad, a representation of the sorrowful Mother of God at the foot of the cross, had been a magnet for pilgrims from the surrounding region, especially on her December 18 feast day. But in anticipation of the Vatican apostolic delegate's placement of a jewel-encrusted crown upon her head on January 18, 1909, legions of the Virgin's followers piled onto rail cars and clogged footpaths bound for the archdiocesan seat. A special festival to honor a venerated local image had immense popular appeal, but its deliberate linkage to the gathering of intellectuals and prelates to address Mexico's "Indian question" promised a confluence of local devotees, provincial elites, and the nation's Catholic luminaries.[1]

On January 15, a chartered train set out from Mexico City, carrying in it Rome's emissary, four archbishops, eight bishops, and approximately fifty priests and Catholic thinkers. After a stopover in Tehuacán, the travelers embarked on a triumphant whistlestop pilgrimage from the archdiocese's northern fringes to the cathedral city. At every town along the route, crowds marshaled by their pastors waited in flower-festooned stations to greet the august passengers. Throughout the afternoon, the train lumbered south, and excited Catholics milled about the Oaxaca City's train station, putting the finishing touches on their decorations. Guilds belonging to Oaxaca's Catholic Workers' Circle busied themselves at preassigned cross streets along Avenida Independencia hanging banners, cascading floral arrangements, and triumphal arches. In the central plaza, Federico Zorrilla, the owner of the city's new electric company, outshone the earnest efforts of humbler Catholics with a blue incandescent arch displaying his initials and the salutation "*Bienvenidos*" in white and gold lightbulbs.

Oaxacans had been girding their souls for months. They participated in rounds of scripted corporate pilgrimage to the shrine, a campaign to inspire mass participation in the sacraments, revivals, and relays of spiritual exercises. But when the guests of honor arrived at 5 p.m. on January 16 and met the welcome committee—Gillow, the bishop of Tehuantepec, the cathedral chapter, and select gentlemen—public piety gave way to a citywide party. The most distinguished churchmen boarded carriages, while others followed in a special tram. Along the way, Oaxacan spectators showered them with flowers, and the Workers' Circle, like a proletarian honor guard, lined the entire route. "Most beautiful was the appearance of the streets in those solemn moments, completely full with a great number of persons from all the social classes, who respectfully greeted and enthusiastically applauded the illustrious prelates," waxed the archdiocese's *Boletín Oficial*.[2] Church dignitaries settled into Gillow's new palace, and other visitors took rooms at the refurbished convent of Carmen Alto or the homes of well-to-do local Catholics. Meanwhile, humble pilgrims camped along the walls of the city's massive colonial churches. That night, a tag team of prelates and canons celebrated Mass at Soledad's shrine, and afterward a group of two hundred indigents enjoyed a banquet served by pious Oaxacan ladies. Clearly impressed, the city's English-language newspaper reported, "Never before in the history of Oaxaca have so many people been congregated in the city at one time."[3]

The next day, January 17, Oaxaca donned blue and white, the Virgin's colors, and put on a performance of local Catholic notions of social order and history. Amidst sprays of flowers and ruffled bunting adorning the aristocratic Centro neighborhood, and banners, bows, and paper decorations enlivening the city's humbler addresses, a *"gran manifestación* [great demonstration]" starring church-affiliated corporations and the region's economic elite set out to demonstrate "the great influence that the Christian spirit exerts in Oaxaca." The girls' catechism centers led the way, trailed by a variety of female parochial schools. They ranged from the Casa de Cuna's orphans to the girls "of the principal portion of society" who attended the Colegio de San José. The boys' catechism centers followed, and behind them marched a similar cross-section of male educational establishments, capped by seminarians. As uniformed children and clerical hopefuls filed down the streets, the men of the Workers' Circle, arranged by guild, joined the manifestation. Finally, the city's devotional organizations and several brass bands paraded in their respective places. Groups identified themselves with unique banners and devotional insignias, and individuals carried huge floral arrangements for the Virgin. According to archdiocesan sources, six thousand Oaxacans participated in the parade, and over twenty thousand spectators witnessed the event. The procession wended its way around Oaxaca before arriving at Soledad's shrine. There, as stipulated on programs posted throughout the city, participants entered the sanctuary, deposited their offerings, and exited the shrine's lateral doors—"in perfect order."[4]

Onlookers applauded this show of Catholic institutional vigor, but the climax of the afternoon, nine *carros alegóricos* (allegorical floats) conceptualized by Archbishop Gillow, inspired the most enthusiastic cheers. Together the floats told a story of Catholic civilization's Mexican expansion, and Oaxaca's progress under the careful guidance of the church. More prosaically, the procession communicated the ranking of members of Oaxacan society: the youths riding on the floats came from elite families, and entrepreneur patrons followed the decorated flatbeds in open carriages.[5] "The Ruins of Mitla" inaugurated the convoy, representing Mexico before the conquest by means of boys and girls clad as the "races of ancient Mexico." Subsequently, "The Revelation of Christianity" appeared, depicting a Spanish caravel arriving in the Americas, and close behind, "Fray Bartolomé de Las Casas" rolled past, carrying a youth costumed as the famed protector of Indians amidst children in native garb. Indigenous dancers in plumed headdresses surrounded the latter float. Then three representations of the "benefits of civilization" followed. On

"Agriculture," local señoritas posed amongst tropical plants and a cornucopia of fruit, and on "Mining" two boys portrayed workers at the entrance of a mine, which was borne upon wheels representing ten-peso coins. Subsequently, "Progress" emerged with Miss Esther Ramos playing the role of Industry, seated before a typewriter and surrounded by machines and other "modern objects."

At the end of the parade, three particularly elaborate floats synthesized the outcome of the preceding historical processes. First, a richly adorned "Oaxaca" emerged, commemorating "the state of civilization under the influence of Christianity." Then the most elegant float of all, "Commerce," swung into view, dramatizing the synergy of wealth, industry, and progress. At its apex, a boy dressed as Mercury presided over other children enacting a tableau of capitalist utopia. Luz Esteva depicted "Riches," and Miss Victoria Zorrilla Barrundia played the part of "Work," while Francisco Villasante and Enrique Baigts appeared as "Shipping" and "Railroads" respectively. Three additional señoritas stood in for modern civilization in the Americas, Europe, and Asia, and a black youth from the coast represented African modernity. Finally the last *carro*, "The Crown," appeared, depicting a cloud full of cherubs and a replica of Soledad's new crown. Following this lesson in history, culture change, social order, and progress, visiting dignitaries and Oaxacan elites retired to a *"lunch-champagne"* at the archbishop's residence. The general populace remained in the streets listening to the bands, marveling at the lights decorating the shrine's façade and domes, and enjoying a fireworks display.

The next morning, January 18, church bells began tolling at 5 a.m. to announce the coronation. By 8:30 crowds began to gather outside of the sanctuary, and dozens of policemen formed a human blockade, screening the entrance to the ample churchyard. Elegant women veiled in black lace mantillas and provincial mourning chic, prominent men in aristocratic suits—"*casacas* [frock coats] *y smoking*"—and over 130 Oaxacan clergymen filed past bystanders, presented numbered tickets, and followed ushers to preassigned sections of the sanctuary. The visiting prelates and the apostolic delegate sat directly before the altar, surrounded by Oaxaca's canons, prominent visiting priests, and the archdiocese's *vicarios foráneos* (head pastors). Gillow occupied his archbishop's throne to the right of the altar. Arrayed before the high clergy, much of the Oaxacan

La Agricultura.
(Beneficios de la civilización.)

Ruinas de Mitla.
(Símbolo de la civilización anterior á la Conquista.)

EL COMERCIO.

Revelación del cristianismo
figurada por un barco que arriba á las costas de América.

4 Archbishop Gillow's allegorical floats. "Agriculture (the benefits of civilization)" and "The Ruins of Mitla," surrounded by crowds at the head of the parade. "Commerce," the most elaborate float of the *gran manifestación* representing the synergy of Christian civilization and modern progress and "The Revelation of Christianity," depicting a Spanish ship bringing Catholic civilization to Mexico (*Álbum de la Santísima Virgen de la Soledad.* Used by permission of the AHAO).

priesthood occupied the left side of the sanctuary, visiting lay intellectuals sat on the right, and seminarians packed the choir. Thus, as the Virgin's crown entered on a gold-embroidered silk pillow born by gentlemen, flanked by two bishops, and trailed by forty-one matrons holding long ribbons tethered to the tiara, everyone—both those inside the sanctuary and the multitudes who amassed in the street and clogged the grand staircase and shady plaza outside—"knew" their place.[6] Several clerical dignitaries celebrated the liturgy, and a full orchestra and choir, incorporating the city's top musicians and seminarians, awed the audience with a Max Filke Mass, conforming to Pius X's recent directives on sacred music.[7] On this day, at least, pilgrims witnessed "appropriate" liturgical music. Finally, the Vatican's representative, Monsignor José Ridolffi, blessed the crown and positioned it on Soledad's head, sparking extended applause, devout *gritos* (such as *"¡que viva la Virgen de la Soledad!"*), joyous weeping, and the pealing of bells throughout the city.

As the Catholic dignitaries decamped to another sumptuous repast at the archbishop's palace, the shrine filled with devotees barred from the actual coronation. At 1 p.m. two rural parishes sponsored a special Mass for the region's Indians. A canon preached on Mary's special love for Oaxaca's natives and solicited their reciprocation. Gillow returned at 4 p.m. and delivered a speech recounting the Oaxacan church's recent accomplishments in the manner of his official histories, but he couched these gains as the Virgin's works. He expounded on all of his pet themes, such as Catholic education, lay associations, and frequency of the sacraments. He also stressed the continuing indoctrination of the region's native population: "Slowly but surely we are overcoming the resistance to receive instruction characteristic of a great majority of them."[8] Finally, he exhorted his audience to unite behind the pope, asserting that together, they would "restore modern society in Christ our Lord." Over the next eight days, a revolving door of scheduled indigenous-parish pilgrimages took turns paying their respects to the newly crowned image.

What are we to make of this event? We can characterize it as an exhibition of Catholic elitism and social conservatism, as well as a repackaging of the church's long-standing historical claims, including aspects of Creole nationalism.[9] These ingredients are readily apparent in the choreographed pageantry, sermons, theatrical blocking of individual participants and corporations, and careful exclusion of indigenous Marian devotion from the official ceremonies. We could also analyze Oaxaca's urban elite performing their identity and marking the differences between themselves and the region's Indian majority. Social differentiation was indeed on stage, as uniforms and insignia distinguished participants from spectators, and ticket holding and a *smoking* or mantilla set certain people apart from the sombrero- and rebozo-clad masses. More importantly, the social group that organized the coronation clearly sought to set a model of religious observance upon a pedestal and highlight the differences between this mode of practice and prevailing Oaxacan customs.

Resting our analysis on the marking of social and religious boundaries, however, leads to the classification of Soledad's coronation as an instance of almost campy elite pomp and a swan song of sorts for a group whose fortunes waned after the revolution of 1910. It leaves us with that smug sense of irony that historians too often assume when we highlight elite arrogance on the eve of social upheaval. It is true that Gillow, the Oaxacan church, and like-minded laypersons faced a series of setbacks in the decades following 1909, but their vision of Catholic society and history survived the revolutionary period.[10]

A detailed examination of this complex public performance of the Gillow model of Oaxacan Catholicism is a necessary complement to the reassessment of the prelate's career. This event distilled a vision and paraded idealized types, roles, and social meanings. It provided a portrait of how some historical actors thought the social order should look and function. The close congruence between the reported event and the Oaxacan archbishop's ideological proclivities may be due to our dependence on archdiocesan sources. It is possible that a less-invested observer might have described a very different coronation. But we must view these texts as components of the overall performance and historical documents. Gillow and his supporters went to great lengths to showcase their ideas and beliefs. It follows that they sought to shape the memory of their endeavors as well.

Any analysis of this event must be eclectic. In some ways, the coronation appears like a Victor Turner–esque ritual drama in which the church staged its interpretation of the social problems and presented its formula for their redress. Its architects drew in the public with a communication of the shared sacra, they critiqued secular modernity, they constructed a regional history, and they projected hopes of an ideal Christian future.[11] Soledad's coronation also lends itself to James Scott's ideas concerning dominant social groups' use of symbolic display to broadcast the "public transcript" justifying their authority.[12] The coronation and subsequent celebrations of its anniversary also bear the markings of an "invented tradition." Although Eric Hobsbawm spoke mostly of nation-states and their use of engineered ceremonies to create bonds of identity between governments and the governed, Oaxaca's high clergy created a festival to communicate their claims and engage the laity.[13] Oaxacan Catholic pageantry also echoes the history of parades examined by Susan Davis, particularly her close attention to public ceremony as an arena where social relations are constructed. Thus, the festivities of 1909 appear as a means of seizing space within the public sphere and demonstrating the dominance of certain social actors and the exclusion of others. Performing expressions of supremacy is an integral part of the meanings communicated by these types of events. In this vein, conventions of public display amount to social identity claims, and observers read them as such. In Soledad's coronation, this is most evident not only in the manner and organization of its grand procession, but in the modes of public religious practice the participants enacted. Furthermore, the celebrations evinced the manner in which societies select from high and low culture the histories, ideas, and symbols that are designated as traditions and incorporated into official cultural repertoires.[14]

The coronation of the Virgin of Solitude represents the Oaxacan clergy's most successful attempt to appropriate local sacred figures as the standards of their Catholic reform project. We see them deploying Soledad's potential as a symbol of regional identity and creating new traditions and symbolic dates around which to rally supporters. It also reveals a careful attempt to delineate the role of every Oaxacan in the civilized Christian social body and to showcase modern orthodoxy as conceived by the church. It was not, however, a cynical ploy. As evident in Gillow's biography, the genuinely effusive piety and conceptions of a divinely ordained social order on display during the coronation festivities were part of the successful modern Catholic resurgence worldwide. It was the performative public complement to other messages. But it was much more than a great megaphone. Like all effective public rituals, the coronation was an experience, both collective and personal. It gave a huge

Exterior de la Soledad en el día de la coronación.

5 The crowds outside the coronation, January 18, 1909
(*Álbum de la Santísima Virgen de la Soledad*, used by permission of the AHAO).

number of participants and observers a sense of spiritual belonging and meritorious fulfillment. Furthermore, it tapped emotions linked to Soledad that are still palpable in the *ex-votos* at the shrine. In addition, the months of activities culminating in the festival served as a long demonstration of the latest fashions of orthodox practice. In this regard, thousands of Oaxacans from across the social spectrum took part in the new modes of religiosity emphasizing disciplined fervor and orderly public display.

But did the coronation have the desired long-term impact that Gillow had in mind? Did it forge a disciplined, regional, Catholic social body united in the quest to Christianize modern society, or did it at least strengthen the resolve of devoted Catholics to stand firm against the errors of the secular age? Did it instill the new orthodoxy in Oaxaca's diverse and stubbornly independent flock? The Oaxacan church succeeded in putting on an impressive presentation of its religious and social vision, but the legacy of this performance is more ambiguous if we consider it alongside the contemporaneous European devotional spectacle or alternative religious visions that emerged within the archdiocese. Linking these poles of comparison reveals a weakness in the strategy of Mexican hierarchs. Their counterparts in Europe galvanized their supporters around narratives of apparitions and miraculous intercession infused with contemporary political significance. In Mexico, indigenous seers inspired committed followings convinced that the Virgin Mary and Christ had appeared in their midst and spoke to their lived experiences in their native languages. In contrast, the Mexican church retooled old devotions. While these acts proved popular, their ability to mobilize the faithful was ultimately ephemeral. The anniversary of a coronation proved a poor match for the emotional urgency inspired by the sense that sacred figures appeared among the faithful in the proverbial here-and-now and commented on society's relationship with God. A crown, regardless of its elaboration and Vatican certification, proved less compelling. In retrospect it appears to have been very successful at motivating the social groups closest to the archdiocesan hierarchy, Oaxaca's urban Hispanic elite and middle sectors. For the larger population, especially the region's indigenous Catholics, it may have represented a one-time blockbuster *feria* and an opportunity to observe high pomp and ritual at its most flamboyant.

DRAFTING IMAGES

The Virgin of Soledad's coronation, however, represents only the most famous part of Gillow's foray into Oaxacan devotionalism. To understand its significance, it pays to explore earlier efforts to canonize the Martyrs of Cajonos, precursors of Soledad's coronation (namely, the apparition of Lourdes and the coronation of the Virgin of Guadalupe), the archdiocesan build-up to the coronation, and efforts to extend the event's impact afterward. The Cajonos case stands as a curious example of Gillow's early efforts to elevate a chosen local tradition to the status of archdiocesan flagship devotion. Gillow failed to leave behind a personal testimonial as to why he seized upon this particular martyr narrative, and its idiosyncrasies suggest that in taking the case to Rome he misread the winds of saint making. The case probably caught his eye because it fit the historical narrative that he employed as the backdrop of his career in Oaxaca and allowed him to employ all his talking points. The story, as told by Gillow, is both simple and classic. Two indigenous *fiscales* (local lay officials in charge of the church in their respective communities) denounced backsliding fellow townspeople to Spanish missionaries in 1700 and died at the hands of idolaters in a subsequent tumult. Almost immediately after his arrival in Oaxaca, Gillow committed himself to collecting local testimony and framing the two heroes, Jacinto de los Ángeles and Juan Bautista, as champions of the region's Christianization and as symbols of Oaxaca's progress toward Catholic civilization.[15]

By his own account, Gillow learned of the *mártires* in 1888 while on a pastoral visit in the Sierra Juárez. What is remarkable is how rapidly he began to champion their cause. In July and August of 1889 he was already gathering evidence in Cajonos and nearby villages. Gillow was also eliciting testimony from doctors in Oaxaca City concerning signs of wear on the martyrs' remains and the prelate's personal, allegedly miraculous cure thanks to the proto-saints' intercession. Before the year's end he published a book on the affair, *Apuntes históricos*, and by February 1890 Mexico's Archbishop Labastida y Dávalos possessed a copy.[16] The rush stemmed from Gillow's impending trip to Rome for the Mexican ecclesiastical reform talks in 1890; while there he hoped to promote the martyrs' cause.[17] The testimony collected in the Sierra Juárez is interesting because it reveals that the hagiography emerged primarily from the family oral history of a priest from Cajonos, Juan Bautista Robles, and this individual's personal crusade to locate documents related to the case and the prospective saints' relics.[18] Robles recalled hearing the story from his parents. Apparently, an aged aunt heard the story some thirty-five or forty years earlier, from the priest's then-living centenarian grandmother, who in turn allegedly knew the martyrs' wives. Gillow failed to find firmer evidence of local devotion, such as a chapel or shrine, or publicly venerated image. Nonetheless, he offered recollections from Robles's family and acquaintances describing the previous existence of a painting depicting one of the *fiscales*, and doctors' tentative assurances that the martyrs' bones may have been the object of relic-centered practice. As for further evidence of the martyrs' sanctity, Gillow avowed that tracing the sign of the cross on his abdomen with one of their skulls had healed his inflamed appendix; his doctors provided supportive written opinions. Finally, the archbishop appended reports on continuing idolatrous practices in the Sierra Juárez.[19]

Why would Gillow, in the early years of his episcopal career, seize upon a devotion well outside of the mainstream of local practice and make it the centerpiece of his pastoral project? There were other options to be sure, such as scores of images with fervent followings, popular legacies of miraculous intercession, and venerable traditions. However, the Cajonos story brought together historical themes that interested the prelate in a manner that few other narratives offered. It included colonial missionaries in the field, specters of paganism, and simple, resolute indigenous Christians defying death. He presented the Oaxacan colonial countryside as a dangerous place for Christians, where social pressures encouraged regression into pre-Christian darkness, and native Catholics faced persecutions if they stood by their tender faith and the righteous missionary fathers. Although it seems an almost laughable stretch today, in crafting this narrative, Gillow transposed notions of the early church and its persecution to colonial Mexico. In addition, by stressing the endurance of indigenous idolatry in the 1700s and the late 1800s, he deployed stereotypes about Indian stubbornness concerning Christian enlightenment. At the same time, however, Jacinto's and Juan Bautista's embrace of the ultimate sacrifice allowed Gillow to certify Oaxaca's Christian foundations as strong and pure. In short, obstacles remained, and Indians were a slow and volatile lot, but the true faith and Christian civilization continued to progress in Oaxaca. The teleological subtext, of course, was that Catholicism's ultimate local triumph was only a matter of time and resolute stewardship.

Gillow's hopes of canonizing Jacinto de los Ángeles and Juan Bautista floundered in Rome in the mid-1890s.[20] (However, Pope John Paul II beatified them on August 1, 2002.[21]) They also inspired scant popular interest in Oaxaca. The archbishop's writings and archdiocesan documentation fail to explain why the canonization campaign encountered obstacles at the Holy See and then lost its luster for Oaxaca's prelate. Gillow was at the Vatican again in the late 1890s, yet he does not appear to have revived the martyrs' cause. In Oaxaca, they also faded from the spotlight. In 1910, the archbishop encouraged residents of Cajonos and nearby towns to mark Jacinto's and Juan Bautista's graves with crosses and then build a chapel to commemorate them, but he did not mention them in other communities.[22] The *mártires*, then, proved a dead end for Gillow, but other means of symbolically communicating his message and portraying his pastoral career presented themselves shortly. In retrospect, the archbishop's attempt to canonize the Martyrs of Cajonos served as a rehearsal for later projects.

As Gillow's interest in Indian *santos* waxed and waned, core groups within the Mexican Catholic hierarchy focused their energies on the coronation of the Virgin of Guadalupe. In fact, the martyrs' case probably floundered in Rome because it threatened to steal attention from Guadalupe's coronation and to muddle the illusion of religious unity promoted by the national patroness's champions. Guadalupe's coronation represents a departure from previous surges of *guadalupanismo* in Mexico. In the past, lay devotees and clerics pushed together for the image's recognition and forged its central place in the national identity. In contrast, the coronation fever that gripped the Mexican Church in the early 1890s emerged solely from the initiative of the Mexican hierarchs who had established strong ties to the Vatican after the Reform. The petitions, preparations, and staging of the coronation on October 12, 1895 took shape without significant lay input beyond a small cadre of conservative elite Catholics. The architects of this process were Mexico's Archbishop Labastida y Dávalos, until his death in 1891, and his nephew José Antonio Plancarte y Labastida. As we have seen, the elder Labastida was Gillow's chief patron within the Mexican hierarchy. His nephew was the Oaxacan prelate's contemporary, and they probably knew each other well. Both received their education in Europe and went to Rome in the early 1860s. Plancarte y Labastida, like Gillow, was also champion of Rome's Colegio Pío Latinoamericano.[23]

Plancarte was a coronation specialist. He participated in the crowning of Michoacán's Señora de la Esperanza (Our Lady of Hope) in 1885 and then turned his attentions to Guadalupe. The entire project drew its inspiration from European trends, particularly the apparition of the Virgin of Lourdes, her image's 1876 coronation, and her role as the symbol of Catholic defiance of secularism. Plancarte and his cohorts went to great lengths to modernize La Guadalupe and link her to the famous nineteenth-century French apparition. The basilica at Tepeyac received a heavy-handed renovation in the late 1880s and early 1890s to update the shrine's appearance, and Plancarte took the controversial step of commissioning the image's alteration to make her more reminiscent of Lourdes and nineteenth-century notions of the Immaculate Conception. In sermons and publications, the Guadalupe coronation's champions linked the Mexican Virgin to Lourdes and depicted them as twin highpoints in Mary's efforts to confound the church's opponents. Thus the "Immaculate of Guadalupe" thwarted Luther and Calvin, and the "Immaculate of Lourdes" foiled Voltaire and Rousseau. The framers of the Guadalupe coronation, of course, viewed Mexico's liberal state as a stand-in for these satanically inspired nemeses. In their view, just as Guadalupe appeared to banish pre-Columbian deities from the young nation, her coronation symbolized the hoped-for return of Catholicism to its central place in Mexico.[24]

While not a central player in the coronation's planning, Gillow was among the guests of honor at the celebration. He led a contingent of Oaxacans to the ceremonies in 1895. According to *Apuntes para la historia*, published in the archdiocese's *Boletín Oficial* in 1909, Gillow organized Oaxaca's first official pilgrimage to Tepeyac in 1893, in which one thousand locals took part.[25] In subsequent years, the archdiocese sent groups to the shrine every January 2, in addition to the May 12 date officially set aside for Oaxaca. Gillow took part in all but three of these official pilgrimages.[26] Most of southern Mexico, though, was not a stronghold of *guadalupanismo*. A glance at archdiocesan documentation reveals that other Marian advocations (Juquila, Rosario, and Soledad) enjoyed much larger followings. But like many of his counterparts, Gillow strove to augment the national patroness's devotion. He dedicated the seminary to Guadalupe and promoted large celebrations of her feast at its chapel. He also decreed her coronation anniversary an official celebration. In the same spirit, new religious associations under his protection usually chose her as their patroness, most notably the Catholic Workers' Circle.[27] In this regard, *guadalupanismo* in a region like Oaxaca often indicated a tie to the official projects of the high clergy. The Virgin of Tepeyac had become the standard of Mexico's Romanizing clergy and laymen who identified politically with the church. Gillow, a pivotal member of this group, proved an effective promoter of the Guadalupe cult.

Guadalupe, then, became the Mexican Mary Immaculate, the international symbol of militant Marianism. This ideology's Oaxacan spokesmen emphasized La Imaculada's role as "*vencedora*" (vanquisher)—the archprotector of the church. In colorful, belligerent flourishes, priests such as José Othón Núñez spoke of Mary splitting the heads of the church's opponents, usually with a clout from one of her dainty feet. He boasted she was the perfect antidote to "the century of Voltairian laughter."[28] In 1903, Pope Pius X decreed that all Catholics celebrate with the utmost fanfare the fiftieth anniversary of his predecessor's momentous declaration. The Oaxacan church leadership fashioned an elaborate commemoration that prefigured the Soledad coronation. In November 1903 the archdiocese published a schedule for the upcoming year, emphasizing a sequence of events centered on the eighth day of each month (a reference to the Immaculate Conception's official feast on December 8). Gillow also decreed a series of official pilgrimages to local Marian images. Slated every other month—from December 1903 to October 1904—and organized by special commissions headed by prominent clerics, these peregrinations honored the images of Juquila, Soledad, and a trio of Oaxacan Guadalupes (Tlacolula, Etla, and El Marquesado). Only Juquila's pilgrimage required an archetypal sojourn to a distant shrine. The rest entailed short trips within the Central Valley. Archdiocesan authorities directed religious associations to organize rounds of spiritual exercises incorporating as many people as possible. In addition, from January to June of 1904, Catholic revival missions took place in city churches and nearby parishes. The archdiocese also sought to schedule the maximum number of first communions during the year and directed parishes throughout the province to celebrate special services on the eighth of each month.[29] The culminating event was a celebration of the Imaculada's feast in Oaxaca City with Domingo Serfini, Rome's apostolic delegate in Mexico. Like his successor five years later, Serfini traveled to Oaxaca in a special charter train and received a triumphal reception at each parish along the route, before joining Gillow and the bishops of Oaxaca's suffragan dioceses in several days of celebrations.[30]

Aside from its role as a precursor of the Soledad coronation, the Oaxacan celebrations of the Immaculate Conception are significant because they included the Virgin of Juquila, the region's most popular Marian image. A diminutive statue, she has been Oaxaca's Imaculada since the seventeenth century. (Soledad is a representation of María Dolorosa.) Archdiocesan officials, however, viewed her strongly indigenous and lower-class devotion with distinct ambivalence. The numerous archdiocesan disquisitions on advocations of Mary and the Marian miraculous rarely even mentioned Juquila, preferring Guadalupe and famous European images. And yet, church archives reveal that Juquila's festival was (and remains) one of the most important pilgrimages in Mexico. Currently, Juquila's devotion dwarfs the Virgin of Soledad's, and middle- and upper-class Catholic discomfort with the hinterland Mary, her devotees, and the practices associated with her is still palpable.

During the Gillow era, Juquila's devotion probably overshadowed Soledad's in terms of the sheer numbers of pilgrims involved. Receipts remitted to the archdiocese reveal that the shrine's clerics typically commissioned thousands of lithographs, medallions, scapulars, embossed ribbons, and chapbook novenas in anticipation of her annual festival.[31] These prints can still be purchased relatively cheaply in their period tin and glass frames at antique flea markets. On December 17, 1899, Oaxaca's Catholic newspaper, *La Voz*, published one of the rare detailed descriptions of Juquila's annual *feria*. In it, an anonymous pilgrim recalled an unforgettable, moving experience among thousands of pilgrims from Oaxaca and Guerrero, who converged upon the shrine in an endless cacophony of devout song, anguished tears, and fervent prayer. Together they kept several priests busy performing nonstop confessions the entire day. Noting the preponderance of rural Indians, mountain laborers, and denizens of the *tierra-caliente* (a veiled reference to Afro-Mexicans), the author claimed that thirty thousand souls gathered before the sanctuary and on surrounding hillsides to witness Juquila's procession on her feast day, December 8. Subsequently, priests performed communion for eight continuous hours. In addition, during the festival pilgrims burned over 7,500 pounds of wax. Invoking international Marianism, the writer opined that most Oaxacans had little hope of visiting Lourdes, but Juquila offered manifestations of piety that defied description and consoled the heart, despite "an ungrateful, prevaricating century that has raised the standard of religious indifference."[32]

The anonymous pilgrim wrote within a tradition of commentary on Juquila pilgrimage practice. There have been only a handful of contributors to this tradition, but they have shaped a legacy of texts describing the rustic body of sojourners, the picturesque route, misfortunes visited upon less-than-devout participants, and laudatory recollections of the effusive piety at the shrine. All of the participants in this tradition write from an elite Central Valley perspective. Invariably, they describe the path to the shrine as originating in Oaxaca City, although they acknowledge travelers from elsewhere. In addition, all of the published narratives of the event

6 The Virgin of Juquila late-nineteenth-century or early-twentieth-century shrine souvenir (author's personal collection).

remain derivative of the text authored in the 1780s by the pastor of Zimatlán at the time, José Manuel Ruiz y Cervantes.[33] In the aggregate, these retellings of the pilgrimage's history and myths comprise what we could term the "White Legend" of Oaxacan popular Catholicism. The Ruiz y Cervantes text set the pattern, describing towns along the route, the Eden-like mountain wilderness separating the shrine from civilization, the intermingling of high- and low-born devotees, the inspirational faith of black, mestizo, and Indian pilgrims, and the din of native languages as the faithful beseeched La Juquilita. Neither he nor his successors tapped into the equally well-established tradition critical of non-Hispanic practice as polluted with the profane, superstitious, and disorderly. According to Ruiz y Cervantes, in the eighteenth century Juquila's feast attracted twenty-three thousand pilgrims and two thousand traders every year. Although this priest and subsequent authors stressed marathon celebrations of the sacraments as focal points of the pilgrim experience, they also underscored mass, unmediated supplication.[34] This kind of intense individual piety, devotion, and mass sacramentalism, however, was not the kind of practice Archbishop Gillow promoted. He was present at the shrine for Juquila's feast in 1900 but did not contribute to the legacy of Juquila commentary. His pastoral writings focused solely on the shrine's management.[35]

Juquila's festival atmosphere, free-form piety, melting-pot crowds, and its role as a trade fair featuring tropical products and horses set it apart from the coronation's regimentation and attention to social hierarchy. Although the attendance figures given by observers can only be considered rough estimates, Juquila attracted at least as many Oaxacans year after year as the Soledad coronation in 1909. Archdiocesan authorities estimated the Soledad festivities drew twenty-six thousand participants and spectators; our anonymous source claimed that thirty thousand pilgrims honored Juquila in 1899.[36] Surely promoting Juquila's devotion in Oaxaca would have been more successful than the Martyrs of Cajonos.

Regardless of Juquila's indisputable popularity, the Oaxacan clergy had other models in mind. The Juquila textual tradition essentially looked back in time to an imagined pious purity, as if Oaxaca's mountains and forests held back the currents of change. It is no coincidence that the editors of La Voz published a description of the pilgrimage festival in the waning days of 1899. As we have seen, the invocation of a colonial past of utopian religious harmony was a key aspect of Gillow's historical claims. Likewise, priests and church thinkers frequently railed against the nineteenth century and hoped the dawning of a new century would bring a religious comeback. This hope was palpable, and often openly expressed, in the sermons, journalism, and Catholic pageantry. In this spirit, the Virgin of Solitude's crowning emerged from the Lourdes/Guadalupe template. This model, however, although it invoked tradition, featured a different style of practice that sprang from the modern era's ethos of order and progress. The coronations of this period were not to be a jumble of the social classes, or a Babel of pious supplication. They showcased the ordered, idealized Catholic social body marshaled by the clergy in the reassertion of its civilizing mission. Indeed, it is difficult to imagine a celebration more symbolic of hierarchy and traditional social order than a coronation.

Oaxaca's coronation preparations began in earnest at least as early as 1906. In that year, Gillow participated in the coronation of Tlaxcala's Virgin of Ocotlán. According to his biographer, as he took part in this event, he was already mulling the coronation of Soledad.[37] During the same year the rector of the shrine published a book detailing the history of the image and adjacent convent.[38] On February 16, 1908, the archdiocese sent the Vatican a dossier of documents, historical texts, and its official request to crown the image. Revealing a much closer congruence with Rome's interests than in evidence in the Cajonos campaign, Oaxaca received a positive response from the Holy See on May 12.[39] On June 1, Gillow published a pastoral letter announcing the upcoming coronation, explaining its significance, and outlining coordinated religious exercises leading up to the climactic event.[40]

Appropriating a metaphor used during the Guadalupe coronation, the archbishop characterized the coronation as a plebiscite in which Oaxacans would affirm his vision of a Christian polis founded on the pillars of authority, obedience, devotion, and Christian love.[41] Only the Vatican could bestow this supreme recognition on a holy image, he noted, but the coronation's objectives exceeded the conferral of honors. Its higher purpose was to inaugurate the Christian "regeneration" of society. The world, he lamented, found itself in a state of profound malaise. Societies and individuals had "rejected the soft yoke of Christ," and found themselves tyrannized by their chaotic personal appetites, and hence doomed to maul each other in the headlong pursuit of riches and unseemly passions. The bonds that held civilization together, "between parents and children, between husband and wife, between patricians and proletarians, between authorities and subjects," lay broken, and the only way to restore them was through Christ. The most efficacious and sure path to the savior, he asserted, was Marian devotion. He then proceeded to outline a route by which Oaxacans would follow Soledad to Jesus and a well-ordered Christian society.

Gillow decided to crown Soledad on January 18, a month after her customary feast. His official biographer claimed that the archbishop decided not to hold the celebrations during her festival so that the "*buenos inditos*" (good little Indians) could visit her on the traditional date with their "habitual customs."[42] Despite his professed concern for indigenous sensibilities, Gillow, like the architects of the Guadalupe coronation before him, organized his staging of Catholic pageantry without significant input from the Virgin's humbler devotees and sought to distance it from the religious practices and low-brow ambiance associated with them. He was well aware that appropriating Soledad's feast day and circumscribing her longtime devotees' actions at the shrine invited embarrassing conflict. The avoidance of public disorder and celebratory intemperance was a paramount concern of archdiocesan authorities, as was evident in the incessant comments stressing "perfect order" in precoronation publicity and subsequent Catholic reportage. In this regard, they responded to a legacy of elite criticism of popular religion as a theater of social ills.[43] The upshot of these efforts was the emergence of what, for a few years at least, functioned like a separate devotion. Soledad's feast day remained an important pilgrimage festival, while the coronation anniversary became a celebration bringing together clergymen, Catholic elites, and Oaxaca City's modern church-affiliated institutions.

As scheduled, the spiritual preparations for the Soledad coronation commenced in August 1908. For the next five months, different churches within the city, parishes close to the capital, Catholic schools, religious associations, and urban sodalities took turns holding "pilgrimages" to the shrine, special spiritual exercises, and public acts of penance.[44] From November 11 through November 29, the city experienced an intense Catholic missionary revival. Every night during this two-week period, crowds gathered at city churches to hear visiting Jesuit and Dominican preachers, and many clergymen were on hand to hear confessions, perform complimentary marriages, and encourage the maximum number of Oaxacans to take communion. The archdiocesan press covered these events with great reverence and proudly trumpeted their orderly, pious demeanor.[45]

The goal, of course, was to create a crescendo of devotional intensity leading up to the coronation, to "prepare" Oaxacans, particularly those belonging to church-affiliated corporations, for the central event. The events also sought to impart the sensation that the faith was indeed changing society. In large measure, the archdiocese succeeded. In the hours and days immediately following the coronation, the church sought to work the rest of the population into the experience, albeit in a manner that relegated them to an after-the-fact role. For the most part, the clergy and visiting Catholic intellectuals turned their attention to the Fourth National Catholic Congress that followed the coronation. This forum became an intense arena of internal debate as the different factions within the church struggled to shape the Catholic sociopolitical voice amidst the presidential succession crisis on the eve of the Mexican Revolution. But elite Catholic political intrigue was of little import to most Oaxacans. Within a few months, Gillow unveiled a plan that positioned the coronation's anniversary as the symbolic hub of archdiocesan religiosity and attempted to institutionalize and extend the scripted fervor of Soledad's crowning.

INDIANS BEFORE THE QUEEN

In a circular published on May 1, 1909, the secretary of the archdiocese announced a permanent rotating schedule of pilgrimages to Soledad's shrine. A less ambitious Central Valley pilgrimage cycle had been in place since at least 1905, but now it theoretically incorporated the entire province.[46] A rough draft of this decree reveals the top-down nature of this project: "Turns that the Illustrious and Very Reverend Archbishop established on this day so that the outlying parishes can successively give homage to the Most Holy VIRGIN OF SOLITUDE."[47] On the eighteenth of each month from February through November, specific regional clusters of parishes, led by their respective pastors, were to come together at the sanctuary. The circular set aside December 18 for Soledad's customary feast and popular devotees, and January 18 for the clergy, Oaxaca City's Catholic corporations, and urban parishes. Church authorities thus hoped that over the course of the year representatives of the entire region would take their turns rendering homage to the archdiocesan patroness, with the provincial capital's urban Catholics taking charge of the region's latest addition to the liturgical calendar—the anniversary of the coronation. It is not hard to see what Gillow and the curia had in mind. Inspired by their successful organization of a dramatic show of Catholic fealty during the coronation festivities, they sought to maintain a rolling pilgrimage/Marian festival. Its yearly climax, the coronation anniversary, underscored the primacy of the archdiocesan seat and church authorities. During the other months, the city's residents would witness controlled, pastor-led Indian fervor as groups trudged into the urban center to worship at the shrine. From the church's point of view, this new pilgrimage cycle had great potential for several reasons. First, it provided a symbolic organizational/devotional focus for urban Catholics, holding them up as the model of appropriate practice for the entire archdiocese. This sentiment bore notions of cultural superiority, the Hispanic civilizing mission, and a sense of political mastery. Second, large groups of Indian pilgrims led by a parish priest in full regalia (Reform-era regulations prohibiting clerical garb in public went unenforced in Oaxaca) allowed the church to depict itself as the natural leader, and tamer, of the region's non-Hispanic rural masses. Third, from a pastor's perspective the pilgrimages brought a core group of individuals from their parishes to the archdiocesan seat for the complete experience of urban high Catholic ritual. The Oaxacan church clearly scripted these gatherings with this in mind. Pastors played the part of the Good Shepherd, bringing in the flock from the wilds, and as they entered the shrine these priests took their place at the side of one or more of the city's canons. In some instances, Gillow himself took part in the services and celebrated with the pilgrims. These events represent, in essence, a kind of schooling in the period's official fashions of religious practice and a display of ecclesiastical hierarchy in action.[48]

According to the Catholic press, for a time the plan enjoyed a modicum of success. In editions of the *Boletín Oficial* after 1909, editors almost always included a paragraph recounting which parishes had come to the sanctuary during the last month. *La Voz* provided more detailed coverage. In January and February, both publications included glowing reports on the celebration of the coronation anniversary. These events were a complement to the rural missions that the archdiocese had been promoting since the mid-1890s. In the missions, several urban preachers, confessors, and often a canon went out to the countryside. Lasting approximately a month, the missions gave rural communities the experience of truly priest-led Catholicism in a revival atmosphere and during a window of time in which the archdiocese suspended customary fees— although parishes or a sponsor paid approximately one hundred pesos to bring the missionaries. During these occasions, clerics organized supercharged Catholic "time outs" from the usual rhythms and doings of daily life. From morning until night, they were busy confessing, giving communion, preaching, teaching the catechism, preparing children to receive the sacraments, and "fixing" marriages.[49] Missions were also a key aspect of shrine festivals. Since most parishes never held them, this may have been the way most Oaxacans experienced them.[50] But bringing the faithful to the state capital and archdiocesan seat was another matter, both for the pilgrims and for the urban Catholics observing them.

As evident in the discursive traditions relating to the Juquila pilgrimage, Catholic writers tended to exoticize rural religiosity. In some instances, they fantasized that they had been transported to the dawn of evangelization and the pure, raw vitality of the early church. These writings reveal that Oaxacan writers, and presumably readers, were fond of the notion that indigenous fervor stemmed from a perpetual state of convert urgency, and they invariably expressed a condescending awe at what they portrayed as primitive and unvarnished religious passion. For example, in *La Voz,* Mariano López Ruís described his visit to the Lenten festival in Teposcolula dedicated to a local image of Christ on the cross.[51] He portrayed it as a return to the time of Saint Dominic and his mission among those completely ignorant of Christianity. Aside from his flights of fancy, Ruís emphatically praised the devotion of Teposcolula's women, arguing that they were living demonstrations of the religious qualities that men should also share. He lauded them as the guardians of Christian purity, whose pious lives amounted to a beautiful, unquenchable, tender protest. In describing the new rotating Soledad pilgrimage, the archdiocese incorporated aspects of this narrative tradition and its favored themes and metaphors, but also infused them with notions of a modern urban Catholic order. In short, they sketched the larger goal and mission of the church hierarchy in regard to Oaxaca's Indians—to fuel the traditions of simple fervent piety and unquestioning faith, but also to put clerics firmly at the head of ritual and practice, and thus bring about its purification and focus.

On February 11, 1910, the pastors of the Sierra Juárez mustered their respective groups of pilgrims after a month of preparations in their communities and Oaxaca City. Pilgrims from Totontepec and Yalálag, and their respective brass bands, traveled together on the first day, and met their counterparts and the parish priest of Cajonos on the twelfth. As they descended toward the Central Valley, they paused for religious talks given by the accompanying clerics, as well as recitations of the Rosary. On the sixteenth, this group met up with another priest and a contingent from communities under his pastoral care. Together, the 1,500 pilgrims and five pastors representing Sierra Zapotecs and Mixes entered the city "in correct formation" and with "indescribable enthusiasm," preceded by one of their brass bands. Up the same avenue that had been decorated for Catholic dignitaries a year earlier, they marched to Soledad's shrine. There, Canon Agustín Echeverría met them and led them in a litany and prayer. On the seventeenth, the pilgrims and a large number of city priests milled about the shrine most of the day as the clergymen struggled to prepare all of them for the sacrament of communion. For the Oaxacan church, this day of preparation represented the true focal point of the events. Ever since the first friars disembarked in Mexico, Catholic missionaries labored to impress upon indigenous peoples the centrality of the Eucharist and the crucial doctrinal linkage between confession, contrition, and communion. Generations of mendicants and parish priests had likewise expressed frustration at the Indian failure to perform "good" confessions and their cavalier attitude toward sin.[52] With this backdrop, and in the context of the modern church's efforts to make sacramental frequency the foundation of practice, large numbers of Oaxacan clergymen sought to convey to 1,500 indigenous individuals the significance of a rigorous examination of one's conscience, genuine repentance, a complete confession, acts of contrition, and making a personal commitment to shun sin in the future. Only after this process, they taught, was the soul properly prepared for the transubstantiated body of Christ.

That evening, indigenous pilgrims filled the sanctuary for matins, led by Echeverría and the orchestral stylings of Oaxacan maestro Cosme Velázquez. Afterwards they enjoyed fireworks and a serenade outside the shrine. On the following day, the symbolic eighteenth, Canon Mariano Palacios said Mass at 7 a.m. Admiring the orderly manner in which pilgrims took communion, *La Voz* exclaimed, "What a beautiful scene! To see hundreds of pious Indians receive Our Lord Jesus Christ. Lucky are the Poor!" Lily-bearing pilgrims from Cajonos—wearing the iconic indigenous homespun white accessorized with devotional medallions dangling on blue ribbons—won the newspaper's highest praise. Following a procession within the shrine, at 9:30 a.m. Gillow and members of the cathedral chapter celebrated a grand service for the pilgrims, with their pastors as attendants, in which the visitors experienced a performance of a Max Filke choral Mass, as at the coronation. They took this step, most likely, because coping with the clash of indigenous sensibilities and new Vatican rules regarding sacred music was particularly frustrating for Oaxacan priests.[53] *La Voz* judged the entire spectacle exemplary and looked forward to the arrival of other parishes and to the benefits that Oaxacan society would reap from their religious edification.[54]

Thus, for a couple of years, Oaxaca's Catholic press reported on the rotating pilgrimages to the Soledad shrine by the region's Indian parishes. All of them followed the same pattern: a triumphant pilgrim procession on the sixteenth as groups arrived at the city, a marathon of confessions and preparatory rituals on the seventeenth, and a high Mass and communion on the eighteenth. In keeping with the pious tradition of writing on Indian Catholic practice, reporters rarely failed to remind their readers of the inspirational simplicity and piety of humble native pilgrims. Yet there was also a crucial difference between these texts and the narratives generated by the previous urban observers of indigenous ritual, revealing an important inversion of perspective. They lack the travelogue-style tone of the writer as representative of civilization traveling back in time to witness primeval traditions and practices, although the authors do continue to champion the intensity of unlettered faith over educated indifference and doubt. Instead, they describe indigenous Catholics guided to the ordered urban center. In this turnabout, discussions of free-form piety and the jumble of prayerful native tongues vanishes, giving way to descriptions of Indian pilgrims as willing clay in the modern Catholic civilizing mold. They arrive "captained" by their pastors, approach the archdiocesan seat and its patroness in tidy devout formation, and acquiesce to "preparation" for the Eucharist. Finally, they partake in the sacrament of communion as mediated by Oaxaca's curia, and absorb the splendors of the latest liturgical fashions. None of these reporters included an opinion or utterance from their subjects—the heralded Indian pilgrims. It is possible that the idyllic scene of orthodoxy and indoctrination existed only in the pages of the Catholic press, but we lack alternate sources. Nonetheless, these narratives preserve a particular vision of Mexican progress and cultural change, and they reveal Oaxaca's Catholic elite asserting its religious and social claims. The coronation of the Virgin of Solitude represented the most complete portrait of the revived church's conception of appropriate social order and reformed practice. The subsequent rotating pilgrimages revealed their prescription of how best to modernize Mexicans. In this view, the church brought the rustic Indian to Western civilization, and "good" Indians—those not addled by their stereotypical rejection of change or seduced by modern error—led by a zealous clergy and a simple but firm faith embraced the opportunity. Through these official Indian pilgrimages, suffused with colonial symbolism and showcasing the coronation-centered model of practice, the Oaxacan church proclaimed a revived potency to all observers, and conveyed its lessons of hierarchy and history to the groups they excluded from the crowning events.

THREE

≋ The Spirit of Association

The Gillow-era revitalization project took place in two stages. An initial phase, between 1887 and the late 1890s, featured the reorganization and expansion of the local clergy, along with the shoring up of finances—in other words, it laid the foundations for more ambitious undertakings. During this period, Gillow and a close-knit group of disciples set about to construct a model of Catholic practice in Oaxaca City that looked, sounded, and felt modern, and yet also evoked tradition. In the second phase, emerging in the late 1890s, the Oaxacan clergy began a determined effort to extend this model to the entire archdiocese. It is crucial, therefore, to trace this process in greater detail through a close examination of one of its most salient aspects: the archdiocesan clergy's approach toward religious collectivities and devotions, particularly their attempt to generalize the *asociación canonicamente erguida* (canonically structured association).

Before we enter into a discussion of preexisting sodalities, new religious associations, and pilgrimage traditions, a few clarifications are in order. First, it is not my intention to identify a specific event dividing a phase A from a phase B. Gillow and his lieutenants approached their task according to the template for Catholic restoration in the Americas that emerged from the Vatican. During Leo XIII's pontificate

(1878–1902), efforts to reform the church in Latin America stressed a crucial role for lay associations integrated and organized within parishes, and under close clerical direction. Ideally, these institutions would champion the church's agenda in secular spheres where clerical action often proved difficult. Vatican planners, however, realized that their hopes of wielding a parish-based lay instrument of policy depended upon establishing better control of distant ecclesiastical provinces and clergymen. When they contemplated Latin America's ecclesiastical corps in the late nineteenth century, they judged local hierarchies too independent and the village clergy poorly trained. In addition, they considered indigenous Catholics only partially evangelized. Hence, the Vatican concluded that the Latin American church required top-to-bottom reform, and it inaugurated a process that included the strengthening of episcopal control, administrative and economic restructuring, the professionalization of the clergy, and a broad movement to educate and moralize Latin American Catholics and integrate them into new ecclesiastically controlled bodies.[1] Gillow was a key player in the codification and implementation of these plans during the 1890s and 1900s.

Although the Oaxacan clergy moved on several fronts at the same time, they followed the Vatican's outline for reform and restoration. The two-part nature of its implementation in Oaxaca was mostly a function of a conventional hierarchy of priorities. When the curia deemed certain goals accomplished and the conditions propitious for the broader array of reforms, they turned their attention to the next level of goals. Hence, the restoration of urban infrastructure, as well as ecclesiastical and fiscal reform, dominated the first decade or so of Gillow's tenure. The ambitious efforts to establish a strong lay institutional network and to reform the laity began almost immediately, but remained in the shadows of other projects for several years. Toward the end of the nineteenth century, however, Gillow and his priests felt sufficiently confident about the state of the ecclesiastical government, the clergy, and infrastructure to give increased attention to the Vatican's call for new religious associations.

Two important gatherings in Rome during the 1890s shaped this agenda: the 1890–91 Mexican provincial reform council and the 1899 Latin American Plenary Council. During the former, Gillow strengthened his ties to the papal court after nearly two decades in Mexico, and emerged as a pivotal figure within the Mexican hierarchy. He returned to Oaxaca to

7   Prominent Oaxacan priests and laymen, circa 1903: José Othón Núñez, no. 4; Lorenzo
    Mayoral, no. 6; the director of Oaxaca's Catholic newspaper, Agustín Espinoza, the
    future secretary of the archdiocese, no. 7 (AHAO, Fotografías, used by permission of
    the AHAO).

press a more clearly articulated, Vatican-inspired agenda than was in
evidence during his first three years in office. Immediately following his
participation in this gathering, he issued decrees on the establishment of
new lay associations. The 1899 council produced the Vatican's official
synthesis of its Latin American reform plan. Gillow returned from this
assembly with even greater prestige. This last event clearly represents a
signpost of transition. Oaxaca's archbishop came back from Rome following his participation in the council and redoubled his commitment to the
Vatican's initiatives, issuing a flurry of directives aimed at the laity. In
these decrees, and throughout the rest of his career, he cited the council's
conclusions as the basis of his actions.

Local events also signaled new directions. Between 1895 and 1900,
Gillow established many new parishes, and in some cases shifted curacies
between towns within the same parish. In 1901, the archdiocese began
publishing its official organ (the *Boletín Oficial*) to keep the village clergy
informed of religious activities in Oaxaca City and the world, and create a

medium expressing official policy on parish administration. Finally, between 1899 and 1902 came the symbolic climax of Gillow's infrastructure renovation program. In October of 1902, Gillow reconsecrated Oaxaca City's lavishly remodeled church of Santo Domingo, thus rescuing the monumental spiritual nerve center of the region's colonial evangelization from decades of government desecration. In the Oaxacan curia's estimation, from Rome to Roayaga, the stage was set. The archdiocese's internal documentation reveals that seminary education, clerical discipline, parish administration, and church finances remained concerns. In addition, urban practice still consumed an inordinate amount of archdiocesan attention. Outwardly though, the curia proclaimed the urban Catholic renewal complete and publicized a push to re-instill Christian morality in the greater population and repair the social order much as it had restored the gilded glory of Santo Domingo.

AN INSTITUTIONAL LANDSCAPE

In the 1890s and 1900s, Catholic prelates and thinkers tirelessly proclaimed the importance of "*el espíritu de asociación*" (the spirit of association). They argued that man's formation of corporations represented the crucial building blocks of Christian civilization and that liberal reforms erred in dismantling these aggregations, be they guilds, religious orders, or peasant sodalities. According to this point of view, outside of collectivities, humans were vulnerable to unscrupulous secular authority and their own passions. A crucial aspect of Catholic revival, then, entailed the renovation of the lay institutional base. The foundations upon which clergymen like Gillow proposed to build, however, were not as weak as they claimed. Oaxacan communities sustained rich religious institutional cultures that seasoned their response to ecclesiastical efforts to alter local organizational structures. During the colonial period, most villages founded a range of *cofradías* (confraternities) and *hermandades* (brotherhoods). The former theoretically possessed an approved charter defining their religious obligations, and the latter were less formal devotional organizations. Particularly in the case of *cofradías*, they collectively managed lands, funds, and other goods in the name of a saint or image. During the Gillow era, however, the most important rural religious institutions were the *mayordomías* of the *cargo* system. Closely linked to

Indian communal identity and politics, and thus resistant to priestly oversight, they served as the organizational epicenters of indigenous Catholic practices. Essentially a nineteenth-century defensive adaptation to reforms banning collective property ownership, *mayordomías* rarely held lands and livestock like their predecessors. Instead, they sustained specific image-centered devotions by transferring the responsibility for local religious celebrations to different individuals (known as *mayordomos* when serving) every year. Much of the economic burden fell upon the individual and his extended family, but in turn the *mayordomo* earned considerable prestige. Some communities maintained dozens of *mayordomías*.

Oaxaca's history of Catholic institution building during this period mirrors broader national trends. Scholarly analyses of Mexico's Cristero Rebellion (1926–29) stress the decisive nature of lay associations in the church's resurgence and their function as the seedbeds of Catholic militance. In some regions, they became the support network of counter-revolutionary insurgency.[2] Lay institutions in the post-Reform period served as refuges for a disgraced conservative opposition and centers of Catholic social life. Liberal laws required that these pious associations proclaim exclusively devotional goals, but their dual emphasis on religious self-actualization and the promotion of a truly Christian order inculcated in participants the church's sociopolitical and historical positions. They began to emerge almost immediately after 1867 and gained momentum in the 1890s and the early 1900s. Catholic educational institutions, and the emerging militant Catholic press, paralleled their growth. Indeed, the same constituencies supported all these developments.[3]

These trends, in part, emerged from broader transformations in Mexican society. Starting in the late 1860s, new institutions emerged and existing ones were strengthened as the most intransigent Catholics attempted to create spaces insulated from secular society. The most obvious example is the expansion of parochial schools and groups like the Sociedad Católica. During the 1890s, a new generation of Catholics—less burdened by the humiliations of the Reform era—began to enunciate a more ambitious goal: the re-Christianization of Mexican public life. Two crucial periods in Catholic institution formation emerged as this movement gained momentum. The first, between 1899 and 1902, coincided with political realignments taking place in the context of Porfirio Díaz's fifth reelection campaign, and the publication of Leo XIII's encyclical *Graves de Communi* (1902). The famous pope's last encyclical enunciated the concept of Christian democracy and inspired many young Catholics to redouble their commitment to "social action." During a relatively short span, the nation witnessed a burgeoning of Catholic study circles, worker organizations, Marian associations, and schools. This flurry of activity represents the Catholic contribution to a general expansion of civil society at this time. In other words, as one sector of society formed *clubes liberales*, another met in *círculos católicos*, or one of the new groups with dramatic and cumbersome names such as the Archconfraternity of the Honor Guard of the Sacred Heart. A second uptick of church-connected institution formation took place between 1909 and 1911, when crisis within the Díaz administration tipped the scales of Catholic opinion toward groups advocating openly religious political mobilization. From this later boom emerged national organizations like the Operarios Guadalupanos, the Unión Católica de Obreros, and the Partido Católico Nacional.[4]

Analyzing this phenomenon in Oaxaca, Daniela Traffano argues that the expansion of new lay associations represents an innovation in the Oaxacan religious scene rooted in an urban-led push to encourage priest-centered orthodoxy. Thus the new *sociedades* and *asociaciones* of the 1870s and 1880s evinced the conspicuous presence of priests as founders and directors, and focused their energies on particular images, the teaching of orthodox doctrine, and "moralization." Traffano attributes their expansion to a synergy between clerical efforts to secure new funding sources and the spiritual void felt by Oaxacans as their traditional brotherhoods floundered in the face of liberal laws.[5] Her conclusion that new religious associations featured the expansion of urban institutions into the countryside and clerical efforts to increase their control of lay religious expression is indeed true, but describing the phenomenon as a meeting, to quote the Mexican proverb, "*de hambre y necesidad*" (of hunger and necessity) oversimplifies its causation and unfairly casts the clergy as predatory.

The impulse behind the expansion of Catholic associations was twofold. On the one hand, the spread of canonically structured associations represents the flow of modernizing currents within the church from urban centers to rural parishes, as facilitated by the clergy. On the other hand, as the new institutions—disengaged from local structures of male civil authority—took root, their infusion with the period's Catholic militance offered devout women a ready-made critique of the status quo. They did not encourage a frontal assault on patriarchy, but in providing an alternate religious patriarchal order, a moral high ground of sorts, standards of public action, and an idealized social model, the new associations supplied a platform from which to comment on public life. Priests, of course, were supposed to lead these institutions, but in practice, local women often held the reins. Equally important, militant Catholic ideology during the period held up women as the standard of proper moral and religious comportment, and the associations supplied acceptable public spaces for like-minded women, a new social niche for enterprising individuals, and an inexhaustible outlet for female initiative and energy. As we shall see, these women proved crucial to the expansion of canonically structured associations.

New pious associations had begun to emerge before the Gillow period in Oaxaca. Church documents demonstrate quite graphically that they took hold quickly in a region with a deep culture of religious collectivities. During the 1870s and 1880s, the mission statements and bylaws of myriad new associations appeared. Today they share archival space with the accounts remitted by older sodalities and the inventories of local brotherhoods. Contemplating similar issues in late-eighteenth- and nineteenth-century Yucatán, Terry Rugeley suggests that we have overstated the demise of the colonial indigenous brotherhood. He argues that clerical oversight historically waxed and waned in sodalities that were probably hybrid in their ethnic and class composition from their inception. Yucatecos experienced the withering of the colonial sodalities with scant protest. The role of outsiders in local religious collectivities probably engendered varying levels of ambivalence, but the fundamental religious and social functions of traditional sodalities endured in new guises. In essence, then, new organizations often felt much like their predecessors.[6]

Oaxacan evidence suggests a similarly less-than-jarring transition and considerable overlap, and even cross-pollination, between "new" and "old" institutional forms and functions. Perhaps the most telling proof of this is the tendency of many clerics and laypersons to use the terms *cofradía, hermandad, mayordomía,* and *asociación* almost interchangeably into the twentieth century. Oaxacan documents also indicate that the priestly preeminence stipulated in regulations may have been a nod to archdiocesan dictates rather than an accurate reflection of reality. Given this scenario, it seems unlikely that enterprising village priests spurred the spread of new associations by taking advantage of local nostalgia for defunct sodalities.

The various new Catholic associations proclaimed distinct goals. For example, the Asociación Pia de la Caridad (Pious Association of Charity) in Ocotlán united in 1870 around the devotion to a Marian painting, care for the sick, and organized mutual aid.[7] In contrast, Oaxaca City's Sociedad Católica de Señoras (Catholic Women's Society) outlined a militant, orthodoxy-inducing mission in 1878. The woman in charge of "branch relations," Maria Santaella, demanded statistics on good works, children taught the catechism, and compliance with the *precepto pascual* ("Easter duty" confession and communion during Lent). According to Santaella, their inspiration emerged from a "Call from God to elevate the spirit of religion and sustain it against the advances of impiety and the corruption of customs that reigns in the current epoch, through the education of children and people of all kinds, procuring in them the frequenting of the sacraments, and also through the protection of divine ritual."[8] Thus, ladies of the Sociedad outlined a dual program for their rural affiliates: to form a bulwark against corrupting cultural change and to bring orthodox order to local practice. But although Santaella's rhetoric emphasizes the defense of tradition, this claim masks the society's attempt to generalize the frequenting of the sacraments, which represented an attempt to alter the dynamics of practice rather than preserve enduring modes of religiosity. Santaella understood her role as part of an ongoing civilizing mission; she and her colleagues targeted society broadly, announcing their intentions to bring their rural counterparts in line with the priest-mediated, sacrament-based faith of Oaxaca City.

Further evidence of the Sociedad's centralizing character and urban origins can be seen in a pamphlet that served as the group's didactic prayer manual and regulations two decades after Santaella's correspondence with the branch presidents.[9] Published in 1899, this document gave even greater emphasis to the efforts to transform and discipline rural practice (and thus society as a whole), stipulating that the goal of the group was the "moralization of the communities by means of religious instruction, the frequency of the sacraments, aid for the needy, the promotion of pious books, and the protection of divine ritual." Accordingly, each branch should function as a doctrine-imparting, civilizing platoon of devout women led by a powerful *presidenta* (female president) who appointed all other officers to safeguard "the best order possible." It makes no mention of feasts, although it stipulates the sponsorship of masses for the group's patrons (the Immaculate Conception and Saint Joseph, both strongly associated with the church hierarchy). Above all, the regulations instructed rural branches to focus their efforts on teaching the catechism and modeling the frequency of the sacraments. Finally, after going on at length about their culture-change agenda, the statutes returned to the discourse of defending tradition. Their ultimate goal, they insisted, was for members to approach the proverbial pearly gates declaring, "I fought the good fight: I have finished my race: I kept the faith."

As in his other endeavors, Gillow distinguished himself as a promoter. His writings reveal that he supported both new associations and the maintenance of preexisting religious collectivities, and they suggest that he felt all of them served the interests of the church. Indeed, in the neo-Thomism embraced by the Vatican and activist Catholics at the time, if the Christian social body comprised many distinct, aggregate parts in orderly harmonious interaction, then it followed that groups would form diverse institutions to foster personal and communal spiritual growth and to organize ritual. But Gillow made a special effort to support organizations, like Ms. Santaella's, that combined militant orthodoxy with the sponsorship of ritual and exhibited the modern organizational culture expanding during the late 1880s and 1890s.

Gillow's actions are interesting on two levels. First, they reveal his attempt to discipline local Catholicism in a manner reminiscent of Bourbon-era prelates. Second, they demonstrate the local implementation of late-nineteenth-century Catholic reforms embodying the characteristically modern sensibilities of bureaucratization, centralization, and standardization, as well as the efforts of elites to expand their control of popular groups. An abiding practicality, however, guided the prelate's actions. He appeared loath to offend traditional sensibilities. In the early years of his tenure he lauded the devout sentiments of Catholic collectivities in general and encouraged their preservation and formation in his formal reports (*autos de visita*) read publicly following pastoral visits.[10] He was rarely specific in his comments on "*las hermandades y cofradías*" at this time. In communities where he found these groups busily celebrating

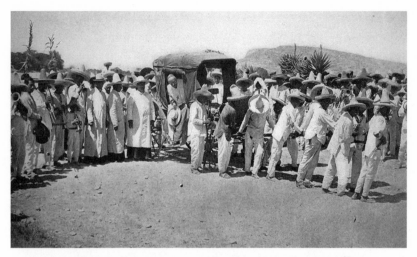

8 Archbishop Gillow on one of his many pastoral visits note how the residents of the
indigenous parish have removed his mules in order to pull the carriage themselves (José
Antonio Rivera G.. *Reminiscencias del Ilustrísimo y Reverendísimo Señor Doctor Don
Eulogio Gillow y Zavalza.* 2nd ed. Mexico: Escuela Linotipografica Salesiana. 1921).

their traditional feasts in cooperation with local priests, he applauded
local piety and spiritual fortitude. Outside of these official declarations,
however, many of his deeper concerns appear in the off-the-record commentary interspersed with the texts of his *autos* in his diaries. Here the
prelate revealed apprehensions occasioned by what he viewed as rampant
religious disorder. He noted rumors of idolatry, insubordinate sodalities,
sloppy administration, rag-tag ritual settings, negligence toward contributions and fees, limited doctrinal understanding, and cavalier attitudes
toward the sacraments.[11]

Throughout the first decade of his career, Gillow emphasized, first and
foremost, his quest to bring order to the Oaxacan church. Focusing on
clerical discipline issues, his first pastoral instruction represented his initial step in this direction. Pastoral visit writings demonstrate that the formation of new associations under close priestly supervision represented
another aspect of this goal, particularly in relation to the tattered aspect
of rural ritual and lay laxities. In February 1895, while touring the Oaxacan Pacific Coast, Gillow held forth on his ideals of priest-parishioner
relations, delineating a crucial role for lay associations. Communities
should treat their pastor with love and respect, and he, in turn, should

be a paragon of charity and zeal. Priests should establish Catholic schools, preach the gospel tirelessly, watch over the community, and safeguard morals by making sure the laity respected marriage. Gillow asserted that the main objective of associations should be the promotion of orthodox ritual. In addition, they should help the "*socias*" (female members) make progress toward personal sanctification, stimulate virtue and peace within and between families, and demonstrate exemplary piety for the community. He directed priests to select the community's catechists from among the most zealous individuals, to form a council of directors for each association, and to convene periodic public meetings, taking care to avoid gossip-inspiring private encounters with female members. In some communities, Gillow occasionally went so far as to decree the establishment of particular associations, noting their crucial role in organizing good works. Devoid of Christian labors to improve the commonweal, lectured the prelate, faith was dead.[12]

In his third pastoral instruction (1911), Gillow elaborated on his conception of the religious association's role in local communities. He revealed that his policies on associations also emerged as a means of organizing the more Hispanized members of communities and encouraging them to follow in the footsteps of colonial missionaries, shouldering a local campaign to Westernize/Christianize Oaxaca's Indians. Pastors, he stressed, should organize the best-educated individuals within their parishes into separate male and female "brotherhoods" that, although working separately, could come together for rituals. These "associations," he proclaimed, would, in turn, become the priests' staunchest supporters and could organize religious education centers to attract "*indios y indias*" (male and female Indians) to pray. Once in the company of their indigenous neighbors, members should teach them the catechism. Gillow cautioned priests not to become complacent about these crucial institutions after their foundation. Mexicans, he cautioned, revealed a peculiar weakness in the "spirit of association." Too often members proved fickle and groups withered after a short time. Thus he directed priests to visit associations frequently, providing them with doctrinal texts and taking care to inspire their evangelical civilizing endeavors. Gillow also stressed the importance of association members as personal exemplars of proper religious practice, opining that modeling orthodoxy would serve to generalize frequenting the sacraments, or at the very least, fulfilling the Easter duty. In a different portion of this document, Gillow revealed what underlay his concerns with Oaxaca's Indians. Simply improving their economic status, as some people suggested, without instructing them in the "healthy principles of morality, order, and religion," would only encourage them to become vagrants and socialists, and hence threats to Christian society.[13] As expressed at the Fourth National Catholic Congress held in Oaxaca in 1909, the root goal was to finish the cultural mission inaugurated by colonial missionaries and to bring Indians definitively into "*la comunión civilizada*" (civilized society).[14]

In a sense, the religious association's role in rural Oaxaca was a local manifestation of the *clase directora/clase inferiór* (leading class/lower class) conception of society bandied about in Catholic circles at the time. But linking practice with clear ethnocultural associations must have been felt acutely in individual communities. In this climate, joining an association or frequenting the sacraments amounted to a statement of religious identity tinged with racial implications. Gillow and his priests rarely spelled this out, but it marbles their writings and commentary on parish administration. For example, Father Vicente González mentioned the founding, in the late 1890s, of a particular association in his parish among "*los de razón*" (those of reason, i.e., Hispanized residents). Neither González nor any of his colleagues, however, established associations specifically for "*los de idioma*" (literally those of language/dialect, i.e., Indians).[15] Frequently, the Westernizing thrust of religious associations in Oaxaca comes through in comments about association members being educated, economically successful, and exemplars of orthodoxy. As we will see, since relatively few individuals frequented the sacraments, it seems that most Oaxacans were not impressed by the models of orthodoxy in their midst, or perhaps felt unwelcome among Hispanic elites.

NEW ASSOCIATIONS

Archbishop Gillow praised many associations, but, in keeping with the centralizing thrust of his administration, he decreed the establishment of a few specific organizations across the entire province. Invariably, they were closely tied to the era's Catholic militance, boasting international bureaucracies and Vatican-approved statutes. Two of these associations merit special attention due to the early effort to implant them in Oaxaca, and the distinct niches they targeted—the Asociación Universal de la Sagrada Familia (Universal Association of the Holy Family) and the Apostolado de la Oración (Apostolate of Prayer).

Founded in Lyon, officially approved by Pius IX in 1870, and based in Rome, the Sagrada Familia sought to inspire poor working families to dedicate themselves to the devotion and emulation of the Holy Family. According to its Vatican sponsors, the savior's family presented humble Catholics with the model of paternal solicitude in Saint Joseph, the epitome of maternal love, feminine submission, and perfect faith in Mary, and the paragon of divine obedience in Christ. Member families could theoretically also find solace in the carpenter-patriarch's struggle for daily sustenance and Christ's participation in manual labor as they contemplated a standardized image of the sacred household and recited a short rhyming prayer. The official regulations stipulated that each ecclesiastical province should assign a cleric to direct the association, and that he, in turn, should communicate with local parish priests in order to keep track of families consecrated in yearly association rituals.[16]

The Sagrada Familia, however, failed to take hold in Oaxaca. Perhaps the clergy promoted it halfheartedly, or its intended audience failed to respond. Nonetheless, its paper trail reveals church efforts to tailor new associations to specific social classes. The association fits a larger pattern of targeting working-class groups, attempting to bring them under clerical supervision, and establishing religious practices with the poor in mind. In contrast to some other associations, rituals in the Sagrada Familia lacked lengthy prayers and spiritual exercises.[17] The devotional requirements involved only displaying the Holy Family's image and praying before it together. Literacy was not required of the membership, and, surprisingly, the regulations do not mention the standard of period orthodoxy—frequenting of the sacraments.

In marked contrast to the Sagrada Familia, the Apostolado de la Oración, an association closely tied to the Jesuit order, intertwined devotion to the Sacred Heart of Jesus and the Blessed Sacrament with a campaign to inspire regular communion. It became ubiquitous within the archdiocese during the Gillow period. The prelate's first act, upon returning from Rome in 1891, was to consecrate Oaxaca and its subject dioceses to the Sacred Heart, decree the celebration of the devotion's feast in every church, and require that branches of the Apostolado be established in each parish.[18] Perhaps due to his personal ties to the Jesuit order, Gillow gave this association enthusiastic and sustained support. During his tenure, the July feast of the Sacred Heart loomed large in the Oaxacan religious calendar, occasioning elaborate novenas. Oaxaca City's all-male branch of the Apostolado became the center of urban elite devotionalism.[19]

Oaxaca, in fact, was participating in the Apostolado's international surge. The archdiocese's 1901 report on the association and devotion to the Sacred Heart reveals the organization's cellular structure, international scale, and religious-reform thrust. The Apostolado boasted 5,225 affiliated associations worldwide, 77 diocesan directors, 100,000 *celadores* and *celadoras* (male and female wards), and 3 million general members. Mexico's data reveals a preponderance of female participation. The nation supported 500 branches, with 1,025 *celadores*, 9,259 *celadoras*, and 250,000 affiliated individuals. In the typical chapter, a director-priest presided over a board of directors, and each *celador/a* oversaw several individuals of the same sex. If these figures are accurate, women outnumbered men in Mexico's Apostolado by nine to one. Aside from the sheer number of participants at different levels, the association's official organ enjoyed a circulation of fifteen thousand issues per month, and its customary services on the first Friday of each month occasioned 740,000 monthly communions worldwide.[20]

In the nineteenth century, devotion to the Sacred Heart became one of the preeminent symbols of Catholic militant revival. It emerged from the seventeenth-century visions of a French nun and arrived in Mexico with eighteenth-century Jesuits. During the early 1800s, an organization called the Pía Unión (Pious Union) nurtured its growth. French Jesuits founded the Apostolado in 1844, and it gained a foothold in Mexico during 1870s, becoming the Sacred Heart's standard-bearer throughout the Catholic world. The devotion emphasized intense meditation on the contrast between the perfect suffering heart of Christ and the sin-stained heart of the devotee. Christ's heart, followers believed, was the source of both divine love and redeeming grace, but suffered tortuous wounds, often rendered as multiple impalings, inflicted by man's indifference and outright contempt for the church's teachings. In the context of nineteenth-century history, the issue of humankind's role in Christ's suffering had strong political connotations. It rendered those political acts and movements that were at odds with the church as torturers of Christ.[21]

Ruminations on personal failings, society's crimes against the faith, and the savior's ideal righteousness logically led to a heightened reverence for the Eucharist, the body of Christ. Thus, a special focus of the Apostolado was to encourage members to take communion and venerate the Host. Frequent participation in this sacrament required equally regular confession, lest the believer profane the Blessed Sacrament. In sum, the Apostolado represents a determined program to establish a distinct, more intense rhythm and individualistic focus within Catholic practice. Although its members celebrated the feast of the Sacred Heart, they made a much deeper commitment than the simple sponsorship of another festival: to contemplate their shortcomings, undertake the stipulated penance, and take communion at least once a month at the association's masses. This was much more than proletarian-targeted devotions required.

Clearly, Gillow and his contemporaries, in promoting the Apostolado, targeted a different sector of the population, one capable of greater discipline and reading the association's organ. In short, the Apostolado aimed to mobilize the elite, educated middle sectors of society both religiously and politically. The Sacred Heart's linkage to conservative politics in Europe and Mexico also gave its flagship association and rituals an added level of social meaning and prestige. The Apostolado, therefore, represents a distilled example of how a religious commitment to a particular devotion and frequent priest-led sacramental practice also entailed a statement of Catholic political identity. In the Mexican context, it also involved supporting the church's Hispanizing project. The political implications of the devotion took on greater significance when the church consecrated the Mexican nation to the Sacred Heart in 1914 with counterrevolutionary dictator Victoriano Huerta's blessing. This act symbolically sealed the church's reactionary reputation in the eyes of revolutionaries and subsequent generations of historians.[22]

Gillow, as we have seen, ordered the extension of specific associations throughout the archdiocese, but in the case of the Apostolado he made a personal commitment to make reality reflect pronouncement. The prelate and his priests, however, encountered a preexisting "spirit of association" difficult to mold to their purposes. Again, Gillow did not suppress older devotional institutions; he treated them as evidence of the endurance of an ostensibly pure faith implanted by colonial missionaries. In his view, the intervening years had brought a variety of "abuses and imperfections," which he and his priests attributed to the independent nature of many devotions. In addition, these clerics tended to view irregularities in local practice, as well as outbreaks of social unrest, as products of the Reform's weakening of church authority over the native population. Their basic premise was that religious and social controls functioned well during the colonial period, when priests, backed by civil authority, had more power to regulate behavior. In addition to validating the expropriation of church property, "the so-called laws of the Reform," as Gillow called them, undermined clerical oversight of the indigenous laity, occasioning a host of social problems.[23] This interpretation predated Gillow, but it became a standard chestnut of priestly discourse and Catholic journalism during the archbishop's tenure. The new associations, they hoped, would help them reestablish the religious and social foundations of stability.

SHRINES AND SODALITIES

Approaching the task of harnessing local practice, Gillow demonstrated a distinct pragmatism. In addition to recommending the establishment of specific associations during his pastoral visits, he often diplomatically granted indulgences to important images, lauded the piety of their devotees, and pressured sodalities to submit to clerical supervision. In some cases he documented the final gasp of the property-owning Indian confraternities and the liquidation of their assets in the 1890s. On a few occasions, he approved new devotions dedicated to local images.[24] When Gillow did promote local devotions, he chose those that fit his centralizing, homogenizing goals.

In Huatulco, for example, Gillow directed parishioners to erect a large commemorative cross where colonial-era English seamen (i.e., Protestants) allegedly tried, and miraculously failed, to remove an outdoor crucifix. He also designated the first Friday of Lent as its official *romería* (pilgrimage) and sanctioned the celebration of open-air masses until residents constructed a chapel. Gillow's biographer commented decades later that the prelate sought to bring this tradition into being, modeling it on a pilgrimage devotion carefully managed by priests in the Central Valley—Etla's Señor de las Peñas.[25] Although he depicted it as a revival of colonial tradition, Gillow's actions, in this case, suggest an attempt to establish a new devotion by decree. The archbishop cited legendary precedent and sought to gain adherents for a new cult identified with archdiocesan patronage. The cross of Huatulco, like the martyrs of Cajonos, represents another example of a centrally promoted and controlled devotion; however, in both cases the archdiocese failed to establish traditions that compared in size, finances, or fervor to numerous local images.

The organizations managing Oaxaca's shrine sodalities predated the cosmopolitan archbishop's arrival in the region and endured despite the Reform. Often interchangeably referred to as *cofradías* and *hermandades*, they continued to attract thousands of pilgrims and traders at their customary fairs and feasts. Documentation pertaining to these groups attests to the presence of several priests who ministered to pilgrims, craftsmen and laborers who adorned and repaired the churches, fireworks masters who designed pyrotechnic displays, and orchestras, bands, and organists who performed at shrine celebrations. In short, shrines collected a steady flow of contributions, and their importance to local economies and religious sensibilities caused both civil and ecclesiastical authorities to treat them with care. Gillow generally tried to increase archdiocesan control over these local institutions diplomatically, without dampening enthusiasm or offending local power brokers. Quite simply, such pilgrimage devotions represented the most elaborate and accessible manifestations of Catholic splendor and fervor outside of Oaxaca City.[26]

Gillow approached them under his rubric of orderly administration, but shrine devotions merited special discretion. For example, in 1888 he found local liberal politico Basilio Rojas in control of the Christ of Cuixtla's funds and brotherhood. Most troubling, Rojas also seemed to direct the activities of San Andrés Miahuatlán's pastor, Julián Luna. The archbishop expressed concern about Rojas's lending out shrine monies at interest and requested through Luna that he submit a proper report on the Cuixtla's *cofradía*. In reality, Gillow just waited for Rojas to die before asserting more direct control over the shrine.[27] Rarely did Gillow undertake drastic measures, but in 1899, after spending several days in Otatitlán, Veracruz addressing a standoff between residents and the priest in charge of the Christ of Otatitlán's shrine, the prelate moved decisively to restore order. Locals had locked their pastor out of the church to protest a long period of minimal ministerial services, high fees, and priestly misuse of alms. Gillow dismissed the priest and a sacristan coconspirator, appointed local interim caretakers, and committed himself to rewriting the archconfraternity's regulations.[28]

For the most part, Gillow asserted control gradually. In 1894, he learned that a district prefect, Octavio Gijón, had been angling for control of the Virgin of Juquila's funds but had thus far been thwarted by the Virgin's four *mayordomos* and their pastor. He also hinted that he had received complaints about the clerical stewardship of the sanctuary. His source, a previous pastor of the shine, informed him that between mass intentions and alms, the shrine collected approximately 2,200 pesos per year beyond other fees and collections in the parish.[29] For the most part, the uses of shrine funds remained at the discretion of Juquila's pastor. In an 1894 decree designed to strengthen the hand of the local priest, Gillow created what amounted to an official charter of the shrine's management, standardizing fees, revival missions, pastoral financial control, celebration of masses, and disbursements of funds for building maintenance and education. He stressed good record keeping to prevent accusations of malfeasance. Gillow noted complaints about the misuse of alms and hence demanded strict adherence to his dispositions. With the regulations, he sought to preempt any moves against the shrine in the name of "*abusos*" (corruption), either in the provision of religious services or use of contributions. Gillow also made sure to invite Gijón to dinner, although Juquila's prefect declined.[30]

In addition, the archbishop issued a pair of directives that must have raised suspicions among devotees and pilgrims. First, he stipulated that all unused wax (Juquila collected vast amounts of wax offerings) be sent to Oaxaca City for use in the cathedral. Wax was essentially used as currency among sodalities. Priests in the colonial period and into the twentieth century frequently listed sodality stores of wax alongside their cash holdings, and hence Gillow's decree amounted to a transfer of resources to the archdiocese.[31] Second, he directed the pastor to remit to the archdiocese the shrine's store of old silver ornaments and *milagros* (small offerings, usually representing a body part cured through the image's intercession) in order to use them to fashion a new throne for the Virgin of Juquila. Gillow maintained that the precious metals involved would be properly weighed and accounted for, but given the fact that the profiteering of shrine *milagros* was a common anticlerical rumor, this portion of the decree must have occasioned some dissent. The archbishop returned to Juquila in 1900 and refined his previous decree. This addendum demonstrates an attempt to secure more of the shrine's yearly earnings for the archdiocesan government and seminary, curtailing the amount of alms allocated for visiting missionary priests and limiting the funds at the pastor's disposal. Gillow stipulated that funds exceeding the amount needed to support shrine ritual should be forwarded to the archdiocese. The archbishop, however, repealed his previous disposition about the shrine's wax, citing the difficulties of transport to Oaxaca City and the poor quality of shrine paraffin. It is also likely that the transport of the wax engendered resentment in Juquila.[32]

Gillow appears to have succeeded in his efforts to increase ecclesiastical control and introduce orderly management practices to the region's most prominent pilgrimage shrines. In places such as Juquila, *mayordomos* became little more than parish priest's employees, collecting alms during the shrine's festival in exchange for a stipend. Yet in Juquila's case, this may reveal the strengthening of church control rather than a Gillow-era sanctuary coup. Colonial sources indicate that the archdiocese asserted direct control over the shrine in the eighteenth century.[33] Sodalities hoping to gain official pilgrimage status, like Tamazulapan's Hermandad del Señor del Desmayo (Brotherhood of the Fainting Lord), acquiesced to priestly supervision in exchange for the curia's approval before Gillow's arrival in Oaxaca.[34] But Gillow's priests often found their efforts to "bring order" to many sodalities and devotions a source of frustration. In 1890, for example, Gillow ordered the brothers of Zimatlán's Cofradía del Dulce Nombre de Jesús (Confraternity of the Sweet Name of Jesus) to submit to their pastor's oversight after several years of resistance. He threatened to suppress their brotherhood and its feast altogether if they continued to flout ecclesiastical directives.[35]

The prelate went over the same ground in 1910 when he encountered a self-sustaining devotion to an image of the Virgin of Soledad in San Melchor Betaza. In his official report, he reveals an effort to bring the devotees into accord with their pastor. As his commentary and official pronouncements reveal, the devotees of this local Virgin controlled considerable funds and spent much of them on ritual and church adornment. They even possessed their own copper printing plates for the manufacture of images of their Soledad. The problem was that the brotherhood refused to inform the priest of the devotion's finances and occasionally spent the "Virgin's money" on nonreligious communal needs. Gillow opted for a diplomatic paternalist tone in this case. First, he flattered them, praising their temple's splendor and the profound piety that its ornamentation revealed. Then he admonished them to avoid profane expenditures and to set aside alms for proper uses, such as addressing their church's structural problems. Finally, Gillow warned that if they continued to spend monies improperly and exclude their pastor, he would be forced to undertake unspecified actions.[36] We don't know if Betaza's devotees capitulated, or, like other sodalities, only went through the motions of compliance.[37]

THE CANONICALLY STRUCTURED ASSOCIATION

Priestly complaints about the secretiveness and recalcitrance of local sodalities, and Indians in general, are practically an evidentiary cliché, but Gillow and his deputies attempted to address the issue through the mechanism of the canonically structured association.[38] For the most part, we have been examining the initial period of Gillow's tenure, when he encountered sodalities and pious associations during pastoral visits, and his early efforts to decree the establishment of certain associations. While he supported the establishment of officially chartered organizations at this time, his priorities encompassed issues of institutional and liturgical order. As the turn of the century approached, Gillow and his priests increasingly turned their attention to the expansion of canonically structured associations as part of the effort to bring orthodoxy to Oaxaca. Although they did not codify it as official policy, documents reveal attempts to force shrine sodalities into the mold of the new religious association at the same time that they began to promote canonically structured organizations with vigor.

As with so many aspects of church history, the issue of canonical statutes for local sodalities was not new. According to canon law, *cofradías* boasted approved charters, while less formal devotional brotherhoods were designated *hermandades* or *devociones pías* and had no such charters. In early-nineteenth-century parish questionnaires, Oaxacan sodalities usually bore the title of *cofradía*, but in the strictest sense they were unofficial brotherhoods. Father Francisco Diez Canseco of San Mateo del Mar commented on this matter in 1802, claiming that Indians erroneously called them by the former title despite lacking "legitimate foundations," and that Oaxaca's bishops tolerated them for the good of the church and its curacies.[39] Diez revealed a mixture of clerical contempt and dependence regarding indigenous sodalities. As his testimony demonstrates, despite their "perverse management . . . and continuous embezzlement," unregulated collectivities funded the better part of the parish's liturgical activities. Within this historical context, the late-nineteenth-century clergy's effort to tame sodalities should be seen as a continuation of attempts to control local religious institutions.

At a basic level, the process of setting up new canonically structured associations resembled the founding of colonial *cofradías*. Individuals in a particular community, often at the urging of the local priest, agreed to form a group dedicated to a particular saint, devotion, or image and to sponsor rituals. In the colonial era, the seed funds typically consisted of the donation of land and/or livestock, with the understanding that any value they produced would support religious activities.[40] In the nineteenth century, asset-holding dwindled due to liberal reforms targeting communal property. Communities developed clever ways to circumvent external efforts to alter local religious institutions and economics, but it was difficult to sustain tradition over the long term. A comparison of parish questionnaires roughly a century apart reveals that while almost every Oaxacan parish boasted numerous livestock-holding *cofradías* in the early 1800s, very few sodalities of this type remained by the early 1900s. Many communities, however, supported large numbers of *mayordomías*, and in some instances, these institutions surreptitiously managed land and livestock. Nonetheless, evidence from Oaxaca and other regions reveals that for the most part, an emphasis on rotating individual sponsorship had supplanted the property-holding sodalities of the past.[41] Priests repeatedly commented on how preexisting sodalities and new associations depended heavily upon member contributions and alms solicitation in the early twentieth century.[42] Still, this transition was gradual and partial.

The addition of the canonically structured association to the local institutional mix represents a definite innovation tied to the interests of the clergy. Archdiocesan documents reveal that during the Gillow era, priests viewed them as a core component of their ministry and the foundation of their support within communities. Indeed, at times an us-versus-them dichotomy characterized the way clerics discussed associations and *mayordomías*. Clergymen defending their own administration, or commenting on another priest's virtues, frequently cited the establishment of associations. They invoked them as evidence of their intent to reform local religion and morals, even if they were having scant success. The founding documents of these institutions appear with greater frequency around the turn of the century.[43] They generally follow a similar pattern: locals gathered by their pastor, and often with the priest writing on their behalf, informed the archdiocese of their interest in a particular association. In some instances, the formation of associations grew out of revival missions organized by the archdiocese. Usually groups asserted that they had already formed an executive council and in some cases included a list of members. Often they stressed their fervent Catholicism and eagerness to obey ecclesiastical authority. They also expounded upon their determination to defend the faith in the contemporary climate of irreligion. The archdiocesan secretary usually gave his approval, citing the benefits new associations produced in other communities, and directed the supplicants to contact the archdiocesan director of the particular association and initiate formal establishment according to canonical statutes.[44] Regional directors, in turn, periodically visited the branches of their organization within the archdiocese, reporting their findings to the ecclesiastical government and to the directorates of the associations.[45]

In many communities, especially larger towns, the formation of new associations closely followed this pattern. Gillow instructed priests during his pastoral visits to first establish associations locally, and, once they demonstrated stability, to then seek formal canonical institution.[46] Echoing colonial *cofradía* history, however, many groups never progressed beyond the first step. Thus, communities boasted active local collectivities bearing the names of new associations without actually gaining formal approval.[47] They may have been more autonomous than their urban counterparts, but the lack of an official charter did not appear to trouble either the curia or village clergy. This suggests that the archdiocese expedited the expansion of these institutions throughout the province rather than adhering to protocol. When new associations did take the final step in formal establishment, they received modestly ornate certificates signed by the national and archdiocesan directors of their organization.[48]

Again, the push to generalize the canonically structured association in Oaxaca came from Gillow himself and was part of his broader effort to spark the rapid growth of lay institutions. For the archbishop, the inspiration appears to have been his participation in the 1899 Latin American Plenary Council in Rome. He had decreed the establishment of some associations after his previous trip to the Vatican in 1891, but when he returned fresh from Rome's elaboration of its official blueprint for Latin American reform, Gillow made the key emphases of the council's conclusions—the fomentation of the Catholic press, the expansion of religious education, and the cultivation of new lay associations—the priorities for the rest of his tenure. There was considerable overlap between these facets of Gillow's program, but the aspect that brought them together was the "spirit of association." It was through the establishment of disciplined, targeted associations that the Vatican and Gillow proposed to re-Christianize society. For example, one of his pet associations was the Sociedad de la Buena Prensa (the Good Press Society, founded in 1896). The focus of this group was to support church-approved publications and convince Catholics to shun the "impious press."[49] Not surprisingly, the voice of Gillow's spirit of association was the archdiocese's new official organ, the *Boletín Oficial.*

In 1901, the archdiocese began to publish the *Boletín Oficial* as a means of explaining and forwarding its agenda. The ecclesiastical government required that clergymen within the archdiocese subscribe and preserve a complete set of issues in their parish archive. The paper's inaugural issue contained Gillow's circular announcing the formal foundation of Oaxaca's Congregación del Catequismo (Congregation of the Catechism) and decreed the establishment of branches of this organization in all parishes. In subsequent issues, the *Boletín Oficial* reported on the Congregation's progress, listing the names of pastor-founders and providing statistics on participation.[50] It also announced the foundation of other associations, such as a mutual aid association for the clergy in 1902 and the Oaxacan Catholic Workers' Circle in 1906. A key aspect of the *Boletín Oficial*'s role was also to publicize the good works, social events, and religious celebrations carried out under the auspices of these institutions, especially in Oaxaca City. For the clergy posted in the remote hinterland, this served as a periodic reminder of the hierarchy's standards of appropriate Catholic social action and practice. It also must have inspired a sense of nostalgia, perhaps bitter for some, for the urban culture that they had left behind as they read reports detailing procession routes, spiritual exercises, and liturgies led by their city-based brethren.

Gillow's pastoral visit diaries also reveal the prelate's personal focus on association formation after 1899. Previously just one among a list of issues mentioned in his recommendations, in the early twentieth century, their establishment and well-being became an issue of primary importance. He also made more declarations as to which associations should be established in different parishes. In one parish after another, the archbishop directed priests to set up separate new associations for men and women. In 1901, for example, he stipulated that the pastor of San Lucas Ojitlán should bolster piety through the establishment of the Hijas de María (Daughters of Mary) for girls, and the Asociación del Sagrado Corazón de Jesus (Association of the Sacred Heart of Jesus) or the Apostolado for boys and men.[51] During his 1907 tour of the Mixteca, Gillow tirelessly promoted the Apostolado, the Apostado de la Cruz (Apostolate of the Cross), the Congregation of the Catechism, and the Hermandad de la Vela Perpetua (Brotherhood of the Perpetual Vigil).[52] In 1910, he demanded that the parish priest of Yalina establish the same associations he had previously encouraged in Ojitlán.[53] In other localities, he decreed the establishment of separate male and female groups affiliated with Apostolado, and he reminded pastors about the mandatory establishment of the Congregation of the Catechism. As in his previous diary writings, he continued to comment on the decorations, local bands, and civil authorities that celebrated his arrival in parishes, but he now added descriptions of the associations and brotherhoods greeting him. Occasionally he praised the colored scapulars, banners, and waist cords that some groups displayed. Time and again, he lectured his flock on the value of these organizations, stressing their role as the front line of combat against the "spirit of indifference" and "modern errors," as well as a means of sanctifying their members, moralizing families, and modeling orthodoxy.

Thus, new associations became the prelate's bellwether of early-twentieth-century local Catholicism. During his visit to Zautla in 1906, Gillow praised missionary priest José Chamadoyra, noting the impressive cast of new associations that celebrated his arrival.[54] With a set of local institutions, Chamadoyra covered all the church's oft-mentioned bases. The Apostolado and the two Sacred Heart associations brought together separate groups of men and women. The Hijas de María and Sociedad Católica de San Luis Gonzaga organized the female and male youths, respectively, and the Congregation of the Catechism served as the catchall association providing all children with access to religious education.[55] Similarly, in Tlacolula four years later, the archbishop declared piety flourishing, as evidenced by the passion with which residents maintained their associations and established new ones. Such was the zeal of the Tlacolulans, according to Gillow, that he encouraged them to expand their activities beyond ritual and to cultivate deeper understanding through the study of religious texts and priest-led instruction. Clearly interpreting the town's embrace of new associations as evidence of support for more ambitious endeavors, the prelate also instructed Tlacolula's pastor to convince his parishioners to establish a Catholic boys' school and an adult night school to complement an already functioning girls' parochial school.[56]

Where canonically structured associations faltered, Gillow's writings reveal his concern about local clergymen and doubts about lay religiosity. In Mitla he complained about the complete absence of brotherhoods (i.e., traditional sodalities) and instructed both its priest and parishioners to form at least one separate association for both men and women. He also ordered its pastor, Ignacio Ortiz, to found the Congregation of the Catechism immediately. Gillow admonished him to exert himself, although he acknowledged the obstacles rooted in his flock's ignorance, "*por ser gente de idioma*" (i.e., Indians). Ortiz's communication troubles were due to the lack of Spanish among most of his parishioners. But it bears mention that in his off-the-record remarks, Gillow also revealed that the townspeople were far from indifferent. They greeted him with great fanfare, distinguishing themselves in the tidy ornamentation of their streets, the great number of candle-bearing well-wishers, and the salvos of fireworks marking his arrival. Furthermore, Mitla's parishioners insisted on removing the mules from Gillow's carriage so that they could tow the prelate into town. In his *auto*, the archbishop also congratulated them for their dedication to the construction of a new church.[57]

In San Francisco Cajonos, the hometown of the prelate's beloved martyrs, Gillow encountered troubling news related to the town's associations. In his pastoral visit report, he praised the town's new "*hermandades*"—the Apostolado and the Asociación del Sagrado Corazón de María (Association of the Sacred Heart of Mary)—and launched into his customary speech about the crucial nature of associations, emphasizing their inspiration of Catholic social action and their edifying example of sacramental frequency and proper ritual. The archbishop informed the pastor and parishioners that he desired the expansion of these institutions. In his private commentary, however, Gillow observed that both of these organizations boasted only a few female members. Far from representing an example worthy of emulation, he noted, they inspired mockery among other parishioners. He opined that ridicule prevented the growth of these institutions.[58]

Nonetheless, the prelate's promotion of canonically structured associations succeeded in spurring a surge in their establishment. Particularly for the period from 1900 to 1910, the archdiocesan archive preserves numerous new official charters for various associations. Among the most interesting documents are those that reveal attempts to impose association-like statutes and standards of practice on sodalities of colonial vintage. They reflect only a partial concurrence with the archbishop's wishes. Clearly, the word was out that the prelate wanted associations formed and bylaws submitted for approval, but what is remarkable about some of these charters is that they do not belong to Gillow's preferred associations, like the Apostolado.[59] Instead, they demonstrate efforts to bring preexisting institutions within the church hierarchy's ideal frameworks of order and practice, or at least provide a sheen of new orthodoxy. In addition, they deviated from the prelate's stipulation that associations be segregated by sex, although women frequently dominated their membership.

In 1903, the pastor of San Andrés Miahuatlán forwarded news of associations functioning in his rural parish: the Hermandad de la Virgen de Guadalupe (Brotherhood of the Virgen de Guadalupe) and the Arch-confraternity of the Honor Guard of the Sacred Heart. He sent in the bylaws of the first and nothing more than a list of members for the second. The names of these organizations demonstrate local manifestations of two of the devotions encouraged most strongly by the Mexican clergy during this period. The regulations of the Guadalupan brotherhood noted, pro forma, the members' commitment to foment devotion to this advocation of Mary. More concretely, the brothers' only obligation was to sponsor a mass every month and celebrate the Virgin's customary feast each December 12. In keeping with archdiocesan requirements, the charter listed the current pastor and his successors as the brotherhood's permanent directors; however, female parishioners held every other formal position (president, secretary, treasurer, and four *celadoras*). The general membership of the Guadalupe brotherhood included thirty-eight women and only five men. The Honor Guard of the Sacred Heart boasted seventy women and only three men.[60]

Associations in Oaxaca City followed protocols more closely. Documents that attest to the foundation and canonical approval of the Archicofradía del Santísimo Sacramento (Archconfraternity of the Blessed Sacrament) also reveal clerical directorship, the predominance of women, and stress the sponsorship of periodic masses, like their rural counterparts. But they also emphasized frequent confession and communion.[61] The Hermandad de San José (Brotherhood of Saint Joseph, founded in 1904) stated in its 1909 regulations that its members committed themselves to daily mass, as well as monthly confession and communion. The Sociedad de la Santísima Virgen de la Luz (Society of the Holy Virgin of Light, established in 1893) also produced its charter in 1909. Its tone and style gives the distinct impression that the priest-director penned these regulations to remind the membership of their obligations. It stipulated their duties to attend a special monthly mass and take communion, followed by group spiritual exercises and a procession. Members were also supposed to take part in the rotating vigils before the Blessed Sacrament. Furthermore, the statutes stressed that members promised to wear the association's scapular and insignia, and celebrate their yearly feast and novena with the utmost splendor.[62]

Here we see the archdiocese under Gillow trying to fuel and channel popular piety. Aside from increasing the frequency of the sacraments, mandating spiritual exercises, stipulating periodic contributions, and requiring the public display of association symbols, the introduction of a cellular organizational structure distinguished these new institutions from older *cofradías* and *mayordomías*. They reveal an effort to discipline religiosity and verify compliance. Usually they listed priest-directors, a president (occasionally a vice president), a secretary, a treasurer, and several *celadores/as*. This latter position represents an important innovation, because it empowered individuals to police their peers' religious observance.

The regulations of the Oaxaca City's Archicofradía de la Preciosa Sangre de Cristo (Archconfraternity of the Precious Blood of Christ) provide a glimpse of a relatively typical new association structure.[63] The *padre-director* imparted ecclesiastical supervision, presided over meetings, and appointed the *celadoras*. Presidential duties included making sure that *celadoras* complied with all regulations, approving group expenditures, and acting on the priest's behalf in his absence. The secretary kept statistics on members and their religious acts, and maintained the schedule of vigils before the Blessed Sacrament. They also signed circulars that the priest-director produced and passed them on to the *celadoras*. The treasurer, of course, maintained association accounts. Finally, regulations stipulated that *celadoras* collect contributions from members in their charge and distribute circulars and secure members' signatures upon their receipt. They also had to make sure that individuals wore association insignias and fulfilled their vigil obligations.

Thanks to Tlalixtac's early-twentieth-century pastor, Felipe Arenas, we can also scrutinize priestly efforts to coax older religious collectivities into the new lay-association mold. Arenas's writings stand out due to the detail he provided about the brotherhoods/associations within his parish, especially the highly successful sodality dedicated to San Andrés Huayapan's reputedly miraculous image of Christ.[64] Father Arenas's testimony is also a dramatic example of how successful priests adopted flexible approaches to lay-institution oversight among their indigenous parishioners and the gendered dynamics of local practice. In a compendium of documents written from 1907 to 1909, he commented on four very different organizations.[65] Two of them demonstrated close adherence to the modern modes of practice encouraged by the Oaxacan clergy and followed by their overwhelmingly female membership, another appeared to be a traditional male-dominated *cofradía*-like sodality, and the fourth originated in a long-standing local pilgrimage devotion but experienced considerable effort to alter its form and function to approximate the curia's new institutional model.

The groups most closely resembling the urban model were the Brotherhoods of the Holy Virgin of Solitude and the Sacred Hearts of Jesus and Mary. They listed forty-nine and eighty-one members respectively, and only thirty-four male members between them. In other words, 73 percent of their members were women. The Marian group, Arenas noted, had been established many years before, but the Sacred Heart association was only a few years old and was "reformed" as of 1906. Both groups practiced the more frequent and restrained piety promoted by archdiocesan authorities and focused their energies on officially sanctioned devotions. Soledad's followers in Tlalixtac sponsored a mass and a vigil of the Blessed Sacrament on the eighteenth of every month, in addition to a solemn mass and exposition of the Eucharist every January 18. Although Arenas did not mention the Soledad coronation anniversary, it is telling that it appeared as the group's devotional high point only two weeks after Soledad's crowning in Oaxaca City. The Sacred Heart's devotees sponsored masses and their own vigil of the Blessed Sacrament on the first day of each month and celebrated an annual high mass on the Friday after the octave of Corpus. At these ceremonies, Arenas claimed, several women usually took communion. In fact, he listed the female members of these organizations as the sole frequenters of the sacraments in his parish. Both groups, he maintained, distinguished themselves in this regard during May, the month of Mary. In marked contrast, Arenas provided scant information about the third sodality, the Hermandad de Nuestra Señora de la Consolación (Brotherhood of Our Lady of Consolation), beyond listing its forty-four members (thirty-five of whom were men) and noting their celebration of a single feast every September.[66] Due to his previous commentary, we can assume that these men did not frequent the sacraments.

At the end of the report Arenas included the elaborate new charter of Huayapan's Hermandad del Santo Cristo y del Santo Rosario (Brotherhood of the Holy Christ and Holy Rosary), outlining its reform. He noted its May 30, 1906, foundation and Gillow's official approval a year later and described the organization's structure in detail.[67] The regulations reveal the Oaxacan clergy's effort to discipline a long-established sodality. The document stipulated the pastor's permanent directorship, obligatory confession and communion at brotherhood feasts, weekly group rosaries, and compliance with all church dictates. Furthermore, the document outlined the duties of officers, gave the pastor veto power over brotherhood elections, and prohibited meetings during celebrations, at members' private homes, or in drinking establishments. All gatherings of the brotherhood, the regulations stressed, must be held in the church or the rectory. These rules suggest that abridging a history of institutional autonomy was one of Arenas's targets. Individual members were also required to maintain strict decorum in their personal lives, risking expulsion for scandalous behavior, drunkenness, or unconsecrated connubial relationships. The regulations also obliged members to don the group's copper cross on a red silk ribbon when they attended rituals, assisted the priest, or joined a procession.

The new rules, however, also hint at some important compromises. They reveal a highly unusual dual focus by pairing devotion to the local image of Christ with that to the Virgin of the Rosary, and making the members responsible for both celebrations. This suggests that Arenas sought to merge two older brotherhoods in one newly reformed body.[68] In addition, although the archbishop consistently pushed clergymen to set up separate organizations for men and women, Huayapan's newly regulated brotherhood remained mixed. Its charter divided the group's sixty-three men and thirty-six women into six male *coros* (choirs) and three female *coros*, each of them with their respective male and female *celador* or *celadora*. In doing this, the brotherhood approximated the cellular structure of organizations like the Apostolado and achieved a semblance of segregated seemliness. The predominance of men in the brotherhood probably stemmed from the history of the Christ of Huayapan and the Virgin of the Rosary's as the most important and prestigious religious collectivities in the parish and their likely origins in colonial confraternities with strong ties to the town's civil administration.

Arenas also provided more information about these groups in his response to the 1908 parish questionnaire, revealing that the new regulations represented more of a statement of ideals than a reflection of reality.[69] He admitted that not a single canonically structured association functioned within his pueblos. The parish did, however, boast twelve brotherhoods and an astounding 47 *mayordomías*. Upon close examination, it appears that Arenas cross-listed most of the brotherhoods among the *mayordomías*. This may indicate that this pastor was trying to pad the list of religious collectivities, but it may also reflect his efforts to push sodalities from the realm of autonomous *mayordomías* toward the idealized, prelate-mandated canonically structured association. Huayapan, for example, still had separate *mayordomías* for their miraculous Christ and the Virgin of the Rosary.[70] Thankfully, this priest included a footnote clarifying what he meant in labeling certain groups brotherhoods. He admitted that his *hermandades* were nothing more than groups of people who agreed to give alms so that a particular image could be celebrated, and that for the most part the members did not confess or take communion and frequently reneged on their commitment to sponsor feasts. Some of these brotherhoods, he declared, were little more than "sketches" (*bosquejos*). In the end, he lamented, some individuals contributed in good faith, whereas many others shirked their responsibilities regardless of the obligations they promised to uphold in the past.

All, however, was not disappointment in Arenas's ministry. The calendar of activities he provided in his responses demonstrates that he was a busy priest celebrating numerous liturgical events in his pueblos throughout the year. He claimed that three of the twelve brotherhoods demonstrated laudable dedication to the sponsorship of their feasts, stipulated masses, and followed the official standards of orthodox practice. In addition to praising the "brothers" of the Virgin of Solitude and the Sacred Hearts of Mary and Jesus in the parish seat, Arenas lauded Huayapan's Brotherhood of the Holy Christ and Holy Rosary's assiduous sponsorship of its celebrations. He claimed that all of its members confessed and took communion during the annual festival. All told, these three brotherhoods accounted for 229 souls who participated in the sacraments at least once a year. Arenas noted that 70 other people fulfilled the Easter duty. Given Tlalixtac's population of 7,141 individuals (as listed by Arenas), this would mean that approximately 4 percent of the parish practiced the faith within the limits of officially prescribed orthodoxy, a figure consistent with many other parishes.

The pastor also mentioned another level of deviation and compromise related to devotions and their management. Every Ash Wednesday, Huayapan's brotherhood held its pilgrimage festival dedicated to the miraculous image of Christ. Arenas estimated that four hundred people attended every year, although he maintained that many came only "*de paseo*" (for the outing). Regardless of pilgrim intentions, though, the festival netted the brotherhood a healthy and regular flow of funds, of which it refused to give its official director, Arenas, an accounting. "*No dan razón al párroco*" (they do not give account to the pastor), noted the padre matter-of-factly. But beyond mentioning this obvious breach of regulations, he did not dwell on the brothers' insubordination or seek the prelate's intervention, as his colleagues sometimes did in similar situations. The cleric reported instead that the sodality invested in its temple's sumptuous ornamentation to such a degree that the parish seat's main church looked poor by comparison. Arenas also professed that the group took charge of all manner of church repairs, even when they were quite expensive.

Father Felipe Arenas and his predominantly Zapotec parishioners, therefore, appear to have come to an accommodation. On file with the prelate in Oaxaca City were the brotherhood's official bylaws depicting a well-ordered, priest-led Catholic lay institution of traditional origin but infused with modern organizational structures and religious sensibilities. In Huayapan, nonetheless, the brothers of the Santo Cristo continued to control their devotion and its pilgrimage without surrendering control. Arenas must have gotten along rather well with the members of this group, as evidenced in his assurances that the entire membership participated in communion and confession and diligently sponsored their feasts. It is impossible to discern if this preceded the writing of the group's charter, but it demonstrates that the members embraced a higher level of sacramental practice than most of their neighbors, even if they rejected full clerical control. The pastor may have had to soft-pedal the principles of hierarchy in the interest of other pastoral goals. Perhaps Arenas felt that it was in the best interest of his parish, and his parishioners' souls, to accept a peripheral role in the sodality's management. In short, he fulfilled his duties: officiating at feasts, as well as promoting reformed piety, frequent sacramental practice, and "official" lay institutional culture. Likewise, the brothers did theirs, organizing and funding the feasts and maintaining and adorning their church. In the end, the strict adherence to archdiocesan mandates and the official charter were of lesser importance.

BROTHERHOODS AND ASSOCIATIONS IN OAXACAN PERSPECTIVE

Thus far we have examined the Oaxacan clergy's efforts to implant a new kind of lay institutional and devotional culture among the region's primarily indigenous Catholics, but it is not surprising that when faced with local realities, they deviated from the Vatican blueprint. In general, communities assimilated the canonically structured association within the field of preexisting religious collectivities, and hence they often failed to function the way their framers imagined. In most cases, they were not Gillow's evangelizing paragons of orthodoxy, inspiring their communities to obey their parish priests and shift the emphasis of local practice from communal festivals to personal, sacrament-centered practice. Should we then judge this endeavor a failure? If our criterion is the achievement of goals expressed by Rome and Gillow, then indeed this program was a disappointment. But if we consider these institutions' local histories and accept that Oaxaca's village clergy probably understood that the association format would be altered in practice, then the program emerges as a significant innovation in local Catholicism.

The canonically structured association's impact can be gauged in the 1908 all-parish questionnaire. The responses to this survey suggest that although outside Oaxaca City canonically structured associations failed to catalyze a thorough transformation of faith and practice, they represented crucial sites of social action, religious innovation, and personal empowerment, particularly for Hispanic and mestiza women. These women, for the most part, could only participate peripherally in village civil administration and *mayordomías*, but they could take up leadership roles in the new associations. In addition, these new institutions functioned as the conduits of different modes of Catholic practice that, like the archbishop himself, carried into the countryside new militant European-inspired notions of pious expression, as well as the church's interpretation of history and vision of social organization. In short, they represented wedges of modernized Catholicism lodged in Oaxaca's predominantly Indian rural communities of the period.

The 1908 questionnaire is a rich source of information, but priest-respondents were inconsistent in the way they addressed the thirty-eight questions. Five questions in succession (numbers 25 through 29) provide most of the data on religious collectivities, asking about canonically structured associations, brotherhoods, *mayordomías*, and local piety. Only a few loquacious clerics provided the kind of dense detail that scholars crave, listing the names of all sodalities, their celebrations, the numbers, ethnicity, and sex of members, and correlating gender and sacramental practice. More commonly, respondents provided only clues about these aspects of devotional life. In addition, at times it seems as if every parish in Oaxaca experienced a unique history that resists comparison. As we have seen, clergymen and local laypersons often used the terms differentiating between kinds of sodalities interchangeably. In part this is due to the lack of linguistic options. For example, what does one call the members of a new *asociación, hermandad,* or *mayordomía*? Both the participants in these groups and the clerics commenting on them frequently used the traditional terminology of *hermanos/as* for all of them, although some preferred *socios/as* for the first two institutions. Thus, it is not without hesitation that I state the following claims.

In the questionnaires, priests conflated *hermandades* (brotherhoods) and canonically structured associations relatively consistently, but they usually differentiated between these two and *mayordomías*. Under the rubric of brotherhoods and associations most clergymen listed groups of post-Reform vintage, revealing the hallmarks of the modern militant Catholic lay associations: independence from civil-religious hierarchies, individual membership, antiliberal sociopolitical postures, and a strong emphasis on frequent sacramental practice. Village pastors tended to provide more information about these organizations than about *mayordomías*, undoubtedly a reflection of these groups' closer ties to priests. Indian communities frequently refused to give clerics even minimal information about *mayordomía* finances, expecting priests simply to officiate in exchange for fees. For most parishes, clerical oversight of Indian sodalities was simply a fiction, despite the fact that their celebrations usually filled the local religious calendar. Not surprisingly, many priests were dismissive of such groups, stating that there were as many of them as there were festivals to be observed, and referring their superiors to fee schedules or the list of feasts instead of mentioning them by name. In contrast, priests fretted about the lack of diligence among brotherhoods and association members, but also wrote hopefully about their progress and provided details about their management. Their testimony reveals a clear congruence with Gillow's statements in his third pastoral instruction that associations and brotherhoods were the mainstays of clerical support in communities, even if they often fell short of the curia's standards. Furthermore, pastors never spurned them with the stock statements about Indian ignorance, uppitiness, and profane debauchery, as they did *mayordomías*.

Of the archdiocese's 151 parishes, only 43 reasonably complete questionnaire responses remain in the archdiocesan archive, and although the Central Valley communities are overrepresented, they allow us to make some observations. Nevertheless, all figures cited here should be taken with a grain of salt. Only four responding parishes lacked brotherhoods or associations altogether. Without exception, these were parishes where priests emphasized the overwhelming predominance of monolingual Indians, and in one case, San Melchor Betaza, the priest noted an almost complete absence of Spanish. All of these towns supported local sodalities, and two of them, Teocoquilco and Mitla, reported a remarkable sixty-eight and sixty-nine *mayordomías*, respectively. Three of these communities provided enough information to compare the frequenting of the sacraments to parish population. Betaza ranked the highest, with 0.5 percent of its residents taking the sacraments at least once a year.[71] These communities were not alone in the cellar of sacramental practice. Sixteen other parishes reported less than 5 percent compliance with this measure of orthodoxy, and only ten parishes revealed greater than 10 percent observance of the Easter duty.[72] Few priests were like Father Antonio Romero, who produced a harsh diatribe about the pathetic state of the faith in his parish. He itemized San Pedro Atoyac's sacramental piety in the following manner: "Those that take communion regularly four times a week and comply with the Easter duty are three boys, five girls, three married women, four widows, three single women, one bachelor, and one married man. In total *they are 23* people" (original emphasis).[73] In a less bleak but almost equally detailed response, the pastor of San Juan Cacahuatepec noted that fourteen people frequented the sacraments, forty people confessed and took communion four to six times per year, and 280 women, eight men, thirty girls, and twenty boys fulfilled the Easter duty.[74] As in other parishes, the great overrepresentation of women is remarkable.

To gain the proper perspective, it is helpful to consider late colonial Oaxacan parish questionnaires. In these documents, priests routinely claimed 100 percent, or near complete, compliance with the Easter duty, although some pastors noted that only half of their flock complied with this requirement.[75] In contrast, not a single Oaxacan parish a century later even approached 50 percent participation in the sacraments. Here is dramatic evidence of an important shift in Mexican culture during the nineteenth century—the transformation of the Catholic sacramental practice from social norm to voluntary act. But it is important not to overemphasize the sacraments as the only marker of Catholic faith and piety. Oaxacans may have had scant interest in the sacraments, but the 1908 questionnaire and other documents indicate their belief in the miraculous power of Catholic images and commitment to local devotions. Most Oaxacans appear to have practiced a brand of Catholicism infused with native Mesoamerican sensibilities, emphasizing propitiation, communal and kinetic celebration, and full calendars of religious festivals. In addition, despite the clergy's efforts, much of the native population had never received the religious instruction required before taking their first communion.

Priests in the field, and prelates like Gillow, recognized this as a reality of their ministry, and they noted the discrepancy between the levels of orthodox practice described by their predecessors and what they witnessed in their parishes. Some of them carped endlessly about indigenous festive practice and stubborn refusals to heed priestly exhortations. Others assumed a more positive stance, accepting their duty to *"sacar sus fiestas"* (bring out their feasts) while elaborating on their efforts to reform their parishioners' *"costumbres"* (customs). Their measure of progress was the state of associations and brotherhoods and the frequenting of the sacraments, rather than the basic Easter duty compliance discussed by their predecessors. The fact that they viewed routine sacramental practice as the chief marker of Catholic propriety and labored to expand it within their communities makes it important in our effort to understand religious culture during the period. They did not talk about piety in terms of percentages. Instead, they concentrated on the realm of optimistic potential and idealistic projection, buoyed by the sincere religious conviction that devout ministerial action would gain divine support. As Archbishop Gillow maintained, with a resolute priest at the helm, and the *socios* and *socias* energetically indoctrinating and displaying exemplary moral and religious comportment, the people would follow.

Who among the laity embraced this mission, and can it be judged as more than a clerical fantasy? According to the statistics and clues provided by Oaxacan priests like the pastor of Cacahuatepec, the reformed Catholic vanguard was primarily female and mestiza, although some Hispanized men and indigenous men and women also answered the call.[76] In general, when priests commented on their institutional stewardship and on the relative zeal of participants, they tended to commend the piety and diligence of Spanish-speaking women.[77] The evidence for these claims is patchy, but palpable. First, towns showing high rates of participation in new Catholic institutions also tended to be regional nodes of economic dynamism and/or municipal seats, where priests also noted larger mestizo populations and widespread bilingualism. For example, Santa Ana

Tlapacoyan's pastor commented on the predominantly mixed-race population of his parish, the general use of rustic Spanish, and the incorporation of 44 percent of the population in associations and brotherhoods.[78] Likewise, in San Pedro Apostol (one of Oaxaca's mining centers), 30 percent of the inhabitants reportedly belonged to its new Catholic institutions, 27 percent upheld their sacramental duties, and both Spanish and Zapotec were widely spoken.[79] Not surprisingly, other parishes with relatively large numbers of residents belonging to associations and brotherhoods were Jalatlaco, Tehuacán, Nochixtlán, Ejutla, and Tlacolula. With the exception of the first, all of these towns served as regional market centers. Jalatlaco, for its part, was once a separate village adjacent to Oaxaca City, but it had been annexed by the growing state capital in the late nineteenth century.

In parishes where clerics reported success and failure, testimonials praising female fervor and lamenting male indifference were common. Tehuacán's pastor, for example, reported that an impressive 32 percent of the predominantly Hispanic population belonged to new associations, and he underscored the pious example of women.[80] A less optimistic cleric posted in Teojomulco admitted that only one brotherhood functioned in his parish, consisting of eleven "*hermanas*" (sisters/members). These women were the only parishioners that frequented the sacraments, he reported, and a paltry twenty to thirty other souls complied with the Easter duty.[81] Likewise, the forlorn pastor of Atoyác struggled to set up a new association devoted to vigils before the Blessed Sacrament, lamenting: "You can only count on a few *mujeres de razón* [i.e., Hispanized women] and some Indian women. Among men vigils are very rare."[82] As noted earlier, the presence of a core group of "*gente de razón*" probably determined where priests concentrated their association-founding energies.

Time and again in the responses to the 1908 questionnaire's query about piety, clerics emphasized female fervor and sacramental piety. The correlation is even more striking if we look exclusively at canonically structured associations. The predominance of women in these institutions and among the most zealous practitioners of the new orthodoxy was particularly clear in towns like Ejutla, where 174 of the 231 members (75 percent) of the Obra de la Propagación de la Fé were women, and 230 of the Apostolado's 243 members (94 percent) were female. In San Sebastián Zinacatepec, the Apostolado and the Asociación de Nuestra Señora del Carmen (Association of Our Lady of Carmen) each boasted four hundred women and lacked men altogether. If there was no overlap in membership, these *socias* accounted for a full 27 percent of the town's population.[83] As we have seen, women outnumbered men in the Apostolado by a ratio of nine to one. Indeed, this most widespread canonically structured association exemplifies the overrepresentation of lay women at the forefront of militant modern Catholicism. In Oaxaca, 51 percent of the parish questionnaires responses noted the presence of this organization, and its size proved directly proportional to sacramental frequency. In other words, the religious mobilization of women in the Apostolado correlated with levels of priest-centered orthodox practice.

The diminutive, predominantly Mixtec parish of San Miguel Peras provides a snapshot of what the rural Apostolado may have looked like at its best. The entire parish was home to 4,857 inhabitants, of whom 1,200 lived in the mostly bilingual (Spanish and Mixtec speaking) municipal seat. The parish seat was home to a well-organized Apostolado branch, mirroring the prelate's preferred organizational structure. Thus, it possessed matching, separate sets of male and female officers (president, treasurer, and secretary), two *celadores* and twenty *socios*, and seven *celadoras* and sixty-two *socias*. All told, they represented 8 percent of the parish seat's population, and 74 percent of them were female. According to their pastor, these women distinguished themselves in their frequent participation in the sacraments, while their male counterparts failed to inspire comment.[84] Again, the Oaxacan clergy does not appear to have sparked a broad revolution in local Catholic practice, but if we consider that these institutions primarily functioned in their respective parish seats, they appear more important. Certainly, in a pueblo of 1,200 individuals, a dedicated core of seventy-two women and a less zealous but supportive assemblage of twenty-five men represented a noticeable subgroup within the community. Their personal identification with the church and clergy, as well as their espousal of the Apostolado's sociopolitically freighted Sacred Heart devotion would have been on frequent display. If nothing else, they served as exemplars of the official modes of practice, new organizational concepts, Catholic conservatism, and devotions infused with militant religiosity. Their social and political impact may have also been even more significant if they counted influential individuals among their members and if Apostolado membership correlated with local factionalism.

Furthermore, our evidence suggests that new associations and brotherhoods also served as important sites of female fellowship. They were platforms upon which women could stake out social space as the guardians of local morality and social welfare under the legitimizing umbrella of religion. They were also socially acceptable public spaces in which women could meet, pool their energies and resources, and express themselves as both women and Catholics. In sum, the canonically structured association and the post-Reform *hermandad* gave women a collective social voice and a realm in which to pursue social prestige outside of male-dominated spheres. This emerges most clearly when *hermanas* sent letters to the archdiocese. Many of these documents openly embraced the church's construction of gendered social roles, artfully deployed the vocabulary of Catholic militance, and fiercely endorsed the archbishop's conservative sociopolitical positions. Indeed, these *socias* appear to have been effectively indoctrinated by the church, but these documents also reveal them demanding to be heard and asserting "rights" as the mainstays of local Catholicism. In addition, they framed local clashes of good and evil as contests between moral women in league with clergymen against depraved secular men.

Excerpts of two letters from Teotitlán del Camino, signed by dozens of women and a few men protesting the removal of their parish priest, demonstrate this phenomenon. The Hermandad del Santísimo Sacramento (Brotherhood of the Blessed Sacrament) addressed a letter to Archbishop Gillow on January 15, 1897, claiming to represent a pious majority opposing the machinations of local men termed "disciples of Voltaire" and "Iscariot enemies." Their opponents, they complained, sought to remove the town's zealous pastor because he opposed their unbridled, un-Christian passions. As if quoting the most strident passages of Mexico's Catholic press, the writers invoked the specter of Teotitlán's perdition: "Communities that believe themselves to be enlightened . . . worship reason, and pursue progress without the charity of religious instruction. Surrounded by the darkness of materialism, these are men of the ephemeral power of the material. Many of them (without admitting it) are the footrests of the throne of the monarch of shadows."[85] Their pueblo, they assured Gillow, had long professed Catholicism but, until recently, had practiced it improperly. Before the arrival of Father Rafael Osorio, parish priests had tolerated the pernicious infusion of the profane in the community's religious celebrations, and parishioners were weak before the lure of sensuality, religious indifference, and usury. Padre Rafael, "a valiant captain in the Christian army," had reputedly turned the tide with decisive pastoral action and his moral example. Teotitlán, however, remained vulnerable, "in the infancy of Christian life," vexed by lingering heterodox fanaticism and modern irreligious apathy.

In a second letter written two days later, the Hermandad de las Ánimas (Brotherhood of the Souls) took a slightly different tack. Instead of detailing their enemies' degeneracy, their pueblo's untoward religious history, or their pastor's virtues, the signatories lobbied the archbishop, arguing, "We women are the majority in most towns: we women suffer with humility the impieties of certain men of the day: we women nurture on our laps the future men of society: we suffering and self-effacing women sweeten the home: we women however, are the weak part of the world: we women on our knees before God, amidst our sorrows, weeping we beg you."[86] Thus they purported to speak for all women, implied a uniformity of female pious opinion, and invoked quasi-democratic rights as the majority of the population. They also maintained that women bore the brunt of modern male error and made their case by invoking the stereotypes of women as the shapers of future men, the tenders of the hearth, the weaker sex, and the bedrock of Christendom. This self-described association of the suffering, submissive, and hence, deserving Catholics, exhorted their prelate to reconsider his past decisions concerning their pastor and grant their request. In doing so, they revealed key reasons why the canonically structured association took root among Hispanized women and served as an important vehicle of militant modern Catholicism. First, it gave women a social space in which to develop as pious individuals and gather as religious women. Second, it provided them with a stage and a potent vocabulary with which to critique secularist patriarchy and assert themselves within the church.

PART II

Revelation

Indigenous Apparitions and Innovations

FOUR

≈ Catholics in Their Own Way

The fifteenth question of Archbishop Gillow's 1908 questionnaire asked pastors, "Do all of the parishioners profess the
Catholic religion? In what areas are there Protestant sects?
Are there Masons? Are there idolaters? Are there superstitious individuals?"[1] From the fringes of the archdiocese in
Puebla's Tehuacán Valley, Father Julián María Miramar replied, "*La religión Católica, a su modo de ellos*" (The Catholic
religion, in their own way).[2] A few years later, in April 1911,
Bartola Bolaños—a Nahua matron from San Mateo Tlacoxcalco, approximately 35 kilometers west of Miramar's parish
—claimed that a well-known local image of Christ appeared to
her and individuals gathered at her home during nocturnal
rituals. El Señor de las Llagas (The Lord of the Wounds),
reputedly angered by the lax devotional attentions of his followers in the town of Miltepec, Oaxaca, had chosen Tlacoxcalco as the site of his renewed reverence. Speaking Nahuatl,
he administered Catholic sacraments, delivered sermons, and
directed his devotees to build a chapel and organize religious
celebrations in his name. Through Bartola Bolaños he also
performed miraculous cures. The emergence of the Lord of
the Wounds' devotion and the central role assumed by an
Indian woman caught the local parish priest, Father Luis Nápoles, by surprise. The diligent young clergymen had replied

in detail to the 1908 parish questionnaire, describing his flock as good hearted and appropriately submissive indigenous Catholics. He enthusiastically predicted the eventual eradication of lingering traces of heterodoxy: "Some superstitions typical of Indian people endure, but they are gradually disappearing."[3] Nápoles even singled out Tlacoxcalco's unparalleled orthodox zeal and piety.

At first, Nápoles treated the rituals in Bolaños's home, the emergent prophecies, the rumored cures, and the requests for his participation as a flare-up of the Indian superstitions he deemed on the verge of extinction. He assumed a noncommittal posture, humored devotees, and waited for the burgeoning apparition movement and its unorthodox rituals to collapse of their own accord. But by September 1911, the usually circumspect clergyman could no longer avoid conflict with the Lord's devotees. In merely four months, Bolaños and her followers had organized a regional brotherhood incorporating communities beyond the parish, staged elaborate liturgical rituals, planned a new pilgrimage festival, and broken ground on a private shrine. Amidst prophecies concerning the misfortunes that would befall the devotion's opponents, Tlacoxcalco celebrated the feast of its patron saint, and Nápoles decided to confront the upstart devotion publicly. From the pulpit, the symbol of priestly authority, he delivered a series of sermons attacking Bolaños and her inner circle. He labeled them frauds, contrasting their movement with officially sanctioned apparition narratives, and lambasting the alleged miracles as tawdry fictions of obvious, Indian fabrication.

Neither Nápoles's oratorical assault, nor the prelate-led campaign to stamp out the increasingly institutionalized popular devotion, succeeded. Today, Tlacoxcalco's Lord of the Wounds remains the center of a regional festival. What follows is an examination of the emergence and development of this apparition movement rooted in female indigenous initiative and revelation, and the responses it inspired among Oaxaca's clergy. Broadly, the actions of the charismatic seer/healer, of the apparition's indigenous devotees, and of local opponents, priests, and prelates offer a case study of local Mexican Catholicism's evolution at this time. More specifically, this case reveals archetypes of early-twentieth-century Catholic culture engaging in a contest of wills, wits, and organizational acumen. Bartola Bolaños represents the region's older devout women, whom the clergy viewed as targets of pastoral opportunity, ideally orga-

nized in pious associations by enterprising priests and deployed as catalysts of Catholicism's revitalization. Nápoles and the priests that succeeded him in Tlacoxcalco acted the part of the church's modern "good
shepherd" figures, seeking to fuel and channel popular piety through
personal zealous faith, new institution building, paternal guidance, and
loving patience.

The history of Bartola Bolaños and the Lord of the Wounds reveals
that within Mexico's oft-cited Catholic revival, deeper struggles took
place, rooted in the relationships between male clergymen and female
and indigenous parishioners. The modernizing church sought to realize
its vision of a righteous masculine hierarchical order stretching from
Rome to Mexico's remotest indigenous villages, yet it depended upon the
devotional and physical energies of the female and Indian Catholics who
made up the majority of the community of belief. Although priests typically characterized these groups as fervent Catholics, this case illustrates
that they maintained independent conceptions of appropriate religious
practice and sometimes worked to establish their own religious movements, paralleling those sanctioned by the church. In short, sectors of
society who were typically viewed as passive subjects of religious revival
instead advanced their own interpretations of Catholicism. Clergymen
and Catholic intellectuals crafted a script of the church's resurgence that
denied a role to active independent Indian and female Catholic agents.
When these pivotal but overlooked Catholics asserted their religious ideologies and rejected the marginal role assigned to them, they inspired a
strong reaction rooted in the church's patriarchal traditions and historical
suspicion of indigenous religious practice. As Oaxaca's clergy faced the
challenge presented by expanding devotion to the Lord of the Wounds,
they abandoned their rhetoric of social unity, pastoral love, and saintly
forbearance and instead attacked the movement and its leadership by
employing stereotypes of Indian superstition and deceitfulness.

To understand the Lord of the Wounds, however, we must set the
stage for his appearance. This requires providing a sociohistorical overview of Puebla's Tehuacán Valley, sketching the region's religious culture,
and scrutinizing Catholic practice in Tlacoxcalco's parish (San José Miahuatlán) and nearby communities on the eve of Bartola Bolaños's visions.
Doing so reveals a continuum of religious practice linked to ethnic identity and economic livelihood in the Tehuacán region during the early

twentieth century. The poles of religious expression are most apparent in contrasting institutional structures, liturgical rhythms, festive traditions, and devotional practices described in the provincial city of Tehuacán and the region's Indian parishes. The intention, though, is not to convey an oil-in-water conception of regional Hispanic and indigenous Catholicism. The evidence indicates that different groups observed, and took part in, each others' devotional practices and celebrations, and sometimes adopted aspects they found meaningful within their own traditions. In addition, looking closely at Tlacoxcalco reveals a history of complex priest-parishioner relationships and lay innovation. In other words, the Lord of the Wounds chose a dynamic milieu for his revitalized devotion.

SOCIETY AND RELIGION IN THE TEHUACÁN VALLEY

When most Mexicans envision the Tehuacán Valley, they think of bottled mineral water, thanks to the marketing of Peñafiel (established in 1928). Among academics, Tehuacán evokes the pioneering research on the origins of maize agriculture. More recently, the region has been the site of studies examining local irrigation and social organization.[4] Water, or its dearth, links these seemingly disparate associations. The Tehuacán region occupies a hot, fertile valley dividing the mountain ranges of the Nudo Mixteco and Sierra Madre Oriental. The surrounding peaks block all but minimal precipitation, but copious amounts of water flow beneath the valley. The arid climate, however, preserves evidence of early agriculture and inspired millennia of valley residents to develop irrigation techniques. Due to the subterranean water sources, would-be irrigators and twentieth-century beverage entrepreneurs have enjoyed considerable success. The valley, which today bridges the states of Puebla and Oaxaca, boasts at least six-thousand years of organized agriculture and continuous human occupation.[5]

Tehuacán scholarship conveys a sense of a valley apart, a virtual intermountain agricultural laboratory. The studies of its prehistory and midtwentieth century agricultural development focus on very local issues, and their accounts of the valley's colonial and postindependence history tend to be impressionistic.[6] Spanish conquerors encountered a network of independent, Nahuatl-speaking city-states (*altepetl*) subject to the Aztec tributary empire in the valley. These polities practiced intensive

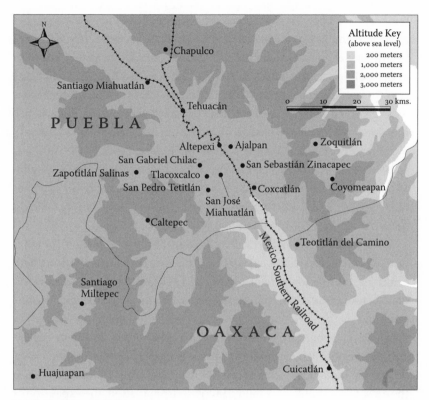

Map 3 The Tehuacán Valley

irrigated agriculture. As in many other regions, Spanish officials adopted the preexisting sociopolitical centers as nodes of colonial administration and parish organization.[7] Contemporary municipal boundaries still correspond to these precincts. During the colonial period, the valley's population remained clustered around the pre-Columbian centers of Tehuacán and Coxcatlán. After independence, the city of Tehuacán became the district seat, and Coxcatlán a municipality within its jurisdiction. Coxcatlán, in turn, administered most of the southern portion of the valley, called the Valle Bajo, including Ajalpan, San Gabriel Chilac, San José Miahuatlán (including Tlacoxcalco), and San Sebastián Zinacatepec. In 1891, these towns became independent municipalities. Ecclesiastically, the parish priest of Coxcatlán also oversaw these subject towns. Mexican prelates and Vatican officials met to redraw the nation's ecclesiastical boundaries in 1891. In 1893, therefore, the Tehuacán Valley was incorporated into the newly formed Archdiocese of Oaxaca. Shortly afterward Gillow moved to rationalize parish jurisdictions. As a result, the new municipalities of Ajalpan, San Gabriel Chilac, and San José Miahuatlán also became separate parishes in the late 1890s, although their pastors remained subject to the parish priest of Coxcatlán.[8] Zinacatepec remained a dependency of Coxcatlán. As we shall see, Bartola Bolaños's movement reunited, at least in a devotional sense, much of the Nahuatl-speaking Valle Bajo that had once been under Coxcatlán. This subregion also boasts the Tehuacán Valley's most intensive hydrological management system and a corresponding legacy of local institution building related to the control and distribution of natural resources.[9]

From the late-colonial period until the revolution, the region's population expanded, especially during the late nineteenth and early twentieth centuries. In 1791 the valley's inhabitants numbered approximately forty-one thousand; by 1891, the population had grown to fifty-eight thousand; and in 1910, eighty-four thousand people resided in the valley.[10] In many ways, Tehuacán experienced the typical Porfirian boom experienced in regions where modern commercial agriculture proved successful. All the ingredients were there: the inauguration of railroad service in the early 1890s, political stability, increasing population, the expansion of hacienda-based cash-crop production, increasing land values, incipient industrialization, and the proletarianization of Indian peasants. Yet the valley avoided the revolution's extreme violent upheavals, in part because the region preserved different production regimes and types of land tenancy as commercial capitalism expanded.[11]

Although the historical documentation discussing Tlacoxcalco's apparition movement makes no mention of natural resource management, the devotion did tap into local traditions of institution building and a culture of innovation rooted in collective efforts to utilize and protect hydrological resources. According to irrigation scholars, the Indian villages of the Valle Bajo waged a long struggle to safeguard their land and water resources against external groups seeking to wrest these assets from them.[12] In the face of resource-use conflicts, the cluster of Nahuatl-speaking irrigating villages that once made up the municipality and parish of Coxcatlán developed flexible organizational strategies. These arrangements demonstrate that far from simply defending traditions and resisting encroachments, Ajalpan, Chilac, San José Miahuatlán, Altepexi, and Zinacatepec responded creatively. They faced two periods of particularly intense resource competition: the classic late-eighteenth- and late-nineteenth-century eras of "agrarian compression."[13] When haciendas expanded and gained control of communal water resources during these periods, Indian villagers increasingly became sharecroppers and peons for these enterprises. Yet they simultaneously pooled resources to regain land and water through litigation and outright purchase. In some instances, neighboring villages cooperated in the quest to recover resources. For example, San José Miahuatlán and Zinacatepec banded together in 1765 to purchase a hacienda on their mutual border. These communities began forming water associations during the nineteenth century in order to increase the available water supply. These institutions developed their own technologies, such as *galerías filtrantes* (chain wells) and locally managed their hydrological resources.

The linchpin of these Indian communities' resilience was the local variant of the *cargo* system. Rooted in notions of communal reciprocity, villages organized the rotation of political positions, religious obligations, land use, and water management between and within quasi-autonomous, wardlike barrios. Four separate barrios comprised each Valle Bajo community, and the heads of households meeting each barrio's specific criteria gained *usuario* ("user," a term denoting full community membership) status. *Usuarios* enjoyed exclusive rights to water allotments and local political participation. They also provided labor and services for water projects and religious celebrations, and accepted civil and religious offices. Within the barrio-*usuario* system, all positions of political and religious importance rotated. Irrigation canals frequently corresponded to these barrio units and bore the name of the barrios that built and maintained them.[14] Within these barrios, numerous *mayordomías* organized religion. Barrios generally divided their membership into smaller groups, often comprising 25 *usuarios*, assigned to the different *mayordomías*. Typically, each *mayordomía* celebrated three functions per year—the saint's feast, its six-month anniversary (*sexagésima*), and another smaller saint's feast. Early-nineteenth-century evidence reveals that *mayordomos* were directly in charge of water allocation, as well as religious festivals. In eighteenth- and nineteenth-century Ajalpan, the chief indigenous political authority, known as the Tetiaxca, appointed *mayordomos* and local church lay officials.[15] He also personally took charge of the town's pilgrimage festival dedicated to an image of Christ, the Lord of Coculco.[16]

The barrio-*usuario* system and the economic and cultural activities that it supported marked ethnic identity in the valley beyond the period of its actual function. Since Indian communities historically barred mestizo residents from *usuario* status, non-Indians frequently stood on the margins of local agriculture and communal religious practice. Commerce, artisanal occupations, Spanish language, Western dress, and priest-centered Catholicism were therefore indicators of non-Indian identity. Conversely, Indian identity distinctions included distinct dress, Nahuatl or Popoloca language use, agricultural labor, participation in local sodalities, affiliation with pueblo structures, and surnames associated with Indian barrios. Some valley residents belonged to an intermediate group of assimilated Indians, labeled *"índios arrazonados"* or *"indios revestidos"* (literally, Indians that have gained reason, or re-dressed Indians). This group preferred Spanish, used Hispanized surnames, and abandoned indigenous dress.[17]

The Valle Bajo's unique social organization faced increasing pressures in the late nineteenth and early twentieth centuries, but the valley's indigenous residents neither surrendered to change nor resorted to violence. Before the revolution, the Tehuacán district government moved against Indian control of water and what they perceived as the wasteful allocation of local revenues, laboring to separate municipal governments and water resources from the barrio-*usuario* system. In towns with larger, economically powerful Hispanized populations, such as Ajalpan, non-Indians gained access to religious sodalities and municipal offices and worked to wrest control of land and water away from Indian-controlled institutions and transfer them to private ownership. These towns witnessed a dismantling of the barrio-*usuario* system amidst polarizing interethnic tensions. In Ajalpan, mestizo interests even succeeded in pushing Indians out of their centrally located barrios. In more homogenous municipalities that remained primarily indigenous, such as Chilac, Zinacatepec, and San José Miahuatlán, Indians successfully blocked non-Indian participation in local governance by denying outsiders *usuario* status. In these communities, the barrio-*usuario* system endured until the 1950s shift to federal control of hydrological resources. Despite pressures and changes, the indigenous communities of the Valle Bajo preserved their traditions of local institution building and collective action. In the twentieth century they formed new, modern-sounding organizations to represent their interests before the revolutionary government: for example, the Society of Small Farmers, the Society of Wells, Canals, and Trenches, and the Society for the Unification of the Indigenous Class. Some villages succeeded in regaining lands through agrarian reform legislation and the formation of *ejidos*, although it proved much more difficult to regain water rights.[18]

A CONTINUUM OF PRACTICE AND PIETY

How is this thumbnail sketch of the Tehuacán Valley's history and social organization relevant to divine apparitions in Tlacoxcalco in 1911? The genius of this particular apparition movement resides in its institutionalization of innovative religious practices in a regional brotherhood that incorporated followers from communities throughout the Valle Bajo. It is clear that when its leaders sought organizational models, the most obvious ones were the sodalities and water-management institutions with which they were already familiar. But the movement's leaders also drew on organizational schemes of recent external origin. The evidence suggests that the Lord's devotees succeeded, in large part, due to their adept hybridization of local institutional and religious traditions, and the organizational and devotional reforms forwarded by the clergy.

As evident in the studies cited above, the Valle Bajo experienced an economic boom in the late nineteenth and early twentieth centuries. The surge in population, the creation of new municipalities and parishes, stress on sociopolitical institutions, the transformation of relations of production, and the increased ethnic and resource tensions were aspects of this process. But the region cannot be analyzed as a traditional hinterland subject to incipient capitalist production. We must look at the Tehuacán Valley as a region long accustomed to commercial agriculture, which was experiencing a series of powerful economic stimuli.[19] Thanks to Archbishop Gillow's 1908 questionnaire, we have snapshots of piety, practice, and institutional culture on the eve of the apparitions. From pastor responses, we can examine the impact of economic development and modernization on religious life. They reveal that these priests ministered in relatively well-to-do parishes, where the innovations of the church's Porfirian revival established a stronger foothold than was in evidence in most of the archdiocese of Oaxaca. The condition of local churches, rich ornamentation, and large numbers of devotional organizations and festivals described in the questionnaire testifies to the region's relative wealth. In addition, the remarkably large number and size of new canonically structured associations suggests that the modern Catholic resurgence exerted greater influence in these communities than in much of the archdiocese.[20]

The best way to put the valley's rural parishes in perspective is to compare them to the regional economic and political hub, Tehuacán. This small provincial city maintained a very distinct Catholic culture within a short train ride of many villages in the valley. According to the archdiocese's 1905 statistics, six priests served the city.[21] In 1908, Tehuacán's pastor Francisco Hernández informed his prelate that twelve thousand individuals inhabited his jurisdiction: ten thousand within the city itself and two thousand in nearby villages. He described the city center as an island of Hispanic piety surrounded by backward Indian communities. Most people residing in town, affirmed the pastor, were "European or Hispano-American." He identified parishioners outside the city as speakers of Nahuatl and Popoloca. In comparison to the smaller Indian communities of the valley, Tehuacán's urbanites had nearly abandoned Catholic festive sodality traditions. Hernández asserted that the only functioning *mayordomía* within the city celebrated Tehuacán's patron saint, and he reported that his parishioners no longer maintained brotherhoods. He listed only ten yearly fiestas but reported an impressive 3,803 active members of seven canonically structured associations. The Apostolado, The Honor Guard of the Sacred Heart of Jesus, and the Asociación de la Propagación de la Fé (Association for the Propagation of the Faith) boasted over 1,000 members each.

The pastor judged piety well developed throughout his jurisdiction but stipulated that his most devout parishioners lived in the city, especially "women of all social classes." Many people frequented the sacraments, he assured the archbishop—estimating that seventy people took the sacraments daily and many more did on Sundays, and that about four hundred people took communion on the first Friday of every month and on feast days. Devout Tehuacanos also took part in many carefully scheduled spiritual exercises, usually linked to their membership in canonical associations. In the aggregate, they provided a consistent hum of devotional activity. In addition to the standard liturgical calendar's rhythms of Sunday services and established feasts, the first of every month featured exercises commemorating Divine Providence, and first Fridays brought together members of the Apostolado for a spiritual retreat. On the twelfth of each month, parishioners gathered for a special service to express their devotion to the Virgin of Guadalupe, and every Sunday afternoon individuals came together for the Rosary, a sermon, and worship of the Blessed Sacrament. Every third Sunday, devotees of the Eucharist held a special mass and procession. If no one in Tehuacán belonged to more than one canonically structured association, roughly 38 percent of the population belonged to these kinds of organizations. Even if the actual figure was much lower, Tehuacán's participation in orthodox piety and the church's new lay institutions was quite extraordinary in comparison to parishes in the rest of the archdiocese. As for confession and communion, Hernández did not even bother to address the issue of the laities' compliance with the Easter duty. Clearly, he felt that his parishioners exceeded their basic sacramental duties at daily, weekly, and festival services.[22]

Hernández also judged his flock well educated in both secular and religious matters. Despite the fact that Catholic schools could not compete with secular schools in terms of sheer numbers, he claimed religious education in the city was a solid, successful enterprise. At 11:00 a.m. every Sunday, children attended catechism classes, and many others went to parochial schools every day. The "best families" sent their male progeny— approximately forty boys—to the reputedly excellent Tehuacán Liceo, which was established in the 1870s to train for careers in law, medicine, engineering, and the priesthood. Up to seventy children attended a religious vocational school, eighty well-to-do girls went to their own Catholic school, and one hundred less-fortunate girls learned under the watchful eye of the Hermanas del Asilo (Sisters of Asylum). In comparison, three hundred boys and two hundred girls attended public preparatory schools in the city, and hundreds more went to municipal elementary schools.

Priests serving in rural, predominantly Indian parishes painted a very different picture. The reply to Gillow's questionnaire by Father Nápoles, the parish priest of San José Miahuatlán and Tlacoxcalco, reveals that he employed a diplomatic approach in his ministry. Nápoles had been

9 Father Luís G. Nápoles (Acervo José F. Gómez, Centro Fotográfico Manuel Álvarez Bravo, used by permission of the CFMAB).

posted in the region since at least 1905, when the archdiocese listed him as the pastor of San Pablo Chapulco—a village near Tehuacán. He assumed the curacy of San José in 1906.[23] His responses demonstrate that he enjoyed a particularly desirable posting. Unlike some of his colleagues who lived in austere quarters, Nápoles inhabited a relatively palatial rectory with comfortable, well-ventilated rooms, two toilets, a spacious kitchen, and a "magnificent breezeway." Perhaps for this reason, he avoided shrill complaints about his flock's attitude toward the clergy or their devotional proclivities. He dispassionately described conditions and local customs as he found them, demonstrating a clear understanding of the limits of his authority.

His parish, Nápoles wrote, occupied a hot, dry portion of the valley at 1,300 meters above sea level. Citing a recent census he noted that the parish seat had 3,000 inhabitants, Tlacoxcalco had 525 inhabitants, and San Pedro Tetitlan and San Gerónimo Axochitlan had only 300 and 22 inhabitants, respectively. The area's soils were rich, but, the pastor assured his prelate, its water rights were limited and poorly distributed.[24] San José did, however, enjoy a telephone link to Tehuacán and a railroad station a scant eight kilometers away. San José gained parish status on January 8,

1897, by Gillow's decree. Within the parish, Nápoles described three Nahuatl-speaking communities (San José, Tlacoxcalco, and Axochitlan), a Popoloca village (Tetitlan), the Hacienda Axusco, and many small ranchos. Tlacoxcalco, the most prominent community beyond San José itself, bordered San Gabriel Chilac, the hacienda San Luis Tultitlán, and Tetitlan. His parishioners, Nápoles professed, were generally good and submissive, although he provided a short list of several disrespectful and less-than-obedient individuals. He vouched for the strong simple Catholic faith of his flock, although some locals haphazardly aped the anticlerical and Protestant doctrines espoused by some regional civil authorities outside of the community.[25]

Economic life in the parish revolved around a mix of commercial baking, cash-crop agriculture, subsistence farming, artisanal alcohol production, and wage labor. This diversified local economy both pleased and troubled the parish priest. He could not say enough about the "magnificent" loaves that sold briskly within the district and beyond. Beans, barley, chilies, and tomatoes also found buyers, and locals subsisted on their own corn and wheat. His parishioners, however, employed their sugar cane yields in the cottage industry production of *lapo*, a beverage concocted from the mixture and fermentation of cane juice, *pulque tlachique* (a variety of maguey beer), and water. Nápoles described this beverage as a potent and disgusting intoxicant, but present-day residents of Tlacoxcalco recall it as a delicious, pineapple-yellow refreshment imbibed by workers at periodic breaks without hampering their tasks.[26] But the dominant economic pursuit in early-twentieth-century San José was hacienda wage labor. Every Monday morning, four hundred men left the parish seat to work on nearby haciendas and did not return until Saturday night. Other communities within the parish also experienced this weekly exodus, although on a smaller scale. The chronic abandonment of the parish by large numbers of its male inhabitants, he avowed, hamstrung the development of local commerce, but more troublingly, it undermined the moral foundations of rural society.

Just as his flock mixed their homebrew from local ingredients, so too the cocktail of masculine migratory labor, weak patriarchal supervision of women, local intoxicants, and atheist civil law produced an unsettling combination of female drunkenness, sexual promiscuity, adultery, and divorce. The pastor felt helpless in the face of what he described as a vicious circle unhinging gendered social order and sexual mores. With their husbands absent six days a week, women indulged themselves in copious *lapo* consumption and, once intoxicated, forgot "their obligations to their husbands." Returning cuckolds promptly abandoned their wives, marched angrily to San José's judicial officials, and procured rapid civil divorces without consulting their parish priest or attempting to save their marriages. These newly minted bachelors immediately sought new companions. It did not take long, Nápoles lamented, for these men, their neighbors' *lapo*-slugging wives, and other recent divorcees to find each other.

Nápoles found his parish's religious life more-or-less typical of Indian communities and lacking in noteworthy devotional traditions. All of the towns in the parish celebrated the official feasts and their patron saints: "The solemnity and splendor of these fiestas does not surpass that which is customary for indigenous pueblos—no pilgrimages exist within this parish." The pastor trumpeted the progress of the Apostolado within his parish. Although they lacked official certification, he underscored the vigor of two local branches of the canonically structured association, especially Tlacoxcalco's. San José's Apostolado boasted forty-three female members organized in the apostolate's standard cellular hierarchy, featuring a president and seven *celadoras* in charge of five women each. In Tlacoxcalco, eighty-six men and women filled out the ranks of this organization dedicated to the Sacred Heart of Jesus and the frequenting of the sacraments. After amassing 107 pesos in 1907, the Tlacoxcalco group purchased a comely sculpture of the Sacred Heart. Both of these associations celebrated the organization's annual feast "with all due splendor," but they had yet to establish the customary masses on the first Friday of every month.

Outside of the 129 souls staffing the Apostolado in his parish, however, Nápoles commented on the weak nature of the church's markers of Catholic culture and pastoral progress. Religious instruction, he declared, was nonexistent among adults, and only slightly better among the children attending Sunday Mass and feast-day catechism sessions. His parishioners, he maintained, lacked access to Catholic schools or the means to establish them. The two municipal schools "teach them poorly and make them believe worse, due to their atheist curriculum." The pastor also divulged that the standard orthodox measures of piety and practice held no allure for most of his parishioners. In his two years ministering in San José, not a single soul frequented the sacraments, and only ninety fulfilled the Easter duty. Given the population figures Nápoles provided for the parish (3,845 inhabitants), only about 2 percent of his parishioners complied with the stipulated minimum level of sacramental observance. In addition to mass, Nápoles led the Rosary on Sunday afternoons and Hora Santa on Thursdays, but only about a dozen people attended.[27] His charges confessed only in preparation for marriage or when they were deathly ill and already deprived of reason. In fact, San José's residents believed that extreme unction guaranteed fatality and hence avoided contacting Nápoles until a death was immanent. Thus, remarked the pastor, they repeatedly strengthened their erroneous perceptions of this important sacrament. In these conditions, Nápoles assured the archbishop, he exerted himself to the limit of his faculties. When significant numbers of people filled the church on Sundays and feast days, he "preached and beseeched with tenacity."

But despite dismal statistics of compliance with official orthodoxy and misunderstandings of doctrine, Nápoles maintained that the bulk of his charges were good Christians at heart. By no means could his flock be tarred as irreligious. San José alone supported twenty *mayordomías*, and subject communities sustained several others. But Nápoles could not supply the details his prelate requested concerning these institutions. Quite simply, he found himself on the sidelines of public religious activity within his parish. All his flock's *mayordomías*, according to the priest, functioned in the same stubbornly autonomous manner. Each *mayordomo* managed his group's funds and stores of wax, and organized its celebrations without informing the pastor beyond requesting liturgical services and paying the appropriate fees promptly and in full. Every year, each community's civil authorities appointed new *mayordomos* and enjoyed their fill of food, dance, and drink at gatherings held after the religious ceremony at the private homes of these individuals. The authorities also refused to consult their pastor concerning the selection of *mayordomos* or provide information on the funds they managed. According to Nápoles, "The parish priest must content himself with nothing more than the receipt of his fees. If on the contrary he were to try to intervene and force them to give a full accounting, everything would end, and the funds they control would be invested in a manner of their choosing."[28]

Here Nápoles recorded the priest's-eye view of the integrated civil-religious system of Tehuacán's Valle Bajo and indigenous practice. Although he displayed no knowledge of the management of hydrological resources by *mayordomos* or local civil authorities, he underscored the interwoven nature of these offices. He missed, or ignored, the deeper importance of the system's celebrations and guarded autonomy, suggesting that their interrelationship stemmed from authorities' predilection for booze, banquets, and fandangos. But in the rest of his report, Nápoles displayed a distinct common sense. He recognized that festive practice, which relegated him to the role of contracted religious specialist, also formed the foundations of religiosity and accounted for a large portion of his ministry. He revealed that the festival system served as the primary sphere of priest-parishioner interaction and surmised that efforts to assert more control over local celebrations and institutions would lead to their abandonment and the reallocation of resources to some other autonomously chosen activity.[29] But his comments on *mayordomía* management and practice demonstrate that the matter-of-fact cleric maintained good relations with these institutions. His assurance that *mayordomos* scrupulously paid festival fees on time and in full is truly remarkable. Many a priest railed against his spiritual charges regarding fees and caution incoming priests to demand prepayment lest they become victims of duplicitous Indian parishioners.

Nápoles's fellow priests posted in other predominantly Indian parishes in the Tehuacán Valley painted similar portraits of local religion.[30] Uniformly they vouched for their parishioners' Catholicism but noted the endurance of "superstitions." Like their colleague, they proudly enumerated the canonically structured associations within their parishes, and relayed statistics on the Church's standard measures of public piety and orthodoxy (sacramental attendance, regular spiritual exercises, organized prayer, religious instruction, frequency of confession, and compliance with the Easter Duty). The questionnaires from Zinacatepec and Ajalpan, communities that supplied a large number of stalwarts of the yet-to-appear Lord of the Wounds, merit close inspection.[31]

The testimony provided by these priests underscores a considerable degree of religious autonomy and innovation in indigenous communities. Quite simply, vibrant Catholic practice revolved around independent *mayordomías* and the feasts they sponsored, rather than priest-centered sacramental observance. In Zinacatepec, a community that grew from 1,900 to 3,000 inhabitants between 1891 and 1908, only 40 people frequented the sacraments and 300 individuals complied with the Easter duty, but they supported two large canonically structured associations, four brotherhoods, and eighteen *mayordomías*. Father Juan Alonso reported that most of these organizations maintained endowments of fifteen to sixty pesos, but six of them had more impressive cash reserves ranging from one hundred to one thousand pesos. Alonso also mentioned the presence of three "private" *mayordomías*; one of apparent great antiquity boasted an impressive four thousand pesos.[32] These sums dwarf the paltry 107 pesos that Nápoles proudly claimed Tlacoxcalco's Apostolado collected and thus raise the possibility that some of the *mayordomías* that refused to give San José's pastor information on their finances may also have controlled similar amounts of money. Alonso also provided a rare glimpse into the gendered identities of rural Catholic organizations. He reported that Zinacatepec's associations, the Apostolado and the Asociación del Carmen, were exclusively female organizations and estimated that each contained four hundred members. He mentioned four male brotherhoods, ranging from eight to fifty members. These figures indicate that female pious energy, and probably church-centered identity, overshadowed its male counterpart.[33] They also reveal that this town contained a core group of publicly devout women and men.

Among Zinacatepec's Nahua sodalities, two reveal recent local incorporation of new devotions—the Sacred Heart of Jesus and Our Lady of Lourdes—associated with the intransigent piety of European Catholicism's resurgence. Nápoles also mentioned the presence of a Lourdes *mayordomía* in San José.[34] Zinacatepec's Sacred Heart *mayordomía* was the town's most wealthy nonprivate sodality (they had one thousand pesos). Alonso considered the pueblo's Lourdes sodality a private *mayordomía* and he reported that it managed a three-hundred-peso endowment. Both of these devotions have their roots in French Catholicism. We have already seen that the Sacred Heart devotion and sacramental frequency formed the centerpiece of practice in the Apostolado. As to Our Lady of Lourdes, evidence of indigenous institutions dedicated to France's famous Marian devotion during this period is exceedingly rare. Emerging from the legendary 1858 Pyrenean visions of Bernadette Soubirous, this advocation of Mary became the international standard of

Catholicism's rejection of secular modernity in the 1860s and 1870s, and it subsequently spread throughout the Catholic world. The adoption of these devotions and their incorporation into the *mayordomía* system of these two towns demonstrates that indigenous communities cannot be pigeonholed as islands of tradition. Their presence is significant for several reasons: first, they show Valle Bajo Nahuas participating in the latest revivalist devotional currents; second, their relatively recent appropriation reveals the *mayordomía* system's sensitivity to larger movements within the church and suggests that the addition of new devotions and festivals, and presumably the subtraction of others, was relatively common.[35] In addition, they demonstrate a rapid Mexicanization of advocations trumpeted as symbols of the universal church and its rejection of secularization.

Ajalpan, a town that experienced a tense standoff between an ascendant mestizo minority (approximately 25 percent of the town's seven thousand inhabitants in the late nineteenth century) and the pueblo's Indian population during this period, provides another interesting point of comparison. This troubled pueblo rated highly in measures of orthodox piety and also maintained a strong *mayordomía* tradition. According to its pastor, Juan Alfaro, thirty to forty individuals frequented the sacraments, eight hundred people complied with the Easter duty, the weekly Rosaries and Hora Santa were well attended, and religious instruction was *"en estado regular"* (in fair shape) despite the absence of parochial schools. This priest also noted the presence of one properly chartered association, the Asociación Guadalupana (established in 1902), with fourteen members of unspecified gender, and an *hermandad* dedicated to the Blessed Sacrament, comprising thirty female members. In addition to these organizations, Alfaro listed thirty-two *mayordomías* in the parish seat and subject villages. The pastor reported that none of the above institutions controlled any funds and that all of them celebrated their fiestas with an identical degree of solemnity.[36]

Given what we know from nearby parishes, this statement about finances and levels of festive practice was probably an admission of ignorance. The parish's sodalities, particularly the indigenous *mayordomías*, probably kept the details of their funding secret from Alfaro. The religious collectivities of Ajalpan were perhaps even more disposed to secrecy due to the ethnic tensions that made the barrio-*usuario* system and its integration of religious practice and resource-management a point of contention. Archbishop Gillow visited Ajalpan in October 1896, commenting on these issues and the local priest's complicity in ethnic tensions. He noted that Indian sodalities possessed independent *alcancías* (cash boxes) and refused to inform the parish priest of their resources. Gillow also described the sharp rift between *"gente de razón"* and Indians and its carryover into local religion. Indians complained to the prelate that an earlier pastor, Epitacio Paredes, ignored their spiritual needs and ministered exclusively to non-Indians, disregarding their requests for sacraments and making no effort to teach the catechism. Gillow's sources also reported that Paredes refused to attend *mayordomía* meetings and keep records concerning them.[37]

It also seems highly unlikely that all the religious functions within Ajalpan inspired the same degree of devotion or the same willingness to pay fees for their respective functions. Most parish priests indicated, in some fashion, which feasts were *"de primera"* (first-rate)—usually only three to five celebrations—and which were celebrated with lesser degrees of pomp and expense. Clerics also tended to list *mayordomías* in order of importance. A similar pattern holds for inventories of images: usually the most valuable images linked to the most important local feasts appear first, followed by the rest. Alfaro did reveal that Ajalpan possessed the Valle Bajo's sole pilgrimage festival. Dedicated to an image of Christ, the Lord of Coculco, this devotion also had its own *mayordomía*. This is the same sodality that Ajalpan's mid-nineteenth century Indian *tetiaxca* personally managed, and which attracted the broadest devotion from the parish's indigenous residents. The pilgrimage was clearly Ajalpan's most important feast in the mid-nineteenth century and probably remained so in 1908.[38] The devotees of the Tlacoxcalco's Lord of the Wounds invoked this image and other local "brother" images of Christ when they sought to legitimize their own new devotion.

For the village clergy of the Valle Bajo, *mayordomías* may have been stubbornly independent and their parishioners' religious understanding primitive, but they did not perceive them as opponents. In general, they viewed them as part of the expected, albeit sometimes frustrating, nature of the church's ministry in native communities. The bugbear for rural clergymen was the percolation of impious ideologies among the faithful, which they asserted originated in external politics and entered their parishes via impressionable indigenous authorities. Indeed, Nápoles critiqued *mayordomía* recalcitrance and festive excesses, but saved his real contempt for the local puppets of outside functionaries who had won recent election. He claimed they distinguished themselves as profaners of the community's traditions and fomenters of anticlerical hatred. The details he provided, however, demonstrate that the "customs and traditions" abridged by these officeholders had little to do with faith and practice, and instead involved the time-honored squabbles of parish economics. Before 1907, civil officials oversaw a general tithe collection (sixty pesos); each of San José's barrios named collectors who jointly provided a weekly stipend (*dominica*) for the priest (five pesos) and organist (one peso).[39] In concert, barrios also organized a bevy of domestic servants and liturgical assistants, and gathered hay, charcoal, and firewood for the priest's household. Nápoles lamented that now priests in San José had to pay for all services and goods they received. Thankfully, he declared, outside of the parish seat a semblance of the old system endured. In Tlacoxcalco and Tetitlan, local officials organized collections and provided personal service for the pastor when he visited their communities.[40]

Such was the general tenor of priestly disquisitions on religion in Tehuacán's rural villages. They portrayed their pastorate as a mixture of promoting the more frequent orderly religiosity showcased in canonically structured associations, attempting to breathe life into "traditions" and practices of little interest to their parishioners, managing declining revenues and degrees of conflict with civil authorities, and officiating at festivals over which they had little control. Nonetheless, for most priests in the archdiocese's rural ministry, these conditions represented the norm. They vented their frustrations concerning the situation and longed for a more hierarchical and better-compensated pastoral ideal, but the conditions as they existed were at least familiar. Priests considered their indigenous neighbors and parishioners to be fellow Catholics, but they tended to qualify their faith; Indians were Catholics, "in their own way."

The responses to the 1908 questionnaire from the Valle Bajo's parishes reveal that priests compared their flocks' piety and practices to a new standard of urban Catholicism. For this particular group of clergymen, the model of religiosity was Tehuacán. Comparing the responses to the archbishop's queries illustrates that the survey was much easier for urban clergymen to answer than their brethren in the countryside. Francisco Hernández, Tehuacán's pastor, confidently replied to each question, providing the archdiocesan curia with detailed and complete answers. In essence, he could tell the prelate what he wanted to hear—Hernández was successfully instilling the militant reformed piety that Gillow hoped to implant throughout the archdiocese. His rural colleagues, however, had to provide somewhat embarrassing explanations as to why they could not provide entire categories of information, why certain practices and institutions did not exist in their parishes, and why local collectivities did not function as stipulated by the church hierarchy. In some cases the questions led them to delve into the peculiarities of local customs that tinctured or hampered parish administration. When these clerics, like generations of priests before them, described their pastoral activities, they listed their standard duties (teaching, preaching, and administering the sacraments) and stressed their role in the construction or restoration of their churches and rectories. In the early twentieth century, however, priests often emphasized their actions as founders and directors of canonically structured associations. In the climate of militant piety pervading urban Catholic circles, these new institutions represented the vanguard of the church's battle for hearts and minds. Parish priests sought to portray themselves as the struggle's leaders in obedient pious communities. Ministers serving in indigenous communities had greater difficulty presenting themselves and their parishioners in this manner. As a result, rural clergymen felt the need to explain why the religious cultures of their parishes differed from the urban environment inhabited by their superiors. In short, they measured their parishioners and their ministry against an idealized modern religiosity of European inspiration. In most cases, clerics attempted to portray a sense of progress toward this goal while invoking stereotypes about Indian superstition, ignorance, and resistance to change to explain the discrepancy between the reigning model and reality. The fact that the predominantly Hispanic priesthood sought to implant foreign models of belief and practice in their indigenous parishes is hardly surprising, but in the process of gauging the distance between observed and idealized religiosity, they left us a record of indigenous religious life during the period.[41]

Tlacoxcalco's apparition movement emerged in a diverse and complex religious milieu. The religious landscape of the Tehuacán Valley reveals a continuum of culture: Tehuacán's staid, sacrament-centered, priest-led piety constituted one pole, while the other resided in the autonomous *mayordomía*-centered practice of San José Miahuatlán and Zinacatepec. Given the rough demographic data provided by our sources, we can also map the percentage of Hispanic and mestizo residents along this scale. Tehuacán was the most Hispanized, followed by Ajalpan, where a mestizo, culturally Hispanic population exerted increased influence. San José Miahuatlán and Zinacatepec represented the most strongly indigenous communities. Lamentably, we do not have more information on the assimilationist religious strategies of more acculturated Indians, the *índios arrazonados.* Our sources are silent on the beliefs and practices employed by individuals and groups that sought to blend in among mestizos. It is likely that many individuals may have "passed" in both Indian and Hispanic social environments and that these intermediary figures may have been conduits of exchange between different religious sensibilities.

Invoking a continuum underscores the evident flexibility, fluidity, and back-and-forth interactions between innovations, traditions, and practices emerging from both Hispanic and indigenous religious practice. By no means can we characterize the Tehuacán Valley as a rigidly divided religious world with Hispanized urbanites, mestizos, and priests practicing one brand of Catholicism, while Indian villages stubbornly protected their own devout traditions against change. Quite to the contrary, the 1908 questionnaire shows that indigenous Catholics in the region were very much aware of the currents of modern Catholicism, adopting certain innovations, devotions, and organizations and adapting them to local norms. Indeed, our data indicate that some members of these communities embraced new associations and their devotions. This newer style of practice—which fused traditional Catholic corporatism with contemporary religious fashions emphasizing more emotional daily, weekly, or monthly expressions of personal devotion—proved relatively easy to adapt to local practices. Nonetheless, devotional preferences did at times amount to an ethnic statement, especially in communities experiencing sharp divisions between Indian and non-Indian residents. Participating in the pilgrimage to Ajalpan's Lord of Coculco, for example, or displaying a print of his image in the home, communicated an indigenous religious identity. Although it may be risky to pinpoint a marker of religious Hispanization and assimilation, the data reported by the Tehuacán Valley's clergy suggest that the numbers of parishioners frequenting the sacraments correlated with the relative size of the non-Indian population. In April 1911, the Lord of the Wounds allegedly wandered into the picture. As we shall see, his devotion drew on the entire range of religious options in the region.

FIVE

〜 Christ Comes to Tlacoxcalco

The scarcity of evidence always limits the reconstruction of popular movements. In this case, the Lord of the Wounds' followers left behind only one text—a petition requesting ecclesiastical recognition of their newly formed religious brotherhood. Thanks to the devotion's endurance, however, we can still examine the physical evidence of their initiative: a life-size image of the crucified Christ commissioned during the summer of 1911, which resides in a large glass cabinet in Tlacoxcalco's church; a small green cross that legend holds materialized during an apparition; a large miraculous stone that allegedly fell from the sky and served the seer, Bartola Bolaños, in curing rituals; and finally, a 1913 typeset flyer advertising a new pilgrimage festival. In addition, present-day residents of Tlacoxcalco, including the seer's grandson, provide details concerning the devotion's history, Bolaños's leadership and curing practice, and the Lord's brotherhood.

We also lack a careful ecclesiastical investigation of the Bolaños's experiences, and hence, a priest's depiction of the seer and analysis of the visions. Perhaps the local clergy failed to understand the religious florescence taking place in their midst. In fact, a succession of parish priests underestimated the attractiveness of the devotion, the strength of its homegrown institutions, and the talents of the movement's organizers. What we do have is a handful of letters written over several years in which clergymen sought guidance from archdiocesan authorities regarding the devotees' persistent efforts to engage their services. The vicar general and ecclesiastical governor, Father Carlos Gracida, repeatedly issued unambiguous orders to priests near Tlaxcocalco banning all participation in the new cult and outlined strategies to gain control of the Lord's image and put an end to its burgeoning career as a focal point of regional pilgrimage and unseemly practice. Archbishop Gillow personally visited the parish in August 1921 and published a strongly worded condemnation of the movement and its leader/seer.

The most detailed account of the apparitions' emergence and its local institutionalization, however, emanates from an acrimonious denunciation written by the movement's religious rivals from the nearby town of Santiago Miltepec, Oaxaca.[1] It was Miltepec's older image of Christ (the Lord of the Wounds), according to Bartola Bolaños, who had abandoned his perch in that village's church to scour the countryside in search of a new home and a more devoted group of sinners. He called on her, she claimed, to organize his relocated veneration in Tlacoxcalco. Seething at the threat to Miltepec's older pilgrimage festival, the anonymous author provided a thorough description of the controversial devotion's development.[2] Aside from omitting his name, the unknown author also left out the standard heading listing his location and the date. Nonetheless, the Tlacoxcalco Christ's critic used the word "*aquí*" (here) when referring to Miltepec, and the last issue the letter discussed is a sermon pronounced at the town's Lenten festival on February 23, 1912. Thus, the report was probably written in Miltepec shortly after this date. The level of detail about the events taking place in Tlacoxcalco and surrounding towns indicates that the author knew the town and its residents very well. It is possible that the person who produced the document, like the chief targets of his ire (Bartola Bolaños and her husband), maintained family ties in both Miltepec and Tlacoxcalco. The language, content, and style of the complaint suggest an educated Hispanic author who ascribed the entire movement to an unholy mixture of Indian ignorance, superstition, and deceit. The author may have been a priest, perhaps the pastor of Miltepec, or a person close to him. This priest and his allies managing the town's venerable pilgrimage devotion had ample motives for under-

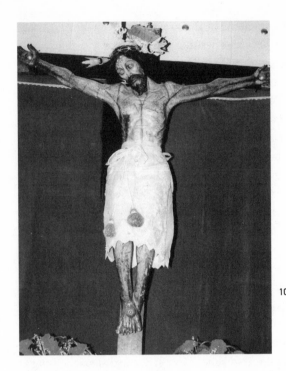

10 A present-day souvenir photograph of the Lord of the Wounds of Santiago, Miltepec, Oaxaca (author's personal collection).

cutting their emergent rivals. The passion and vitriol of this document make it both fascinating and problematic.

Weighing the truth claims of the various texts proves a fruitless task, but the arguments embedded in them allow us to explore how individuals and groups practiced their faith and contested the control of images, the pilgrimages they inspired, and the social meanings attached to apparitions. The goals of particular actors shaped their testimony and therefore provide us with specific kinds of information. For example, the author of the Miltepec denunciation alleged that the devotion to Tlacoxcalco's Lord of the Wounds sheltered a cynical scam and a hotbed of immorality organized by Indian miscreants. Thus the author endeavored to "pull back the curtain" on the apparition movement and expose the machinations behind the miracles. The degree to which the author embellished this diatribe must remain a mystery, but the careful detail and chronology it preserves suggest that its author recorded a great deal of accurate information. From a historian's perspective, it offers a glimpse of the local religious and sociopolitical groundwork related to institution building, myth making, devotional innovation, and religious propaganda vital to the establishment of new devotions. In short, the anonymous author crafted an exceptionally rare historical document: a detailed description of a popular religious movement's emergence and early development.

Examining a historical popular movement through the testimony of its opponents is always problematic, but these types of sources often represent the richest available evidence. Reading a document such as this "against the grain," we can find in the anonymous author's bitter condemnation of Indian credulity evidence of growing popular support for the visions and their controversial seer. Likewise, the author's claim that the devotees deployed a regional network of spies suggests that the movement enjoyed substantial backing beyond Tlacoxcalco. Accusations that Bolaños tricked ignorant villagers into contributing money, goods, and labor indicate that the new devotion voiced a significantly unifying religious ideology.[3] With evidentiary foundations such as these, any reconstruction of the movement that coalesced around Bartola Bolaños remains fragmented, and yet, the Lord of the Wounds and his intermediaries manage to be heard.

BARTOLA AND THE LORD OF THE WOUNDS

The miracles began as a family affair. Feliciano Lezama and his wife, Filiberta, discussed Mrs. Lezama's persistent health problems with their relatives, María Bartola and her elderly, one-eyed husband, Anastasio Bolaños. The social origins of the Bolaños couple are difficult to determine. Ms. Bolaños was apparently illiterate, but her husband could read and write. This suggests that Mr. Bolaños was perhaps from one of the more successful families in Tlacoxcalco, although the family was by no means rich by regional standards. Nonetheless, as the following pages will demonstrate, both Bartola and Anastasio enjoyed considerable respect in their community. On April 18, 1911, at 11:00 p.m., Mr. Bolaños and a figure wrapped in a blanket entered a dark room within the Lezamas' house and sat on a bench. The mysterious figure blessed the Lezamas, offered advice, and blew on them. Filiberta requested a cure for her maladies and received a prescription for herbal remedies. On the next night, the Lezamas and a group of acquaintances went to the Bolaños home for further treatment. Upon arrival they found a figure sitting on a large box in complete darkness. The enigmatic person blessed them with flowers and indicated that they kiss his hand and perform other displays of veneration. Then he told those gathered in the house that he was the Lord of the Wounds, and declared that the residents of Miltepec no longer cared for him, and therefore he had been suffering the elements as he wandered in search of more dedicated followers. He explained that he had finally chosen Tlacoxcalco.[4] When the apparition ended, the visitors heard a great clanging of metal, and as the witnesses left, Mr. Bolaños handed them framed prints of the Lord of the Wounds, instructing his guests that it was no longer necessary to undertake the pilgrimage to Miltepec. The Lord, he proclaimed, now came to Tlacoxcalco in person.

As in most apparition movements, suspicions on the part of some observers contrasted with credence on the part of others. Allegedly, Feliciano Lezama assumed trickery from the very beginning. Apparently he identified the mysterious voice he heard on the first night as Bartola altering her speech and recognized her on the second night as the figure shrouded in darkness. According to our informant, Anastasio Bolaños provided the cacophonous touches to the apparition by rattling a box of tools, while his brother, a member of the original Lord of the Wound's brotherhood in Miltepec, supplied the framed images. Nonetheless, on successive evenings more people visited the Bolaños home, until upwards of fifty people were in attendance every night. Within approximately a month, the gatherings took on a distinctly Catholic character. They began with the Rosary, a litany of saints, and a hymn before the organizers extinguished all the lights and prohibited the lighting of matches. The apparitions commenced after a devotee circulated with a hyssop, as priests do, sprinkling visitors with water. Suddenly the Lord of the Wounds would appear and deliver a sermon in slow deliberate tones, causing many of those present to beat their chests, weep, cross themselves, and shout pleas of forgiveness without daring to look up. "*El aparecido*" (the one that appears) informed them that illness, poverty, and divine acts of arson awaited those who failed to believe in his apparition. Furthermore, he commanded that all of Tlacoxcalco's Catholic brotherhoods render him homage. As he spoke, the entire house trembled. The conspirators achieved this feat, our indignant informant assured us, by having one collaborator surreptitiously shake the walls of the simple structure, while another stationed outside rattled the roof with a long stick. But in the dark, he carped, gullible visitors believed they witnessed a miracle.

On May 29, at 7:00 p.m., a fire consumed the home of Filomena Gómez, a resolute critic of the Lord's apparitions, while she was away. Villagers rushed to extinguish the blaze, but a widow named María Julia blocked their path, warning that the blaze served as a lesson to doubters. Gómez subsequently filed a complaint with the town's civil authorities accusing Bartola Bolaños of arson. The accused scoffed at her opponents, claiming that they could not proceed against her because she was immortal. Even in the remote possibility that they succeeded in incarcerating her, Bartola allegedly boasted, "all the people would see with great amazement that she would become a resplendent crucified Christ, and escape without leaving the slightest trace." According to the Miltepec denunciation, these astounding claims went untested. Apparently Tlacoxcalco's authorities, avowed "slaves of the *santo*," chose witnesses from among the devotees, resulting in Bolaños's exoneration.

During approximately the same period, the nocturnal Christ's devotees sought the support of Father Luis Nápoles in San José Miahuatlán. The pastor appeared to toy with the believers; he listened to their retellings of miraculous happenings and even accepted gifts, but carefully avoided participation in the Lord's rituals. First Tlacoxcalco's authorities requested that he come to the village and bless the house where the apparitions were occurring, and although he visited the site, he withheld the blessing. The next day they visited the padre again and told him that the Lord wished to speak to him. Nápoles simply instructed them to tell their *santo* to send him a sign. They returned on the following day bearing a "relic," a common silver peso coin wrapped in a handkerchief. Nápoles accepted the money and told the devotees that he would await the Lord's orders. The devotees stipulated that Father Nápoles come alone, but apparently the summons never materialized, and hence the priest and the Tlacoxcalco's Christ never conversed.

The nightly apparitions continued to evolve and gain complexity. On May 30, the devotees revealed to those visiting the apparition site a green cross measuring eighty centimeters, which they maintained had miraculously appeared during one of the Lord's previous visits. Our anonymous informant opined that they stole it from the home of a local blind man. That night, the Lord summoned Tlacoxcalco's sacristan and detailed the arrangement of images, candles, and flowers for an upcoming mass in his honor. He also issued instructions about the foods to be prepared for visitors coming to the service. Then he delivered more threats, warning that during the consecration, those who still failed to believe would sprout horns and tails. In addition, he would call on three local "brother" *Cristos*: Tlacoxcalco's Lord of the Sanctuary, the Lord of Tlacotepec, and Ajalpan's Lord of Coculco. The former still resides in Tlacoxcalco's sacristy but was not the focal point of an established devotional. The other two had long served as important local pilgrimage images in the Puebla-Oaxaca border region.

The individuals lobbying Padre Nápoles probably had his officiation of this Mass in mind, but if they failed to convince the priest to meet the Lord, they had no trouble finding willing clerics for the Mass. On June 3, 1911, a trio of priests celebrated a service in honor of the Lord of the Wounds. The ability to stage a three-minister Mass (the maximum pomp for rural Catholic services) and sponsor an elaborate feast demonstrates that the movement had successfully marshaled resources and organized people at a level rivaling the most established local religious festivals. At the Mass, the unnamed priest who delivered the sermon avoided the polemical topic of Christ's apparition in Tlacoxcalco. Instead, he preached on the topic of Christ's suffering, death, and love for mankind. Scores of visitors attended this service, including residents from other communities within Tlacoxcalco's parish, and others from towns further afield, such as Zinacatepec and Chilac.

Tlacoxcalco's emerging devotion appears outrageously heterodox in the reconstruction provided by its anonymous critic. We have no way of knowing if there is any truth to the fantastical statements its author attributes to Bartola Bolaños. At several junctures, the author of the Miltepec denunciation strives to convince the archdiocese of Oaxaca that most locals rejected the Lord of the Wounds devotion outright or lost interest in it as they slowly perceived the unholy truth behind the miracles. According to this rendering, the movement was so bizarre and corrupt that only the most gullible Indians persevered in their support for Bartola's revelations. Nonetheless, the detailed narration of the movement's growing resources and power repeatedly undercuts claims that it was unpopular. The author carefully records the doubts that observers expressed and details the disenchantments of one-time participants. Yet he also describes ever-expanding gatherings. In addition, aside from denigration of the apparitions and pronouncements emanating from the Bolaños' home, the Lord's nameless detractor documented the establishment of the movement's institutional presence in Tlacoxcalco.

This transition began in earnest shortly after the June 3 Mass. It is what sets the Lord of the Wounds devotion apart from the majority of apparitionist devotions, which often flounder and collapse within a few years of their inception. In early June the movement was broadening in scope and thus inspiring greater opposition. The nighttime apparitions continued, but less frequently, taking place only once a week. One evening two hundred people arrived at the Bolaños house to witness the Lord's appearance, but Bartola Bolaños turned them away, claiming that he was too tired to carry out a purification ritual for all those in attendance. Some visitors questioned why Christ failed to appear during the day, and devotees countered that the Lord spent the daytime founding brotherhoods in Oaxaca. Witnesses began to criticize Bolaños, noting that she often disappeared, or that a stand-in furtively took her place during the apparitions and sermons. Despite these complaints, sometime in mid-June the nocturnal Christ started emphasizing his desire for a private chapel and exhorted visitors to contribute cash, building materials, and labor. He also supposedly announced that men could thenceforth have two women, and his followers began to stage processions with the green cross in the large yard surrounding the Bolaños's house. According to our informant, the organizers enjoyed considerable success collecting alms during the day and at the nighttime gatherings, and many supplicants also brought fruit, candy, and other foodstuffs to the seer.

In late June, the Lord stepped up his demands for a shrine and began to perform priestly functions. During his customary 11:00 p.m. sermon on June 22, the Lord summoned the municipal president and the judge, instructing them to support the construction of his chapel and promising to guide them to great quantities of buried treasure. The *aparecido* demanded that they ring the church bells for him and boasted that rich men of the past had gained their wealth from him. That night, claimed our source, another person assumed the part of the Lord and directed Bartola to undergo harsh public penance. Hence, as Tlacoxcalco's Christ heard confessions, baptized a devotee, remarried some previously separated couples, and dispensed advice, Bolaños lay tightly bound to a large clay pot in full view of visitors.[5] Not long after this eventful night, some female devotees began to withdraw from participation. Apparently they realized that Bartola was behind the "pantomime," claiming to recognize her voice, body, rough hands, and other attributes that propriety prevented our informant from recording. Despite the defection of some believers, the Lord of the Wounds movement continued to gain new adherents, and on July 7 and 8, 1911, they sponsored two more Masses officiated by three priests. Again, priests delivering the homily avoided discussing the apparitions, and instead the unnamed clerics held forth on the need to obey God's laws and the dictates of the church.[6]

It was also on July 8, 1911 that the leaders of the movement penned a petition to archdiocesan authorities, allegedly in the presence of Father Nápoles, detailing their desire to establish a formal brotherhood.[7] This document reveals a deliberate attempt by the upstart devotion's leaders to lobby church authorities according to the guidelines dictated to pilgrimage-managing sodalities seeking official recognition. It also demonstrates that within a few short months, they had crafted an innovative rotating pilgrimage brotherhood that ultimately proved more enduring than ecclesiastical attempts to set up an archdiocese-wide rotating pilgrimage to the Virgin of Soledad. The supplicants underscored their commitment in contractual terms, stressing that they would accept the sanction of civil authorities and the confiscation of their material possessions if they failed to adhere to the seven points outlined in their petition. In a nod to modern institution building, they promised to form a "board of directors." Second, they pledged to build a chapel of adobe and mortar (i.e., a proper house of worship) and, if possible, grace the structure with a dome. In addition, they vowed to keep their pastor abreast of the sodality's income and expenses related to the construction project. In reference to formal observances, they promised to hold services on the first Friday of every month, with devotees from nearby Zinacatepec sponsoring *sexagésima* (the six-month anniversary) festivities every July. Tlacoxcalco's branch of the brotherhood assumed responsibility for the Lord's yearly feast on the first Friday of Lent, promising the utmost solemnity. In essence, these new festivities promised the church a new set of monthly fee-generating celebrations and spiritual gatherings that would have been the envy of many rural parish priests.[8] In their sixth point, stipulating that Nápoles would be their official director, they acknowledged the church's clerical oversight requirements for officially recognized lay organizations. Finally, echoing the timeless haggling about infrastructure maintenance and construction in community-archdiocese relations, the devotees reemphasized their commitment to the chapel construction project.[9]

Following the petition's promises of diligence and submission to ecclesiastical authority, the list of signatures reveals marked male-female collaboration in the Lord's developing devotion. The first two names belong to Anastasio Bolaños and Rafael Marrero. Bolaños, of course, was Bartola's husband and a key figure in the movement. Marrero was also one of its leaders. Oddly, Bartola's name does not appear among the signers, but on the third and final page of the petition, the names of four more men precede those of seven women. Then six more men affixed their signatures, followed by four more women, and the last name at the bottom belonged to a lone man. In total, eleven of the twenty-four signing "brothers" were women. The gender balance and order of the signatures on the Tlacoxcalco petition is anomalous compared to the hundreds of village petitions sent to Oaxaca's curia during this period. Most of these documents display only the names of men, usually a community's civil authorities and occasionally religious officeholders. In instances when women's names do appear, they are usually among the last. In contrast, when the period's new lay associations—such as branches of the Apostolado or the Congregation of the Catechism—sent reports to church authorities or applied for canonical recognition, they frequently listed their members. Individually, or more rarely, in small groups, women wrote to the archdiocese, but these letters usually address issues frequently identified with women, such as requests for a priest in their community, concerns about the management of official devotional organizations, and complaints about clerical conduct.

The Tlacoxcalco petition's structural and numerical balance indicates that this movement deviated from the patriarchal policies and gender segregation advocated by the clergy during this period. This is especially noteworthy, considering that in all the other documentary evidence and oral testimony commenting on the Lord of the Wounds, Bartola Bolaños, and not her husband, emerges as the movement's primary leader. We know that she was illiterate, but this does not explain why someone else failed to sign for her, as was commonly done during the period. Perhaps

her role was too polemical by July of 1911 for her to appear before Nápoles and sign the petition. It is also possible that in representing themselves before the archdiocese, Bartola's supporters shaped their petition
with patriarchal prejudices in mind.

The petition also represents an early example of the devotees' strategic
savvy in the negotiations taking shape between the Lord's followers and
the clergy. In this discussion, the devotees assumed a discursive posture
that diverged from their actions. Undoubtedly aware of the church hierarchy's public claims to unmitigated authority in religious matters, they
laced their communications with submissive overtures and expressed
their goals in orthodox terms. Outwardly, they offered their time, toil,
and money to foment devotion to Christ. As well, these local devotion
managers promised to defer to their pastor. They made no mention of
tensions between themselves and other residents, emphasizing only their
interest in forming a brotherhood, building a chapel, and sponsoring
ritual. Given the rest of the movement's history, however, this document appears much more ambitious than a simple appeal for official
sodality establishment. As the struggle wore on, the believers unflinch-
ingly battled priests and ignored prelates. Along the way, these innova-
tors invested their energy and funds in the Lord's devotion. Despite their
noncompliance, at no time did they engage in the typical letter-writing
campaigns that disparaged individual clergymen and demanded their removal. Some of their pronouncements, as reported by their anonymous
antagonist, oozed anticlericalism. Yet documentary evidence attests to
their seeking a place within the church, not independence from it. In this
quest for inclusion, public protocol required that they affirm their allegiance to the clergy. Nonetheless, in terms of religious practice, they
pressed the clergy to make concessions.[10]

Broadly speaking, they employed a strategy of relentless lobbying for
clerical participation and a tactical deafness toward ecclesiastical intervention. In practice, this amounted to jealously controlling their homegrown devotion, refusing to acknowledge ecclesiastical demands that
they abandon their "superstitious" cult, and cajoling individual clergymen
in the region. For over a decade they parried ecclesiastical censure with
repeated requests for masses and priest-officiated blessings, gestures of
submission, generous fee payments, and stubborn persistence. Clearly, a
form of negotiation rooted in a history of Mexican priest-parishioner

interaction was taking place. In essence, their actions demonstrate an insistence that the church accommodate a new pilgrimage devotion rooted in indigenous revelation, yet they phrased these demands as humble requests.

According to the Miltepec denunciation, tensions continued to mount in July 1911. During the latter portion of the month, Tlacoxcalco's authorities, in league with the Lord's followers, began to persecute those in town who still refused to support the apparitions, jailing opponents and threatening to beat them. As we have seen, our informant described the town's civil officials as the Lord's "slaves" and argued that they had orchestrated Bartola Bolaños's acquittal, but now they undertook more direct actions in support of the movement. As this more menacing phase began, apparitions occurred still less frequently—every ten to fifteen days—and Tlacoxcalco's Christ stepped up his demands for a chapel. On August 16, the devotees broke ground on their private shrine and commissioned a life-sized wooden image of Christ from Justo Ruiz, a renowned sculptor in Tehuacán. Apparently, Bartola Bolaños stipulated that Ruiz leave a cavity in its chest so that the "soul" from Tlacoxcalco's older image of Christ, the Lord of the Sanctuary, could be transferred to the newly carved Lord of the Wounds.

Erecting a structure devoted to the talking Christ, combined with the commissioning of a new image, symbolized an escalation of the religious challenge that the apparition's followers represented for their opponents. A private shrine in Tlacoxcalco would give the upstart devotion a concrete physical presence in the community and an alternative devotional space outside of the church and well beyond the pastor's control. Its location on the Bolaños's property gave increased weight to the seer's local stature and further undermined clerical authority. Various clergymen clearly felt threatened by it, and in subsequent years, they habitually denigrated the Lord's new home. The commissioning of a high-quality, up-to-date depiction of Christ on the cross represented a different kind of challenge. It would give the devotees control over a fully orthodox, modern rendering of the deity and a Christian symbol steeped in traditional devotional culture that could serve as the centerpiece of ritual, a magnet for pilgrims, and a standard for devotees. The Lord's opponents must have viewed the devotees' efforts to silence their opponents, and give their devotion a more orthodox sheen, as an aggressive two-pronged strategy.

These moves probably goaded Father Nápoles into action. Initially, Nápoles may have felt that his best option lay in humoring the devotees and playing along with their miraculous assertions, while avoiding any commitment to the emerging devotion or confrontation. Our sources do not indicate which clerics officiated the elaborate three-priest Masses, but Nápoles probably took part. It is doubtful that three other priests would enter a colleague's jurisdiction against his will without sparking a quarrel. Our informant noted that in their homilies, these priests previously eluded the issue of the talking local Christ. This fits the pattern of Nápoles's previous dealings with the Lord's followers. It is plausible, then, that Nápoles simply granted the devotees' request for Masses with all the liturgical extras—such as two other priests, vespers, matins, and sermons —and charged them the fees that these special services required, according to the established fee schedule. For rural priests, such observances amounted to a welcome financial windfall. These devotee-sponsored Masses capture a new pilgrimage practice establishing itself among other local devotions in the religious calendar. The ability to fund elaborate religious services, break ground on a new chapel, and commission religious art also reveals that Bartola Bolaños and her supporters enjoyed considerable success in their fund-raising efforts. These activities, in turn, reflect their ability to strong-arm their more timid neighbors and foment broad popular support. In short, the movement was continuing to gain steam.

This thriving new heterodox devotion finally forced Nápoles to confront it publicly. Tlacoxcalco's pastor did not leave us a statement illuminating his change in approach, but Bartola Bolaños was making her stand in the middle of the pueblo, and hence she could not be ignored as a bush faith healer. It seems likely, then, that the prospect of the devotion's dynamic seer independently managing a private chapel with its own miraculous image of Christ and coordinating a pilgrimage festival represented a comprehensive challenge to his own role in the community. Although local religion often escapes the confines of priest-mediated practice, the devotion's strength threatened to make glaringly apparent the violation of this central tenet of church dogma. Furthermore, the movement's growth assured that sooner or later it would come to the attention of his superiors. No longer treating the Lord of the Wounds as a simple fee-generating Indian superstition, Father Nápoles took to the pulpit on September 8, 1911, and began to attack Tlacoxcalco's apparition movement.[11] According to the Miltepec denunciation, by this time thirty-seven apparitions had taken place. Twenty-two of them occurred in public rituals at the Bolaños house. The seer also publicized fifteen "secret" apparitions in which the Lord appeared to her alone, sometimes in the form of a talking, hovering dove.[12]

Nápoles began by invoking the time-honored juxtapositions of day and night and good and evil. The pastor warned his parishioners not to believe the lies and hocus-pocus emerging from nocturnal gatherings at the Bolaños home. Christ, he assured them, performed miracles in broad daylight, and the Bible never mentioned saints acting in darkness. Laboring in the shadows, he cautioned, was the specialty of Lucifer. Nápoles, however, did not argue that demonic agency powered the appearance of the Tlacoxcalco's Christ. Instead, he underscored the discrepancy between established miracle lore and the events sponsored by the Bolaños couple to expose them as native charlatans. "Furthermore," he preached, "all of the statements attributed to the apparition, reveal that they are produced by the Indians of these pueblos."[13]

It is difficult to overemphasize the extent to which the Lord of the Wounds' opponents played to ethnic stereotypes concerning religion. Among the clergy and non-Indian society, simply invoking indigenous religion amounted to an accusation of heterodoxy. By extension, discussions of independent Indian-led ritual and devotion usually occurred in the context of complaints about "abuses" or outright fraud. Lamentably, our informant was not more specific about Nápoles's sermon. It is likely that the priest highlighted the statements attributed to the Lord of the Wounds that marked them as Indian cultural references. Considering the information we have about the Lord's pronouncements, they do indeed telegraph a strongly local religious worldview. For example, the Lord proclaimed his ability to call on his "three brothers," in reference to other images of Christ known as primarily Indian devotions.

The contest of wills became especially intense as Tlacoxcalco prepared to celebrate the feast of its patron saint, San Mateo (Saint Matthew). On September 12, Nápoles again assailed the Lord of the Wounds and his followers during Mass. Saint Matthew's feast falls on September 21. Since the 12th is nine days before the feast, Nápoles was probably in Tlacoxcalco to inaugurate the patron saint's novena. The combination of the village's traditional feast day and the contention surrounding the upstart devotion must have made for a festival fraught with tension. The priest warned those present to reject the "fables and gossip" suggesting that Christ had appeared in a local "shack." The apparitions, Nápoles insisted, were simply outrageous lies, and the perpetrators nothing more than swindlers. Furthermore, he threatened to denounce them to the civil authorities. If the alleged miracles had merit, he assured his parishioners, he would have personally championed the cause and invited the entire cathedral chapter to visit the apparition site. But the stories were false, he inveighed, and thus he prohibited all participation in the superstitious cult.

Six days later, on September 18, Bartola Bolaños picked up the padre's verbal gauntlet. She announced that the Lord told her that by the feast of Saint Matthew, September 21, he would set fire to the homes of three unbelievers and others would suffer grave illness and death. Bolaños also declared that upon the chapel's completion they would hold a solemn celebration with the archbishop himself. After this ceremony, the Lord of the Wounds would celebrate masses and administer the sacraments without need of the parish priest. In addition to the threats of arson and prophecies of Father Nápoles's impending irrelevance, our informant asserted that Bolaños and her husband employed a propaganda and espionage network to bolster Bartola's claims. Allegedly supporters traveled to villages throughout the region broadcasting news of the miraculous events in Tlacoxcalco and collecting information about the actions and statements of the movement's critics. Our source maintained that Bolaños used this information to great effect, dramatically quoting her opponents during nighttime rituals as if she had preternaturally received word of their activities. None of Bolaños's dire prophecies came to pass, crowed her epistolary adversary, "because Our Lord God does not comply with the whims of *pilhuanejos* (parasitic underlings/religious ignorants)."[14]

Heedless of threats, Nápoles continued to attack the Lord of the Wounds. Seething at their pastor's criticisms, supporters of the apparition movement accosted the priest personally with indignant recriminations, to which he retorted that he cared little for their advice or suggestions. His duty, he proclaimed, required him to protect God's truth. On September 22, he again publicly blasted the apparitions.[15] This time he sought to expose their falsehoods by contrasting them with official

Marian apparitions, specifically those of Guadalupe, Lourdes, and Pilar. Three days later, Nápoles continued his campaign against the Lord in a sermon detailing its fraudulent history. Bartola Bolaños and her supporters countered that Nápoles was not truly Catholic, and they spread rumors that he had three wafers dividing his heart and hence could not risk meeting the Lord. The priest knew his heart "was not clean," they maintained, and therefore he feared Tlacoxcalco's Christ and maligned his devotees.[16]

This issue of having a single heart, a divided heart, or two hearts appears commonly in image-centered devotion in Oaxaca. According to Oaxacan priest-ethnographer Enrique Marroquín, the region's indigenous Catholics use this terminology in discussions of purity of faith and intentions; those who go before powerful images or to sacred places with untoward intentions, or while hiding less-than-devout sentiments, risk personal catastrophe. Present-day Juquila pilgrims warn that approaching the image with "two hearts" can result in divine castigation.[17] Conversely, facing church efforts to suppress their cult, the devotees of a recent Marian apparition movement scrutinized visitors at the apparition site to see if they experienced some mishap in order to gauge their intentions, or rather, the state of their hearts.[18]

It would seem that venting these accusations and counteraccusations would have opened a deep rift between the devotees of Tlacoxcalco's Christ and the clergy, but that appears not to have happened. On October 25, the faithful went to Tehuacán and returned bearing their new, life-sized crucified Christ. The sculptor, our informant admitted, produced a rather attractive image, and the Lord's devotees began publicizing that their *santo* had appeared for all to see. Five days later, three unnamed priests blessed the image and presided over a Mass without a sermon. After being the target of several homiletic diatribes, the devotees undoubtedly decided not to pay for this liturgical extra. Shortly afterwards, on November 21, three ministers and the devotees celebrated another Mass, and later, they paraded the image to a devotee's home. There, Bartola Bolaños made the dramatic pronouncement that after ten such Masses, the Lord would come to the altar in his new chapel to be crucified, flanked by saints Peter and Paul and surrounded by angels. The author of the Miltepec denunciation probably attributed this claim to Bartola in a stark literal manner to strengthen his case for how far beyond

11 The Santo Niño Hallado (photograph by the author).

the pale of orthodoxy the indigenous matron had drifted. However, this statement may have been more symbolic than miraculous. Perhaps Bartola simply stated that the new Christ on the cross would soon reside above the chapel's altar, flanked by other images, saints, and cherubs. Regardless of Bartola's alleged pronouncements, evidently some priests in the region were still willing to participate in this controversial new devotion. But after the acrimonious exchanges between Nápoles and the devotees, it seems logical that he was not among them. The devotees, however, had not given up on their pastor.

After an earthquake on December 16, 1911, the followers of the Lord of the Wounds summoned Father Nápoles to examine a large stone. They announced that it miraculously fell from the sky during the tremor. On Christmas Day, Nápoles viewed the rock. According to the Miltepec denunciation, the stone had letters or figures on its sides, although there are none visible today. Named El Santo Niño Hallado (The Holy Discovered Child) by the faithful, our informant described the rock as an old stone that had long been worshipped in the town of Malinalco and the countryside around San Luis. Allegedly many people recognized it, and stones of the same appearance abounded on a nearby mountain. Nápoles left no record of his reaction, but his successors found its role in subsequent devotion particularly bothersome.

As 1911 came to a close, Tlacoxcalco settled into a long religious stalemate. The practices associated with *el aparecido* still featured late-night rituals at the Bolaños home. Over the course of the year, averred the devotion's anonymous adversary, seven different women became pregnant during the nocturnal gatherings. The "false Santo," the anonymous critic groused, referred to these children as his gifts to lonely women and proffered Anastasio Bolaños as their guardian. The devotees maintained orthodox expressions of devotion, such as processions with the miraculous green cross and reverence to the new image of Christ, but they also added the Santo Niño Hallado to the ritual mix. The leaders of the movement kept warning that unbelievers faced death and eternal damnation. Some participants withdrew, but new people also joined in what emerged as standard initiations. The devotees brought neophytes into the completely dark house, whereupon the Lord ordered them to lay face up on the floor with their eyes closed and their mouths covered. Tlacoxcalco's Christ asked if they were willing to submit to him and dedicate themselves to the construction of his chapel. Further conjuring stereotypes of Indian heterodoxy, the Miltepec denunciation emphasized that all of the rituals, sermons, and initiations took place in Nahuatl.

The Lord's nemesis closed his harangue on a sanctimonious, partisan note. He reported that on February 23, 1912, Miltepec celebrated its Lenten festival dedicated to the original Lord of the Wounds. Despite propaganda and repeated threats of arson issued by followers of Tlacoxcalco's parvenu *santo*, he asserted, the usual numbers of pilgrims arrived. In his festival sermon, Miltepec's parish priest attacked claims that Christ wandered the region's mountains and *milpas* and spoke to a woman in Tlacoxcalco. Invoking dogma stipulating that the revelations in the New Testament were complete and unalterable, he argued that the savior had already passed his trial in mortal flesh and communicated his message to mankind. The competing fiesta and devotion, he declared, constituted an underhanded attempt to sap Miltepec's devotion, the sale of mass intentions, and alms gathering. The indignant priest even suggested that it was common knowledge that Father Nápoles had been duped by scoundrels employing darkness and tricks to fleece the ignorant.[19]

With the closing of the Miltepec denunciation ends the detailed, almost day-by-day rendering of this polemical female-led indigenous Catholic apparition movement from April 1911 until February 1912. Its author invoked the classic stereotypes that cast Indians and women as innately superstitious and overly credulous. The report alluded to female and Indian independence and defiance as evidence of impious worldly motivations and nonclerical ritual as the seedbed of fraud, pagan resurgence, and sexual immorality. Furthermore, the text invoked the supposed Indian and female penchant for mendacity and chicanery. In short, he presented the apparition movement as a hothouse of social ills and a threat to priest-mediated devotion and patriarchal order. The report argues that most of Tlacoxcalco's residents, "more-or-less educated and raised with a holy fear of God," shunned the notion that divine marvels took place in a "*casucha de mala nota*" (a hovel of untoward reputation) and intimates that the movement depended upon threats to silence critics and tricks to hoodwink a passel of simpletons. Throughout the document, the author remains oblivious to evidence that suggests otherwise.

From Oaxaca's prelate to the anonymous poison-pen chronicler, all the Lord of the Wounds' critics took pains to juxtapose the events taking place in the Bolaños's home with official teachings regarding apparitions. Mexican cultural prejudices undergirded much of the opposition to the Lord of the Wounds (i.e., they essentially implied that the devotion was too Indian to be authentic). More specifically, Bartola's critics stressed her unseemly comportment and the agency of the Lord's devotees as evidence of the new cult's illegitimacy. After the mid-nineteenth century, a single model served as the standard by which church authorities and many lay Catholics judged miraculous validity—Our Lady of Lourdes. The stories and legends related to this French apparition circulated so widely that Lourdes became a template of sorts, shaping both the style and content of new claims of divine apparition. Lourdes, then, served as the touchstone of a new apparitionist idiom.[20] As we have seen, parishes in the Tehuacán Valley, including Tlacoxcalco, formed sodalities dedicated to this advocation of Mary and clearly knew of the latest fashions of the Catholic miraculous.

This French apparition pivoted on the image of the church's paradigmatic modern seer, Bernadette Souloubris. According to Catholic doctrine, and exemplified in the official narrative of the Pyrenean girl's visions, true visionaries experience a divine charism and merely relay the grace received to ecclesiastical representatives.[21] As such, its veracity and the seer's inherent sanctity should be obvious. Furthermore, the idealized visionary epitomizes proper obedience and submission to church authorities. Although self-effacing, the model seer professes an unshakable, innocent faith in the divine nature of her own experiences. Bernadette played the role to perfection.[22] As had happened with many other apparitions, the seer's claims sparked the emergence of a new devotion, but the visionary's residence near the apparition site represented a problem for the development of an official cult. Both human weakness and charisma can undermine the emergence of new shrines: either less-than-saintly behavior inspires doubt about the alleged miracles, or the seer, often viewed as a living saint, threatens to become the object of devotion. Bernadette obeyed her clerical handlers and shunned the limelight, but nonetheless pilgrims came to Lourdes in hopes of seeing, or better yet, touching her. Finally, eight years after her visions, she entered a convent and never returned to the apparition site. This allowed the church to proceed with its massive shrine-building and devotional-marketing campaign unencumbered by the seer's presence. While still alive, but at a safe distance, Bernadette became the visionary standard and a pivotal image of Catholic propaganda. The church even sold romantic photographs of the seer wearing stylized rustic outfits and assuming pious poses in studio reenactments of her visions.[23]

Bartola, however, was no Bernadette. Neither obedient to archdiocesan dictates, nor shy and unassuming, she remained a powerful, compelling presence at the head of the Lord of the Wounds devotion until she died over three decades later. In the Lourdes tradition, neither Bernadette nor her popular supporters organized institutions to promote the miracles' cause. Theoretically, a divine hand shapes truly miraculous apparition movements. Thus, critics of emerging devotions frequently seize upon human initiative as evidence of profane motivation, most commonly alms profiteering. The church invariably accuses deviant apparition movements of miracle mongering in order to bilk simple believers. This line of criticism engages widely accepted assumptions that financial concerns and authentic piety are somehow mutually exclusive. The church employs this argument somewhat duplicitously against those apparition movements it seeks to suppress while simultaneously promoting and managing myriad alms-generating shrines.[24] Ideally, from the perspective of clerical managers, once an allegedly miraculous apparition gains ecclesiastical sanction and the machinery of shrine management is in place, devotional folklore ignores the unseemly details of its emergence. Consequently, processes of contestation, ecclesiastical politics, religious propagandizing, and fund-raising do not figure prominently in official or popular narratives.[25]

From 1912 to 1924, the history of the Lord of the Wounds movement emerges primarily from ecclesiastical correspondence generated in the context of archdiocesan suppression efforts. The clerical hand-wringing and complaining in these letters demonstrates that priests faced a determined movement with an astute leadership attentive to the limits of ecclesiastical authority. Although we lack documents from the devotees arguing their case at the time, a 1913 flyer filed among the archdiocese's parish administration documents speaks volumes.[26] Beneath the heading "Lord of the Wounds that is venerated in the town of San Mateo Tlacoxcalco, District of Tehuacán on the First Friday of Lent" appears a photograph of the newly carved crucified Christ surrounded by four beribboned candles and sprays of roses. And at the bottom of the page, a poem/prayer titled "Nueva despedida" (New Leave-Taking) celebrates, in orthodox, sentimental verses, the passion of Christ and bids Tlacoxcalco's image a pilgrim's farewell. Here we have incontrovertible evidence that the devotees of the talking Christ invested in Catholic pilgrimage advertising. Clearly, they had learned from more-established festival organizers. Purchasing an attractive image both to focus devotion in Tlacoxcalco and to serve as an orthodox "logo" symbolizes an essential step in the movement's development. The hiring of a photographer and commissioning mass-produced graphic art represents an even more ambitious act of expansion. In essence, it reveals Bartola Bolaños and her supporters working to attract pilgrims and laying claim to a place on the religious calendar.

Significantly, the devotees elected to publicize their pilgrimage via modern photography instead of the cheaper, more traditional lithographs and block prints still widely in use at the time.[27] Image reproduction and marketing has long been a staple of Catholicism, but it surged with the advent of modern technologies. In Mexico, religious printmaking was a

standard part of urban printshop commerce during this period, especially
among those set up by Catholic interests to produce *"la buena prensa"*
(the good press), in contrast to *"la prensa impía"* (the impious press).
Oaxaca's archdiocesan archive is full of receipts attesting to the production of thousands of *estampas* (images ranging from full page to octavo
size, to be framed and sold at festivals) in the late nineteenth and early
twentieth centuries.

In the long run, this kind of pious boosterism provided an aura of
antiquity and legitimacy, even if the devotion's origins were rather recent and suspect. The 1913 flyer also demonstrates that the Tlacoxcalco
movement remained determined to compete with Miltepec for devotees
on the first Friday of Lent. They may have continued to employ threats
and misinformation about the rival Lord of the Wounds, but now they
also sought the upper hand through a publicity campaign.

Oral history provides further clues to the movement's staying power. The anonymous author of the Miltepec denunciation mentioned the issue of faith healing and made vague, sarcastic references to the Lord/Bartola prescribing herbs and performing purifications. But he omitted the continuing importance of cures in the movement, especially the growing reputation of its seer as a religious intermediary skilled in the healing arts. Bartola Bolaños's grandson, Pablo Cervantes Bolaños, a present-day resident of Tlacoxcalco, described his grandmother's curing practice as central to the devotion. He recalled her employing the image of the crucified Christ, the green cross, the miraculous stone, and herbs in her well-known curing practice. He compared her methods to today's homeopathic medicine. Her cures were "natural," he maintained, and word-of-mouth testimony brought many prospective patients to see her after standard medical interventions failed.[28] People believed that in her hands the Santo Niño Hallado functioned "like a curing crystal ball." But Bartola was very sincere, Cervantes recalled. She informed some of her visitors that they could not be cured and spared them the expense of her treatments.

In Catholic lore, miraculous cures represent a kind of stamp of divine authenticity recognized by the laity and clergymen.[29] It is hardly surprising that Bolaños's critics would downplay reported instances of miraculous healing. But the movement's broad appeal and endurance implies that her followers, and visitors from beyond the region, had faith in her herbalist talents and divine connections. This discrepancy between oral testimony and the written denunciation also suggests that a devotee's interpretation of the events at the Lord of the Wounds' nocturnal appearances would have emphasized a climate of supplication and effervescent healing ritual, rather than bizarre séance-like performances. As Cervantes indicates, Bartola Bolaños was indeed the center of attention and action, but not because she manipulated the faithful. Rather, she mediated the granting of divine grace with the help of "tools," such as the image, cross, and stone. Unfortunately, our sources do not lead us further into these alternative narratives.

The Lord of the Wounds movement showed no signs of fading between 1917 and 1921, when priests outside San José Miahuatlán wrote their superiors seeking guidance. Father Nápoles no longer served in the Tehuacán Valley. In fact, he died on October 15, 1912, while ministering hundreds of kilometers south in Ocotlán, Oaxaca, just over a year after his dramatic sermons from Tlacoxcalco's pulpit.[30] Perhaps the Miltepec denunciation inspired ecclesiastical authorities to transfer him to the opposite end of the archdiocese. We have no evidence that his erstwhile opponents in Tlacoxcalco knew of his death. But if they did, we can be sure they interpreted it as evidence of the Lord's powers and incorporated it in their devotional lore.

The letters of the late pastor's successors indicate that it was the devotees' repeated efforts to gain priestly participation in the image's cult, and an official blessing of the recently finished chapel, that caused them to request their superiors' opinions. These letters also reveal an internal struggle within the church to maintain clerical discipline and mediate personal disputes between priests in the countryside. Priestly correspondence demonstrates that the church faced a well-organized, religiously motivated movement in Tlacoxcalco, but it also documents that their own personnel contravened orders and adopted independent policies toward heterodox practices. The church hierarchy demanded complete and unconditional submission from Bartola Bolaños and her supporters, rejecting repeated gestures from the faithful seeking accommodation. Realizing that the devotees could not be swayed by one-dimensional invocations of Catholic hierarchy and obedience, archdiocesan authorities adopted a liturgical/sacramental siege strategy concretized in a complete ban on clerical participation in any of the movement's rituals and threats to withhold the sacraments from the devotion's leaders. Above all, priests were not to say masses dedicated to the image or accede to the devotees' unrelenting requests for the consecration of the Lord's chapel. This type of approach remains a common church response to popular revelation. Ideally, it denies the dissident movement the trappings and settings of orthodoxy—such as priest-led services, the use of churches, religious utensils, images, and sanctified spaces—while the church waits for the new devotion's energies to fade. This approach also represents an effort to insulate the church from the criticism that popular religious movements inspire among other members of society. But this policy has an Achilles heel: clerical discipline. The hierarchy sought to shun the Lord of the Wounds, but some priests elected to remain engaged with the evolving devotion. Not surprisingly, other clerics sometimes accused them of profiteering. But arguably, some of them simply followed older traditions of tolerating the idiosyncrasies of local practice while attempting to guide their parishioners in more orthodox directions. This somewhat deviant strategy, of course, was eminently pragmatic. Living among the devotees while condemning their cherished beliefs, and refusing to officiate at requested services, guaranteed priest-parishioner conflict; turning a blind eye to heterodox practice, or otherwise accommodating it, developed a modus vivendi between pastor and flock.

From 1914 to 1921, Gillow remained in exile, but the able vicar general and ecclesiastical governor, Carlos Gracida, dealt with Bartola and the Lord of the Wounds. Thanks to his frequent correspondence with Gillow, we have an excellent record of the Oaxacan church hierarchy's concerns and activities during much of the revolutionary period. In 1917, Gracida requested a report from Father J. Velasco in San Gabriel Chilac on the Lord of the Wounds movement. Unless it has been lost in the archive, he failed to produce a detailed account. But in a rather sloppy note, dated April 25, 1917, Velasco related a personal experience in Tlacoxcalco.[31] On April 8, he visited the village and the "room that María Bartola calls a chapel." His goal, he assured the vicar general, was to remove the devotion's miraculous stone from the altar and cast it out of the chapel. He claimed that, unseen by the devotees, he hefted the offending rock to the door before concluding that it would be unwise to simply throw it into Bolaños's yard. Instead, he set it on the floor by the door and left. He must have hidden it, because subsequent visitors reported its absence to the military garrison of San José Miahuatlán. According to Velasco, soldiers proceeded to Tlacoxcalco to search for "the Zapatistas that had stolen the treasure." Fearing an altercation, the cleric sought out the captain of the investigating troops and explained the situation. He contended that the gentlemanly officer agreed that the matter corresponded solely to the priest's religious authority and did not pursue the issue further. Afterward, Father Velasco alleged, Anastacio Bolaños announced that it was his "*gusto*" (pleasure) to worship the stone and that no one could force him to abandon his endeavors.

Velasco's missive is a curious document. As he neared the end of his message, he apologized for involving himself in an issue that was not his business, then signed off, "waiting for superior orders." This suggests that a suspicious Gracida may have been questioning him about possible participation in the banned cult and had upbraided him for meddling outside his jurisdiction. His presence inside the private chapel is certainly suspicious. It seems doubtful that the Bolaños family would have welcomed an unfriendly cleric into their private house of worship and given him unaccompanied access to the devotion's sacred objects. Was Velasco's assertion that he had crossed into the neighboring parish on an iconoclastic mission a dubious alibi? It may have been, but there was probably some truth in it. The Lord of the Wounds had supporters in Velasco's parish of Chilac, and like other priests in the region, he had probably received solicitations requesting his participation in masses dedicated to the image. For obvious reasons, priests were loath to dampen local religious fervor, since their livelihood depended on the devotional energies, money, goods, and foodstuffs allocated by communities toward their passionately held beliefs. Velasco may have thought that the devotion could be pulled toward orthodoxy. If so, removing the supposedly heaven-sent rock from the altar and ritual practice would have been a logical place to start. Official norms of practice could easily incorporate the Lord's image and the allegedly miraculous cross, but not the Santo Niño Hallado. Velasco sent another note to Gracida on May 25, 1917. In it he pleaded for understanding of his "involuntary" inaction in providing his superior with a report on the Tlacoxcalco affair, blaming the poor mail service. The excuses failed to satisfy the vicar general: shortly afterward, he removed Velasco. On July 20, 1917, Father Mauro Rodríguez wrote from Chilac notifying Gracida that he had received, and would obey, the vicar general's order to reject petitions for religious services from a brotherhood in Tlacoxcalco "that maintains a superstitious cult to a stone and an image of the Lord of the Wounds."[32]

The testimony of Pablo Cervantes sheds a different light on these issues and provides a unique interpretation of the same events. He maintained that one of the movement's most important faith-inspiring miracles took place in a confrontation between Bartola Bolaños and federal soldiers over the Santo Niño Hallado and its pivotal role as a divinatory tool in her curing practices. Cervantes never mentioned Father Velasco's attempts to remove it from the chapel, but he recalled an event that echoes the story that this priest told his superior involving San José's revolutionary-era garrison.[33] According to the *curandera*-seer's grandson, federal troops and their captain went to Tlacoxcalco to confiscate the stone, arrest Bolaños, and put an end to her expanding fame. As she underwent interrogation and the captain prepared to take her into custody, Bolaños calmly revealed the infamous rock. At that very moment, in the presence of many bystanders, a glowing golden heart began to shimmer on the side of the stone. Awed by this show of supernatural power, the captain eschewed arresting its keeper. According to Cervantes, these events so moved an eyewitness from Ajalpan, Calixto Reyna, that he became one the movement's greatest stalwarts. For the rest of his life, Reyna led yearly pilgrimages to the shrine and headed the largest branch of the Lord's brotherhood outside Tlacoxcalco.[34]

Two years later, a new pastor of San José Miahuatlán, Cenobio Mendoza, became the object of the devotees' attentions. On September 4, 1919, he wrote Carlos Gracida stating that Bartola Bolaños, "the woman in charge of the image of the Lord of the Wounds," had solicited the blessing of her chapel during the upcoming festival of Tlacoxcalco's patron saint, and also the celebration of some masses in the name of the image. He told her that he could not accede to her requests, since archdiocesan authorities prohibited all devotion to the image. But, Mendoza revealed, Bartola expressed an interest in negotiation. When he inquired about her willingness to obey ecclesiastical orders, she replied that she "was open to anything." In light of her apparent readiness to submit to authority, Mendoza asked Gracida for new instructions.[35] On November 19, 1919, Mendoza wrote Gracida again, prodding him to respond to his previous letter. He repeated his assertions that Bolaños was willing to comply with the hierarchy's dispositions, adding that Anastasio Bolaños and another man had approached him reiterating the appeal for the chapel's consecration, and seeking to engage him as the celebrant of the Lord's feast on the first Friday of Lent in 1920. Bartola's husband, the priest asserted, also professed a willingness to obey the vicar general's orders.[36]

Gracida replied on January 30, 1920. Citing the "superstitious origin" of the Lord's cult, he reaffirmed his ban. In addition, ignoring the pleas from Bolaños and her husband, he ordered Mendoza to abstain from participation in the image's cult both inside and outside the church. In response to the Bolaños' professed respect for archdiocesan authority, he instructed Mendoza to tell them that they must surrender the image, along with all the ritual utensils that had been paid for using alms. If they complied, he declared, Mendoza was to deposit the crucified Christ and his accoutrements in the parish church of San José for an unstipulated period of time, and the priest was to prohibit any organized devotion to the image beyond individual reverence and prayer.[37] Bolaños, her husband, and their followers did not abide by the vicar general's demands. A year and a half later, Gracida had to explain to the recently repatriated Archbishop Gillow his policies toward the insubordinate devotees.

Returning to Oaxaca from exile, Gillow envisioned a triumphant homecoming. Approaching Oaxaca's cathedral in stages, visiting the rural parishes that lay in his path, he orchestrated a dramatic series of pastoral reunions with his priests and flock. Among the first stopovers was San José Miahuatlán. On July 26, 1921, as the prelate prepared to depart from Tehuacán, the vicar general provided him with a brief sketch of the movement's history and his approach to the dissident devotion. For the most part, his rendering of the devotion's history matched the interpretation offered in the Miltepec denunciation. In an interesting discrepancy, however, he claimed that Father Nápoles tried to correct the abuses and superstitious nocturnal rituals by commissioning the large image to "provide an object to the cult that was developing." Devotion to the image took root, affirmed Gracida, but instead of improving, it became more superstitious. The crowds and commotion caused by the image's yearly feast on the first Friday of Lent, he admitted, enveloped the entire region in what had become a formidable, unofficial pilgrimage festival. These celebrations featured the image's procession back and forth between the Bolaños' "special room" and Tlacoxcalco's church. Like other movement critics, Gracida avoided the term "chapel." He reported that the residents of Zinacatepec (the town specifically mentioned in the devotees' 1911 request to establish a brotherhood) were particularly well represented among the pilgrims. Gracida accused Bartola Bolaños and her principal assistants of fomenting the most "disgusting and ridiculous inventions," such as claims that the image sweated, spoke, and gave all manner of orders. The vicar general also alluded to sexual deviance at the devotion's nocturnal rituals.[38]

Gracida maintained that the repeated requests from devotees in Tlacoxcalco and Zinacatepec for the blessing of the "*sala*" (room) aroused his suspicions, because they lacked the support of San José's pastor. Once he received more information, Gracida avowed, he forbade the consecration of the room/chapel, ordered that the devotees hand over the image to the parish priest, and banned all public devotion to the image and title of "The Lord of the Wounds of San Mateo Tlacoxcalco." The devotees had not complied, but he claimed that his actions had led to the cult's decline. It would have been extinguished, he insisted, had it not been for its promoters' impertinence and support from the people of Zinacatepec. Providing a telling glimpse of the high clergy's approach to popular revelation, Gracida offered suggestions for his prelate's impending visit to the troublesome parish. Gillow should first insist on the devotion's extirpation and wrest control of the image from the movement's leaders, depositing it in San José's church. Then, once in possession of the crucified Christ, the priest in charge should make sure that the image received no special cult for the time being. Never again, moreover, should parishioners call it the Lord of the Wounds. Later, if the archdiocese deemed it fitting and proper, it could tolerate a local devotion to the image under a different name. Otherwise, Gracida declared, the Lord should be destroyed or sent to another community far from Tlacoxcalco.[39]

Ten days later, on August 5, 1921, Cenobio Mendoza met Gillow at Zinacatepec's railway station, eight kilometers from San José. During his sermon the next morning, the archbishop lectured parishioners about the need to establish Catholic schools so their children could "withstand and counter the impious propaganda of socialism and Protestantism, which tend to destroy all moral and social order." Probably alluding to Tlacoxcalco, he also stressed the laity's religious duty to respect and submit to all the precepts of the church.[40] While still in San José, on August 7, 1921, Gillow penned the pastoral visit report decreeing, as was customary, that it be read during Mass on the next feast day.

The report is extraordinary in its dedication to a "superstitious cult" and its censure of an individual parishioner—Bartola Bolaños. It also demonstrates that either the archbishop was oblivious to the limits of his power or he believed that a dramatic and unequivocal condemnation of the deviant devotion would carry enough weight to dampen local support for Bolaños and the pilgrimage festival that she had brought into being. As if willing a period of long-gone ecclesiastical potency back into existence, Gillow attempted to circumscribe the nature, manner, and even vocabulary of nonchurch religious ritual, and he commanded his priests to impound private property. The archbishop, however, eschewed the more powerful and risky option of attacking the cult of the Lord of the Wounds during a sermon, as had Father Nápoles. In fact, the edict does not reveal whether the prelate even set foot in Tlacoxcalco during his visit.

Preferring the safe distance of a decree read by Father Mendoza after his departure from the parish, Gillow left behind a textual denunciation of Bartola Bolaños's movement. Labeling the Nahua matron the "inventor" of the cult, Gillow savaged her for pretending to be a medium of revelations and passing off her pronouncements as the Lord's instructions. The heterodox cult, he insisted, inspired scandalous behavior and grave sins that endangered the participants' souls. He claimed that Bolaños had refused to comply with an order to appear before him and "submit to the dispositions of the prelate." Hence, the archbishop issued a set of stern directives. Deviating from the advice of his vicar general, Gillow demanded the immediate transfer of the offending image to the church in San José Miahuatlán, and rechristened Tlacoxcalco's Christ "El Señor de las Agonías" (The Lord of the Agonies). Second, he condemned all image-centered rituals that took place in the Bolaños home, warning that attendance at these ceremonies and any assistance rendered Bartola represented a grave, sinful act. He also ordered her to surrender all the utensils and religious objects purchased with alms monies, as well as any cash contributions still in her possession. Failure to conform to his exact instructions, he announced, would result in a complete withdrawal of the sacraments from Bolaños and any others who opposed his rulings. Finally, he directed Father Mendoza to seal the "house or chapel," which he contended would remain at the disposition of ecclesiastical authorities.[41]

Gillow's attempt to silence the apparition movement fared miserably. Indeed, the movement outlived the peripatetic prelate. Nine months after his stopover in the Tehuacán Valley, Gillow died while on a pastoral visit in the southern arm of Oaxaca's Central Valley.[42] The ruling he left behind in San José failed to deter the dissident devotion, gain control of the cult's image and ritual paraphernalia, cow its leaders, or shutter the Lord's shrine.

Secular society in the city of Tehuacán was also critical of the apparition movement in Tlacoxcalco and troubled by its endurance. In his village-by-village history of the region published in 1921, the city's leading intellectual and journalist, Joaquín Paredes Colín, assailed the devotion and its leaders.[43] The author labeled the very notion of twentieth-century apparitions anachronistic and opined that they had been ham-handedly fabricated in this case. Arguing that it was important to set the record straight, lest "fanaticism seek to disfigure the facts later," Paredes identified Bartola and her husband as the "authors" of the "so-called miracles," and implied they had engaged in fraud. This critic, however, maintained that the devotion, although lingering, was in full decline. Subsequent documentation, though, proves him wrong.

On September 1, 1922, another new pastor, Everardo Gracida, composed a letter to the archdiocesan secretary, Agustín Espinoza, commenting on the persistence of the popular cult.[44] Father Everardo contended that his local superior, Antonio de P. Valencia, flagrantly disregarded orders from both the vicar general and Gillow regarding the dissident devotion. This document illuminates several different issues: tensions between clergymen in the field, the limits of clerical discipline, rumored change in the hierarchy's approach to popular revelation, and an individual priest's checkered past.

The subtext of Everardo Gracida's personal failings pervades this curious letter. He alluded to the fact that in criticizing other priests' conduct he knew his credibility was weak, but he attempted to make up for this by describing a quasi-mystical bond with the recently deceased Gillow, owning up to his legacy of broken vows, and pledging to reform his conduct. The fragments of his personal history that emerge in archdiocesan documents suggest that his once-promising ecclesiastical career had suffered from a scandalous appetite for carousing and the attentions of women. His past merits discussion, because it sheds considerable light on priest-parishioner relations and the Lord of the Wounds devotion.

We have no firm evidence that Father Everardo was a relative of the vicar general Carlos Gracida, but he may well have been. His writings reveal that he maintained a closer relationship to Gillow and Espinoza, and sought Espinoza's protection. If he enjoyed strong family ties to the powerful Father Carlos, it seems logical that he would have tapped into the traditions of familial patronage, unless his history of misbehavior had turned the vicar general against him. The two Gracidas must have known each other well, regardless. In 1906, when Father Everardo was only a deacon, he served as the prefect of Oaxaca City's prestigious Catholic boys' school, the Colegio del Espíritu Santo.[45] This educational institution had been the pet project of the elder Gracida long before he became vicar general. He was its founder, director, and principal champion for most of his career. Older Oaxacans still recall it as "Father Carlos's school." Everardo Gracida appears to have had enviable connections to other high clerics as well. In 1908, the soon-to-be Bishop of Zamora and future Archbishop of Oaxaca, José Othón Núñez, listed the newly ordained Father Everardo as a participant in the Catholic Workers' Circle's religious celebrations.[46] Thus the young clergymen's career began auspiciously in Oaxaca City, and it would seem that he was in a prime position to work his way up the urban archdiocesan ladder of teaching assignments and chaplaincies. But in January 1913, the archdiocese transferred Everardo Gracida to a distant parish along Oaxaca's Pacific Coast.[47] Most likely, a pattern of moral failings began to emerge while still in Oaxaca City, eventually occasioning a fall from grace and the young priest's banishment.

The well-documented saga of Everardo Gracida's transgressions in a series of postings near Jamiltepec, Oaxaca, befits a present-day Mexican soap opera. In 1921, angry parishioners sent two letters to the archdiocese detailing Gracida's immoral and outrageous behavior.[48] Seventeen male signers accused their priest of a violent, depraved temperament, but above all, they complained about his scandalous relationships with women. They argued that amidst the persecutions Catholicism suffered in the current political climate, it was incomprehensible that the church should allow a lecher in priestly garb to undermine popular faith and morals. They alleged that Gracida organized bacchanalias with his lover, a widow named Modesta Aguirre, and certain local elites. On September 10, 1921, the priest's festive stupor apparently led him to appear naked in public. Rankled parishioners claimed Gracida's perversions endangered the moral development of their children and scandalized the "feminine element." Furthermore, distracted by Aguirre's attentions, he neglected his sacramental duties. Such was the harm caused by this living "symbol of temptation" that they accused him of apostasy and Protestantism. Some parishioners, the letter cautioned, had begun contemplating violence. However, in a postscript dated October 5, 1921, they revealed that Gracida had hastily sold his properties, fled Cacahuatepec, and rendezvoused with his inamorata in Putla, because a previous mistress, Esther Iglesias, had initiated legal proceedings against Padre Everardo for child support.

Iglesias also wrote two letters to the vicar general, relaying a personal and tragic story.[49] She claimed that her legitimate husband had fled the region several years prior to escape revolutionaries controlling their hometown, Pinotepa de Don Luis. Alone and persecuted by her husband's enemies, she fell prey to the feigned gentlemanly compassion of Everardo Gracida, who was then the pastor of the pueblo. According to Iglesias, she firmly resisted his advances, but he broke into her home and raped her. Her husband subsequently disowned her, and she had no option other than accepting Father Everardo's "protection." She had since born the priest two children, and she affixed a photograph of their daughter to her letter. She refused, though, to accompany the priest to Cacahuatepec upon his transfer. Destitute and disgraced, Iglesias pleaded with Carlos Gracida to force Father Everardo to support his children.

When the younger Gracida wrote Secretary Espinoza in 1922, he essentially confirmed this story, bemoaning his past transgressions and pleading for his superior's compassion.[50] This letter reveals that the wayward priest felt isolated and vulnerable in San José Miahuatlán. Ironically, a dispatch that purported to denounce a colleague's dalliance with a heterodox Indian cult began on a strongly superstitious note: "The news that I am about to give you is from a soul in eternity." Father Everardo then announced that on that very morning, the late archbishop had visited him in a dream. Gillow, apparently in the process of boarding a flaming coach, admonished his priests, particularly the letter's author and Secretary Espinoza, for forgetting him so quickly. Noting a deep personal debt to the late prelate, Gracida asserted that Gillow needed the support of their supplications to mitigate his travails in purgatory, and furthermore, the priest claimed to write Espinoza at the dead archbishop's request. On the surface, this otherworldly invocation can be seen in a relatively benign light—Gracida enjoining Espinoza to join him in prayer for their late mutual benefactor. But in the context of the rest of the letter, we can perceive this young priest's attempt to secure ties of patronage amidst interclerical conflict and fears that his ex-mistress would discover his whereabouts and scuttle his efforts to start anew.

After his visionary introduction, Father Everardo turned to the news from Tlacoxcalco. Throughout his report, he reveals that he identified the root of the problem in the devotees' Indian heritage. He referred to them solely as Indians, not individuals or even parishioners, and labeled their interests "Indian demands." Noting that Espinoza was probably familiar with "the famous Bartola of San Mateo," he announced that

Father Valencia, the nearby pastor of Coxcatlán, was flouting authority by sustaining the cult of the Lord of the Wounds and telling the devotees that the recently promoted Archbishop Núñez would grant the consecration of the contested chapel.[51] Despite the prohibition of participation in the cult and the unlikely prospect that Núñez would approve the devotion, Valencia (one of the few priests that spoke Nahuatl, the devotee's native language) led a group of Indians to meet the new prelate at the local rail stop, where they presented the new archbishop with approximately sixteen pesos. The Indians, asserted Padre Everardo, viewed this gift as a deposit toward the eventual authorization permitting the blessing of their much-maligned private shrine. Subsequently, they pestered Valencia every fifteen days, asking if the license had arrived; to allay "the exigencies of the Indians," Valencia informed them that the archbishop's approval required much more money. Claiming to play the fool in order to track their activities, Padre Everardo maintained that the devotees had begun to whitewash the walls of the chapel in anticipation of its official dedication. He listed Valencia's misdeeds: he contravened vows of obedience and principles of authority; he compromised the archbishop by arranging his meeting with the devotees and propagating illusions that official sanction was forthcoming; he sustained the "idolatry, or fraud, of those people"; he undermined Padre Everardo's ministry; and finally, by insinuating that the prelate demanded cash in exchange for the chapel's blessing, he fueled notions among the church's enemies and Indians that the clergy's infamous reputed greed emanated from the highest levels of Catholic administration.

Padre Everardo also complained about his frustrating efforts to reform his parishioners, or as he put it, "*meterlos al orden*" (put them in order). Revealing much about the church's approach to Indian communities and the difficulty of imposing the official model of lay religiosity and behavior, he maintained that he had searched in vain for a way to influence his parishioners. He lamented how difficult it was for priests to be heard, much less heeded. The only arena in which he enjoyed a minimal response to his ministrations was the attendance of a handful of girls and boys at catechism. Tepid support and rebelliousness, he claimed, plagued the parish's brotherhoods because certain women sought to dominate them. In addition, he found no means of decreasing *lapo* consumption. Slighting his parishioner's Christianity, he mused that perhaps God would favor a different priest with their "evangelization." Everardo Gracida insisted that his failure was not for lack of effort, but he admitted feeling demoralized. Revealing that he was in a difficult position as Valencia's subordinate, he begged Espinoza to keep his complaints secret. In the classic language of patronage (and in hopes of simultaneously escaping Valencia, the Lord of the Wounds, and his ex-mistress), he asked for "a grace": a transfer to a more remote parish in the region.[52]

Father Everado's correspondence with a fellow cleric in the Tehuacán region, however, reveals a different side of the reformed humble stickler for hierarchical obedience. Seven months prior to his principled criticism of Padre Valencia's flirtation with indigenous superstition, Gracida lightheartedly beckoned select colleagues to join him at the Lord of the Wounds' Lenten feast.[53] The letter demonstrates Father Everardo's duplicity and also reveals the way some priests approached unorthodox Indian religious practice. He opened his dispatch with a tongue-in-cheek reference to the church's Indian ministry, addressing Father Estanislao Rodríguez, the priest in Zinacatepec, in colonial-vintage, missionary Nahuatl: "*Estimado teopixque*" (Esteemed priest). Clearly writing a close friend, he continued: "I permit myself to invite you on Friday because I want you to come so that we can go to San Mateo by donkey and celebrate the First Friday of Lent. Just imagine, I agreed to celebrate their fiesta, but in the church, and since it is said that most of their supporters are from San Sebastián [Zinacatepec] and from the mountains, I want to invite the *tractable families* from here [San José Miahuatlán] to go as if it were an outing."[54] Here Everardo Gracida disclosed that he had little concern for issues of orthodoxy or archdiocesan authority regarding popular religious practice. He conveyed his disdain for the Lord of the Wounds devotion in his affected reluctance toward celebrating *their* fiesta. First, he stipulated that he would celebrate in the church—that is, not in the Bolaños's chapel. Second, noting that the festival's public hailed from his colleague's parish, San Sebastián, or were mountain dwellers ("*serranos*," i.e., especially rustic Indians), he outlined a plan to whitewash its indigenous/heterodox reputation by bringing along "tractable families" from the parish seat. He indicates that he sought to win this group's participation by pitching the independent Indian festival as a mere picnic. In a later portion of the letter, he joked about withholding his crony's share of the fees.

In sum, Padre Everardo displayed little interest in reforming his indigenous parishioners. His missive evinces no effort to engage the devotees in order to harmonize their beliefs and practices with the archdiocese's model of faith and worship. Nor does he demonstrate any anxiety about violating the vicar general's and Gillow's prohibitions. Instead, he projected an air of breezy contempt in his humoring of indigenous "superstitions" and exhorting Rodríguez to join him for fun, fees, and fellowship. Comparing Padre Everardo's two letters suggests that his differences with Valencia resided in a dispute over jurisdiction and fees, rather than heterodoxy and vows of obedience.

Estanislao Rodríguez had his own troubles with his indigenous flock. In fact, a shared frustration with their non-Hispanic spiritual charges, personal legacies of pastoral dereliction, and problems with their superiors may have drawn these two priests together. In late summer and fall of 1922, self-described Indian parishioners of Zinacatepec complained to the archdiocese about Rodríguez's less-than-paternal attitude toward Indians.[55] The root of their complaint was excessive clerical greed. They claimed that Rodríguez's thirst for cash forced many couples to live in sin, because they could not afford his capricious application of marriage fees. In one instance, he scandalously combined the marriage of two parishioners with the funeral of another in order to hold only one service, but charge twice. They also accused him of physically abusing Indians and ignoring requests for Extreme Unction. According to the signatories, Rodríguez practiced an unholy dual ministry: he served a small number of privileged Hispanic parishioners well, while treating the indigenous poor with contempt. Father Antonio de P. Valencia (the same priest that Everardo Gracida complained about) went to Zinacatepec to collect testimony and file a report about the accusations concerning Rodríguez. The testimony he forwarded to the archdiocese confirmed the allegations.

Rodríguez, in turn, accused his critics of a history of lies, half-truths, and specious attacks against the clergy.[56] He admitted pummeling the parishioner in question but argued the man had suggested that Rodríguez interfered in his repeated spousal abuse due to his own carnal intentions. Rodríguez claimed that the cad's sarcastic offer to resolve their differences by giving his wife to the priest elicited his violent response. The great irony of this case is that the Indians of Zinacatepec cited the demeanor of San Jose's Everardo Gracida as their pastoral ideal. It appears Padre Everardo assumed different masks for his superiors, colleagues, and the natives of the Tehuacán Valley.

Father Everardo failed to gain a new post, but reports filed in 1924 reveal that archdiocesan authorities had made some personnel changes in the region and had altered their approach toward Bartola Bolaños and her followers.[57] A different prelate was carrying out pastoral visits now. Francisco Campos y Ángeles, a bishop banished from neighboring Tabasco by that state's anticlerical governor, had taken refuge in the Archdiocese of Oaxaca. Under the newly created title *visitador arqudiocesano*, he became Archbishop Núñez's eyes and ears in the province. He also brought with him a diplomatic approach toward issues of indigenous practice. By the mid-1920s, Valencia no longer served as the regional head parish priest in Coxcatlán, although he returned to the parish in the 1930s. In his place, Isidoro Palacios, an experienced priest known for his energy and prudence, was amidst an ambitious, and undoubtedly contentious, crusade to reform the town's wayward brotherhoods and church musicians.[58] Campos praised Father Everardo's patience and dedication in pastoral matters and the material improvement of parish buildings. But Campos also ordered Padre Everardo to modify his approach to the Lord of the Wounds of Tlacoxcalco: "We strongly recommend that he treat the issue of the devotees of the Lord of the Wounds that is worshiped here in an extramural chapel in the town of San Mateo with charity and prudence, working directly with the Ecclesiastical Government, in order to develop a paternal tolerance concerning what is done by ignorant and misadvised devotees, and hopefully lead abuses toward pure and beneficial ritual practice among those involved."[59] With this pronouncement, Campos offered a truce. Gone were the attacks on Bartola Bolaños, threats to withhold the sacraments, demands for the surrender of the image, accusations of fraud, and efforts to change the image's appellation. Instead, he articulated a policy of accommodation, directing Father Everardo to treat the devotees with respect and to cultivate a relationship with them rooted in paternal tolerance, charity, and prudence. Alluding to preceding years of conflict, he outlined a policy that amounted to gradual negotiated reform—an approach that, while rarely articulated, has been historically at the center of religious change in Mexico.

The key metaphor in Campos's order is the priest's role as a loving father addressing his children's innocent misdeeds and misinformed bad behavior. Padre Everardo, he declared, should tolerate and forgive the members of his flock's failings, and by developing a close paternal relationship with them, gently transform religious abuses and wayward practice into a "pure and beneficial cult." This pronouncement also contains a crucial discursive surrender. For the first time, the clergy ceased to belittle the devotion's house of worship, calling it an "extramural chapel" instead of a shack, house, room, or parlor. With this discursive concession, the church accepted the building on Bartola's property as a site of local piety, albeit one outside of the church's direct control. Henceforth, Campos's announcement manifested, the clergy would gradually seek to bring the independent pilgrimage devotion into the church, literally and figuratively, rather than demand its extirpation.

A NEW TRADITION?

Bolaños and her followers must have greeted Campos's revision of church policy toward the Lord of the Wounds as a victory, even if they failed to secure the immediate consecration of their chapel. Essentially, the visiting prelate instructed their pastor to change his ways without requiring the faithful to do anything. Or perhaps we should look at this outcome as the hierarchy's tardy acceptance of a policy already in place locally. Thirteen years' worth of stonewalling tactics gave way to a strategy of open engagement. In large part, Campos's reform of the Oaxacan church's position merely harmonized the hierarchy with a fait accompli. The new devotion had demonstrated its ability to thrive despite archdiocesan and local opposition. Regional clergymen repeatedly adopted their own approaches to the devotion, which amounted to participation and engagement in disregard of their superiors. Campos probably recognized the futility of the archdiocese's unenforceable prohibitions and decided to put the issue to rest. He may have consulted with Archbishop Núñez, but we do not have any evidence of this. Again, he was not really fashioning a new policy, but rather reasserting the church's long tradition of tolerance toward heterodoxy, in hopes of steadily leading "misguided" devotional energies and beliefs toward more proper religious observance at some undefined moment in the future. The church's detractors had long seen this as little more than the shameful exploitation of crypto-pagan practice. Indeed, as we have seen, some clergymen showed little interest in fomenting the close paternal relationship with their indigenous flock that Campos prescribed in order to wrest orthodoxy from "abuses." Many pastors appeared content to preside over indigenous celebrations, collect fees, and ignore the details of belief and practice. But as far as the parish of San José Miahuatlán and the village of San Mateo Tlacoxcalco were concerned, the visiting bishop relieved tensions.

Despite the apparent rebuke, Padre Everardo also emerged victorious. Campos removed a divisive issue from his parish administration that must have contributed to his frustrations. Now he could work openly with some of the most energetic members of his parish, preside over their services, and maintain that he was gently modifying their superstitious practices, without fear of sanction from his superiors. Given his already precarious position with the curia, this must have been a great relief. Moreover, the strongly positive assessment that Campos provided of Gracida's parish administration demonstrates that he ingratiated himself with the visiting bishop. The transfer of Father Valencia from Coxcatlán probably also cheered the young pastor. Evidence that Campos planted the seeds of a lasting accommodation resides in the absence of the Lord of the Wounds, Bartola Bolaños, and priest-parishioner squabbles over this new pilgrimage devotion in the archival record after this point. Pablo Cervantes Bolaños provided further proof, recalling almost eighty years later that although his grandmother and her followers always had opponents in the region, they counted Padre Everardo and one of his successors, Father Federico Castilla, among the devotion's supporters.[60]

It could be argued that rising national and local tensions between the Catholic Church and the Mexican state in the mid-1920s inspired the archdiocese to mend fences with this dissident apparition movement in hopes of shoring up popular support. Yet there is no evidence of a policy to this effect. Although this may have motivated Campos to act as he did, or Archbishop Núñez to direct him to do so, it is important to keep in mind that the policy of engagement represented a return to a traditional means of managing tensions between local religion and the universal church. The outcome of this accommodation is visible today in Tlacoxcalco on the first Friday of Lent, when hundreds of pilgrims join the village's Catholic residents in honoring the Lord's feast. The rotating brotherhood still "cares" for the image, as branches from different towns

13 Tlacoxcalco's Lord of the Wounds today, amidst the flowers and candles. In front of the image stands the miraculous green cross and a small cashbox featuring a framed copy of the 1913 flyer (photograph by the author).

in the region take their turn patronizing services. Bartola Bolaños remained at the head of the devotion and sustained her reputation as a skilled local healer until she died in the mid-1930s. After her death, other individuals took up the maintenance of the private chapel, but no one assumed Bolaños's healing practice. When the private shrine fell into disrepair in the 1950s, the residents of Tlacoxcalco transferred the image to the village church, although some feared that the Lord expressed his displeasure with the move when it began to rain as he exited the crumbling chapel.

Today he resides in the far end of the transept, to the right of the main altar, inside a large glass case surrounded by vases of natural and artificial flowers, candles, a diminutive statue of Saint Martin of Porres, and a small, red, wooden alms-collection box with gold trim. The upper part of this box displays a framed copy of the 1913 flyer announcing the newly carved Lord of the Wounds and the pilgrim's farewell poem surrounded by tinsel flowers. Inside the glass cabinet with the actual image, a large circular stone rests at the foot of the crucifix, holding a central, although obscured, place of honor. Amidst the floral and wax décor, a simple green cross, inserted in a nondescript stand, occupies the center of the Lord's altar, draped with a pink lace stole with gold tinsel fringe. In short, Bolaños's persistence and Campos's reversal of church policy bore slowly ripening fruit. Priests participated in the "extramural" cult, and its seer held on to her spiritual and leadership role until her death, but steadily the devotees' relationship with the church improved. It was not until the remarkable Bartola Bolaños died and two more decades passed that the Lord of the Wounds took up residence in Tlacoxcalco's church. It is doubtful that he will ever be taken to the parish seat as stipulated by Archbishop Gillow and Vicar General Gracida, and even less likely that he shall be renamed "The Lord of the Agonies." Today the festival seems no different from the numerous Friday Lenten festivals held throughout the region dedicated to different images of Christ, except that on the first Friday of Lent in Tlacoxcalco, the small green cross and the Santo Niño Hallado still precede the Lord of the Wounds as his devotees carry him in solemn procession.

Looking back at the history of Tlacoxcalco's Lord of the Wounds, we could argue that it does not, in actuality, represent a new devotion. The practices, modes of expression, institutional structures, and beliefs have clear local antecedents. The Lord's devotees brought personal pilgrimage histories to their efforts in Tlacoxcalco; most of them had probably participated in celebrations associated with Ajalpan's Lord of Coculco, and their rival devotion, Miltepec's Lord of the Wounds. From these, and everyday Catholic practice, they appropriated liturgies, vocabularies, and traditions related to the Passion and the cross. Of course, they even borrowed the name of their image. From sources within and beyond the Catholic tradition, they drew on conceptions of image-centered faith healing and miraculous intercession, indigenous curing and divinatory practices, and enduring popular devotion to sacred objects like the Santo Niño Hallado. They also tapped into the barrio-*usuario* system and its *mayordomía*-centered practice and organizational structure, along with the new canonically structured associations' emphasis on frequent pious expression and monthly commemoration. Both local organizations and the clergy were fond of rotational systems. The building of a private chapel and independent management of local brotherhoods also had regional antecedents.

The great innovation of this new devotion resides in the creative recombination of all of these elements in a movement that adamantly asserted its Catholic and indigenous identity and went to great lengths to envelope its rituals in the trappings of orthodoxy. In organizing a devotion that sponsored monthly services centered on the devotion to the crucified Christ and incorporating several communities, the devotees succeeded in shaping rural Catholicism to a degree that eluded the revivalist clergy. Subverting church concepts of patriarchy, Bartola Bolaños and her cohorts led a revival of their own, and their initiative, determination, and grassroots savvy allowed them to outmaneuver the archdiocese. Like the local irrigation canals built to distribute communal water resources, pious energies flowed where the region's Indian Catholics guided them, rather than obeying the course traced by Hispanic clergy. Unable to embrace or suppress the movement, the church chose to employ a strategy with deep roots in Mexico's colonial history. They gradually accommodated the devotion, trusting time to obscure its heterodox roots, and death to humble its independent-minded leadership.

SIX

~~~ The Second Juan Diego

"At first it is impossible to see anything, but if everyone prays with devotion the Virgin Mary and an angel appear instantly; she gives her blessing and disappears. Then the stone suddenly becomes a screen and on it pass images of the Virgin of Carmen, of Solitude, and of Juquila." Thus, nearly five years after the Oaxacan archdiocese made peace with Bartola Bolaños, a reputedly successful merchant, Mr. Sánchez Alcántara, returned to his home in Oaxaca's Central Valley trumpeting the wondrous happenings he witnessed in the mountains above the Pacific Coast. In January 1929, Sánchez completed an arduous pilgrimage over difficult terrain to a region whose fame had been spreading for several months. Words, he maintained, could not do justice to his visions: multitudes of moving images, apparitions of a vast temple within the mountain, and glimpses of the entire celestial court.[1] For the reporter who interviewed him and published his claims in *El Mercurio,* a secular Oaxacan newspaper, one word sufficed to characterize Sánchez's experiences, and similar accounts of many other pilgrims: "*absurdo.*" Beneath the headline, "In the caves of Ixpantepec, Juquila, Naive Believers See Strange Visions Appear," he called for government intervention, noting that hundreds of people from the Central Valley were making their way to the region in hopes of experiencing these wonders for themselves. But Sánchez and his pilgrim cohorts had further cause for undertaking the journey. Beyond their hopes of experiencing their own visions, they also sought to consult the Virgin Mary through a young Chatina Indian girl who allegedly held frequent conferences with the Mother of God in an alpine grotto above the village of San Francisco Ixpantepec. A proud Sánchez Alcántara exhibited a document upon which he swore were written the exact questions he had asked the Virgin, along with her answers. Our skeptical source, though, failed to elaborate on them.[2]

When this edition of *El Mercurio* hit the stands on February 7, 1929, a florescence of Oaxacan apparitionism secured its place in the public record. In retrospect, this account reads like urban society's formulaic denigration of the superstitious ignorance of the indigenous countryside. Many residents of the city, in actuality, probably learned of the apparitions long before this report. Ixpantepec resides near Juquila and just a handful of kilometers from the pilgrimage/trade route linking the state capital, the famous Marian shrine, and the Pacific Coast. The correspondent listed important valley towns such as Zimatlán, San Andrés Miahuatlán (not to be confused with San José Miahuatlán in the Tehuacán Valley), and Ejutla as nodes of apparitionist fervor. If mass, impromptu pilgrimages were setting out from these communities, people in the state capital were bound to hear about it. In fact, by 1929, a healthy number of urbanites may have trekked to Ixpantepec of their own accord. The secular press's account, although dismissive and incomplete, alludes to the complex set of issues that make it worthy of our attention. Amidst the sociopolitical turmoil of the late 1920s, a cross-section of Oaxacan society, exemplified by the Indian girl and the merchant pilgrim, came together around the notion of Marian apparitions in the state's Chatino heartland. The reporter's grasp of local geography was somewhat feeble—he implied that all the paranormal events were taking place at the "grottos of Ixpantepec," when, in fact, he spoke of events in two distinct communities, Ixpantepec and Temaxcaltepec. Unwittingly, he revealed that by early 1929, the apparitions had become a regional phenomenon.

The visions, in fact, began in Ixpantepec in the late spring or early summer of 1928, when the eight- or nine-year-old seer, Dionisia (or Nicha, as she was called) reported her divine encounters and consultations in the small cave above her village. News of apparitions were (and still are)

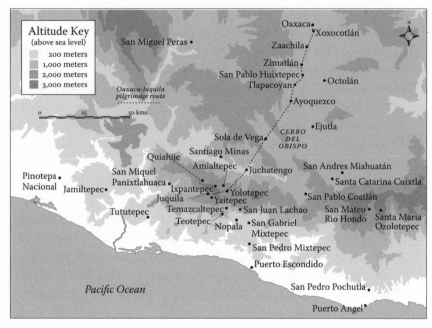

Map 4 Juquila, Ixpantepec, and Southern Oaxaca

relatively common occurrences in Oaxaca, but Nicha's proclamations of
impending divine chastisement reached local society at a moment when
several factors primed the laity for revelation. In some parts of Mexico, the
church-state struggle of the late 1920s fueled antigovernment insurrection and state-sponsored, antichurch violence. Catholic activists viewed
the clash as a modern-day version of early Christianity's persecution. They
spoke of President Plutarco Elías Calles as Mexico's tyrannical Caesar and
praised the faith's martyrs who perished opposing him. Throughout the
summer of 1928, newspapers obsessively chronicled the suspected Catholic conspiracy behind president-elect Álvaro Obregón's assassination.[3]
Oaxacans were living through an uneasy period of instability as factions
jockeyed for power in the unpredictable climate of revolutionary state
formation, and the region experienced a redefinition of its relationship to
the nation. For the archdiocese, the apparitions could not have arrived at a
more delicate time. The hierarchy approached them carefully as Catholic
rebels in other parts of the country fought federal troops and their auxiliaries to an atrocity-plagued standstill in the so-called Cristero Revolt

REVELATION

(1926–29). Above all, the Oaxacan church sought to avert open conflict with the government while attempting to protect the archdiocese's economic base, personnel, and institutional infrastructure. The region did not experience a broad, religion-fueled rebellion like Jalisco and Michoacán, but it was far from calm. The archdiocese labored to maintain clerical discipline, outmaneuver local anticlericals, and avoid entanglements with small bands of Catholic dissidents.

But more than armed resistance was on the minds of the communities and clergymen surrounding Ixpantepec when pilgrims began to hail Nicha as the "second Juan Diego." Several disconcerting tremors and two devastating earthquakes struck the region between 1928 and 1931. The first large quake, on August 4, 1928, leveled most of the public buildings and many homes along the coast and in the nearby mountains and coincided closely with the public emergence of the Ixpantepec visions. Torrential rains followed shortly afterward, leaving many roofless households to face the deluge without shelter while what remained of their homes washed away. Nicha apparently also predicted the great earthquake of January 14, 1931, that destroyed much of Oaxaca City, many Central Valley towns, and Juquila and its shrine.[4] As a result, many communities in the region were destroyed twice, and rattled several times, whilst the seer and her supporters warned of celestial punishments, called for fervent expiation, and lobbied for official recognition.

In truth, devotional and doctrinal concerns had shaken the region's Catholics in advance of the seismic events. The national hierarchy responded to the revolutionary state's efforts to enforce anticlerical portions of the 1917 constitution by suspending all religious services in 1926. They also pressured ecclesiastical provinces to force rural clerics to respect the ban. In Oaxaca, some clergymen feared that their indigenous parishioners would lapse into idolatry and thus sought means to continue their ministry. In a parish adjacent to Ixpantepec, and in other communities in the region, accusations emerged about certain priests conspiring with local officials to maintain religious services in defiance of their superiors. This, in turn, inspired rumors of a religious schism and worries about the validity of the sacraments. In concert, the Chatino girl's visions, intense seismic activity, and the prevailing climate of turmoil appeared to match the prognostications of a legendary eighteenth-century seer whose visions were a staple of Mexico's popular devotional literature. La Madre

Matiana, as she was called, allegedly foresaw the Wars of Independence, the church's international loss of power and prestige in the nineteenth century, anticlerical violence, and the triumph of secular liberalism in the nineteenth century. She also predicted a great conflict and the ultimate triumph of the church thanks to a new female-led devotional movement in a year ending in eight.

For most Oaxacan Catholics, divine apparitions are an article of faith. The region has a rich legacy of apparitionist lore and deep indigenous visionary traditions. To this day, shrines dedicated to miraculous images and apparitions dot the landscape, their pilgrimages traverse the spaces between them, and together they fill local and regional ritual calendars. For several decades prior to 1928, church publications and teachings fueled belief in the Catholic miraculous, trumpeting official apparitions as evidence of the enduring relevance of the church and the folly of secularism. The faithful expected marvelous demonstrations of their faith, despite the fact that the clergy remained leery of popular revelation. The issue for priests and many laypeople was veracity. Were the Ixpantepec visions truly divine apparitions? If so, what did they mean?

For a time, thousands of Oaxacans surmised that the Indian girl's visions were indeed divine. They rushed to Ixpantepec and began calling Nicha the "second Juan Diego." In doing so they made her the legendary seer's successor and linked the events in Oaxaca to the Virgin of Guadalupe narrative. Giving Nicha this new identity represents a dramatic statement. The national hierarchy had been energetically promoting Guadalupe's devotion, originally confined to the central highlands, throughout Mexico during the late nineteenth century. They made her the symbol of militant Catholic nationalism and reformed piety. As part of this process, they also generalized the characters and themes of her apparition legend, particularly the notion that Guadalupe appeared as a mestiza to an older indigenous man in order to coax Mexico's native peoples into the Christian fold. In 1928, though, many rural Oaxacans embraced a young Chatina girl as their own Juan Diego, and proclaimed a new advocation of Mary, La Virgen de Ixpantepec.

Regrettably, all we have are tantalizing hints concerning popular understandings of the Ixpantepec apparitions. At several decades remove, we know that Nicha and her supporters, unlike the devotees of the Lord of the Wounds, failed to establish an enduring devotion. Currently, their endeavors teeter on the verge of oblivion. As with the Tlacoxcalco case, we must rely on rich but problematic evidentiary materials. There are three sources of documentary evidence produced by participants in the struggles surrounding Nicha's apparitions. Each of them provides a divergent interpretation of the events from essentially mestizo outsiders' perspectives: Matilde Narváez, the longstanding Catholic activist, argued that the apparitions were authentic miracles meriting recognition; Father Ausencio Canseco, Juquila's pastor, concluded that Satan lay behind the rash of visions in his parish; and Hilario Cortés, Canseco's protégé and close assistant, claimed that Nicha and others concocted an elaborate hoax to bilk gullible locals at a time of heightened unease. Although their respective theses clash, each of these sources provides crucial information about the apparitions and rural Oaxacan society at the time. Unfortunately, Nicha died in 1999 without documenting her point of view. In addition, there are no documents to consult in Ixpantepec. Hence our knowledge of the apparitions as a Chatino event must remain impressionistic. In the present chapter, I will describe how Oaxaca experienced the Mexican Revolution and subsequent church-state conflict, and detail how Narváez, Canseco, and Cortés analyzed the visions and depicted the movement surrounding the Chatina seer. In the subsequent chapter, I will examine the discursive strategies of these actors, and employ oral history and recent ethnographic studies to hazard an interpretation of the Chatino origins of Nicha's visionary career. Then I will sketch the historical development of Madre Matiana's prophecies, and delve into their construction of female pious agency. Finally, I will explore the motivations of the pivotal figure of Matilde Narváez, and the gendered dynamics of rural Oaxacan Catholicism evident in the apparition movement's ultimate collapse.

OAXACA'S MEXICAN REVOLUTION AND CRISTIADA

At the broadest level, the Mexican Revolution and postrevolutoinary development sharply increased the political and economic power of northern Mexico and hence represented a drastic change for Oaxaca.[5] The region never emerged as one of the chief revolutionary conflict zones, but the collapse of the Díaz regime inaugurated the state's marginalization. Oaxaca had enjoyed a position of prominence before and during the

Porfiriato, and Oaxacans liked to think of their state as a cornerstone of the nation. The dictatorial president looked after his fellow *oaxaqueños*, and many of them gained important positions in the federal government. Investment in infrastructure, commercial agriculture and mining also flowed into the state. As a result, Oaxaca City, long simply a provincial administrative center, became a hub of Porfirian entrepreneurial activity, foreign mining ventures, and commerce. Beyond the state capital, development evolved in a patchwork fashion. Capitalist modernization transformed certain districts and passed others by. Regions like Pochulta, Juquila, Cuicatlán, and Tuxtepec emerged as centers of commercial agriculture. For the most part, though, agricultural development was decentralized and oriented toward markets outside Oaxaca. Coffee growers from Pochutla and Juquila shipped directly from ports on the Pacific, Cuicatlán's farmers marketed their crops via railroad though Puebla, and Tuxtepec's produce went to Veracruz. Other districts like Octotlán, Ixtlán, and Tlacolula were the focus of mining investment, although the mines never matched promoters' glowing projections.[6] The transformation of some communities in these regions, the concomitant alienation of resources, and the exploitation of workers fueled diffuse unorganized discontent. The dislocations and social turmoil associated with capitalist modernization were simply not that widespread. Aside from Tuxtepec, commercial haciendas and plantations never dominated Oaxacan agriculture the way they did in the state of Morelos, the epicenter of revolutionary agrarianism. Most communities endured as small peasant societies outside the full embrace of economic modernization, and villages continued to control land and other resources. In sum, Oaxaca's Porfirian transformation was uneven, and the state lacked the conditions that fueled extensive peasant revolt.[7]

The revolution came to Oaxaca from outside the state, and when local unrest took shape, it developed along the lines of preexisting rivalries. This is not to say that Oaxacans were counterrevolutionary; however, they tended to view national political upheavals from parochial perspectives. Francisco Madero and his anti-reelection movement gained only tepid support in the state. The elite, particularly in the state capital and the surrounding region, was firmly *porfirista*. The emergent middle sector, a key constituency of *maderismo* throughout Mexico, was small and wielded only limited influence.[8] Armed revolt in other parts of Mexico led to a sustained crisis among Oaxaca City elites, as rebel groups from Puebla and Guerrero penetrated the Mixtec highlands and Pacific Coast, regional strongmen asserted themselves, and parts of the state harboring longstanding antagonism toward the state capital—such as the Isthmus of Tehuantepec—rebelled to gain greater autonomy. In short, the state government's ability to control areas outside the Central Valley began to disintegrate. Díaz's ouster in 1911 led to a period of sustained instability as elite factions maneuvered to preserve the sociopolitical status quo, pinning their hopes on various politicians associated with the defunct regime, among them don Porfirio's nephew Félix Díaz. Some of these individuals attained the governorship, but few lasted long. In general, they failed to navigate the twists and turns of revolutionary politics while simultaneously coping with local challenges. Some influential clergymen, such as Agustín Echeverría and José Cuevas Ramírez, made their sympathies known by leading a rally for the younger Díaz and placing his portrait next to the Virgin of Solitude at her shrine. In many places, power simply reverted to local strongmen backed by loose regional coalitions. Many strange-bedfellow alliances between Oaxacan groups and external political movements emerged and dissolved in this environment.[9]

In 1915, a coalition of militias from the Sierra Juárez and Central Valley elites fearful of the increasing national power of Venustiano Carranza and the Constitutionalist army, declared the state's provisional autonomy. Led by José Inés Dávila, a newly elected governor of established *pofirista* and *felicista* sympathies, they argued that Oaxaca had to withdraw from the nation to protect its institutions from anarchic revolutionary politics threatening to dissolve state's social foundations. In the interim, they promised to rule in the spirit of the 1857 constitution and return to the union once order had been restored. At the time of the declaration, Constitutionalist forces occupied the Isthmus, Tuxtepec, and parts of the Pacific Coast. In these areas, revolutionary commanders and their local collaborators openly challenged state authorities. In hopes of bolstering their position, the leaders of the sovereignty movement even cultivated ties with Zapatista groups. The root of this ill-fated maneuver resides in the Oaxacan elite's desperate effort to retain their privileged perch in national politics. According to Oaxacan historian Francisco José Ruiz Cervantes, the movement should be understood as an attempt by the state's elite to carve out a strong bargaining position in its dealings with the emerging revolutionary state, rather than as a full-blown counter-revolution.[10]

Initially the move enjoyed considerable support in Oaxaca City, the Sierra Juárez, and the Mixteca, but it proved no match for the Constitutionalists. Groups aligned politically with the Catholic Church and many priests were enthusiastic supporters. Convinced by newspaper coverage of the Constitutionalists' entrenched anticlericalism, they opposed the new government as a threat to the religion, property, and family.[11] For the Oaxacan church, this stance added to their reactionary reputation. Archbishop Gillow had already fled to the United States due to his ties to Victoriano Huerta's brief dictatorship. Less than a year after Dávila's declaration of Oaxacan sovereignty, the movement began to disintegrate when federal troops defeated the poorly equipped local militias and occupied Oaxaca City in March 1916. Urban elites learned that they could sustain their status under the new regime, and soon became willing collaborators. A few months later, the Sierra Juárez also fell to the Constitutionalists, and the federal government made conciliatory provisions to incorporate some Oaxacan militias within the national army. Dávila and others tried to sustain opposition in Tlaxiaco, and the state's stability remained tenuous for a time, but support for the sovereignty movement gradually withered. Soon General Álvaro Obregón's agents were seeking allies amongst sovereignty's supporters in his growing conflict with Carranza, a man widely disliked in Oaxaca. After Obregón defeated Carranza and secured the presidency in 1920, he sent Oaxacan General Manuel García Vigil to govern the state. This appointment set the stage for rapprochement. Obregón needed to cement regional alliances, and the Oaxacan elite and the Sierra Juárez strongmen needed to secure new ties to national power holders.[12] Before long a mutually beneficial relationship emerged.

Like other groups that had aligned themselves with the sovereignty movement, the Oaxacan clergy escaped harsh retribution. Perhaps the Constitutionalists avoided conflict with the Oaxacan church because they remained insecure about their position in the state, but there is no documentary evidence revealing such a policy.[13] Catholics and historians in Oaxaca claim that the vital figure during this period was Vicar General Carlos Gracida, the churchman entrusted with the archdiocese's administration during Gillow's exile (i.e., the same official who tried to suppress the Lord of the Wounds). In the late 1920s, Archbishop Núñez, like his predecessor, also left the archdiocese temporarily because of church-state tensions. Thus Padre Carlos, as he was called, was the steady hand at the helm during two critical periods for the Oaxacan church. Due to his long-standing, diligent administration of Oaxaca City's most prestigious Catholic boys' school (El Colegio del Espíritu Santo) he enjoyed close personal ties with many influential men. Besides using this network of contacts, Gracida worked long hours in his offices adjacent to the cathedral, and crisscrossed the city on foot to carry out archdiocesan business, personally engaging in careful diplomacy with secular authorities.[14] One of his relationship-building tools was officiating at marriages bringing together traditional Oaxaca elites and the new caste of revolutionary leaders. He is given considerable credit for Oaxaca's relative calm, soothing prochurch passions and negotiating sagaciously with the government.[15] He even personally intervened to avert a riot when rumors surfaced that the government was planning to sell the Virgin of Solitude to foreign collectors.[16] This balancing proved difficult to sustain under more anticlerical civil authorities in the 1930s, but successfully navigating the turbulent 1920s was no mean feat.[17]

Gracida's ability to control events in the countryside was limited, but still Oaxaca escaped the assassinations of priests, temple desecrations, and iconoclasm that polarized other regions and fueled antigovernment mobilizations. While violence convulsed states like Jalisco and Michoacán, the Oaxacan church continued to function with remarkably little difficulty thanks to a "gentleman's agreement" between the high clergy and civil officials. The key ingredients in this arrangement were the personal relationships between clergymen and officeholders, flexibility in both camps, Catholic sympathy at all levels of civil administration, and the lack of large-scale Catholic unrest. One of the more fortuitous events leading to this outcome was Calles's appointment of Genaro V. Vásquez as governor in 1925. Vásquez, a native of Oaxaca City and one-time Constitutionalist congressman, was a close friend of the secretary of the archdiocese, Agustín Espinoza. Through this contact, he developed good relations with Gracida. In addition, Vásquez, unlike some of his counterparts in other states, had little interest in extreme anticlericalism or aggressive expropriations. He focused on progressive educational reform, restrained agrarianism, and up-beat, moderate leftist-nationalist cultural programs. Throughout this period, archdiocesan administrators remained in constant contact with their secular counterparts. They took care that the clergymen complied with federal rulings, such as the establishment of an official registry of priests and the turning over of all church buildings to civil committees. Government officials, in turn, modified or only partially implemented anticlerical directives. For example, contravening federal instructions, they allowed priests to remain in their posts and continue with their pastoral duties and permitted the seminary to reopen. They were able to do this as long as antigovernment Catholic mobilization did not threaten stability or embarrass them. This kind of improvisation, of course, also undermined support for antigovernment activity.[18]

Beyond the city of Oaxaca, some rural areas lived their own histories of civil-religious conflict and accommodation. State archives in the early 1920s reveal a modest degree of popular anticlericalism in complaints about illegal public worship, but the unabashed openness of the violations that found their way into the archives suggests that tolerance of these kinds of infractions was, in fact, the norm.[19] Nonetheless, according to archdiocesan correspondence, a number of village priests, like Juquila's Ausencio Canseco, felt besieged. The state's edicts regulating the number of priests in its jurisdiction, and summoning clerics to the state capital to be registered, caused some Catholics to suspect the impending permanent removal of their priests. Independent-minded municipal governments sometimes sought to "reconcentrate" priests to their own liking or oust them from their communities.[20] In some parishes like Tututepec, priests and civil officials sparred throughout the 1920s and early 1930s. On one occasion, the town's officials imprisoned a priest for an extended period and refused to allow a new cleric to staff the parish. Archdiocesan officials sent Father Canseco from Juquila to investigate in 1932 and he feared local anticlericals were plotting the pastor's murder. In early 1933, this group burned the parish church to the ground, and worried Tututepec Catholics beseeched the church for help.[21]

In addition, two nodes of armed Catholic resistance sustained a tenuous campaign against the federal government, one near Huajuapam in northeastern Oaxaca, and another in the mountains where Ixpantepec resides. These groups failed to garner sufficient peasant backing or urban Catholic financial support like their counterparts in the west-central

Mexico. They were more a nuisance than a threat to federal authority, but they occasionally caused very real local problems. According to *El Mercurio*, the mountains around Tututepec, Juquila, Sola de Vega, Miahuatlán, Pochutla, and Putla were home to various small *cristero* groups. In some cases, these bands attacked important towns. The newspaper noted that Catholic rebels sacked Juquila on September 9, 1928.[22] Journalistic claims that priests led these rebels, however, turned out to be false.[23] Nearly a month later, on October 3, *cristeros* carried out a daring attack on San Andrés Miahuatlán during the town's celebrations honoring the late president and favorite son Porfirio Díaz.[24] In response, federal patrols occasionally harassed rural clergymen. In 1929, correspondents followed federal efforts to exterminate bands of *"fanáticos"* in the coffee-growing region between Miahuatlán and the Pacific Coast and claimed that troops operating in the Mixteca showed them captured arms and a banner emblazoned with, "Long Live Christ the King."[25] In the winter and summer of 1929, *El Mercurio* noted the surrender of some bands and their leaders in the region.[26] The dates and geography of Cristero activity indicate that the Ixpantepec apparition movement took shape amidst the most concentrated Oaxacan religious unrest, although oral history sources suggest that popular support for religious rebellion remained weak in the southern mountains.[27]

In reality common Oaxacans found other, more effective, ways to defend Catholicism. According to recent research by Jean Meyer, Oaxaca's relative quiescence owes a great deal to a broad lay commitment to the faith, which manifested itself as a vast uncoordinated project of passive resistance. He argues that the church hierarchy focused on diplomacy and challenging legislation through legal channels while trusting the laity to quietly sustain the faith. This worked because the region's deep religious institutional culture functioned largely on its own without priestly involvement. Quite simply, the dense network of *mayordomías*, brotherhoods, and associations proved to be the church's secret weapon. There is a certain irony in this phenomenon: the same stubbornness that priests often complained about in local religious institutions and communities with long experience circumventing laws and external attempts to alter local practices helped sustain and protect the clergy.[28] Sometimes, however, individuals went much further in their efforts to defend the faith.

In 1928, Ixpantepec was a small, poor village connected only by a narrow trail to the municipal seat of Juquila, approximately twenty kilometers away. At about two thousand meters above sea level, it has a relatively cold climate. A statistical survey in 1883 listed 194 inhabitants.[29] Demographic data suggest that Ixpantepec was relatively important in the sixteenth century and, presumably, before the colonial period. It is actually one of the few local settlements for which Spanish authorities compiled statistics. In 1544, colonial tribute documents listed 460 tributaries in the pueblo. Statistics published in 1978 record only 291 residents.[30] It remains small both in actual size and in the minds of outsiders. Hilario Cortés, the self-styled historian and eyewitness of events at the apparition site, referred to the town as *"miserable,"* implying abject poverty and hopelessness. He described the community as a monolingual, autochthonous Indian backwater, whose residents "have not Castillianized themselves and live without evolving."[31] Ixpantepec lacks a historical or contemporary claim to fame like its neighbors. Juquila is a shrine center drawing thousands of pilgrims from much of southern Mexico; Amialtepec, its closest neighbor, has achieved a certain status as the original site of the Virgin of Juquila's appearance. For the most part, in contrast, Ixpantepec is just overlooked.

Visiting the village today and contemplating the tiny plaza, humble church, rustic school, and the scattered houses perched on the steep slopes, it appears that the bleak portrayal by outsiders is somewhat exaggerated. But it is also evident that the dry, stone-laden soils cannot support a large agricultural community. The village historically depended upon low-yield, subsistence corn farming, the cultivation of maguey and its fermented products, and fruit collection. Due to its elevation, cool temperatures and low rainfall, Ixpantepec failed to attract the entrepreneurs who brought coffee production and increasingly Hispanized the Chatino region over the last 125 years. Like many Oaxacan villages, today it exports people. Despite its present state, from 1928 until some time in the early 1930s, the heir of Juan Diego presided over the village's moment in the sun.

Although Nicha left us without her testimony, we can glean some clues about her experience through her mestiza ally, Matilde Narváez.

This woman, an elderly spinster at the time of the apparitions, epitomizes the period's devout women who were crucial assets of the church. Her biography reads like a central casting request for the Hispanic archetype of the black-clad, fanatically proclerical unmarried *beata*, or *ratón de iglesia*.[32] For much of her life she appears to have played this role in all of its particulars. A long-time resident of Juquila from a reasonably well-off mestizo family owning lands and cattle near Tututepec, she was the right-hand woman of Juquila's pastors, and widely recognized for her piety and loyalty to the church. Father Canseco noted that he and his predecessor, Manuel Ramírez, had such confidence in Narváez that they entrusted Juquila's Catholic school to her. Older residents of Juquila still recall her with affection as the schoolmarm, "doña Matildita."[33] The fact that she administered the parochial school and taught classes for many years demonstrates that she possessed a relatively high degree of education and inspired respect among Juquila residents. She also donated land for a shrine hostel.[34] But the school principal and benefactoress did not escape the 1920s with her reputation intact. Narváez's standing as a Catholic stalwart and her relationship with the clergy soured thanks to her championing of Nicha's visions, as well as a financial dispute. As we shall see, church-state tension aside, conflict over events in Ixpantepec took shape as a struggle between Catholics. Nicha's village even enjoyed its own reputation as a prochurch bastion prior to the apparitions. When Father Canseco and Cortés fled from revolutionaries in 1919, they chose this out-of-the-way community as their refuge.[35]

In the 1920s, the Chatino region was amidst a gradual but profound transition.[36] From the 1880s onward it served as a destination of the Central Valley's mestizo entrepreneurs seeking opportunities in coffee, cattle, and rubber. Chatino municipalities still controlled land in the region, but faced state-backed expropriations, as well as pressure to grant lands to newcomers or privatize them among community members. Juquila, a municipal seat, district government capital, and parish seat, had become the center of the non-Chatino population and the node of state power in the region. It was also a target of indigenous uprisings. As a result, Chatinos gained a fearsome reputation in Oaxaca City. Archbishop José Othón Núñez's father, a previous district prefect in Juquila, was killed by Chatino rebels in the "War of the Pants" in 1896. Apparently, the state government sparked unrest in many communities when it raised taxes on small properties. Rebellion was most intense in the Chatino region, where angry insurgents sacked Juquila during Holy Week shouting "Death to those that wear pants!" They also killed every government official they could find, including the elder Núñez.[37] Authorities brutally repressed the rebels, however, and political and economic transformation of the region continued.

One of the more remarkable aspects of this process was the seemingly mundane mechanics of transition. For example, a strategy among entrepreneurial families in the region was to have a son take up residency in an Indian community in order to gain access to communal land. Strategic intermarriages (or less formal unions) greatly aided this process. Priests even took part. A Juquila pastor in the early 1890s, Francisco Zorrilla, gained access to parcels of land, started a coffee plantation, and raised a family with a local woman. He undoubtedly benefited from his status as parish priest in getting the land, and his descendants remain prominent in local politics.[38] In the early 1930s, one of our protagonists, Father Canseco, arranged for his nephew Rafael León to gain some choice coffee lands, and in 2002 León's grandson was serving as Juquila's municipal president.[39]

Still we cannot characterize this process as an outside imposition of commercial capitalism. Many Chatinos and bicultural locals took part. The pace of change, as well as intercommunity and intracommunity violence, became more intense in the 1930s, 1940s, and 1950s, when coffee production, land privatization, and social differentiation within villages surged in tandem. Between 1916 and 1930, local factions proclaiming allegiance to national revolutionary groups were sparring for political control. In the late 1920s Juquila's Hispanic/mestizo population was in the process of definitively replacing the town's historically Chatino municipal officials. Local church-state issues insinuated themselves into this dynamic and muddied what might otherwise be interpreted as a simpler economic and ethnic struggle. Chatinos in Juquila tended to side with conservative Hispanic Catholics, like Canseco and Matilde Narvaéz, in opposition to the new municipal president and factions who claimed to be local representatives of the victorious Constitutionalists.[40]

Since doña Matildita had been a close ally of Canseco in this environment, their falling out was particularly rancorous. According to Canseco, during the revolution he entrusted 1,900 pesos of the shrine's capital to

the loyal spinster, expecting that she would protect the funds from soldiers and nosy officials. When he sought to recover them in 1926, Narváez informed him that she had spent the money in the intervening years.
Revolutionary unrest in Oaxaca's coastal mountains lingered into the
mid-1920s, and hence it is not surprising that Canseco waited to request
these funds. This dispute was simmering for two years before Nicha's
apparitions and remained a thorny issue after 1928 when the *beata* and
her one-time ally were simultaneously at variance over the appearance of
Mary and the disappearance of money. Canseco tried to pressure Narváez
to repay him for five years before he brought up the issue with the archdiocese.[41] Such was his frustration that for years he threatened to deprive
her of the sacraments and denounce her before the archbishop, but he
restrained himself out of respect for her family.[42] In 1931, he overcame
his reluctance. He cut Narváez off from the sacraments, and convinced
the same auxiliary bishop who smoothed things over in Tlacoxcalco,
Francisco Campos, to take up the case with her family. All this took place
outside of the public eye. By law, priests were not supposed to have the
resources Canseco sought to regain.[43]

While this was taking place, Narváez threw her energy behind the
effort to gain ecclesiastical recognition of Nicha's visions and promote
devotion to the Virgin of Ixpantepec. Her 1932 report to the ecclesiastical
government is the only document that offers a detailed reconstruction of
Nicha's visions. She depicted a heady early period when many people,
including Canseco, seemed convinced of the legitimacy of the apparitions
and keen on following Nicha's indications. The exact date when Nicha
began to consult with the Virgin remains a mystery, but sometime in late
July or early August 1928, the news reached Juquila. Narváez and a group
of women rushed to Ixpantepec as soon as they heard about the apparitions. Canseco had preceded them. In an atmosphere of considerable
excitement, Canseco said a mass of rogation, as requested by village
officials, and then led a large group to the grotto. This included the entire
complement of Ixpantepec's authorities, many villagers, and probably
Narváez, her female companions, and Canseco's assistant, Hilario Cortés.
Upon their arrival, Nicha entered the grotto and remerged telling Canseco that the Virgin was indeed present. The priest proceeded to bless the
grotto and pray the Rosary with all those present. This act soon took on
special meaning for believers, whom Canseco later maligned as "*los inter-*

esados."[44] Nicha claimed that the Virgin had intended to move to the village of Ixpantepec, but once Canseco blessed the grotto, she considered it her temple and planned to remain. Over time, belief that the Virgin physically inhabited Ixpantepec's grotto and desired a shrine on the site became an article of faith for devotees and a sign of heterodoxy for Canseco.

Nicha also communicated frightening news. The angel accompanying Mary, she said, told her that her efforts on behalf of the Virgin had enraged the devil, and he planned to accost her in a horrible fashion. Narváez asserted that this indeed took place. But the angel also told Nicha that if she and her entire family received confession, the demonic apparitions would retire. Nicha apparently had not yet received the sacraments of confession and communion. According to Narváez, Canseco immediately ordered a woman to begin preparing Nicha and her mother for confession. But Nicha refused, saying that the angel already taught her what she needed to know. Canseco, Narváez maintained, discovered this to be true when he confessed the girl.[45]

These details were a crucial part of Narváez's documentation of Nicha's credentials as an authentic Catholic seer. They revealed the dramatic opposition of Satan to Nicha's fulfillment of her "service" to the Virgin, the girl's natural piety, and her miraculous preparation for the sacraments. The latter is especially significant: Nicha represented the indigenous blank slate of evangelical lore, supernaturally guided toward orthodoxy. Oral testimony adds further complexity to Nicha's paranormal encounters within the grotto. A present-day Ixpantepec resident recalls that her grandfather told her about the frenetic excitement caused by Nicha's visions, and a subsequent building boom when Ixpantepec became a magnet for pilgrims. He concurred that civil authorities sent for Canseco and then accompanied him to the apparition site, along with many others. But he maintained that nobody in the village, beyond Nicha, ever witnessed any miracles. In addition, our informant's grandfather claimed to have administered curing rites to Nicha after her visions. According to this account, the girl returned from the grotto in a state of dazed hysteria, babbling fearfully about a beast in the town's church that threatened to consume her and the people of the village. This man succeeded in exorcising this panic by praying over her and performing unspecified rituals.[46]

While Ixpantepec oral history does not contradict Narváez's testimony, it reveals that she either did not witness all of the rituals that emerged from Nicha's apparitions, or else chose to omit them from her report. Regardless of these unknowns, it is clear that different ritual specialists took part in the ministrations linked to Nicha's visions and that more than one religious tradition was in play. It is likely that in much of the Chatino region, people like Narváez, our informant's grandfather, and Canseco perceived this overlap of religious practice as routine, even if they disapproved of it. Common sense suggests that Narváez would mute even the slightest hint of heterodoxy in her report to church hierarchs, but Canseco did not mention Chatino rites either. It is also possible that they took place before outsiders heard about the visions or during rituals from which they were excluded.

Our sources indicate that the apparitions had been occurring in Ixpantepec for at least a few weeks before news of them spilled beyond the community. Something enabled this local happening to breach linguistic and cultural barriers and emerge as a regional phenomenon. Certainly, the frenzied action in Ixpantepec during these days emanated from the ominous message of impending chastisement, which Nicha brought from the Virgin and the angel. The seer warned of "God's justice" if they did not turn their efforts toward divine supplication. Perhaps these warnings would have been ignored at a different time, but in the summer of 1928, they coincided with an intense earthquake on August 4 that pummeled Oaxaca's coast. Several aftershocks followed, and other earthquakes ensued in March and April of 1929.[47] Nicha, apparently, emphasized the linkage of these events to looming divine punishment, and the earliest date that Matilde Naváez provided in her narrative, June 16, 1928, concerned a vision following a small tremor. It was the combination of Nicha's dire prophesies and the August 4 earthquake, most likely, that inspired Ixpantpepec's authorities' call to Canseco.

When the priest and other outsiders descended upon the village, Nicha told them that the Mother of God asked for thirteen masses to be said during August 1928 to avert doom. Narváez maintained that Canseco complied with the exact number of masses requested, celebrating some at the grotto and others in private homes due to the church hierarchy's suspension of public religious services. She indicated, however, that he officiated four of them after August. Narváez also listed miraculous events and prophetic statements to impress archdiocesan authorities, and these form the basis of a chronology of the apparition movement's development.

After the earthquake of June 16, Nicha announced that the faithful should come to the Virgin of Ixpantepec on their knees and beseech Christ for forgiveness, worship the Blessed Sacrament in her temple (the grotto), and redouble their devotion to the Virgin of Juquila. Twice Nicha allegedly entered a mystical subterranean sanctuary with the Virgin. On one occasion, Nicha went into the grotto and passed into a magnificent rose garden. There, the Virgin told her, "Look my daughter what I have here. If I give you these roses and you take them as a sign, it will bring about another result." During another visionary experience on August 15, 1928, Nicha described seeing a great number of "santos" when she entered the enchanted sanctuary.

Increasing numbers of pilgrims arrived at the grotto as the fall of 1928 progressed. Most of them came with a fervent desire to catch sight of the Virgin. Nicha assured visitors that the Virgin intended to reveal herself, and many of the queries addressed to the Virgin through Nicha broached the issue of when, and under what conditions, this would take place. On All Saints' Day, gatherers learned from Nicha that if all of them, "large and the small," could come together and form "a single heart," the Virgin would appear in a sensational manner for the New Year. As in Tlacox-calco, the issue of having unquestioning faith was important to the de-votees.[48] Once again it emerged in a contentious environment surround-ing an unofficial apparition when devotees suspected that some visitors sought to discredit the new devotion.

By this time, Narváez revealed, tensions with Father Canseco were mounting. On November 4, 1928, Nicha proclaimed that the Virgin wanted a small altar beneath a cross inside the grotto. She instructed those gathered to pray the Rosary there the next morning so that the Virgin could come down and bless them, and added that if Canseco would celebrate another mass at the grotto, all those "who were graced" would see her.[49] By this time, however, Canseco was distancing himself from the devotees. Not only was he probably increasingly uncomfortable with the emergent devotion, but its growth was also undoubtedly threat-ening the older Marian devotion centered in Juquila. Indeed, rumors were circulating that the Virgin of Juquila had decided to move to Ixpantepec.[50] With Juquila's festival approaching on December 8, the parish priest refused to say more masses at the grotto.

Anxiety and activity peaked in December as this anniversary neared. At the grotto, the faithful begged the Virgin to show herself. Nicha sought to calm them, saying that she was busy representing other towns and people before God. The faithful organized a novena scheduled to climax on the 8th. At this point, Nicha relayed that the Virgin wanted a priest to bring the Blessed Sacrament and celebrate Mass in Ixpantepec. But Canseco refused, arguing that he was too occupied with festival preparations. In his absence large numbers of people gathered at the grotto and recited the prayers of mass together. They sent Nicha to secure the Virgin's blessing, and she returned instructing them to kneel. Then, according to Narváez, as another woman invoked the Trinity, flashes of miraculous light shone on the faithful.[51]

Here doña Matildita's report fails us. The extant text is incomplete, ending abruptly when Narváez began to describe her own queries addressed to the Virgin. She claimed that Canseco had prohibited her from visiting Ixpantepec, and as a result, she suffered a "great burden on my conscience that left me profoundly unsettled." In May 1931, Narváez defied her pastor and went with Nicha to the apparition site to ask the Virgin if she could take up her cause with the visiting bishop.[52] We may never know more about her request, but its very existence suggests that Nicha and the Virgin approved.

THE VISIONS ARE DEMONIC

Narváez's testimony underscores the energy and anxiety—both in Nicha's visions and devotee actions—focused on Father Canseco. Repeated gestures and pronouncements broached securing the pastor's mediating/ sanctifying ritual presence, and no one emerged as a popularly ordained substitute when it became clear that Canseco sought to suppress the devotion. In addition, none of our sources mention efforts to find a different priest to officiate, as was the case in Tlacoxcalco. It is also notable how much Nicha stressed devotion to the Blessed Sacrament, a key aspect of the reformed piety emphasized by priests and canonically structured associations like the Apostolado in the decades before 1928. It is possible that the movement's epistolary voice, Narváez, exaggerated the devotees' orthodoxy, or simply expressed her personal concerns. Alternatively, perhaps she merely sustained her role as a Catholic educator, and inculcated pilgrims, and even Nicha, with these ideas. In any case, Canseco's testimony provides a very different picture of the Virgin of Ixpantepec and *los interesados*.

Born in Oaxaca City in 1870, Ausencio Canseco emerged from the reformed Oaxacan seminary and expressed his desire to embrace the clerical state in November 1893 when he petitioned to receive minor orders. He had entered the seminary in 1887, the inaugural year of Eulogio Gillow's crusade to revamp clerical education and produce a bumper crop of priests steeped in ultramontane revivalism. Canseco earned exemplary grades and enjoyed a sterling reputation. His ordination file demonstrates that he weathered an academic (and one wonders if also vocational) slump in 1891 and 1892 when his grades dipped bellow "excellent" to "very good" and "good." But he completed his final year of preparation in 1893, and as diaconal ordination loomed, he maintained extraordinary focus, getting the highest possible marks in Holy Scripture, moral theology, dogmatic theology, and ecclesiastical history. In addition, witnesses testified formulaically, but nonetheless emphatically, that he frequented the sacraments, avoided profane pursuits, and came from an honorable family.[53]

His class origins are unclear, but he was not from a wealthy family. Like many of his fellow priests, he was probably a studious boy from the urban middle sector of society. A photograph of him made when he was perhaps in his late twenties or early thirties reveals a resolute, slightly portly cleric enveloped by a cape. Besides a round face of strongly Hispanic features, only a pair of sturdy boots peer out from beneath his dramatic black wrap. Archbishop Gillow noted in his pastoral visit diaries that he ordained Canseco in 1896. Subsequently, he served briefly as assistant pastor in Etla before gaining his own parish in Tecomastlahuaca. In 1898, the prelate found him happy in his new post, living with two of his sisters.[54]

In 1902, the archbishop sent the promising young priest to the important shrine parish of Juquila. That year the often-lauded pastor, Father Manuel Ramírez (later elevated to canon), gained a transfer from Juquila to a Central Valley parish. Ramírez had written to the ecclesiastical government during his tenure in Juquila complaining about how difficult it was to minister there. He claimed that the parish experienced great difficulty recovering from the brutal repression of the 1896 Chatino Revolt. Many men had been killed or imprisoned, and few families could afford the usual fees and offerings that supported him. He described a general indifference toward the church beyond the residents' interest in making money during the Virgin of Juquila's feast. His parishioners lacked affection for the priesthood, he asserted, and habitually charged him extra for goods. He also complained about the district prefect's sustained efforts to undermine him.[55] Nonetheless, Ramírez's impending exit from Juquila inspired petitions from Catholic associations begging the archbishop to repeal his transfer.[56]

It is a testament to Gillow's high opinion of Canseco that he assigned him to the difficult parish. The young priest did not disappoint him, serving admirably for the next thirty-one years in Juquila. His career demonstrates that the ecclesiastical government felt the need for a trustworthy, strong-willed pastor there. As we have seen in the case of Tututepec, they relied on him to investigate his fellow priests in the region who had trouble administering their parishes, engendered excessive complaints from parishioners, or maintained conflictive relations with civil authorities. His letters to his superiors indicate that he worked hard, often administering other parishes in addition to Juquila. Like many of his counterparts in rural Oaxaca, Canseco maintained a ministry on horseback, visiting many communities separated by large distances and harsh terrain. Writing to the secretary of the archdiocese from his circuit in 1931, he described a nomadic existence, *"doctrinando, predicando, y sacramentando"* (indoctrinating, preaching, and administering the sacraments) in two different parishes.[57] In fact, the reliable padre died on the road. On August 24, 1933, he fell off his horse and drowned in the flood-swollen Sola River as he hurried between communities.[58]

When Father Canseco confronted news of apparitions within his parish, he was coping with the local manifestations of the late 1920s church-state conflict, which Catholics at the time simply called *"el conflicto religioso."* Like many other regions in Mexico, this clash evolved as part of the revolution. Residents of Juquila struggled through a long period of turmoil that does not correspond to conventional dates associated with the storied political upheaval. Rival armed groups professing allegiance to Zapata and Carranza fought over Juquila several times in the late 1910s, and self-described Zapatistas still roamed and raided in the region as late as 1927.[59] Father Canseco's letters reveal him deploying a triage-like approach during this period, seeking above all to maintain regular services and sacraments in the parish seat, along with the Virgin of Juquila's festival. In addition, he also guarded the funds and ornaments "belonging" to the revered image. Like his colleagues throughout Oaxaca, he had to cede control of the parish church and its contents to the newly legislated local juntas in the fall of 1926. Attesting to his skills, Canseco stacked Juquila's church committee with supporters, although a few allies of the municipal president also served on this body. The parish priest maintained that this politician was bent on plundering the shrine and controlling the Virgin's festival. He fretted that his allies might be tricked due to their simple indigenous nature.[60]

Canseco considered himself a victim of "true religious persecution." He claimed that the municipal president found praying and singing at the shrine irritating, reported private baptisms and domestic worship to state authorities, and when possible, confiscated religious objects. Despite these details, however, Canseco's reports indicate that the real apple of discord was economic. In Oaxaca there is an adage linking holy images and public works: "*Santo milagroso . . . que coopere!*" (Miraculous image . . . ante up!)[61] Local factions in Juquila believed they sat atop a gold mine and angled for access to the Virgin's wealth. According to the pastor, his opponents argued amongst themselves about how to use the imagined windfall of church funds in 1926; different groups lobbied for their use in underwriting legal disputes with neighboring towns, public education, instrument purchases for a town band, public salaries, or as loan capital for private entrepreneurial activities. In the end, they commandeered small amounts of cash and goods such as wax, furnishings, and curtains. Apparently, Canseco outmaneuvered them while they bickered. He mentioned spiriting three thousand pesos to the archdiocese, and as we saw in the Narváez case, he hid sums with trusted locals. Counting on factionalism, he placed Juquilita's jeweled clothing and accessories in a special room under municipal seal and protected by two locks. The keys remained with chosen, separate committee members. Canseco also engaged in a certain degree of intrigue himself. He coached supporters, spied on opponents, tapped the church hierarchy's political connections in the state capital, and arranged for his allies to receive preferential treatment whenever possible. In one instance, he secured the ecclesiastical waiver of impediments to a helpful lieutenant's marriage aspirations.[62] In another instance, he managed to get an antagonistic tax official transferred out of the region.

Canseco's other pastoral duties suffered during this period, but he did not abandon Juquila's villages, and, as we saw in Tututepec, the archdiocese sent him to check on nearby colleagues. At times he strategically scheduled visits to villages to avoid Juquila's intrigues.[63] One of his more interesting tasks, however, was investigating allegations of religious schism in the neighboring parish of Teotepec. In Mexico City, the Calles administration attempted to create an independent Mexican Catholic Church and recruited dissident priests to staff it. The initiative proved a failure, but it raised the specter of rupture within the church.[64] In rural areas far from Oaxaca City, the archdiocese's ability to control its ministers had always been limited, but in the late 1920s, the hierarchy became especially sensitive to news that priests ignored the suspension of religious services. In a somewhat paranoid leap, the thinking was that if individual priests said masses and celebrated public festivals in spite of the ban, then they must have come to terms with the government and schismatics. The rural laity had more intimate concerns. If a priest disobeyed the church, were the sacraments he performed valid? If not, the devout feared, souls were in danger. Priests wrote the archdiocese asking for guidance when concerned individuals came to them from other parishes demanding repeat baptisms and claiming their pastor had defected to the government.[65] The vicar general, Carlos Gracida, sent stern letters to suspected turncoats, appealing to their sense of kinship as brothers in the priesthood and alluding to the ultimate spiritual sanction if they did not repent.[66]

Canseco's investigation of Teotepec's Father Aureo Castellanos, a priest in a parish where apparitions linked to those in Ixpantepec later emerged, is perhaps the best documented of such cases in the archdiocese. Rumors that Castellanos "had surrendered to the government" came to light in 1927. Worried parishioners surreptitiously copied documents in Teotepec's municipal archive and sent them along with an anonymous denunciation, to archdiocesan authorities.[67] As a result, Canseco went to Teotepec several times to investigate. He reported that Castellanos was indeed celebrating fiestas and masses in the churches of his parish by arrangement with local officials and found his colleague combative. Castellanos criticized the hierarchy's policies, claiming they were insensitive to his ministry in Teotepec. Faulting the preeminence of the church's national political concerns, he maintained that the suspension of religious services threatened to undermine the faith of his pueblos. According to Castellanos, the prohibitions perhaps made sense in Mexico City, but in distant Indian communities, ritual continuity was imperative. He insinuated that his Chatino parishioners would return to their idolatrous past in the absence of regular services. Furthermore, he maintained that what took place in his remote parish should not trouble authorities. Canseco excoriated his colleague's attitude toward his vows of obedience, and Castellanos agreed to amend his ways. Juquila's parish priest continued to relay information on him to the archdiocese over the next few years.[68]

Amidst investigations and administrative tasks in neighboring parishes, and politicking in Juquila, Canseco felt besieged when he heard that a girl in Ixpantepec held periodic consultations with the Virgin. In his correspondence the padre portrayed himself as a righteous, spiritual soldier in the church's hour of difficulty. He described his frustrations and tribulations as the Virgin's way of testing him. Assuming there were no earlier letters that have perished from the archives, he waited almost six months before reporting to his superiors on the matter. The long delay in sending his report to church authorities, and his minute descriptions of the visionary testimony, indicate that Nicha's purported conferences with the Virgin, and the apparitions reported by visiting pilgrims, unsettled the seasoned clergyman.

Canseco's actions and analysis of the apparitions show him grappling with the conundrum of Catholicism in modernizing society. Dogma dictated that visions validated Catholic belief in earthly divine action. This belief was especially important among Catholics sensing their faith under rationalist assault. Yet Canseco, a native of the state capital, must have known that reports of supernatural visions among an infamously rebellious indigenous group in the midst of church-state tensions would arouse suspicions. In addition, it would be difficult to convince his superiors that the Ixpantepec visions were indeed divine. A full archdiocesan investigation posed significant risks for the padre, arising from his participation in earlier rituals at the grotto. Moreover, official validation of the miracles would have occasioned many potential problems for the

Oaxacan church, ranging from interpreting their meaning and controlling devotional practices, to explaining the miracles to modern urbanites and managing the political fallout. These larger issues must have been on his mind in 1928 and 1929. But if we accept his word, Canseco believed wholeheartedly that supernatural visions were taking place at the grotto. He also had to explain the apparitions in his own parish among people less encumbered by secular rationalism. This issue was crucial, since his long-time henchwoman, Matilde Narváez, had begun to champion the visions. He must have wondered if the Mother of God had indeed chosen to speak to her troubled flock through a young Indian girl. The officially sanctioned apparitions, such as Guadalupe, Lourdes, and Fatima, could be construed as precedents. Perhaps Mary chose his parish for a campaign to strengthen the resolve of the faithful and conquer the hearts of Catholicism's enemies during the church's hour of need. By the time he sent in his detailed reports in January 1929, he had made up his mind, but mindful of protocol, he left the final analysis to his superiors: "The fact of the apparitions of the divine images is true, very true, but not everyone sees them. Hence, it is necessary to determine if the cause of these apparitions is good or bad; either it is God through the ministry of his angels, or it is the devil planning some evil outcome."[69] Thus he assured authorities that the visions indeed took place, but he structured his report to emphasize the unholy anomalies within the visions and Nicha's claims, and hence made his case that demonic agency powered these paranormal occurrences.

Canseco's adamant assertion that real supernatural visions were taking place, however, necessitated detailed description.[70] On January 12 and 16, 1929, Father Canseco penned letters to the archdiocesan government detailing the events of Ixpantepec and the emergence of visions in other towns. In his latter dispatch, Canseco relayed his interpretation of the same visionary scorned by the Oaxacan press—the pilgrim merchant from San Andrés Miahuatlán, Mr. Sánchez Alcántara. Perhaps the presence of numerous pilgrims in the region, and the certainty that news had reached the Central Valley, induced the priest to send his reports to the curia at this time. Canseco assumed the voice of a cautious, expert observer and faithful subordinate. His testimony reveals a remarkable visionary diversity and complexity in action at Ixpantepec and Temaxcaltepec (a village within the parish of Teotepec). Describing a crescendo of visionary claims and pilgrimages since early November 1928, the pastor emphasized the experiences of male visitors while relegating Nicha to secondary status. In fact, he minimized the role of women in general in his rendering of the events. Above all, he sought to convince his superiors of the great number and extraordinary nature of the visions reported and to underscore disturbing characteristics and doctrinal errors indicating that dark forces were afoot.

In his first letter dedicated to the visions at the grotto of Ixpantepec, Father Canseco described three distinct types of grotto experiences. One set of visitors saw nothing out of the ordinary. These were not skeptics, but rather participants in the rituals established at the site. They approached the cave on their knees, praying, singing and doing penance, and yet perceived nothing unusual. A second group observed images in the patterns produced by the combination of water seeping across the stones inside the grotto and the multitude of candles crowding the entrance. A third group described three-dimensional moving images in sizes ranging from tiny to natural human scale. They abruptly appeared and disappeared, and were often seen best by those looking at the grotto from a distance. Visionaries most often claimed to see manifestations of Mary (Soledad, Guadalupe, Juquila, Carmen, and Monserrat). They also described shimmering lights within the grotto, the Blessed Sacrament in the monstrance, and the Christ Child of Atocha. Some visionaries told of entire processions, such as the Virgin of Solitude leading a group of saints, or the Blessed Sacrament heading a glowing parade, while others reported seeing Christ crucified. Still others described seeing the Virgin of Solitude bless them, making the sign of the cross with her hands held together and then opening her hands like a priest at Mass. Canseco, however, noted that this apparition signed the cross from right to left instead of left to right.[71]

He also listed several visions of *"figuras malas"* (bad or evil figures). Among them he described a fire-breathing monkey and a wounded devil. In one instance, a man saw a dapper figure seated on an altar inside the cave surrounded by natural flowers. This supernatural *charro catrín*—a version of the iconic, dandy-like Satan of Mexican folklore—was dressed in black, with a long, pointed white collar. He sported rakish sideburns and a stylish, wide-brimmed hat with iridescent little points around the rim, which glimmered as he moved his head. Other visionaries maintained that they had seen hell and purgatory, and one witness noticed a wheel turning inside the cave, with demons and souls dangling from its perimeter. Another observer described an archangel wearing ammunition belts and leading many armed followers.[72]

The variety of visions and inconsistencies astounded Canseco. In exasperation, he recorded strange or incomprehensible apparitions, such as a loosely saddled neighing horse, large snakes, a woman with a tall ghost on her head, and flying flowers, before giving up and writing, "etc, etc . . ." He also noted almost laughable discrepancies. In one case two men praying together saw a figure emerging from the grotto: one of them saw the Virgin of Juquila, while the other reported only a chicken. In addition, people in groups would often see sacred figures that others failed to perceive, no matter how much their companions coached them.

In the second half of his report, Canseco turned his attention to Nicha. The priest described her as an uncouth, poor, taciturn, eight- or nine-year-old native of Ixpantepec. He also relayed his suspicion that the girl's hovering mother controlled her actions. Since the beginning of the apparitions, he reported, Nicha maintained that she met with the Virgin and one or two angels in the small cave. The Virgin, apparently, seldom spoke, relying on an angel to transmit her dispositions. Typically, visitors would congregate before the grotto, and Nicha would enter it with their petitions, seeking blessings, responses to a wide variety of questions, and cures. Some pilgrims needed a translator to communicate with Nicha.[73] Then the girl would enter the small opening in the stone while the anxious pilgrims waited in front of the cave. From there they could only see her from the waist down as she presented their requests. Canseco tartly remarked, "It seems that this small cavity serves as the conference room of the Virgin, the angel, and the girl." In many cases, Nicha returned suggesting that the supplicants take the water that emerged from the cave and drink it, bathe in it, or apply it to afflicted areas of the body. Some witnesses observed miraculous transformations in Nicha's attire while she was in the grotto. Instead of her usual lowly, unshod appearance she reappeared brilliantly clad in white stockings, good shoes, and a rich dress. Canseco, however, asserted that many supplicants left unsatisfied. Nonetheless, despite these failures and the fact that they could not see the angel or the Virgin, others professed a blind faith in Nicha's pronouncements.

A lack of certifiable cures became a key component of Canseco's argument against Nicha's revelations. Calling miraculous healing "the seal of the divine," he tested the seer. He suggested that Nicha cure three individuals, which he selected. The padre clearly chose a symbolic range of supplicants: a man with stroke-induced partial paralysis, another man with a mental disorder, and a blind woman. Canseco stressed that all of them made the journey to the grotto with great sacrifice. Nicha returned from a consultation in the grotto, however, saying that none of them were worthy of a cure. Insinuating some divine sanction was the source of their afflictions, she stated enigmatically that the first two should remember the cause of their illness.

The suspicious parish priest cited other problems with Nicha's testimony and comportment. He was particularly critical of the unbelievable nature of statements that Nicha attributed to the Virgin, deeming these worthy of quotation. She occasionally denied requests, saying, "The Virgin is not here—she will return later," or "She is too busy," or "She is making arrangements with him who rules." Sometimes she kept pilgrims at a distance, claiming: "The Holy Virgin says not to bunch up in the cave." She even asked some supplicants to wait, claiming, "The Holy Virgin went to take a bath, but she will bathe quickly." Still most damning in the cleric's eyes, Nicha announced, "The Holy Virgin says that the girl should be in charge of all the alms collected at the grotto." Furthermore, Canseco underscored Nicha's attempts to obstruct church protocol. Apparently he caused great concern among believers when he announced that he would submit a report to Oaxaca's ecclesiastical authorities, and secure an official determination on the visions. Devotees immediately asked Nicha to consult with the angel and she informed Canseco, "*it would not be a good idea, or that I not notify the archdiocese.*"[74]

Canseco defied Nicha, *los interesados,* and the Virgin of Ixpantepec, and contacted his superiors. He offered his "humble opinion" that a grave doctrinal error had emerged. Many of the visitors, including "educated people," believed that in the cave, or within the rock itself, the Virgin Mary resided in body and soul, "as if she lived there." Some of them claimed that the celestial court also dwelt there. Canseco identified the key propagator of these ideas as a pious woman from Juquila (clearly Narváez) who attended pilgrims as they arrived at the site. This person, he claimed, inculcated them with the notion that the Virgin inhabited the very stones, and that within the mountain itself, she maintained a magnificent, supernatural shrine.[75]

The oral testimony of present-day Juquila resident Justina Vásquez reveals that others beyond Canseco found Nicha's statements and visions troubling. Vásquez was born after the apparitions, but her mother, father, and sister joined the rush to the apparition site and described the events years later. Revealing the tensions these apparitions must have caused among devoted Catholics, Vásquez reports that Matilde Narváez was her mother's godmother and a blood relative. Furthermore, Vásquez's mother was also a teacher at Juquila's Catholic school under doña Matildita, and the two women were close collaborators, laboring together in support of the church. Quite likely, Vasquez's mother was among the women Narváez led to Ixpantepec. The Vásquez family approached the apparition site with great reverence but became suspicious when Nicha announced that the Virgin was unavailable because she was visiting other nations. Concerns evolved into outright alarm when other pilgrims reported visions of faceless figures in procession. This informant contradicts Canseco's claims that Nicha's statements were simply trivial or odd. Vásquez maintains that Nicha's proclamations inspired great respect, especially when she predicted the earthquake that leveled much of Oaxaca on January 14, 1931. But, falling in line with Canseco, Vásquez cautioned, the devil also knows what the future holds.[76]

Canseco's January 12 report is missing its concluding page, or pages, but on the last extant page, he appeared to conclude his remarks by listing some parting "other strange details." Nicha, he claimed, went back and forth from her supposed celestial consultations without demonstrating any change in her emotional state or manifesting any abnormality. She remained cold and indifferent both coming and going from her meetings with the Virgin. He also mentioned that another girl sometimes fulfilled Nicha's role as the Holy Mother's human intermediary. Some witnesses told him that on at least one occasion, this child emerged temporarily transformed from the cave in the garb of an angel with a white sash covering her torso, and with wings, a diadem, and fair skin. But, added the perplexed priest, she also emerged with a white beard.[77]

Canseco's account stressed that the apparitions were real but questioned their provenance. He also added that rumors of new apparitions in other places had begun to emerge in different communities.[78] According to Vásquez, Canseco performed a ritual test at the apparition site in order to expose the force behind the visions. Apparently, the padre recited some incantations and sprinkled holy water on a boulder at the site, rending the stone in half. This indicated to the priest, and presumably others, that *"el enemigo"* (the enemy) was at work in Ixpantepec.[79] Canseco never mentioned this test in his reports, but he was clearly leaning toward a demonic hypothesis when he wrote the January 12 report.

Four days later he sent another letter to his superiors, detailing a vision from Temaxcaltepec that provided further evidence that evil forces were at work. Although Canseco did not name his source, the vision he related and other details he supplied indicate that the visionary in question was none other than Mr. Sánchez Alcantara, the same pilgrim-seer who had been at the center of *El Mercurio's* story on the apparitions. The pastor described him as a knowledgeable, well-respected, pious man. Apparently he claimed that apparition sites near Juquila were more important than the sacred places in Jerusalem. He maintained that he had seen the entire celestial court and the Virgin "in body and soul," declaring his intentions to organize a great pilgrimage from his hometown. Canseco indicated that this seer had visited the "three places" attracting pilgrims (presumably Ixpantepec, Temaxcaltepepc, and Nopala) and had witnessed marvelous things at each locale. His most powerful supernatural experience, though, took place at a grotto near Temaxcaltepec.

According to Sánchez Alcántara, while praying the Rosary on his knees, the Virgin appeared to him in the opening of the cave and then vanished. Subsequently, the Christ child appeared on a bed of flowers, and a pair of white hands materialized to comfort him before a female saint undertook his care. Then the Virgin Mary returned and picked up the baby, and the entire scene began to glow with resplendent light. Suddenly he perceived a magnificent temple within the stone, and at that moment, a multitude of priests and bishops emerged. Standing out amongst them, a prelate appeared wearing a miter that towered above all others. The pilgrim asked for the Virgin's blessing, but the clergyman with the impressive miter blocked her effort to bestow this grace. Shortly thereafter, clerics in the vision offered the seer a book with gold letters, which he refused. But later he accepted a smaller book. Then as he called out, "Lamb of God who takes away," all of those present beat their chests and the vision vanished. Awestruck, Sánchez Alcántara collapsed to the ground. But when he redirected his gaze toward the cave, the Virgin appeared again, this time from another part of the rock face on the mountainside. She blessed him and disappeared.[80]

THE VISIONS WERE DELINQUENT

In Oaxaca's archdiocesan archive and Juquila's parish archive, there is no record of an official pronouncement on Nicha's conferences with the Virgin or Sanchéz Alcántara's visions in Temaxcaltepec. The hierarchy probably decided to deal with these phenomena quietly. The most likely source of more information would be Canseco's personal correspondence, but none of his letters remain at the shrine. As was common, the archdiocese probably conveyed its determinations through trusted emissaries. This paperless communication, while frustrating for today's scholars, was a crucial tool, especially during tense times like the late 1920s. It may not have been efficient, but it was more secure than the mail, and added a level of authority in the person of a trusted messenger who frequently outranked the recipients. It also gave the archdiocese another opinion on events far from Oaxaca City.[81] Thus, aside from a short note written by the vicar general to Canseco's successor in 1934, we are dependent on the letters written to the ecclesiastical government from Juquila.[82]

By the time Canseco wrote his reports in January 1929, and probably earlier, he and his one-time ally, Matilde Narváez, were at loggerheads over the apparitions, and after 1931, the issue of her misuse of shrine funds also appears in both of their letters. In earlier reports he had refrained from naming her, although he alluded to a woman from Juquila as the leader of *los interesados*. In May 1930, though, the pastor openly attacked doña Matildita with passion. Demonstrating that there is no dispute as bitter as a challenge within the fold, Canseco maligned Narváez's character and apparitionist crusade, implying that the hierarchy supported his interpretation of the visions. He referred to the ex–school principal as the "fomenter and soul of the disturbances at Ixpantepec's cave" and asserted that she misled others, teaching that "those diabolical visions" were indeed divine apparitions of the Virgin. Still worse, carped Canseco, Narváez openly challenged his religious authority in Juquila, claiming that just as Catholics believed in the sanctity of Mass, they should trust in the presence of the Virgin at the grotto. Thus in his view, she propagated the error that the Virgin physically inhabited the cave. The parish priest warned that she refused to heed the archbishop's "sagacious resolution" and threatened to take her case personally to Oaxaca and even Rome. Indeed hoping to outmaneuver Canseco, she undertook the four-day trek to Oaxaca in April 1930. She attempted to conceal this journey from her pastor, but people saw her in transit and alerted him.[83] Two years after this letter and Narváez's surreptitious trip to the state capital, the persistent local religious intellectual and apparition devotee sent her report on Nicha's visions to the archdiocese. We have no firm evidence of the curia's reception of the intrepid, devout lady or its response to her 1932 report, but it was most likely negative—or perhaps an indirect rejection, reminding her to submit to her parish priest.

A couple years later, the struggle was over. Canseco was dead and Narváez had given up. On February 8, 1934, the champion of the Ixpantepec apparitions wrote a heart-wrenching letter to the archbishop.[84] She appears to have renounced hope of the apparition's official recognition, but her tone reveals a deep sense of spiritual and personal angst related to her standing in the church, and a passionate, enduring faith in Nicha's visionary calling. First, she solicited an extension of her debt, stressing the tribulations buffeting Juquila: the death of Canseco, cold weather, sickly cattle, and an acute shortage of money. She then pleaded to be freed from the prohibitions barring her from visiting the apparition site so she could go with Nicha to "speak with the Virgin of the grotto of Ixpantepec to see if we can communicate with His Majesty, and I will inform him. In this region there is sickness, and we are threatened by earthquakes and other calamities; for these reasons I would like to go with the girl that speaks to her so she can tell us what to do."[85] Narváez also alluded to negotiations with Canseco before he died, and a pending agreement related to her petition concerning the Virgin. The pastor, she claimed, had promised to lift the sacramental ban, and she beseeched the archbishop to allow her the sacred benefits of communion. Finally, Narváez rhetorically threw herself at the archbishop's feet, reiterating her desperate desire to go back to the apparition site and secure the Virgin's assistance.[86]

Those inclined to believe in Nicha's visions may have interpreted Canseco's untimely drowning as a divine punishment, but popular support for the visions may have already faded by the time of his death. Not long after Narváez wrote her final letter, the vicar general outlined his response in a terse, bureaucratic letter to Canseco's successor, Tereso Frías, dated February 23, 1934.[87] Gracida appended a typed copy of Narváez's 1932 report (the only extant copy) and mentioned her more recent letter. He said that Narváez had been instructed to address all further inquiries to Frías, who would, in turn, receive instructions from the ecclesiastical government. Gracida told Frías that Narváez had previously been informed of the archbishop's emphatic ruling against the visions. Moreover, she remained prohibited from returning to the apparition site. With this dispatch, the vicar general simply invoked the church's principle of hierarchical obedience and refused to address Narváez directly. He did not even mention the sacramental ban. Afterwards, the archdiocesan documentation on Nicha, doña Matildita, and visiting visionaries ceases.

In Ixpantepec and Juquila, life lumbered on. Nicha stayed in her hometown and raised a family. As for Narváez, her campaign to legitimize the apparitions may have collapsed, but her faith had not. She died an impoverished, neglected spinster sometime in the 1940s, absolutely convinced of the sacrality of the events she witnessed in 1928.[88] Canseco's nephew, Rafael León, expressed pity for Narváez seventy years later, declaring that the elderly doña Matildita's obsession with the Ixpantepec apparitions initiated her mental deterioration.[89]

One individual, however, sought to record an account of events. In the late 1970s and 1980s, Hilario Cortés undertook a history of Juquila and the region. In all likelihood, he attended the school run by Matilde Narváez. Cortés accompanied Canseco on his rounds in the 1910s and 1920s and noted in his diary that he went with the pastor to Oaxaca City in 1912.[90] As mentioned previously, León, Canseco, and Cortés briefly fled to Ixpantepec together in 1919. In the early 1920s, Cortés entered the seminary in Oaxaca City, only to return to Juquila when authorities temporarily closed the institution in 1926.[91] There he started an eclectic career and developed an eccentric reputation. Recalled as *el pingüino* (the penguin) for waddling about town in a black suit, hat, and matching umbrella, he was a scribe-for-hire and served as municipal secretary for various towns. In this capacity, he gained renown for inventing surnames for those who lacked them, still a common phenomenon among indigenous Oaxacans in the early twentieth century. Cortés also worked as a schoolteacher, hired prayer leader at funerals, and even enjoyed a reputation for curing.[92] In short, the civil-religious turmoil of the 1920s short-circuited his plans to become a priest, but he nonetheless became a local intellectual and religious specialist.

Cortés never realized his dream of publishing a regional history, but fragments of his manuscript endure in private hands.[93] He conceived of his opus in the nineteenth-century manner of town-by-town descriptions of climate, economy, history, and customs. Luckily, his analysis of the Ixpantepec apparitions survived. Although he assumes a third-person voice in the beginning of his narrative, as he progresses he drifts into the first-person plural, revealing that he was on hand. His analysis at a distance of fifty or sixty years diverges from that of his mentor and provides important details about the ambience of the apparition site that contradicts Narváez.

Cortés argued that there were no miracles of either divine or diabolical origin. He depicted the entire episode with a distinct smug disdain, describing a backward Indian village and a con artist's moment of fame before a rapid, and deserved, return to obscurity. He claimed that a conniving Nicha availed herself of intense popular unease and succeeded in deceiving thousands of ignorant believers with her fraudulent visions and consultations. According to Cortés, the sham began when Nicha returned from her daily chores, claiming to have been surprised by the Virgin, who instructed her to tell the people of Ixpantepec that they should immediately build a temple and render homage at the grotto. But many people refused to believe her, prompting the girl to issue threats of imminent divine punishments. Cortés asserted that it was the synergy of Nicha's threats, a profound popular apprehension rooted in 1928's earthquakes, and Madre Matiana's apocalyptic prophecies that inspired the explosion of visionary fervor among "*el vulgo*" (the ignorant rabble). It was Cortés who recorded that people called Nicha the "second Juan Diego." He also described a remarkable social reversal. For a time, he averred, the poor Indian seer enjoyed a level of respect uncommon for a country girl of her "social class."

Cortés emphasized an environment of intimidation at the apparition site, claiming that Nicha and her cohorts maintained that those who failed to see visions faced eternal suffering. He declared that he and others were interrogated about what they saw, and since they feared being classified among the damned, they gave vague replies, such as "we saw what everyone sees." In other instances, Cortés asserted, visionaries fell victim to their own ignorance and imputed supernatural agency to the visual effects caused by the mirror-like aspect of water seeping over the cave's walls, the flickering light of hundreds of candles, and the patterns produced by the bryophytic plants growing on the stone. He also claimed that Nicha and her supporters chastised any visitor who had the temerity to call the grotto a "cave"; they demanded that all refer to it as the Virgin's temple. Finally, Cortés noted, after consultation with archdiocesan authorities, Canseco condemned the apparitions as diabolical, and someone burned all the structures built on the site by the peddlers of candles, religious trinkets, and foodstuffs. Petty entrepreneurs, Cortés scoffed, were the real beneficiaries of Nicha's visions.[94]

SEVEN

≈ The Gender Dynamics of Devotion

Several vans in present-day Oaxaca City leave for Juquila every day. They lumber through traffic, slip into the southern arm of the Central Valley, and retrace the venerable pilgrimage route leading from the provincial capital to the shrine pueblo perched in the mountains. If you brought along a copy of *Memorias de la portentosa imagen de Juquila*, you could follow an eighteenth-century account of the journey and devotional traditions, noting landmark towns, rivers, and mountains.[1] It used to be an arduous four-day trek. Over the last century, the trip became progressively shorter, as infrastructural improvements inched into the Oaxacan countryside. First a railroad spur penetrated the southern Central Valley, and later, bus service followed sporadic road construction toward the Pacific Ocean, coffee plantations, and the Virgin's sanctuary. Today you can reach the shrine in about four hours.

If you inquire about the Virgin of Ixpantepec in Juquila and nearby villages, you can expect a three-tiered response. First, people will attempt to correct you: "You mean the Virgin of Juquila?" Then, they will suggest that you have mistakenly attributed to Ixpantepec its neighbor Amialtepec's claim as the original site of Juquila's appearance and devotion. Finally, if you persist, a few older residents will concede that they recall stories of apparitions in Ixpantepec; however, they stress, the visions proved false. For many, that ends the discussion. Indeed, the failed apparition movement is almost a cliché throughout the Catholic world—a popular revelation emerges and inspires hope and heightened devotion, only to be stifled or fade, and become a parable of popular superstition in historical memory. The events then languish in the silent shame of disgraced seers and geriatric recollection before being forgotten altogether. In Ixpantepec, most people proclaim complete ignorance of the miracles and prophecies that made their community a center of Marian devotion and pilgrimage, while lamenting the community's recent loss of several elders—including Nicha—who were alive at that time. Civil authorities lack knowledge of the apparitions or documentation from the period. In fact, they broke into spontaneous laughter upon hearing that Nicha, an old woman they had all known, claimed to have seen and spoken to the Virgin as a child.[2] Thus, the fruits of the "second Juan Diego's" revelations: seventy years later, they inspire humor seasoned with a dash of contempt.

The previous chapter approached this ill-fated apparition movement from the divergent viewpoints of three participants: Matilde Narváez, Ausencio Canseco, and Hilario Cortés. Here I would like attend to other issues manifested in the apparition's history, scrutinize our sources, explore possible Chatino interpretations and the broader ethnocultural ecology of the visions, and discuss the complex gender norms at play. I will also address the relationship between Nicha's visions and the pre-existing prophecy narratives of Madre Matiana, and plumb the issues surrounding the movement's ultimate collapse.

What really happened in Ixpantepec? Did a young Indian girl hatch a theatrical, attention-getting scam? Was she in league with a coven of crones—her own mother and Matilde Narváez—to exploit gullible pilgrims, or were they all duped by the devil? Alternatively, could this be a case of a community's shrine-founding gamble as prevailing economic and cultural currents left it behind? To establish with certainty "what happened" in Ixpantepec during these years is impossible. But even if we cannot hold up a "true" version of events, there is still much to learn from the fragments we can piece together. A strict rationalist interpretation might render the seer as a con artist, the *beata* as an old fool, and the priest as a money-grubbing hack. But this type of analysis casts the event

14 Nicha's overgrown grotto in present-day Ixpantepec (photograph by the author).

on the scrap heap of unimportant past happenings, perpetuating the silencing of nonelite, indigenous, and female historical voices, and belittling the deeply religious worldview of all these actors. The most valuable analysis emerges if we suspend scholarly cynicism and examine the sources as a reflection of their authors' honest appraisal of the events, without losing sight of their respective roles in society.

CHRONOLOGY AND SOURCES

Upon first glance, the apparitions at Ixpantepec seem simple. A girl reported having visions, word spread, and a pilgrimage devotion began to take shape. Then doubts emerged about the seer, the local priest refused to support the visions, prophecies failed to materialize, and the once-burgeoning popular movement ebbed over time. But the devotion had a more complex gestation. The earliest date cited in the sources is June 16, 1928.[3] This was probably not Nicha's first vision. According to Hilario Cortés, Nicha frequently collected firewood near the grotto prior to the polemical miracles, and one day reported having visions after one of these outings. Cortés, however, did not provide a firm date.[4] Nicha may have had a series of visions at the grotto before she shared them with others. Once the visions became public in Ixpantepec, villagers probably pondered them in light of Chatino visionary traditions, but we have no way of knowing when Nicha's relatives and neighbors first heard about the girl's experiences or what was their initial reaction. The fact that none of our informants provided an exact date suggests that there may have been considerable lag time between her first claims of revelation and when they began to cause concern in Ixpantepec. The mid-June date provided by Narváez and its linkage to seismic activity may indicate that at this point Nicha's visions were at least a village-level issue.

None of our sources record the exact date when Canseco answered the summons to witness Nicha's visions. It is possible that Ixpantepec officials notified their pastor after news of the apparitions began attracting outsiders. But Juquila is only a half-day's walk from Ixpantepec, and thus it seems unlikely that word of the visions would have spread far without the priest's knowledge. Moreover, Narváez's account implies that news of the apparitions reached Juquila with this summons and inspired a dash to Ixpantepec among devout Catholics. This moment signaled the transformation of the apparitions from a local village concern into a regional phenomenon. It brought with it an influx of outsiders, setting the stage for a change in visionary content as a broader array of cultural traditions came into play. Essentially, it inaugurated the *mestizaje* of the apparitions. Once Narváez, a respected local thinker and leader in her own right, was on hand, it appears that she assumed an integral role in shaping the understandings, practices, and visionary experiences. She probably influenced Nicha's subsequent visions and pronouncements.

Our evidence hints that the Ixpantepec visions made the transition to regional importance in August 1928. Since we know the region suffered an intense earthquake on August 4, 1928, it is tempting to assert that this event moved Ixpantepec authorities to send for their pastor. Both Narváez's and Cortés's testimony linked the acceptance of Nicha's claims to seismic prophecy and very real earthquakes. Perhaps rattled by the tremors of early August, Ixpantepec's residents were driven to seek Canseco's guidance by fears of further prophetic fulfillment.

Oaxacans visiting the apparition site, as well as those contemplating news of apparitions and natural disasters from afar, drew on Mesoamerican and Hispanic traditions of divine chastisement and supernaturally induced calamity. In Mesoamerican religiosity, problems such as natural disasters, evil, and social unrest suggest disequilibrium in the relationship between human society and the divine that must be ritually addressed. The supernatural has to be propitiated through communal ritual and sacrifice. Indigenous collective ritual therefore focuses on maintaining or restoring cosmic balance in order to avert or mitigate natural or social disasters.[5] European notions of a wrathful God bent on punishing wayward polities emerge from the Old Testament. The tales of floods and pestilence—seasoned with Revelation's enigmatic prognostications—serve as a well of symbolism for Christians contemplating calamity, social conditions, and turbulent politics. Church authorities have a long history of organizing devotion to address these issues. They are part and parcel of the dynamics of personal sin, collective soul-searching, atonement, and notions of the communal experience of God's grace and wrath. These concerns permeate Narváez's letters. It follows that in a religious social environment like rural Oaxaca, believers would inaugurate a movement of penance and expiation.[6] These themes were also at the forefront of international militant Catholicism in the nineteenth and early twentieth centuries, as the church cautioned that the fruit of secularization and modern error would be harsh divine retribution. As we shall see, notions of impending punishment, and the need for devotional mobilization to avert it, were very much present in popular prophecies circulating in Oaxaca.

The apparition movement in Ixpantepec gained momentum throughout the fall of 1928. From September through December, Nicha, doña Matildita, and an expanding number of pilgrims focused their efforts on expiatory devotion. As we have seen, excitement mounted in anticipation of All Saints' Day in November, and a second crescendo of anxiety and activity took shape in early December. According to Canseco, Cortés, and the Oaxacan press, visions also emerged in Temaxcaltepec and Nopala by early January 1929. The mounting tensions of November and December stemmed from the developing conflict between the new devotion and Juquila's festival. The antagonism must have occasioned a taking of sides among the parish's Catholics.

After these dates, we only have snippets of information about what was happening at the grotto. At some point in 1929, Canseco received word that the archdiocese supported his evaluation of the apparitions. In May 1930, vowing to overturn the ruling, Narváez made her visit to the state capital to lobby church authorities in person, but we know nothing of what transpired there. In May 1931, she violated the ecclesiastical prohibition banning her visits to the apparition site, and in April 1932, she filed her petition for official recognition. Presumably, devotional activity took place at Ixpantepec throughout these years, but neither Canseco nor Narváez provided us with any details. Neither of them mentioned further activity at the other visionary sites either. Finally, in her last letter, written in February 1934, Narváez appeared to relinquish hope of official recognition but pleaded for permission to act on her personal beliefs and consult the Virgin, with Nicha's help, in hopes of assuaging local economic problems and natural disasters. The gloom of this letter suggests that between 1932 and 1934, devotional activity at the apparition site had begun to fade, even if the redoubtable doña Matildita remained firm in her faith.

Regrettably, we cannot count on more-detailed accounts from present-day residents of Ixpantepec. The only eyewitnesses of the events that recorded their own interpretations were mestizo residents of Juquila (Narváez, Cortés, and Canseco). Narváez committed herself wholeheartedly to the project of legitimizing the apparitions and the seer, and therefore her testimony focuses closely on events taking place at the grotto and on Nicha's experiences. Her stature as an orthodox stalwart, her religious knowledge, and the prestige rooted in her service as a Catholic educator must have been deployed at the apparition site. Thus, Narváez played a twofold role in editing and shaping the Ixpantepec apparitions (and our understanding of them): first, as a prominent participant and religious authority at the grotto; and second, as the author of the report sent to archdiocesan authorities. One aspect that is immediately evident in her testimony is the complete absence of visions beyond Nicha's. Indeed, she suppressed them in her report. She renders the scene at the grotto as an orderly gathering of devout pilgrims hoping for a personal glimpse of the Virgin and intent on communicating with her through a blessed seer who shared her extraordinary grace. Clearly, Narváez wanted to convince archdiocesan authorities of straightforward Catholic fervor linking a band of faithful believers, Nicha, and the Virgin Mary. In this regard, she assumed the pivotal on-the-ground authorial role observed in more recent apparition movements.[7] Her letters reveal how she fashioned a single coherent narrative from a complicated, multifaceted, regional happening.

Cortés and Canseco described the apparitions very differently than Narváez. Several decades separate Cortés's account from the Ixpantepec apparitions, and his tone as a self-appointed historian infuses his testimony with aloofness, but, nonetheless, he provides us with invaluable information about the popular mood, the experience of skeptics at the grotto, and the issues influencing the visions' reception. But in many ways, his retelling is more a condescending narrative about the region's retrograde Indian towns and gullible rabble than a careful description of the events. Canseco's testimony has its own unique emphases. If Nicha starred in Narváez's depiction of the miracles, she played a suspect, supporting role in the priest's rendering. He slighted the Indian girl both in the structure of his reports and in his depiction of her character and experiences. When he turns his attention to Nicha, it is only to sow doubt about her credibility. In addition, when he finished discussing the seer, he returned to the bizarre visions experienced by others. In contrast with Narváez's portrait of orderly devout fervor, the pastor depicted a visionary free-for-all.

Ubiquitous ethnic and gender biases also shape Canseco's report. With the exception of Nicha, he never mentioned another female visionary, while noting several times that the source of a particular vision was male. In fact, all the women that enter his narrative fare poorly: Nicha, the dubious seer; her mother, a shadowy manipulating force; and Narváez, the fomenter of error. The parish priest made no mention of the indigenous community surrounding the apparition site, and the vague chronology he provided reveals that he did not consider the apparitions worth reporting until they drew "*gente entendida*" (people of understanding). In the context of the rest of his testimony, this label applied to Spanish-speaking men who possessed some education and social rank: hence the weight he placed on the testimony of Sánchez Alcántara, who also attracted the attention of *El Mercurio*'s correspondent. Canseco, in fact, described the apparition movement as if it began with the visionary claims of non-Chatino visitors.

On the surface, Nicha's visions fit the standard description of Latin American and Oaxacan apparitionism. They involve the sacralization, or resacralization, of a concrete place on the local landscape, and they occur at a paradigmatic locus of spiritual activity—a mountain cave or fissure from which water emerges.[8] There are also some interesting resonances between this early-twentieth-century visionary movement and Tzeltal apparitions and social unrest in the eighteenth century.[9] But general similarities to visionary conventions or other apparition movements provide limited insight into the events that came together at Ixpantepec in the late 1920s and early 1930s. Nicha's visionary experiences emerged from a homegrown apparitionist tradition. In all likelihood, she was very familiar with the Virgin of Juquila's and the Virgin of Guadalupe's apparition stories. The Juquila legend is particularly important, since it unfolds in the neighboring village of Amialtepec. According to Chatino legend, the image "was born" in a stone crevice behind a waterfall and appeared to a devout man from the village. The site is still revered in Amialtepec and among other Chatinos, who associate it with the moon, water, and earthly fertility, despite the church's appropriation of the image and management of its devotion in Juquila since the eighteenth century.[10] One of Nicha's visions clearly alluded to the Guadalupe narrative. If doña Matildita faithfully recorded Nicha's visionary experiences, then the Virgin's invocation of the "results" an armful of roses could produce attests to the Chatina girl's personal identification with the original Juan Diego. Nicha may have also known of contemporary unofficial Oaxacan apparitions.

More importantly, Chatino culture maintains a deep visionary tradition overlapping with, but distinct from, Hispanic Catholic conventions.[11] Overshadowed by their more numerous Mixtec and Zapotec neighbors and, until the advent of coffee production, hidden in the remote districts of Juquila and Sola de Vega, Chatinos have sustained a coherent religious tradition across their scattered alpine communities.[12] To date, they maintain a syncretic system whose complexity makes it difficult to categorize in relation to Hispanic Catholicism. According to ethnologists Alicia Barabas and Miguel Bartolomé, Chatino religion and Catholicism endure in a "strange coexistence" rooted in mutual incomprehension.[13] In contrast, James Greenberg describes Chatino religion as a reworking of Catholicism within a preconquest nexus of rituals and ideas.[14] Regardless of how odd their interaction may seem, or how strong preconquest sensibilities remained, at the foot of Nicha's grotto monolingual Indians and orthodox mestizas, and presumably many pilgrims in between these poles of acculturation, felt they were experiencing sublime events of spiritual import.

The Chatino cosmos is a classic Mesoamerican multilayered ecological system, conceived as a sacred entity maintained by ritual interactions, exchange, and reciprocity between cosmic regions. Rituals take place at "doors" separating the various sacred spheres, and Chatinos locate these portals on the landscape. Religious practice is so tied to natural features that it is difficult to separate the Chatino belief system from the local geography. Chatinos consider the entire area where they predominate as a linguistically and sacredly defined region, and within this zone they demonstrate an unlimited ability to generate individualized new religious meanings and rituals focused on geographical features, such as mountains, caves, the confluence of rivers, and springs. Caves are particularly important, since they form entrances into the earth. Thus, they frequent them to contact various mountain, forest, and place deities, as well as ancestors, the devil, and the Virgin.[15]

When scholars contemplate the layered Mesoamerican cosmos, they often depict a two-dimensional cross-section divided into celestial, surface, and subterranean bands. But Chatinos also construct the universe as a system of nested "houses." Linguistically, the words *house* and *body* differ only in tone, and metaphorically, they are interchangeable. Like bodies, human houses and other social structures have hearts, heads, and other corresponding parts. Thus, villages are bodies/houses, and within them, the church, municipal buildings, and the cemetery occupy locations symbolically analogous to body parts. Beyond the community, the universe is both the great house of God the Father and God's body, and mountains are both the homes of local deities and the sacred beings themselves. The very landscape, therefore, is suffused with corporeality and is itself made up of individual supernatural bodies. Extending the concept of house to the entire cosmos projects an idea matrix, rooted in settled human society, onto the supernatural world and the ecosystem, and in doing so, establishes the framework for transactions between them. Chatinos invest a considerable amount of energy on rituals at the "doors" and "houses" located on the landscape. Frequently linked to forces of nature, such as the wind, rivers, mountains, fire, and rain, these gateways/beings have local names like "Santo Dueño," "Dueño del Cerro," and "Dueño de los Animales."[16] Chatinos invoke them to gain access to the bounty of the natural world and to protect community boundaries, lands, and livestock. In true Mesoamerican monist fashion, Chatino religion offers a great number of sacred places/figures/forces within a unified, sacred whole.

Our sources, when commenting on devotional practices centered on the Virgin of Ixpantepec, mention the placement of a cross and an altar at the entrance to the grotto. In addition, they note the presence of hundreds of candles, flowers, and other offerings at the Virgin's temple/cave. Chatino practice revolves around the ritual manipulation of saints, crosses, and candles at sacralized locations governed by a complex ritual calendar. All houses and places have patron saints, and Chatinos buy Catholic images and treat them with great care. They also pay close attention to the arrangement and placement of crosses and candles accompanying the manipulation of images. The metaphorical and symbolic associations of crosses are particularly rich. Linked to pre-Columbian directional concepts and color symbolism, as well as to rain deities, crosses are also bodies, but largely free of associations with Christ. Metaphorically describing the placement of crosses as sewing or planting, Chatinos employ them to mark boundaries, liminal areas, and kinship relations. Burning candles symbolize the human life force, and their consumption of wax represents the steady ebb of life. Almost all Chatino rites involve the placement of candles in patterns mirroring conceptions of the cosmos. Frequently, the appropriate number of candles is thirteen. Thirteen is also the span of days typically required for ritual purification.[17] Thirteen, incidentally, was the number of masses that the Virgin requested at Ixpantepec.

Matilde Narváez emphasized certain pivotal dates that have considerable resonance in Chatino cosmology, and some of Nicha's visions lend themselves to distinctly indigenous interpretations. Chatinos maintain local versions of the Mesoamerican ritual calendar, employ shamanic practices—including the broad use of hallucinogens—and believe in nagualism (protective animal spirit companions). Adapted to the Catholic liturgical calendar, their most important religious event is the All Saints' festival, which coincides with the end of the 260-day ritual cycle centered on distinct new-year themes of order versus disorder, death, and renewal. Men lead all significant public rituals in Chatino communities, although women are usually present. In curing rites and propitiatory rituals, shamans serve as intermediaries who engage sacred entities at the interstices between sacred regions. Many rituals involve psychotropic mushrooms. Shamans use these substances to filter out the extraneous sounds of the world, which allows them to "hear" the supreme deity, the Holy Father Sun. In addition, common people seek personal contact with the divine through hallucinogenic visions. Anthropologists estimate that almost all men and women do so three to four times during their lifetimes. Chatinos perceive these experiences as valuable cathartic exercises allowing individuals to reorient their lives and perceive their destiny.[18]

In all likelihood, Nicha's family and other residents of Ixpantepec viewed the girl's early visions in terms of Chatino thought and practice. First, it seems probable that the grotto had long been a site of ritual, since it contained the attributes that connote sacredness in Chatino tradition— an alpine fissure/cave from which water emerges. There it could be argued that she encountered the "Santa Abuela," a maternal earth/fire deity associated with fertility and ancestor rituals, whom Chatinos believe has an angel *nagual*. Or perhaps they surmised that Nicha stumbled upon the Chatino conception of the Virgin Mary, who is associated with the moon and sources of water. When she continued to have these visions at the grotto, Nicha began to develop a reputation as an intermediary between humans and the supernatural, a time-honored tradition in Mesoamerican cultures. We could also interpret beliefs that the Virgin physically inhabited the mountain as an extension of the Chatino house-body concept. In many ways, this interpretation squares with Nicha's comportment throughout the ordeal. She never attempted to deliver a definitive celestial message, nor did she produce a physical image that could serve as the center of more orthodox Catholic devotion in Ixpantepec's church or a shrine at the apparition site. Many devotions have prospered when an image allegedly miraculously appeared, or alternatively, as in Tlacoxcalco, devotees commission an image to commemorate previous apparitions. Nicha, however, simply positioned herself as a go-between within a cosmology mediated by patron-client relationships and briefly enjoyed a career as a spiritual facilitator.

It is crucial to consider the first days, weeks, and perhaps months when presumably Nicha, her family, and other individuals constructed a local interpretation of the apparition narrative. Sources identify at least two other important players: the seer's mother and the man who performed rituals to relieve Nicha of the paralyzing fright stemming from the darker aspects of her visions. In most apparition movements, a seer's local circle serves as the first level of interpretation and dissemination, as well as the initial shapers of meanings ascribed to the visions. The sense of heightened anticipation at the grotto before All Saints' Day provides a clue about the reception of the apparitions among Chatinos. The coincidence of Nicha's prophesies of the Virgin's public appearance with the All Saints' Day festival marking the end of the Chatino ritual calendar cycle suggests that her visions drew strongly on indigenous practice. Much of the excitement fueling mass peregrination, fervor at the apparition site, and the girl's expanding fame at this stage probably stemmed from their link to Mesoamerican calendrical traditions. In this context, the new Virgin, new seer, and New Year synergies were probably compelling to Chatinos and possibly other indigenous groups.

Perhaps the root of the visionary chaos described by Canseco lay in his inability to understand the visions' indigenous roots. Such bizarre images as those of a bearded girl and strange animals could be explained as manifestations of the Santo Dueños, but they are not easily accommodated within orthodox Catholicism. We could also interpret the visions of the demonic dandy, which Canseco reported, as a manifestation of the classic Mesoamerican depiction of Satan as a rich mestizo *catrín* (i.e., a conspicuously wealthy non-Indian).[19] In addition, the Virgin's request for thirteen masses, the cross, and an altar at the grotto, and the scores of candles around them must have had powerful significance beyond Hispanic Catholic tradition. But the truly remarkable quality of Nicha's visions and those that took place around her was that they did not obey cultural boundaries. In fact, they straddled them and gave birth to multiple interpretations. It is as if the apparitions were tailor-made for cultural code switching. Or perhaps more accurately, they emerged from a multiethnic milieu and hence reflected the complex transcultural multiplicity of meaning and symbolism at play in Oaxaca. Again, a crucial moment was when Ixpantepec's civil authorities called on Father Canseco. Once understanding and interpreting Nicha's visions became a regional issue, the apparitions before the grotto became much more complex religious events that could not be controlled by Nicha, Ixpantepec's authorities, Narváez, nor Canseco.

Clearly, a synergy of issues and events propelled Nicha's visions through linguistic and cultural barriers. Among these factors were intense seismic activity from 1928 to 1931, anxiety over the national church-state conflict, local military and Cristero action, the suspension of religious services, fears of schism, and doubts about rites performed by rumored schismatic priests. As we have seen, the regions of Oaxaca most often mentioned in relation to the apparitions and their pilgrim devotees correspond to the areas where federal troops and antigovernment Catholic groups were most active. These were also the zones where alleged renegade priests practiced in violation of the church's ban on religious services. As the Teotepec case demonstrates, authorities in at least one Chatino community sought the continuity of priest-officiated religious festivals and thus negotiated with their pastor to evade the hierarchy's dictates. Judging from contemporary ethnographies, Chatinos were probably less concerned than their nonindigenous neighbors about the validity of Catholic sacraments, but this issue certainly would have troubled Catholics such as Matilde Narváez. In addition, the 1920s environment of political transition and intermittent violence formed the backdrop of the visions. In fact, one of the visions described by Canseco contained a clear reference to armed hostilities—the gun-belt-wearing Archangel.

Examining an additional preexisting visionary narrative deployed amidst events in Ixpantepec further deepens our understanding of responses to Nicha's visions and illuminates several crucial issues related to the Virgin of Ixpantepec. First, it pushes us to move beyond the discussion of sociopolitical and materialist factors to examine issues of belief spurring social action. Second, it forces us to contemplate an extraregional sphere of religious thinking at play in Ixpantepec. Third, it requires an examination of the gender dynamics of Catholic resurgence and the social norms embedded in local Catholicism. And finally, it helps us understand the pivotal role of Matilde Narváez.

Why would a Catholic woman of doña Matildita's station support the visionary experiences of a poor Indian girl in opposition to her church's religious authorities? Long before Hilario Cortés penned his commentary on Nicha's apparitions, he was Canseco's protégé, and almost certainly Narváez's pupil. He knew both of them very well. Although he never mentioned Narváez specifically, in all likelihood he was thinking about her when he wrote that the concatenation of Nicha's ominous warnings, intense popular apprehension brought on by powerful earthquakes, and the prophecies of La Madre Matiana inspired people to hail the girl as the "second Juan Diego" and converge upon the remote village.[20]

Sources relevant to this legendary seer are sketchy, but appear in two basic categories: references mocking popular superstition, and devout commentaries interpreting the prophecies and their relevance to historical events. In the first group, a revolutionary-era satirical newspaper appropriated "La Madre Matiana" as its title; and she has become a humorous, anthropomorphic nickname for death (as in La Flaca, La Pelona, La Madre Matiana, etc.). She also occasionally appears in the mordant rhymes known as *calaveras*. In a 1930s broadside, entitled "The Doctrine of Madre Matiana," she appears as a rotund, one-eyed fortuneteller with copious freckles and a sagging lower lip. The verses accompanying her likeness lampoon Catholic prayer and fatalism in an acid commentary on postrevolutionary politics.[21] Thus, it appears, a renowned popular seer secured a place in Mexico's rich tradition of irreverent satire as the female incarnation of doom-and-gloom Catholic fanaticism.

Gauging the prophecy's role in Ixpantepec, however, requires attention to documents that approached Matiana seriously. At least three texts on the prophecies probably influenced the apparition movement centered on Nicha and the Virgin of Ixpantepec. They include an 1861 pamphlet published in Mexico City, claiming to be the original text of the prophecies; an 1889 book by Luis Duarte published by Mexico City's Círculo Católico, integrating an allegedly faithful copy of an 1857 text of the prophecies along with in-depth commentary; and a 1910 article in Oaxaca's official archdiocesan organ.[22] The pamphlet stressed that numerous versions of Matiana's prophecies were in circulation throughout Mexico, and indeed she appears in nineteenth-century popular almanacs as well.[23] Many people in Oaxaca probably read about them in cheap printings such as these or listened to local retellings of the visions and ominous portents. Matilde Narváez must have been very familiar with Matiana's prophecies. Chapbooks and pamphlets on the famous prognostications probably sold alongside images of the Virgin, prayer books, and scapulars at Juquila's pilgrimage fair. In addition, Catholic preachers leading annual revivals at the shrine most likely held forth on their contemporary relevance. It is also likely that Narváez knew Duarte's analysis. Market stalls around the Virgin's sanctuary probably sold religious books at the time, as they do today, or it may have found its way into the parish archive thanks to one of Juquila's priests. It is almost certain that Narváez read the article in the archdiocese's *Boletín Oficial*. Since the emergence of this publication in 1901, regulations required that all parish priests in Oaxaca keep a complete set of the archdiocese's official organ. As pastoral visit reports attest, Father Canseco enjoyed a reputation for scrupulous compliance with archdiocesan dictates.[24] Narváez, Juquila's parochial school principal, had access to the parish's collection of books and publications.

In spite of their distinct origins, these three texts are remarkably consistent in their renderings of the prophecies. The 1910 Oaxacan article only glosses them and cites the Duarte text as the definitive interpretation of the visions. Duarte truncated Matiana's prophecies into discreet ideas/ issues and composed nineteen separate chapters examining each of these points. The visionary narrative in this book, nevertheless, is nearly identical to the 1861 pamphlet. According to these sources, the prophecies emerged from Mexico City's Hieronymite convent oral history. Matiana apparently died in the late eighteenth century due to ardent practices of self-mortification, but she entrusted her visions to two disciples. They, in turn, shared the visions decades later with María Josefa de la Pasión de Jesús, known as Madre Guerra, whose testimony on January 18, 1837, is the "original" testament of Matiana's revelations.

Matiana lived most of her life as a servant (*criada*) in various convents. Of humble origins in Tepotzotlán, the young seer caught the eye of a nun at San Juan de la Penitencia. While in this woman's service, she began to gain a reputation for miracles. When her benefactress died, she lived briefly in another convent before the Virgin led her to the Hieronymite order.[25] There, a demented, gluttonous nun hired the budding visionary. Matiana embraced her station with great abnegation, forfeiting her wages and allotment of food to her voracious mistress, and subsisting on stale bread proffered by fellow servants. In addition, she revived a floundering devotional sodality within the convent that emphasized care of the sick and personal humility. Apparently, her stature grew such that the prioress obeyed the *criada* and vice-regal ladies sought her preternatural insights.[26]

In moments of rapture, Matiana communicated with the Virgin and experienced her frightful visions. Within the Hieronymite convent, the Virgin instructed Matiana that an innovative religious order would emerge dedicated to "*el Desagravio de Jesús Sacramentado*" (the Expiation of the Blessed Sacrament). As described by Madre Guerra, the new aggregation of women was to be something of a super-order, with three initial Hieronymite members and others selected from different convents. This new institution, Matiana learned, would be the last establishment of a religious order before the final judgment. These nuns dedicated to acts of expiation were destined to lead a movement of religious renewal emphasizing fervent devotion to the Body of Christ in order to placate the righteous anger of God. The Virgin, Madre Guerra stressed, promised Matiana that the founding members of the order would attain the same stature as the original apostles. Through these nuns' personal piety and the acts of expiation they inspired among others, Mexico would regain divine favor. Old religious orders would resurrect their primordial fervor, lax churchmen would rediscover their pastoral zeal, and sinners would plead for mercy.

Aside from instructing her on the establishment of the Hermanas del Desagravio, the Virgin showed her seer the source of God's looming wrath. Matiana witnessed a secret meeting in hell of demons frustrated by the "Christian peace" of the colonial period: "They formed a congress, and together they made the constitution and the legal code; and Lucifer directed the demons to spread those constitutions throughout the world to pervert everyone."[27] Matiana then glimpsed the outcome of this assault: she saw the violence and destruction of Mexico's Wars of Independence and the expulsion of Spaniards; she envisioned Iturbide's blundering imperial venture and the Parián Riot in 1828; and she also perceived the invasion of North American armies and the arrival of protestant sects and Masonic orders. She even foretold Mexico's suffocating indebtedness. Most galling, Matiana prophesized the ex-cloistering of the nation's female religious orders.

Thus our sources tell us Matiana anticipated the dawn of a painful period in which Mexico and faithful Catholics would suffer martyrdoms, poverty, humiliation, and persecution. Matiana presaged epic battles and fire in the streets of Mexico City, but at some vaguely defined point in the future—just prior to emergence of the new order of nuns in October of a year ending in eight—Mexicans would reunite with their Spanish Catholic brethren and reestablish a trans-Atlantic Christian empire ruled by a Spanish king. In this restored monarchy, however, the sovereign would rule from Mexico. Facing a vigorous Hispanic devotional and military phalanx, the Anglo-Americans and their heretical sects would retreat, without offering struggle or demanding the money owed to them. The restored monarchy would rule from a new palace next to the Basilica of the Virgin of Guadalupe, and the Hermanas del Desagravio would take up residence in the shrine's cloister. Furthermore, all ex-cloistered nuns throughout the nation would rejoin their congregations and find their convents miraculously restored to their exact condition prior to expropriation. Thenceforth, all of Mexico's religious orders would prosper in peace and unity.

Pondering these prophecies today, it is difficult to suppress the notion that they represent a fabrication of intransigent Catholics pining for the return of church-state unity and the extirpation of liberalism in Mexico. The publication of the earliest known Matiana texts in the late 1850s and early 1860s—amidst intense liberal-conservative violence, and the promulgation of the 1857 constitution and the reform laws—arouses suspicion. Matiana's prophecies could simply be a product of conservative propaganda. They invoke a colonial society of religious and social harmony, and juxtapose this idealized past with the turmoil that Mexicans experienced between 1810 and 1860. The prophecies portrayed civil strife, foreign invasion, and economic turmoil as divine punishments for the nation's separation from Spain and abandonment of church teachings due to a satanic plot ensconced in ascendant liberalism. In this light, the visions foretold that an Armageddon-like conflagration was in the offing. Matiana's visions, however, also provided the possibility of redress: "*el desenojo de Dios*" (the un-angering of God) through female-led expiatory fervor. If Mexicans returned to the bosom of the church and devoted themselves to acts of atonement, God's righteous anger could be calmed. The theme of a society that is at odds with divine will, and thus is courting world-ending disaster, has been an apparition staple for millennia. But amidst the advent of secular modernity, the "dragons of the apron [Masons], the basilisks of liberalism, and the great serpents of materialism" emerged as the pernicious enemies of Catholic civilization.[28] The faithful, however, could support the Virgin's merciful efforts to stave off the final judgment if they demonstrated remorse and repentance. In this quasi-millenarian worldview, the Catholic Church emerges triumphant regardless: either society turns away from the blasphemous antagonism toward God and his church, or God annihilates the wicked and resurrects Christian order on his own.

Mexican liberals probably saw Matiana's prophecies as a transparent ploy to scare the nation's "superstitious" public. Militant Catholics, however, portrayed these criticisms as proof of their veracity—prophets and visionaries, they assured their readers, always suffer scorn in their own time. The later Matiana texts sought to reassert the contemporary relevance of prophecies, fuel fears of the United States and Protestantism, strengthen the laity's identification with Hispanic Catholicism, and generalize notions of Christian civilization's perilous existence. Furthermore, they gave even greater importance to devout females as the protectors of religious purity, devoting extensive attention to women and girls as the Virgin's stalwart visionaries and depicting faithful women as the catalysts of male repentance.

Thus, Luis G. Duarte's *Profecías de Matiana acerca del triunfo de la Iglesia* (*Prophecies of Matiana Concerning the Triumph of the Church*) represents a dramatic recasting and amplification of the visions.[29] In contrast to the popular publications of Matiana's visions, this book donned the trappings of official ecclesiastical scholarship. In addition to Duarte, a reputedly learned Catholic scholar named Antonio Martínez del Cañizo provided explanatory footnotes and secured canonical license to publish the book and ecclesiastical opinions supporting the prophecies. *Profecías* linked Matiana's visions to nineteenth-century European Catholic lore, burgeoning intransigent devotionalism, and the church's critique of secular modernity. Duarte argued that Matiana had foreseen the Mexican experience of an international anti-Catholic, Masonic/demonic conspiracy that first came to light during the French Revolution and subsequently enveloped the world. Successive chapters of the book employed the various themes in Matiana's prophecies as starting points for the author's disquisitions on historical events and the contemporary issues. In short, Duarte wove Matiana's prophecies into the fabric of nineteenth-century international Catholic militance. Much of the text describes the visions of other Catholic seers, primarily European girls and women, whose visions echoed Matiana's warnings of an impending chastisement and subsequent Catholic renaissance. Modern societies, particularly educated men, Duarte averred, were in a state of open rebellion against God, and thus invited annihilation.

Drawing from Matiana's emphasis on expiation, Duarte launched into a discussion of the Virgin's role as the "general" rallying Catholics against the church's enemies. He specifically linked the seer's call for acts of ritual indemnification and veneration of the Eucharist to the chief devotion of late-nineteenth-century militant Catholicism—the Sacred Heart of Jesus. Intertwining the visions of different seers and notions of Christ's sufferings occasioned by society's iniquity, he argued that through Mary's advocacy and the blood of martyrs, God's vengeance repeatedly had been postponed. The Virgin, he claimed, feared that modern men would only respond to the lash of divine retribution, and yet she beseeched the world through her stalwarts, laywomen, and nuns. Men, he suggested, had become so blinded by the quest for secular power and riches that only mass repentance and expiation, as described by Matiana, could avert impending punishment.

Discussing the Hermanas del Desagravio and their apostle-like status, Duarte underscored the "manly vigor" of devout women in Catholicism's epic struggle. First, they clung to Catholic virtues and nurtured the faith in their children. Second, they contended with recalcitrant fathers and husbands in a heroic battle to steer men aright.[30] In fact, during the impending conflagration, some men would repent when they realized that their lives had been spared by relics and sacred images which their wives, sisters, or daughters had hidden in their clothing. For Duarte the establishment of the Hermanas del Desagravio, the emergence of new saints from their ranks, and their pivotal role in the church's triumph represented a grace bestowed upon Mexicans of the "pious sex" in recognition of their exemplary sacrifice.

In April 1910, the Oaxacan curia endorsed Duarte's interpretation in the archdiocese's official organ.[31] Prophecies, the archdiocese argued, were God's method of conveying to the faithful the outlines of his divine plan. This text did not offer a new analysis, but it glossed Matiana's pronouncements and Duarte's book, asserting that the Mexican visions had all the hallmarks of truly divine prophesy. It was only natural, the archdiocese maintained, that God should inform impious nations of what awaited them. Pondering the state of affairs in Juquila in the late 1920s, Matilde Narváez, and others inclined toward visionary thinking, would have found ample evidence that a great crisis was upon them. Matiana had predicted a great final conflict between Catholics and the Mexican church's constitution-wielding, anticlerical nemeses in a year ending in eight. In the summer of 1928, when reports of Nicha's visions reached Juquila, devout individuals could point to the revolutionary bloodshed, the 1917 federal constitution and its anticlerical articles, the postrevolutionary persecution of the church, the Cristero Revolt, local conflict and violence related to religion, and rumors of schism. Facing news of Marian apparitions in her parish and mulling the world around her, doña Matildita faced a momentous decision. She undoubtedly plumbed the depths of her faith and considered her extensive knowledge of Catholic lore. Once she embraced Nicha's visions, she did what came naturally—she led.

MATILDE NARVÁEZ AND FEMALE CATHOLIC ACTIVISM

We know now that Matilde Narváez paid a high price for her independent initiative. She died alone, impoverished, and disgraced, but the Catholic school principal and apparition-movement leader can teach us about women and the church's modern resurgence. According to historian Thomas Kselman, the key to broadening our understanding of Catholicism is examining the role of "belief in history."[32] In Matilde Narváez, we have a church activist who, for much of her life, was an important agent of Catholic action in rural Oaxaca. Inspired by fervent faith, women like her taught catechism, administered parochial schools, led new Catholic associations, and marshaled the laity throughout Mexico. In some cases, *beata* figures like Narváez emerged as local religious intellectuals. Her relationship with her pastor suffered due to their financial dispute, and Canseco may have brought this issue to the attention of archdiocesan authorities in the early 1930s to undercut Narváez's reputation, but it is doubtful that Narváez embraced the Virgin of Ixpantepec simply out of spite. Nor is it likely that she succumbed to pious hysteria. Even Canseco avoided such facile explanations.

Doña Matildita clearly believed that Nicha's visions were legitimate divine miracles. The foundations of this faith and her subsequent movement-leading gambit make even more sense if we factor in the apocalyptic feminism of Madre Matiana's prophecies. We lack evidence of Narváez specifically invoking Matiana, although Hilario Cortés stressed her pivotal role in the response to Nicha's visions. Given the prophecies' wide popular dissemination, their militant reinterpretation by Duarte, and the Oaxacan curia's efforts to promote them, Narváez certainly knew of Matiana's visions. In fact, heeding the colonial seer's warnings, finding evidence of their veracity in contemporary life, and practicing fervent expiatory devotion was precisely what the archdiocese encouraged.

A personal conviction that the Virgin spoke through Nicha, and a sense that she had an important role to play in God's plan, are the only logical explanations for Narváez's actions. Of particular import in this case is the militant discourse within Matiana's prophecies, which portrayed devout women as the saviors of a society suffering the consequences of modern error and religious indifference forced upon it by irreverent men. This interpretation of the nation's history pervades Catholic newspapers and popular devotional literature of the period, and found a receptive audience among the Catholic women in rural Oaxaca, and presumably much of Mexico. As we have seen, Narváez's contemporaries in other Oaxacan towns reproduced this gendered militancy in conflicts with local men whom they labeled "disciples of Voltaire." They lashed out at the "worship" of reason and notions of progress without religious instruction. They professed horror at the way in which materialistic men became the devil's instruments.[33] In addition, their deployment of notions of pious feminine abnegation and the pivotal role of women as the shapers of men merits reemphasis: "We women are the majority in most towns: we women suffer with humility the impieties of certain men of the day: we women nurture on our laps the future men of society."[34] Like these women, Narváez practiced her faith in an environment steeped in the notion that women were the primary protectors of the faith from male malevolence and folly, as well as a deserving and enlightened constituency within the church.

Catholic newspapers and the Matiana texts that Narváez probably knew are replete with references to women as the Virgin's preferred agents. The oft-repeated maxim is that God chooses the lowly to forward his great designs. Commentaries on Matiana's prophecies invoked this tradition and, in doing so, sought to convince readers to suspend social prejudices against lower-class female servants and women in general. The Duarte book introduced a long list of humble female seers and religious women leading the global fight against impiety and error. In these texts, male clerics appear as the facilitators of female revelation and pious fortitude. The Matiana prophecies even asserted that stalwart, devout women would revitalize "lukewarm ecclesiastics," as well as other wayward men.

This superheated reactionary feminism was probably tremendously motivating for women like Matilde Narváez. In Juquila's tumultuous 1920s, Narváez probably saw her own experience as part of the grand struggle described in Matiana's visions and elaborated by Duarte. It is possible that the echoes of Matiana in the visions at Ixpantepec—such as the emphases on expiation and devotion to the Blessed Sacrament—are a product of Narváez's narrative interpretation of the Chatina girl's experience. When Nicha's visions came to light, it was but a short step to view the Chatina seer and herself as the Blessed Mother's humble instruments. When she took up the Virgin of Ixpantepec's cause, the Juquila *beata* essentially stepped into the Matiana legend and its ethos of gendered reversal. Nicha spoke for the Virgin and warned the people to repent, and thus avert disaster. Canseco played the part of the tepid cleric. Narváez became Nicha's spokeswoman, interpreting the visions, leading the faithful in expiatory ritual, and getting the Virgin's message out. In short, the coming together of Matiana's prophesies, gendered militancy, and Nicha's local visions allowed doña Matildita to perceive a divinely ordained role for herself in the larger struggle. In this context, pastor opposition, archdiocesan sanction, and patriarchal social pressures failed to deter the resolute lay Catholic leader. The Virgin of Ixpantepec offered this redoubtable woman a more personal connection to the ultimate paternal figure through the mediation of an Indian girl. In essence, she answered the call to lead the devotional activities that could forestall divine retribution, revive the church, and right society. As we endeavor to understand Catholicism's international resurgence and the events in Ixpantepec, doña Matildita's decision suggests that the sense of a world-saving mission reserved for Catholic women served as a powerful mobilizing ideology for individuals like the remarkable Narváez. It could inspire devout women like her to dedicate their lives to the Catholic cause, but it could also empower them to lead the faithful where the clergy was unwilling to follow.

VISIONS OF WOMEN

In early-twentieth-century Mexican society, notions of the fanatical religiosity of older women and the superstitious, gullible nature of Indians were standard clichés. The clergy, however, depended on the religious energies of these maligned actors while at the same time holding their theology and testimony in low regard. Church publications lauded Indians for the stubborn maintenance of devout tradition and public shows of humble devotion, whilst they rendered religious women as exemplars of unshakable piety. The underlying link between these characterizations is their emphasis on submissive, essentially instinctive faith rather than deep thought. For the hierarchy and larger society, it was plausible that a female Catholic school principal could fall prey to a clever Indian girl and her own angst, but if men were having visions and spouting heresies it was a matter of greater concern. For the pastor and *El Mercurio*'s censorious correspondent, popular female revelation could be ignored, but a reputedly learned Hispanic merchant having visions and planning large pilgrimages represented an alarming development. Canseco's reports echo colonial-era concerns about the contamination of Spanish speaking *"gente de razón"* (people of reason) by heterodox Indian practices. In fact, a fear of spreading doctrinal contagion emerges in Canseco's writings. The January 12 letter describes the visions in Ixpantepec and mentions the emergence of visionary claims in other places, but Canseco devoted his entire January 16 dispatch to a vision experienced in the neighboring town of Temaxcaltepec. Together, they create the impression of a rapidly expanding rash of troubling visions and doctrinal error. The church hierarchy must have noted that they also showed the spreading of visionary fervor from Canseco's parish to Teotepec, the parish of Aureo Castellanos, the alleged schismatic. In the latter report, Canseco implied that a popular pilgrimage circuit of three Chatino locales (Ixpantepec, Temaxcaltepec, and presumably Nopala) had taken shape, and he presented his interpretation of Sánchez Alcántara's visions. Stressing this man's knowl-

edgeable reputation, Canseco provided more evidence of expanding heterodoxy as he described the merchant's elaborate visions. He also presented the hierarchy with a visionary critique of the clergy. Specifically, he
recounted the merchant pilgrim's vision of a prelate directing him to sign
a suspicious book and obstructing the Virgin's blessing.

For Canseco, the unfavorable portrait of Catholic hierarchs was the
work of the devil in his tireless efforts to mock the church.[35] His emphasis on a non-Indian, educated male's experiences represents a crucial
piece of evidence in his interpretation of the visions. But beyond the
devil's possible trickery, the here-and-now risks that Canseco faced in the
Ixpantepec apparitions merit further attention. The loss of allies like
Narváez, and perhaps the other women she led to Ixpantepec, indicates a
significant weakening of his position in Juquila, where they must have
been key supporters. Furthermore, the emerging sites of Marian devotion
just a handful of kilometers from Juquila's shrine represented a problem
for the priest and other residents of the parish seat, who depended on the
income generated during the town's venerable pilgrimage festival. In the
mid-1920s, Canseco complained to his superiors about the dwindling
number of pilgrims in recent years due to the suspension of services,
political instability, and the efforts of civil authorities to increase revenues generated from festival commerce.[36] Geographically screening Juquila from the Central Valley and the southern sierra, a new devotional
circuit encompassing Ixpantepec, Temaxcaltepec, and Nopala would sap
interest in the traditional trek to Juquila.

Although Canseco did not mention this threat to the shrine, it was
probably clear to archdiocesan authorities reading his reports. But why
did the parish priest settle on a demonic-inspiration hypothesis instead of
simply accusing Nicha, her supporters, and other visionaries of fraud and
greed, or hysteria and superstition? He hinted that Nicha and her mother
may have been swindling pilgrims, but did not openly accuse them. His
tactics centered on alluding to their impure motives, and then proceeding
to ignore these women. But this still does not explain why he suggested
demonic agency and supposedly performed an exorcism at the site. We
must allow, therefore, that the priest truly believed that the devil was at
work in his parish. The confusion and complexity of visions that he
describes stemmed, in part, from the broad cultural roots of the experiences he recorded. Canseco probably did not understand the indigenous

content of apparitions steeped in Chatino visionary tradition. Hence, he deemed them strange and ominous, and imputed the presence of a dark hand in their emergence. To him they signaled malignant entropy instead of divine order. Supernatural disorder could only be attributed to "the enemy." In short, the Ixpantepec apparitions, and even Nicha's comportment, clashed with reigning Hispanic models strongly influenced by nineteenth-century European apparitions and violated Canseco's cultural assumptions about appropriate visionary behavior.

Another reason for Canseco's conclusions concerning the visions was that among his flock, especially non-Indians, a straightforward accusation of fraud was probably not credible. The combination of popular unease, the timing of the visions, and the commitment of an influential, respected Catholic resident like Narváez required that the priest forward an explanation portraying the visions as real but dangerous. In fact, doña Matildita's fervent support of the apparitions may have convinced Canseco that real paranormal events occurred at the grotto. The oral testimony of Justina Vásquez underscores the power of his demonic-intervention thesis. She noted that her family—prominent mestizos and active supporters of the church—had been very close to Narváez before the apparitions and remained so afterward, despite their acceptance of their cleric's interpretation. Simply calling Nicha and Narváez profiteers would not have won over those who respected the Catholic school principal and knew her well. Canseco could have wielded the evidence of Narváez's misuse of funds as evidence of personal avarice, but he did not. However, asserting that genuine demonic apparitions had caused her to err was plausible. In sum, the priest's bedrock supporters in Juquila—those that maintained a Catholic political identity—could accept the idea that one of their own had fallen prey to the devil's ruse, but they would not have accepted a greed-based scam as the root of the extraordinary events in Ixpantepec and the tensions in the parish. The demonic-inspiration thesis allowed Catholics in Juquila to explain the rift in local Catholic opinion. They could pity doña Matildita for being tricked by the devil, as Vásquez does to this day, or simply claim she had lost her mind, as Canseco's nephew asserts. Many decades later, Cortés proclaimed the apparitions a fraud, but he identified the perpetrator as the uppity Indian girl without mentioning Narváez, and we have no evidence of what his opinion had been when the apparitions were in full flower.

As implied in this discussion, facets of the Ixpantepec visions, and the different responses to them, have roots in the social norms of Mexican Catholic culture. On one level, it is impossible to separate how actors interpreted the visions from gendered notions about the visionaries and their supporters. But on a deeper level, two spheres of gender norms related to Oaxacan religious practice are of particular importance: the relationships between activist Catholic women and priests, and the dynamics of Indian communal religious institutions and practice. The Ixpantepec apparitions subverted traditional roles in both of these spheres. By Canseco's admission Matilde Narváez had been one of his most trusted allies in Juquila since he began his ministry there, and during the difficult years of the Revolution. And in the village of Ixpantepec, it is likely that the social reversal evident in an eight-year-old girl's elevation to the status of female Juan Diego, and the high-profile roles played by her mother and a prominent mestiza from the municipal seat, unsettled other residents.

Women have always been important in the Catholic Church, but especially after the sundering of church-state unity, parish management has depended heavily on the bonds between activist women and priests. The pairing of young priests and older female parishioners recreates the symbolic dyad rooted in notions of Jesus Christ and the Virgin Mary as the mother-son/male-female tag team of divine action. This construct also bears expectations of social roles and behavior: priests are to emulate the chastity, purity, compassion, and divine vision of Christ; older women are to act the part of the Virgin, purified and humbled through a life's travails, obedient, and purged of a sexual identity.[37]

Within parishes, the women who developed close relationships with their pastor rooted in shared faith and socio-political alliance gained prestige and a time-honored identity as confidants of one of Mexico's salient paternal figures, "*el padre.*" Especially in rural areas, priests occupied a key node of influence that extended beyond their religious activities, and prominent lay women gained a palpable degree of power by virtue of their ties to the pastor.[38] Typically, these women came from relatively privileged social origins. People needing the priest's support in spiritual matters, social arrangements (such as marriages), or issues of local political and economic import would often seek the council and mediation of prominent Catholic women. Priests in small-town Mexico are still important local figures today, but their status was even greater in the past. In a parish like Juquila, where a shrine festival is the heart of the local economy and cultural life, the pastor's role as a social, economic, and political actor, and likewise, the standing of women in his confidence, is even more pronounced.[39] It is tempting to see the devotees' repeated efforts to convince Canseco to say Masses as Narváez's attempt to patch things up with her pastor. But although Canseco may have appeared to support the visions at the beginning, by early November he had turned firmly against Nicha, Narváez, and all the people he labeled *los interesados*.

The censure of the local priest certainly made the survival of a popular apparition movement more difficult, but as we have seen in Tlacoxcalco, church suppression efforts did not necessarily doom emerging apparition movements. Narváez was naïve to think that she could circumvent Canseco with her petitions to the archdiocesan curia. In doing so, she not only subverted patriarchal norms governing the relationships between pious Catholic women and priests, but she also violated Catholic institutional culture stipulating that the laity defer to their parish priests. In Ixpantepec, however, Nicha and her mother stumbled on an additional gendered roadblock.

In the nineteenth century, Catholic religious practice may have become a predominantly female sphere of social action in Europe and among Mexican urbanites, but in Oaxacan indigenous communities male-dominated institutions embedded in the *cargo* system remained the backbone of Indian Catholicism. Although contemporary ethnography suggests that women were important participants in religious ritual, the overwhelming body of evidence on twentieth-century indigenous religious institutions suggests that they were male-dominated social structures.[40] These collectivities were more sensitive to socio-economic and religious change than scholars had previously believed, but they remained primarily masculine spheres of action. Recent studies stress the flexibility of the *cargo* system in the face of popular revelation and the ebb and flow of religious devotions. Some sodalities cease to function for economic reasons or the loss of popular interest for particular saints, and sometimes local apparitions lead to the creation of new brotherhoods, like the Lord of the Wounds.[41] Unlike their counterparts in Tlacoxcalco, the devotees of the Virgin of Ixpantepec failed to develop an institutional framework that included the men of Ixpantepec and other communities.

Narváez mentions a couple of men who visited the apparition site and asked Nicha to procure the Virgin's blessing, but no Bartola-like figure emerged to create a local brotherhood that could be incorporated among previously established sodalities and bring important local men into the devotion's management. It is precisely this type of institutionalization that can ease the acceptance of new devotions and integrate them into existing social structures, and thus create mechanisms that sustain them in the face of clerical opposition and long after the initial excitement has faded.

The process of the apparition movement's failure, like much about Nicha's visions, remains shrouded in mystery. Our sources left large gaps in the story. For example, we know almost nothing about what transpired at the grotto between January 1929 and April 1932, beyond the fact that Nicha was still communicating with the Virgin when Narváez went to see her in 1931. We do not know who the throngs of pilgrims were beyond vague statements, such as Cortés dismissing them as *el vulgo*. Even though Justina Vásquez asserts that Nicha predicted the January 14, 1931 earthquake, we do not know how believers marked that event at that apparition site or in the village of Ixpantepec. We have Cortés's assertion that the makeshift market erected at the grotto was burned down in keeping with Canseco's determination of demonic agency, but he did not provide us with a date or an agent of this act. It could have been done by the civil authorities of Ixpantepec with encouragement from Canseco, but we cannot be sure. From the evidence that we have, it appears that *los interesados* pinned their hopes on official recognition, and neglected to form a movement that incorporated local men and institutionalized their devotion. Perhaps Ixpantepec's influential men felt slighted. Whatever transpired, when authorities refused to support the apparitions and time passed, perhaps as the mood of devout anticipation began to fade, so did the climate of credulity. It is also tempting to speculate that the passing of 1928—and thus the passing of prophetic synergies—led to the waning of interest in Nicha's "conferences" in the grotto. We will probably never know with certainty, but without a physical image to focus devotion, or a sodality to organize Nicha's followers and carve out a niche in the region's ritual life, the Second Juan Diego and the Virgin of Ixpantepec began a slow slide toward obscurity.

~~~ Picturing Mexican Catholicism

Recovering the history of Nicha and her visions took shape amidst dusty boxes and loose papers at Oaxaca's archdiocesan archive. First, I plunged in to the 1908 parish questionnaires and what seemed, initially, like idiosyncratic, priestly concerns. Seeking perspective, I moved on to the boxes labeled simply "*parroquias*" (parishes) and began plodding, page by page, from the 1860s to the 1900s. Each box overflowed with missives, memos, fragmentary financial reports, and hundreds of scrap-sized papers documenting various purchases and payments. At first glance they seemed trivial. Gradually, though, I began to perceive patterns in the sea of fee schedules and receipts. The various "investments" made it apparent that organizing religious events represented a crucial social nexus. To put it another way, so much energy was expended in these happenings and so much cultural interaction was worked out in these endeavors: indigenous villagers engaged their pastors for festivals, local clerics paid urban preachers to inspire the faithful, humble supplicants purchased mass intentions and priests traded them with each other, loads of wax came and went, hundreds of artisans and laborers maintained and adorned ritual spaces, fireworks maestros and orchestras plied their craft, and urban printers pumped out endless numbers of *estampas* (images). Branching out to newspapers revealed more complexity: traders hauled merchandise to festivals, bandits/rebels preyed on commerce, authorities tried to secure byways and tinker with fiesta tax rates, and pilgrims sought sites of miraculous import. Thus I realized that tracking the emergence of new devotions and attempts to maintain or reshape longstanding ones revealed the institutions, both large and local, and the individuals taking part. Feeling I was "on to something," I started to work through the boxes marked "*correspondencia.*" There I learned to search out longer dispatches—generally, any letter over three pages meant that somebody was exercised about some aspect of devotion.

The archdiocese also preserves a small collection of photographs residing in a single, grimy box. There, a lone snapshot of one of Archbishop Gillow's pastoral visits remains. Remarkably, it appears to bring the actors populating *parroquias* and *correspondencia* together. In this picture, the archbishop, local leaders, and a large number of indigenous villagers arranged themselves around the massive façade of a crumbling colonial landmark. In short, captured on film is a portrait of provincial Mexican Catholic society, from blue-blooded prelate to indigenous peasant, arrayed before a physical testament of the nation's religious history. If we consider only the bottom two thirds of the image, it reveals a real-life enactment of the Catholic order that the Oaxacan curia energetically promoted. Beneath the canopy we can make out Gillow. He stands in line with the pole farthest to the right, looking directly at the camera, with his pectoral cross just discernable on his chest. His diaries' discussion of hundreds of gatherings like this one allows us to surmise the roles of the people with him.[1] The individuals clustered around the archbishop in positions of prestige probably include the local pastor, other priests working in the region, economic elites, and civilian officials; perhaps the municipal president and even the district prefect are among them. On the fringes of the shaded group at the hub of the gathering, the individuals we can see may be local church officials, respected laymen, and the *mayordomos* of the communities' most important sodalities. The portrait of patriarchal order, hierarchy, and deference in this portion of the photograph is extraordinarily complete. Almost every person in the front row is identifiably male, and each of them removed their wide-brimmed hat out of respect for Gillow. In addition, the persons in the picture tend to decrease in physical stature as they appear more distant from the central

15 Early-twentieth-century pastoral visit
(AHAO, Fotografías, used by permission of the AHAO).

canopy, particularly to the left of the prelate. Even the little boys leaning against the colonial ruin to the far left took off their diminutive sombreros for the solemn, quintessentially modern moment—posing for a photographer. In addition, on the edges of the gathering and poking up in the back, we can see the leafy *palmas* and a great decorative arch celebrating the archbishop's presence.

Gillow was probably pleased with this photograph. It suggests the Catholic social body in harmony; all the participants—rich and poor, priest and parishioner, Hispanic and indigenous—seem to know their place and acknowledge the social and spiritual deference owed to the archbishop and the church. They stand with their prelate in front of a monumental colonial edifice, a symbol the Oaxacan clergy frequently cited as proof of the region's bedrock Catholic piety.

What, though, can we say about the indigenous community's brass band along the crest of the impressive, though roofless, structure? There they are arrayed from the low brass on the far left, to reed and wind instruments on the far right. Did the photographer or their parish priest send them up there to "frame" the composition? Or did they perhaps select this location to make sure they stood out above the crowd? We know that long before the Gillow era, bands had been fixtures in Oaxacan indigenous society and important representatives of individual communities.[2] Gillow's writings attest to their omnipresence. Bands usually met him outside of town and provided a triumphal musical entrance; they also served as his retinue as he proceeded to the local church, and sometimes they escorted him until another ensemble met him at the outskirts of the neighboring parish. The prelate complained about their stubbornness concerning when and how to play during his visits.[3] In addition, around the time that this picture was taken, priests struggled to implement regulations barring brass bands from the liturgy and the sanctified space inside churches.[4] Given this context, it is possible that the bearing and superordinate position of the thirty-four-piece band may imply a symbolic expression of community prerogatives in tension with the idealized hierarchical assembly in the foreground. Perhaps the combination of their stance and the arrangement of their fellow townspeople bellow represent a physical manifestation of the intricate relationships between communities and the clergy I had found in reports and letters.

A third and final aspect of this photograph also merits our attention: almost all of the individuals that we can see are clearly male. Where are the devout women who were such pivotal participants in the shaping of religious culture during the period? If we look just behind the front row and to the left of archbishop, two unmistakably shawl-covered heads peer out at the camera. We know from Gillow's diaries that women were usually among the groups that welcomed him; sometimes they approached him as members of the new associations he promoted, such as the Apostolado and the Sociedad Católica.[5] Here, perhaps inadvertently, the posing of the social body expressed the church hierarchy's conception of the appropriate social and religious role of women in society. They were to form a supporting cast that avoided the limelight reserved for the clergy and important laymen.

Where would Bartola Bolaños or Matilde Narváez have stood if an analogous event had been recorded in Tlacoxcalco or Juquila? Perhaps they would have remained obscured from view like most of their counterparts in the archdiocese, or they may have been among the few that found a place in the composition by stepping into the gaps between local men.

Of course, they might have made their presence felt in other ways. Matilde Narváez probably would have been directing local Catholic school children or leading a group of devout women honoring Gillow in the background. In Bolaños's case, once she became a local religious celebrity and the target of censorious episcopal summons, even her absence would have represented a statement of defiance. If we could miraculously view the crowds behind the featured subjects of this photograph, we would probably see many more women. In all likelihood, they are "in" this photograph, proudly wearing the scapulars, crosses, and colors as *socias* of their respective devotional associations.

Does this photograph, then, simultaneously reveal the enactment of idealized traditional order, an assertion of indigenous cultural identity, and the veiled but pivotal role of devout women in late-nineteenth- and early-twentieth-century Mexican Catholicism? I suspect that it does. But without knowing much more about the individuals in Gillow's august memento and the history of this community, it is impossible to prove. Nonetheless, just as priests and parishioners came together and took their places for this picture, their counterparts elsewhere converged in processions commemorating the Virgin of Solitude, pilgrimages celebrating Tlacoxcalco's talking Christ, and fervent gatherings at Ixpantepec's grotto.

Archbishop Gillow's life and career led us to the world of high churchmen, pueblo pastors, and priestly institutional culture. The historical evidence he left behind demonstrates that he distinguished himself as a diligent practitioner of the pastoral visit, a skilled political operator, and an agent of Vatican-conceived Catholic revivalism. His multivolume diary, penned during his sojourns, remains an invaluable source of information on the Mexican clergy in the field and the nation's diverse laity. Simultaneously, he took up a major role in institutional and religious reform, as well as church-state relations. In other words, Gillow remained engaged in the Vatican and Mexico City, as well as Oaxaca's state capital and remote parishes. As a result, he represents a crucial mediating figure. He was not the only priestly middleman in these pages. Carlos Gracida and Francisco Campos had firsthand experience in the upper circles of ecclesiastical hierarchy and regional political negotiation, and also formulated the church's response to heterodox local challenges in Ixpantepec and

Tlacoxcalco. In addition, clerics like Ausencio Canseco, Everardo Gracida, and Luis Nápoles entered Oaxaca's reformed seminary as youths and were thus formed at a center of Mexico's Catholic resurgence. Subsequently, each of them proceeded to spend their careers ministering in rural indigenous communities. Their writings provide us with a unique glimpse into the lives of a central, enduring figure in Mexican culture, *el cura del pueblo*.

In this book we have first charted the priestly conceptions of religious reform and revival that shaped the outlook of these actors from the 1880s to the 1930s, and then explored the history of apparition movements championed by lay agents during the same period. The 1930s, though, brought new challenges for all of these groups. As we have seen, in 1934, Matilde Narváez gave up her quest to establish an official Marian devotion at Ixpantepec. Not long afterward, Nicha lost her vaunted status as the second Juan Diego and returned to the unheralded life of a poor Chatina. Around the same time, Bartola Bolaños ceased to lead the devotees of Tlacoxcalco's Lord of the Wounds. After fending off opponents, maintaining the shrine on her property, and curing the sick for more than two decades, the Nahua healer and seer died in the mid-1930s. In Oaxaca City, Vicar General Gracida ably led the archdiocese again, because the state government forced Archbishop José Othón Núñez to stay in Mexico City. But the Oaxacan clergy was but a shadow of the proud ecclesiastical corps showcased on January 18, 1909, when the province's priests took their places for the Virgin of Solitude's coronation. On the eve of the crowning event, Archbishop Gillow and his cadre of priest-journalists boasted that over two hundred zealous clerics tended the flock and sustained the robust health of the Oaxacan church. They maintained that priests, laypersons, and outsiders alike recognized Catholicism's Oaxacan rejuvenation after its ignominious persecution in the nineteenth century.[6] By 1934, however, only seventy-one clergymen ministered to Oaxaca, and many rural areas were acutely understaffed.[7] In Oaxaca City, the seminary had finally succumbed to a second, more intense wave of state anticlericalism and closed its doors. Its edifice, as well as many other buildings housing the Catholic schools, charities, and associations of the Gillow era, fell victim to government expropriations and soon sheltered their secular rivals.

In a sense, then, by the mid-1930s, the three distinct envisionings of

Catholic revival at the center of this study had run their course. The Virgin of Ixpantepec's advocation-founding campaign collapsed in the face of clerical opposition and her followers' failure to graft their devotion to local structures and practices that could sustain their movement. The devotees of Tlacoxcalco's Lord of the Wounds succeeded in establishing an enduring devotion to the new image of Christ, but without Bartola Bolaños's role as the faith-healing caretaker at the shrine, their movement became more like other image devotions in the Tehuacán region. It lost the unique presence of the controversial seer and spiritual leader. As for the ecclesiastical hierarchy's plans to spark a regional Catholic transformation and reassert church teachings in public life, Gillow and his inner circle expanded the clergy, bolstered religious education, founded militant associations, resacralized the streets and plazas of the archdiocesan seat, and transformed urban ritual spaces and liturgy into models of Romanized modern Catholic practice. In short, they succeeded to a remarkable degree before losing steam in the face of an increasingly powerful, fiercely anticlerical federal government, as well as Oaxaca's economic stagnation.

Still, these endeavors from Oaxaca's past can help us see Mexico's cultural history more clearly. Although we commonly begin discussions about Catholicism in Mexico with the trauma of conquest and early evangelization, the more useful starting point is actually a later, very gradual, multigenerational time span during which Mesoamerican everyday experience became infused with Catholic meaning. It was in the late sixteenth and seventeenth centuries that a culture of Christian devotion formation and reproduction evolved into a central dynamic of social life. It was then that the relationships between priests, sodalities, *beatas*, and common parishioners took on their cultural salience. It is no coincidence that "traditional" devotions, such as the Virgins of Juquila and Soledad, emerge from of this period. Simultaneously, Christianized notions of divine involvement in nature and the human social order put down dense networks of roots, which have proved exceedingly durable. Very gradually, then, Catholic ritual became imbedded in a liturgical-agricultural cycle, and the acts of Christian supplication, curing, and pilgrimage—as well as the sacred images associated with them—became integral to the way individuals and groups understood themselves and expressed their social identities. Indigenous traditions endured in these religious cultures, and local practices evinced the same cultural tensions that suffused colonial life. Nonetheless, over time priests and laypeople understood baroque complexity, including certain levels of heterodoxy, as "Catholic."

In many ways, Oaxacan documents from the late 1800s and early 1900s reveal an enduring "colonial" society. Priests talked about indigenous religiosity as their predecessors had, and villages engaged clergymen as had their forbearers, even though the context of local Catholicism had shifted. It remained a world of *gente de razón* and *gente de idioma*—a world where colonial social structures appeared firmly entrenched. Practice had changed, though. Sacramental compliance fell precipitously, the *cofradía* gave way to the *mayordomía*, and liberal reforms inadvertently gave communities greater leverage in their dealings with priests. Nonetheless, most Oaxacans were still deeply religious. What remained stable was the interest in sustaining ritual and the perennial tensions over who controlled religious "obligations." This does not mean that priests and parishioners sought simple preservation. Sometimes, as we have seen, they altered traditions or added new practices. In other cases, home-grown mysticism brought innovation. Clerics talked of *"metiéndolos al orden"* (cleaning up popular religious practice) but often just agreed to *"sacar sus fiestas"* (celebrate their feasts). Conversely, communities harbored varying degrees of anticlericalism but nevertheless valued the sanctifying role played by priests. Thus, the struggles of Matilde Narváez and the dilemma's faced by Father Luis Nápoles corroborate what Fernando Cervantes labels Mexico's "ritual constant"—a persisting, flexibly conceived, elevated importance placed upon the local maintenance of communal rites, regional religious calendars, and life-cycle rituals.[8] This was not because of an addiction to clerical pomp, as reformist critics complained from time to time, but rather a lasting commitment to collective ritual prerogatives. According to Cervantes, the reluctance to let outsiders manipulate or expunge this aspect of social life—more than issues of belief, doctrine, or religious social norms—has repeatedly sparked conflict in Mexican history.

Although I stress broader, long-term processes, what we learn here about Gillow's initiatives, the Virgin of Ixpantepec, and the talking Christ of Tlacoxcalco should also capture the attention of scholars interested in the revolutionary state's efforts to reshape Mexican culture between 1920 and 1940. During the dust-settling, postrevolutionary decades, scholarship tended to chart the expanding state's achievement of dominance over the church. The greater the distance from the revolution, however, the more suspect and oversimplified this interpretation appears. Just as Oaxacan devotional movements demonstrate that Mexican Catholics were not religious in an easily characterized or homogenous manner, there was nothing simple or standard about the anticlerical actors and secularizing government institutions.[9] In addition, we now know that like many religious actors, postrevolutionary reformers were often quite heterodox in practice. When deemed expedient in terms of pressing economic goals and consolidating power, they compromised their secularizing principles.

Perhaps we should look at Catholic religion and Mexican revolution in terms of dialectic interaction and trace how innovative religion accompanied radicalization.[10] It is true that the "bundling" of anticlericalism with government rural development schemes and public education exacerbated deep tensions within Mexican society. Likewise, the state's efforts to create and consolidate a broad popular base, while trying to neutralize competitors, guaranteed conflict where the Catholic clergy was thick on the ground and integrated within powerful social sectors.[11] For religious individuals, however, the ability to explore new ideas and practices, and the opportunity to shape ritual, expanded during the period's general social opening. With the clergy harried, it was often the laity that fashioned the creative strategies of resistance and sustained ritual in the face of secularizing pressures.

Could we ascribe the emergence of apparition movements like Tlacoxcalco's and Ixpantepec's to this phenomenon? In some ways perhaps, but it remains difficult to prove. We do not have many comparative early-twentieth-century cases, and documentation for these kinds of movements is always sketchy. As Oaxaca demonstrates, claims of miraculous revelation are relatively common in Catholic social environments, but lasting devotional movements only occasionally take shape around them. The revolutionary period, with its radical rhetoric, anticlerical campaigns, sustained violence, economic turmoil, and loosening of social mores, most likely stoked the climate of credulity and urgency awaiting apparitionist claims surfacing at this time. The Lord of the Wounds devotion may have benefited from a heightened openness toward new revelation, but neither the devotees nor their detractors hinted at revolutionary unease. Nicha's visions and prophecies, it is probably safe to say, would have garnered much less interest in a prerevolutionary context. Moreover, the conflicts stemming from the revolution exerted a clear impact on actors like Matilde Narváez and Ausencio Canseco, and the disagreements that emerged between them.

At least tangentially, Oaxacan evidence also addresses patterns of resistance to the new revolutionary state's projects. As we have seen, the archdiocese evinced considerable Cristero sympathy but failed to produce broad antigovernment insurgency. Alan Knight has color-coded the map of Mexico into white, pink, and red zones, denoting the likelihood of resisting or embracing anticlericalism.[12] In broad brushstrokes, Oaxaca appears pink, a region where both the institutional church and the state have been weak, and where relatively autonomous, vibrant, indigenous folk Catholicism has deep roots. According to this characterization, Oaxaca lacked the levels of priestly social assimilation that made other regions respond with such violent intensity to state anticlericalism. Likewise, religion, though prevalent, was integrated in small indigenous communities that largely ran their own religious affairs. Much of southern Mexico simply lacked the clericalized culture that state agents targeted, although some scholars caution that this level of generalization overlooks subregions where Catholicism was simultaneously priest-centered and accommodating to indigenous practice.[13] Hence although the "pink" designation fits in some ways, perhaps we should be wary of the connotations of intermediacy. The more important variable, in the Oaxacan case, is the relative weakness of the state. First, the national government of the 1920s was not fully confident of its hold on the region, and it pragmatically focused its attentions on other areas where it faced direct challenges. Second, the Oaxacans working in government institutions proved reluctant to press anticlerical actions due to prevailing Catholic sympathies. Even in the 1930s, amidst more intense anticlerical measures, inflammatory actions—such as saint burnings—remained rare in Oaxaca. In addition, the handmaidens of postrevolutionary anticlericalism—state-sponsored agrarianism and public education—spread very slowly and unevenly in Oaxaca. Thus, aside from the issue of clericalized religiosity versus more autonomous folk cultures, the Mexican state simply did not impinge upon Oaxacan local religion to the same extent that it did in other regions.

Pulling back to a present-day historical perspective, though, we must conclude that Jacobin legislation and government-sponsored "defanaticization" fared poorly throughout Mexico. The state failed to uproot Catholicism's solid historical foundations and never countered the value much of the population placed upon the spiritual mediation offered by the church. Straightforward assertions that salvation, miraculous intercession, and performative ritual were simply pabulum failed to impress legions of individuals who may not have been particularly orthodox but who found Catholic practices deeply meaningful.[14]

Catholicism remained vibrant. In important ways visionaries and devotional impresarios, brotherhoods and associations, as well as pastors and hierarchs succeeded in "moving the faithful": they engaged them emotionally, mobilized them politically, focused them spiritually, and put them in motion physically. These motivating endeavors came together in efforts to inspire participation in religious collectivities, image-centered worship, and pilgrimage to official and unofficial shrines. In short, these actors brought religion to life. They infused ritual, pious display, and even the preparatory actions related to religious events with passion and daily relevance. It should be clear that so-called popular religion in Oaxaca was not necessarily oppositional, nor was there a hard and fast popular-official divide. In fact, the most meaningful way to look at the devotional movements emerging from Tlacoxcalco and Ixpantepec is as struggles within the church and among avowed Catholics. The events charted here highlight the efforts of clergymen to change the way laypeople practiced their faith, and, in turn, they reveal common Catholics attempting to bring priests around to alternative approaches to the sacred. Both the laity and the clergy remained committed to engagement, despite tensions and conflict.

We can approach the different visions of Catholicism in various ways. Concerning the high clergy's conception of ordered religious renaissance and the restoration of the church's sociopolitical prestige, the most common way of viewing these developments has been to emphasize an unofficial conciliation pact between President Díaz and prelates like Gillow. From this standpoint, the liberal strongman allowed activist Catholics to reassert themselves in the public sphere in exchange for political support from the church. In other words, Díaz consolidated his dictatorship with help from an institution intent on regaining its pre-Reform standing. In regard to the movements that coalesced around Nicha's and Bartola Bolaños's claims of visionary experience, it is tempting to describe them as resistance movements, devotional entrepreneurship, pastiche-like cultural revivals, or alternative modernities. Whereas aspects of them can be adduced as evidence of these characterizations, none of these labels provides a satisfying description of the complex interlinkages between the church hierarchy's project and homegrown apparitionist devotions. It is ultimately more useful to think of them as interconnected arenas of Mexican culture change and to resist the urge to disaggregate them or pit them against each other.

For some time it has been fashionable, in Mexican studies, to describe patterns of sociopolitical and cultural change in terms of negotiated construction. The point has been to uncover the agency of subaltern groups in large-scale social transformations, even when they are not clearly represented among power holders. When we apply the concept of negotiation to situations where there does, indeed, appear to be sustained communication between historical actors, the characterization is apt. But sometimes the concept loses useful meaning if we lack evidence of give-and-take between the parties. In Oaxacan devotionalism, however, negotiation in a relatively narrow sense applies. In rituals, questionnaires, petitions, sermons, and even processions and pageantry we can perceive running historical "conversations" between priests and laypersons centered on working out how ritual practice would look, feel, and sound, as well as what social meanings would be attached to it.

Beyond strictly religious matters, these interactions reflect how Oaxacans deployed religious belief and practice amidst their engagement of modernity. It is relatively straightforward to chart the Oaxacan church's transformation as evidenced in the Gillow-era initiatives. In the broader historical sense, this reformist program reached back to late-eighteenth-century attempts to purge popular culture of its baroque sensibilities and substitute a more austere, individualistic interior piety in place of community-centered, fiesta-based religiosity. Ironically, liberal reform and Mexican anticlericalism had roots in the same movement.[15] More directly, though, Gillow's platform represents a Mexican articulation of the church-revitalization and modernization blueprint outlined by the

Vatican in the 1890s. Rome called for internal reforms encompassing bureaucratic reorganization and centralization, professionalization of the clergy, ultramontane obedience and stricter discipline, rationalization of ecclesiastical jurisdictions, and standardization of parish administration. Regarding the faithful, Gillow worked from Vatican plans aimed at organizing the laity in clerically controlled institutions targeted at particular social niches—such as the Apostolado and Catholic Worker's Circles. Rome also promoted popular practice centered on personal identification with militant devotions like the Sacred Heart and increased sacramental observance. The Virgin of Solitude and other select local devotions also proved adaptable to these goals. In its efforts, the church hierarchy availed itself of the latest tools at hand. Oaxacan clergymen and their lay supporters became fervent newspapermen, propagandists, and advertisers. They promoted the mass production and marketing of Catholic images and symbols. They also did their best to organize the faithful and arrange their technologically eased transport to well-ordered mass gatherings at staged devotional events. These ostensibly religious celebrations doubled as demonstrations of Catholic sociopolitical power.

In addition, they labored to renovate and refurbish the region's religious landmarks and alter the feel of ritual. This entailed presenting the clergy's claims of a glorious colonial past, nineteenth-century persecution, and unfolding spiritual and sociopolitical revitalization by means of parades, architecture, and liturgy. They restored dilapidated structures, redecorated interiors, and implemented Rome's latest regulations concerning the mass. These endeavors were most extensive and successful in Oaxaca City. There, a large clerical presence, a predominantly Hispanic laity, a conservative elite, and a small middle class favorably disposed to European cultural trends formed the social base of Gillow's reform program.

The period, however, did not witness a simple "out with the old and in with the new" metamorphosis. The Oaxacan clergy was by no means monolithic, and like their counterparts in much of Mexico, they realized that they had to accommodate local sensibilities. Moreover, there was a considerable amount of social and religious tradition that both the laity and clergy sought to preserve. The process in specific localities, therefore, was often improvisational, and naturally, the end results were patchy. Modernity, in this context, was more of a set of options than an integrated package of ideas and practices. Churchmen, religious intellectuals, and devout laypersons approached it selectively. In general, they rejected aspects associated with the secularization of public life, but they availed themselves of other ideas. For example, Catholic newspapers and devotional literature tapped the modern discourse of rationalist advancement, although they reveal telling accommodations in their use of such concepts as "true Christian progress," "Catholic sociology," and "pilgrim science." Gillow and his inner circle strove to modify devotional themes, generalize distinct rhythms of practice, and shape understandings of the social order without erasing links to idealized tradition. They wanted Oaxacan Catholics to celebrate a particular version of the past, rooted in notions of an unchanging forefathers' faith and Christian civilization's moral and socioeconomic advancement. Moreover they maintained that this inexorable, divinely ordained process had been shepherded by an infallible church. But they also sought to imbue history, faith, and practice with contemporary relevance, prestige, and style. As described in Chapter 3, they even introduced new kinds of institutions—"canonically structured associations"—boasting cellular structures designed to discipline lay practice and encourage personal, sacrament-centered piety. In short, they sought to Christianize modern notions of order, progress, and individualism, and to generalize them among the populace.

It is tempting to suggest that Oaxaca's Catholic resurgence floundered because of the clergy's inability to accept new local devotions and indigenous visionaries or to fully embrace female religious leadership. Indeed, the Oaxacan priesthood failed to anchor their vision of Catholic revival in popular religious enthusiasm, in contrast to their European counterparts. But taking this line of reasoning too far leads us toward anachronistic judgments. Neither revolutionaries nor churchmen countenanced truly empowering Mexican indigenous or female actors. To this day, the church is cool to notions of an indigenous *"iglesia autóctona"* (autochthonous church) as championed by relatively radical priests like Chiapas's former bishop Samuel Ruiz García.[16] Likewise, the hierarchy remains unwilling to incorporate women fully within the church.

In truth, despite its considerable accomplishments, the clergy's reform project remained relatively shallow. Gillow and his priests achieved success in Oaxaca City and among the relatively small urban Hispanic population, but they approached indigenous and rural Catholics from an essentially colonial perspective. Then the Mexican Revolution interrupted their plans. When Gillow returned from exile in 1921, and after Núñez succeeded him as archbishop in 1922, they did not know what was in store. The 1917 constitution and the anticlerical rhetoric of revolutionary politicians troubled them, but the ultimate character of the postrevolutionary state was still a mystery. As the emergent order became clearer, instead of returning to the ambitious projects of their youth, Gracida, Núñez, and their Gillow-era cohorts simply made do in the face of expropriations, shrinking revenues, and flagging vocations.

Lay actors observed this project in action all along. They accessed new ideas about the meanings and modes of religious devotion forwarded by the clergy but channeled popular pious energies according to their own judgment. In Bartola Bolaños and Matilde Narváez, we have two mature women of organizational talent, obvious intellect, and popular esteem who inspired and led the faithful. They also tried to convince the clergy to embrace local visions of Catholic revitalization. Together with the thousands of devout women who embraced Catholic activism in canonically structured associations, these women's noteworthy lives suggest that historians need to examine the issue of female religious activism and leadership more carefully. We often talk about the feminization of piety almost as if it was a by-product of modernity, but the mechanics of this transformation remain murky. Nonetheless the evidence of marked female overrepresentation in the church's new revivalist institutions and their pivotal role as agents of resistance to radical state projects is incontrovertible.[17] This takes on added importance, since scholars tracking Mexican revolutionary anticlericalism stress that its adherents were almost exclusively male.[18] What does this mean, then, if the two sides in this storied clash of institutions and sociocultural projects were largely divided along gender lines? This can be taken too far, of course. We do not want to fall in to clichés about a society of traditional, religious women and revolutionary, anticlerical men. Still, these polarities demand that we explore more closely the complex interrelationship of gender and Catholic identity. It is high time we balanced our longstanding interest in male-dominated brotherhoods and *mayordomías*, although there is important work yet to be done examining pious expression and masculinity. A good place to start would be in the social history of female-dominated canonically structured associations and the devotions they championed, such as the

Sacred Heart and the Blessed Sacrament. There were certainly many women like doña Matildita in Mexico, and perhaps several like Bartola Bolaños. Maybe, if we look hard enough, we will even turn up a few more girls trying on the visionary mantle of Juan Diego.

The Lord of the Wounds devotion represents a case where we can perceive the interaction of popular devotion-formation and gender. Not unlike the priests and prelates who censured their movement, Bartola Bolaños, her husband, and their supporters proved adept at recombining the traditional and modern. The Lord of the Wounds movement in Tlacoxcalco reveals a creative synthesis of ideas and practices. In essence, the Lord's devotees beat the clergy at its own game. Building on local conceptions of image-centered worship, miraculous intercession, faith healing, and religious social organization, they structured a pilgrimage devotion that resonated in local tradition and yet evinced distinctly modern sensibilities. We can see this most clearly in the rotational brotherhood and the devotees' grassroots religious advertising. The Lord of the Wounds sodality represents the emergence of an innovative indigenous institution—a branching organization with central leadership in the shrine community and member collectivities in surrounding villages. Moreover, this novel brotherhood embraced a more frequent and structured rhythm of organized worship, rooted in a coordinated monthly rotation of pilgrimage devotion and special priest-led masses. It is no coincidence that in many ways it appears to be a local reinterpretation of the canonically structured association.

In order to bolster their devotion they fashioned a promotional campaign tapping into the cachet of modern aesthetics. They commissioned a sculptor from the nearby city of Tehuacán to carve an image in the reigning romantic style, and—at a time when outsiders frequently disparaged indigenous images—even their critics attested to its attractiveness. Then the devotees hired a photographer to take a picture of the newly carved Christ and engaged the services of a printer to produce flyers. They then proceeded to promote their upstart devotion with this mass-produced photographic likeness and effusive religious poetry. Crucially, in Bartola and Anastacio Bolaños, Tlacoxcalco's apparition movement boasted a female and male leader, although the former was clearly in charge. The new brotherhood also included many local men, and often

Mr. Bolaños appeared as the devotion's representative before the church. Bartola, at least outwardly, assumed the vaunted role of healer and spiritual leader. Because of this dual nature, the Lord of the Wounds devotion was able to navigate patriarchal norms quite effectively. On another level, however, Tlacoxcalco's seer transgressed gender norms and appropriated the voice of Christ. Only priests were supposed to speak for Christ. Critics argued that Bartola was simply impersonating the Lord of the Wounds in her nighttime gatherings and duping gullible Indians. The devotees most likely knew full well that Bartola Bolaños was the voice of the Lord. For believers, this woman's embodiment of the masculine figure of Christ and mediation of miraculous cures may have been precisely what made the devotion so compelling.

The movement that coalesced around Nicha and Matilde Narváez demonstrates less of this creative savvy and flexibility. In fact, in addition to its failure to develop a self-sustaining institutional structure and meaningfully incorporate local men, perhaps another reason for the devotion's collapse was its leaders' failure to take up the new modes of organization, expression, and religious boosterism that proved effective in the hands of church hierarchs and indigenous Catholics in Tlacoxcalco. At a distance of several decades, it seems inexplicable that the devotees failed to commission or "find" an image on which to center an enduring devotion. Narváez's role and the influence of Madre Matiana's legendary prophecies at Nicha's grotto, however, demonstrate the potent impact of the period's militant Marianism and apocalyptic feminism in the church's resurgence. Doña Matildita's life, career, and vigorous support of Nicha's visions exemplify the prominent part devout women played in modern Catholic activism. For most of her life, she dedicated her energies to the church's revitalization; she was a generous benefactress and a model of pious orthodoxy. Furthermore, she was a local agent of celebrated Vatican projects, Catholic education and the coordination of lay social action. In short, Narváez embraced the gendered role outlined for her by the church: indoctrinating children and supporting the male clergy. But for clergymen, like Narváez's erstwhile ally Father Canseco, the dynamic school principal and Catholic organizer imbibed the period's militant gendered piety too deeply. She embraced the notion of devout women as the pious vanguard holding back secularizing error (gendered male), keeping divine chastisement at bay, and serving as the expiatory catalysts of the church's ultimate triumph. Amidst the context of late-1920s turmoil, the synergy of Nicha's visions and Madre Matiana's prophecies appear to have convinced the *beata* to risk a break with the clergy in order to make this pious victory a reality. In a sense, then, Narváez was out in front of the revalorization of women within Mexican society. However, she violated one of the least flexible patriarchal tenets of the clergy—doña Matildita began interpreting doctrine.

Piecing together the history of the Virgin of Ixpantepec may perhaps forestall the devotion's extinction in local memory. At the very least, some present-day residents have talked about Nicha and her visions with an inquisitive historian and guided him to the apparition site. Like the once-popular devotion, the grotto itself seems nearly forgotten. Plants and trees almost obscure the cleft in the rocks, but a steady stream of water still burbles to life there and flows down the mountainside. Decades of erosion and more recent earthquakes have likely altered the site. Observing Our Lady of Ixpantepec's "temple" today, it is hard to imagine an eight-year-old girl fitting inside the grotto, or hundreds of candles, offerings, and an altar arranged at its entrance. Nor are there intuitive locations for the food sellers and souvenir vendors, or an obvious gathering place for hopeful penitents. Nonetheless, the locale provides a splendid panorama of Oaxaca's rugged mountain scenery, and perhaps a generation or two of ingenuity and hard work could have made this a shrine site worthy of a lasting pilgrimage tradition. A devotion's survival or collapse, though is not what makes it worthy of analysis. Nicha's visions help us see into Mexican Catholic culture a century ago and gain an appreciation for local religious dynamism and complexity. Parts of what we perceive must remain veiled in uncertainty, but other aspects appear in nuanced detail.

In the Tehuacán Valley, Tlacoxcalco's Lord of the Wounds endures, but his devotion may be in trouble. Although he withstood archdiocesan censure in the past, his brotherhood is currently struggling with a more recent avatar of religious innovation in Mexico—the expansion of evangelical Protestantism. It is the arrival of a new kind of religious competition in Mexican pueblos that may lead to a secularization of local culture where nineteenth-century liberals and twentieth-century revolutionaries failed. As the Lord's present-day caretakers point out, Protestant converts refuse to take part in the image's festival and pressure local officials to withdraw their customary support as the celebration approaches its centennial. In addition, if the current pastor is a barometer of the institutional church's opinion, the brotherhood cannot count on clerical support if popular commitment falters. Thus the Lord of the Wounds may join the Virgin of Ixpantepec in the pantheon of forgotten devotions. In his case, however, his image and the innocent-looking green cross could remain in Tlacoxcalco's church indefinitely, although the Santo Niño Hallado (the miraculous, divinatory stone) may not fare as well. Then again, there is always the possibility of new revelation and revival.

INTRODUCTION MOVING THE FAITHFUL

1 Matilde Narváez to Archbishop José Othón Núñez, AHAO, DGC 1934–1939, February 8, 1934.

2 Mexico's state of Oaxaca is renowned for the diversity of indigenous cultures. Chatinos represent one of sixteen distinct formally recognized ethnic groups, although there are many more distinct subgroups. The largest, the Zapotecs and Mixtecs, historically dominated the area and remain the most well known. Approximately 20,000 Chatinos inhabit a network of villages in Oaxaca's southern sierra near the town of Santa Catarina Juquila. They speak an Oto-Manguean language closely related to Zapotec. For an English-language ethnography, see Greenberg, *Santiago's Sword.*

3 Andrés-Gallego, "Catolicismo social mexicano," 19–27.

4 In particular, see Joseph and Nugent, eds., *Everyday Forms of State Formation*; Scott, *Domination and the Arts of Resistance*; and Scott, *Seeing Like a State.*

5 For a clear, concise overview and texts from this period see Harrington, *A Cloud of Witness.*

6 Misner, *Social Catholicism in Europe*; and Mel Piehl, "A Wealth of Notions."

7 Blackbourn, "The Catholic Church in Europe since the French Revolution."

8 See Jonas, *France and the Cult of the Sacred Heart*; Kaufman, *Consuming Visions*; and Kaufman "Selling Lourdes."

9 See Taylor, *Magistrates*, chap. 3.

10 Ricard, *The Spiritual Conquest.*

11 See Klor de Alva, "Aztec Spirituality and Nahuatized Christianity," and "Language, Politics, and Translation."

12 See Brenner, *Idols*. See also Madsen, *Christo-Paganism*; and Madsen, *The Virgin's Children*.

13 See Taylor, *Magistrates*, 53.

14 For an interesting discussion of the scholarly terminology of mixture and a nuanced discussion of hybridity, see Dean and Liebsohn, "Hybridity and Its Discontents."

15 Compare Burkhart, *The Slippery Earth*; and Gruzinski, *The Conquest of Mexico*. In addition, compare Greenberg, *Santiago's Sword*; and Ingham, *Mary, Michael, and Lucifer*.

16 See Taylor, *Magistrates*; and Inga Clendinnen, "Ways to the Sacred."

17 See Farriss, *Maya Society*. See also Chance, *Conquest of the Sierra*, although he leans heavily on Farris; and Rugeley, *Wonders and Wise Men*.

18 This chronology and the delineation of these phases of sociocultural change form the basis of Lockhart, *Nahuas after the Conquest*. For his summary of the phases, see pages 429–35. Of course, Oaxaca's relative isolation from the centers of Spanish colonial rule and population slowed cultural interaction. Phase 1 probably lasted much longer, but clearly, by the nineteenth century the region found itself amidst phase 3–like transformations.

19 The classic nineteenth-century conservative history is Alamán, *Historia de México*. The nineteenth-century liberal perspective is best expressed in Sierra, *Evolución política*. For early-twentieth-century examples, see pro-church historian Cuevas, *Historia de la Iglesia*; and liberal historian Toro, *La Iglesia y el estado*.

20 For liberal and conservative historiography, see Hale, *Mexican Liberalism*. See also Matute, Trejo, and Connaughton, eds., *Estado, Iglesia y sociedad*.

21 Karl Schmitt, "Church and State in Mexico."

22 On Mexican liberalism, see Hale, *Mexican Liberalism*; and Hale, *The Transformation of Mexican Liberalism*. See also Knight, "El liberalismo mexicano."

23 See Mallon, *Peasant and Nation*; Guardino, *Peasants, Politics, and the Formation of Mexico's National State*; Thompson and LaFrance, *Patriotism, Politics and Popular Liberalism*; and Thompson, "Popular Aspects of Liberalism."

24 Schmitt, "Church and State in Mexico."

25 Hale, *The Transformation of Mexican Liberalism*.

26 Bazant, *Alienation of Church Wealth*; Costeloe, *Church Wealth in Mexico*; Costeloe, *Church and State*; Knowlton, *Church Property*; Knowlton, "La Iglesia mexicana y la Reforma"; Lavrin, "Mexican Nunneries"; Rodríguez O., "The Conflict between Church and State"; Sinkin, *The Mexican Reform*; and Staples, *La Iglesia en la primera república*.

27 See Adame Goddard, *El pensamiento político*; and Ceballos Ramírez, *El catolicismo social*. See also Schmitt, "The Díaz Conciliation Policy," and "Church and State in Mexico."

28 Schmitt, "The Díaz Conciliation Policy." For Oaxacan examples, see the 1907 cases from the districts of Jamilitepec and Cuicatlán, AGPEO, Porfiriato, leg. 35, exp. 8; and leg. 42, exp. 32.

29 Meyer, *La cristiada.*

30 Curley, "'The First Encounter.'"

31 Butler, *Popular Piety.*

32 See Jrade, "Counterrevolution in Mexico"; Meyer, *La cristiada*; Purnell, *Popular Movements*; and Butler, *Popular Piety.* For North American Catholic responses to these events, see Redinger, *American Catholics and the Mexican Revolution.*

33 On the Wars of Independence, see Van Young, *The Other Rebellion.* On Tomochic, see Vanderwood, *The Power of God.*

34 Connaughton, "La sacralización de lo cívico."; and Martínez Assad, ed., *A Dios lo que es de Dios.*

35 See Adame Goddard, *El pensamiento*; Ceballos Ramírez, *El catolicismo social*; and Ceballos Ramírez and Garza Rangel, eds., *Catolicismo social en México.*

36 Butler, *Popular Piety*, stands as a notable exception.

37 Hewitt de Alcántara, *Anthropological Perspectives.*

38 For example, see Wolf, "Types of Latin-American Peasantry," and "Closed Corporate Peasant Communities."

39 See introduction to Monaghan, *The Covenants.* See also Mulhare, "Mesoamerican Social Organization and Community."

40 Greenberg, *Santiago's Sword*, 2. See also Greenberg's *Blood Ties.*

41 For the internal conflict–management thesis, see Wolf, "Closed Corporate Peasant Communities." For the "legitimation of the status quo" argument, see Cancian, "Economics and Prestige in a Maya Community," "Political and Religious Organizations," and *The Decline of Community.* Marvin Harris argued that the cargo system existed to pump resources out of indigenous communities; see Greenberg, *Santiago's Sword*, 148–49. Works emphasizing reciprocity and nonmarket exchange include Aguirre Beltrán, *Regiones de refugio*; Carrasco, "The Civil-Religious Hierarchy in Mesoamerica"; and Dow, *Santos y supervivencias.*

42 See Chance and Taylor, "Cofradías and Cargos"; and Rugeley, *Wonders and Wisemen.* See also Cancian, *Decline of Community*; and Chance, "Changes in Twentieth-Century Mesoamerican Cargo Sytems."

43 To gain a sense for the extraordinary diversity of practices in indigenous communities, see Barabas, ed., *Diálogos con el territorio.*

44 Mulhare, "Mesoamerican Social Organization and Community after 1960."

45 Monaghan, *The Covenants.*

46 Ibid; and Greenberg, *Santiago's Sword.* The latter describes a similar conception of the community among Chatinos.

47 Monaghan is referring to the notion of a deep, enduring pact between the

supernatural/the Earth itself and human society within Mesoamerican monism. In doing so he builds on the work of Hugo Nutini, Miguel de León Portilla, and Marcello Carmagnani. The idea is that many indigenous groups in the region speak of their interaction with the divine in terms of mutual obligation. The emphasis on rituals and services is not worship or the quest for salvation in the Western sense. Instead, Mesoamerican indigenous groups frequently describe religious activities as "work." Civilized life, then, is accomplished through a covenant in which humans are constantly laboring to "pay" an unpayable debt to the Earth and sacred forces that allow them to endure. Society and the cosmos, in this conception, are maintained through ritually mediated exchange.

48 Larraín, *Identity and Modernity*; and Alonso, *The Burden of Modernity*.
49 Gaonkar, ed., *Alter/Native Modernties*; and Holston, "Alternative Modernities." Overmyer-Velázquez, "Visions of the Emerald City," employs this approach in his analysis of the city of Oaxaca's history.
50 Viqueira Albán, *Propriety and Permissiveness*.
51 Voekel, *Alone before God*.
52 Guardino, *The Time of Liberty*.
53 Larraín, *Identity and Modernity*.
54 Here I am thinking about Lomnitz, "Nationalism's Dirty Linen," in *Deep Mexico, Silent Mexico*.
55 Alonso, *The Burden of Modernity*.
56 See Hobsbawm, *Primitive Rebels*, and "Peasants and Politics." See also Worsley, *The Trumpet Shall Sound*. For an example of the cultural-crisis school, see Burridge, *New Heaven, New Earth*.
57 See Barabas, *Utopías indias*. These phenomena have received considerable attention among the Maya: see Bricker, *The Indian Christ, the Indian King*; Gosner, *Soldiers of the Virgin*; and Patch, *Maya Revolt*.
58 See Comaroff, *Body of Power*. Comaroff's analysis echoes the "cultural crisis" school of religious movements but also incorporates aspects of the political school.
59 Holston, "Alternative Modernities."
60 Fields, *Revival and Rebellion*.
61 Ibid.
62 Vanderwood, *The Power of God*. For more on popular millenarian thinking in Mexico, see Van Young, *The Other Rebellion*.
63 Austin-Broos, *Jamaica Genesis*.
64 Ibid.
65 Christian, *Moving Crucifixes*; and Christian, *Visionaries*. See also Brown, *The Cult of the Saints*.
66 Turner and Turner, *Image and Pilgrimage*.
67 See Blackbourn, *Marpingen*; Christian, *Moving Crucifixes*; Christian, *Visionaries*; and Harris, *Lourdes*.

68 Turner and Turner, *Image and Pilgrimage*, 210.

69 See Blackbourn, "The Catholic Church in Europe since the French Revolution"; and Kselman, "Introduction."

70 Kselman, *Miracles and Prophecies*.

71 See Pessar, *From Fanatics to Folk.*

72 Blackbourn, *Marpingen*; and Christian, *Visionaries.*

73 Blackbourn, *Marpingen.*

74 Ibid., 360–76.

75 Christian, *Moving Crucifixes*, 82–90.

76 For example, see Fray Francisco Ximénez, *Historia de la provincia de San Vicente*, as quoted in Patch, *Maya Revolt*, 15.

77 See Barabas, "La aparición de la Virgen en Oaxaca." In addition, while researching events that took place in Tututepec during the 1930s, I met devotees of a recent apparition of the Virgin in the countryside near town. They faced pressure from the church hierarchy to abandon their devotion but had already built a private shine and requested that I speak to the archbishop on their behalf.

78 Christian, *Visionaries.*

79 See Blackbourn, *Marpingen*; Christian, *Moving Crucifixes*; Christian, *Visionaries*; Harris, *Lourdes*; and Kselman, *Miracles and Prophecies*. See also Della Cava, *Miracle at Joaseiro.*

80 See Brading, *Mexican Phoenix.*

81 If Oaxacan documentation is any indication of broader trends, the push to generalize the Guadalupe devotion throughout Mexico dates from the 1880s and 1890s.

82 Christian, *Visionaries.*

83 Apolito, *Apparitions.*

84 On the local intellectuals who shaped the voice and policies of the Juazeiro apparition movement see Della Cava, *Miracle at Juazeiro*. For more on the crucial editing and shaping role of intellectuals see also Christian, *Visionaries*; and Apolito, *Apparitions.*

ONE AN ENTERPRISING ARCHBISHOP

1 AHAO, Impresos Religiosos, 1880–1899. Gillow's Oaxacan supporters republished this text without removing references to his Puebla candidacy.

2 Gillow, *Apuntes históricos.*

3 Mariano Palacios, "Apuntes para la historia," *Boletín Oficial*, October 1, 1908, through January 1, 1910; and Rivera G., *Reminiscencias.*

4 Scholars frequently mention this relationship, citing Adame Goddard, *El pensamiento político*, whose footnotes reveal that his source was Oaxacan historian Jorge Fernando Iturribaría, who in turn cites Rivera G., *Reminicencias*. See Iturribaría, "La política de conciliación." Daniela Traffano uncov-

ered letters underscoring Díaz's efforts to secure Gillow's appointment in Oaxaca, revealing definitively that he enjoyed the president's patronage; see Traffano, "Indios, curas, y nación."

5 *Reminicencias* remains the primary source of this interpretation. Oaxaca lacks a thorough church-sponsored history; however, the church's point of view can be gleaned from writings of the Gillow period and texts like Medina Villegas, *Monografía de Nuestra Señora de la Soledad.*

6 Esparza, *Gillow.*

7 Ibid., 96.

8 In all fairness to Esparza, Gillow was indeed deeply involved in commercial agriculture. Gillow merits analysis as a landowner, economic modernizer, and prelate, but Esparza's impassioned attack on him as the "landowning bishop" deprives us of a more nuanced understanding of this historical figure. See also Overmyer-Velázquez, "Visions of the Emerald City." Overmyer-Velázquez asserts that the main thrust of Gillow's administration in the city was the merger of religion and capitalist modernization. He suggests that the formation and direction of the city's Círculo de Obreros Católicos under the archbishop stalled effective urban labor organizing.

9 See Hamnet, *Politics and Trade in Southern Mexico*; and Sánchez Silva, *Indios, comerciantes, y burocracia.*

10 Berry, *The Reform.*

11 José Mariano Galíndez, as cited in ibid., 11–12.

12 Berry, *The Reform.*

13 See Chassen-López, *From Liberal to Revolutionary Oaxaca*, 88–105.

14 See AHAO, DGP 1868 through 1871.

15 Christian, *Local Religion.*

16 For coverage of these issues in Oaxaca, see Traffano, "Indios curas, y nación."

17 For example, AHAO, DGP 1868, Manuel A. Casterán, Cudrante provisional para la parroquia de Santa María Jaltepec, September 30, 1868.

18 AHAO, DGP 1868, José Manuel C. Villa Alta, September 19, 1868.

19 For example, AHAO, DGP 1872–1873, Negocio de Nochixtlán con Apoala.

20 AHAO, DGP 1868, Casterán, Cudrante provisional para la parroquia de Santa María Jaltepec, September 30, 1868.

21 See AHAO, DGP 1880–1881, for many examples of fervent requests for priests; nearly every box during the period contains several such letters.

22 AHAO, DGP 1868, Juan María Muñoscano, Arancel aproximativo que actualmente rigen en la parróquia de San Francisco Cajonos, August 25, 1868.

23 See the receipts and reports from Juquila and Cuixtla in almost every box in AHAO, Parroquias, from the 1860s to the early 1900s. Similar documents can be found for Etla's Señor de las Peñas during these years, but a detailed account book covering 1871 to 1885 resides in AHAO, DGP 1885–1886.

24 AHAO, DGP 1880–1881, José Antonio Mendoza, Datos sobre las fiestas del Señor de Esquipulas en Zaachila, 1855–1881. In this remarkable document,

Mendoza, the secretary of the *cofradía* (brotherhood), divided the fiesta's history in three phases: 1855–66, 1866–72, and 1873–79. In the first, costs and festivities appear stable for over a decade and the sodality's members sustained it, soliciting contributions. In the immediate post-Reform period, costs increased, but the brotherhood not only kept supporting their devotion but also added the sponsorship of the feast of the Holy Cross and spent more on musicians. During the third period, costs climbed further and brothers set up a special fund to sustain the fiesta. They also began putting on more elaborate fireworks displays. In 1880 and 1881, spending declined to nearly pre-Reform levels and contributions grew scarcer, but the brothers kept the fiesta going.

25 Traffano, "Indios, curas y nación," chaps. 4 and 5.
26 See Adame Goddard, *El pensamiento político*; Ceballos Ramírez, *El catolicismo social*; and Ceballos Ramírez and Garza Rangel, eds., *Catolicismo social*.
27 Ceballos Ramírez, *El catolicismo social*, 27–40.
28 See Harris, *Lourdes*. Surprisingly, Gillow never mentioned visiting Lourdes.
29 Rivera G., *Reminicencias*, 3–40.
30 Ibid., 113–25. Gillow considered his estate a model of Christian rural development. Along with modern machinery, he introduced a uniformed corps of thirty-six Mexico City orphan boys in hopes of "awakening the love of order and work" among the young toughs and getting his machines out of the "hands of inept Indians." However, most of these individuals refused to abandon their scandalous tendencies and had to be ushered off the estate. He also experimented with wage levels but claimed that raising them encouraged vagrancy and vice. Instead, he advocated for estate chapels, religious schools, and nonprofit stores, as well as patronizing a resident priest and hacienda religious festivals.
31 There was a faction within the Mexican hierarchy opposed to Romanization. Gillow labeled this group *"la familia tapatía"* due to its epicenter in the Jalisco region; see O'Dogherty, "El ascenso de una jerarquía eclesial intransigente."
32 These were published in the archdiocese's *Boletín Oficial*, which can be consulted in the AHAO, and also as pamphlets and handbills. Some of these other printings also reside in the *folletería* collections of the AHAO and the FLCG.
33 Gillow's pastoral visit diaries reside at the FLCG.
34 Knight, *The Mexican Revolution*, 1:424–34.
35 See Rivera G., *Reminicencias*.
36 O'Dogherty, "El ascenso de una jerarquía eclesial intransigente."
37 For a history of this institution, see Edwards, "In Science and Virtue."
38 O'Dogherty, "El ascenso de una jerarquía eclesial intransigente."
39 Esparza, *Gillow*, 23–26.
40 See AHAO, DGC, boxes dated 1887–1922. Vicar General Carlos Gracida's

letters, written to Gillow under the alias Mr. Gibbs and Gibis during his exile, form an almost daily chronicle of the Oaxacan church hierarchy's tribulations during the revolution.

41 Ceballos Ramírez, *El catolicismo social*, 256–57. Ceballos Ramírez maintains that social Catholic activists counted Gillow as one of their few supporters within the high clergy. He also notes that Oaxaca was one of the few provinces which enacted the suggestions of the Catholic congresses.

42 See "La biografía de José Othón Núñez, Obispo de Zamora," *Boletín Oficial*, August 1, 1909. It emphasizes his role as the father figure for the Worker's Circle, where he held weekly talks on Catholic sociology.

43 The Catholic paper in Oaxaca, *La Voz de la Verdad*, covered his visits. In a letter written in 1911, Núñez wrote to Gillow telling him that during his recent visit with the members he found some of them beginning to drift from the church's teachings on appropriate worker politics and ideology due to "recent political struggles." He assured his mentor that he would delay his departure from Oaxaca in order to carry out a *"misioncita"* (little mission) to right the wayward workers; see AHAO, DGC 1911, Núñez to Gillow, September 6, 1911.

44 AHAO, DGSM, boxes 1889–1925.

45 AHAO, DGC 1890, Antonio Labastida to Eulogio Gillow, March 9, 1890. Labastida noted that he was amazed to see that after the previous ordinations, Gillow still had another seventeen aspirants ready for the coming year.

46 See Mariano Palacios, "Apuntes para la historia," *Boletín Oficial*, January 1, 1910.

47 The archdiocesan archive is full of paperwork related to the establishment of new parishes in the mid- and late 1890s; See AHAO, DGP 1893–1899.

48 Rivera G., *Reminicencias*, 207–11, provides a gloss of Gillow's three formally published pastoral instructions. See also Gillow's second pastoral letter in its entirety; FLCG, Folletería, Eulogio Gillow, *Segunda instrucción pastoral a los señores curas de la arquidiócesis de Antequera* (Oaxaca: Imprenta de la Voz de la Verdad, 1897).

49 See AHAO, DGP 1894–1896.

50 Eulogio Gillow, "Tercera instrucción pastoral," *Boletín Oficial*, April 1 and May 1, 1911.

51 Esparza, *Gillow*, 135–42.

52 Oaxaca's Catholic journalists referred to the PCN's foundation as "the great triumph of the revolution"; see *La Voz de la Verdad*, June 18, 1911. Throughout June, July, and August of 1911 *La Voz* discussed the party's formation and editorialized about the right of Catholics to bring their faith into the democratic arena. They also published tracts on Catholic approaches to issues such as land tenure and social policies concerning Indians. On agrarian issues, they supported the legislation to limit the amount of land held by individuals. They argued that although Divine Providence established the social

order and private property, an individual's right to control vast extensions of land ceased when that ownership impinged upon the common good. On Indians, the newspaper called for a national educational and moralization campaign to regenerate the masses; see *La Voz*, August 8, 1911. According to the *Boletín Oficial*, Oaxaca established its own branch of the PCN on October 1, 1911, and other branches around the state in 1912; see also *Boletín Oficial*, November 1, 1911, and March 1, 1912.

53 Gillow, "Tercera instrucción pastoral," *Boletín Oficial*, April 1 and May 1, 1911.

54 Ibid. Of course, political uncertainties may have inspired Gillow to publish this document a year before the twenty-fifth anniversary of his consecration.

55 For a description of Gillow's return, see *El Mercurio*, March 6 and 7, 1921.

56 Pontificia Commissio Pro America Latina, *Actas y decretos*.

57 Lira Vásquez, "La ciudad de Oaxaca," 380–83.

58 Gillow, "Carta pastoral," *Boletín Oficial*, June 1, 1908.

TWO CROWNING IMAGES

1 The main primary sources on the coronation and the Fourth National Catholic Congress are the Catholic weekly newspaper *La Voz*, Oaxaca's English-language daily *The Oaxaca Herald*, the monthly organ of the Oaxacan archdiocese, the *Boletín Oficial*, and a book published by the archdiocese, *Albúm de la Coronación de la Santísima Virgen de la Soledad que se venera en Oaxaca*. *La Voz* and the *Boletín Oficial* should be analyzed as two faces of the same archdiocesan journalistic project. The former targeted the general lay readership and the latter the province's clergy, but they were produced in the same workshop outfitted by Archbishop Gillow and guided throughout much of their respective histories by José Othón Núñez. His correspondence with Gillow reveals Núñez as the conduit of the archbishop's directives concerning *La Voz*'s content; see AHAO, DGC 1901, caja 2, Núñez to Gillow, July 14, 1901. Many of the clerics who wrote for the *Boletín Oficial* also contributed to *La Voz*, but the use of pseudonyms obscures their identities. The *Albúm* was also printed at *La Voz*, and its writers were the same cadre of cleric-authors.

2 *Boletín Oficial*, April 1, 1909.

3 *The Oaxaca Herald*, January 17, 1909.

4 FLCG, Folletería, Programa de las fiestas con que sera solemnizada la coronacíon de la Santísima Virgen de La Soledad, January 1909.

5 *Boletín Oficial*, May 1, 1909.

6 Among the men listed as pillow-bearers, three of four also sponsored *carros alegóricos*. The archdiocese also published the names of the coronation's *madrinas*. For the most part, these patronesses were matriarchs of Oaxaca's elite families. See *Boletín Oficial*, June 1, 1909.

7 In 1903, newly elected pope Pius X published his *Motu Propio* on church

music. The regulations allowed for orchestral accompaniment of choirs under strict guidelines and with special license from ecclesiastical authorities. Among the composers that wrote works conforming to the new rules was Max Filke; see "Musical Instruments in Church Services," *The Catholic Encyclopedia*, vol. 10 (New York: Robert Appleton Co., 1911). http://www.new advent.org/cathen/10657a.htm. Evidently the Oaxacan archdiocese was also modeling the latest Vatican directives on sacred music.

8 *Albúm de la Santísima Virgen*, AHAO, Biblioteca.

9 See Brading, *The First America*.

10 Medina Villegas, *Monografía de Nuestra Señora de la Soledad*. The most dramatic evidence of this resides in the anniversary celebrations of 1959. Once again, in a gathering of national Catholic luminaries and Vatican representatives, the Oaxacan church fêted its patroness and staged a parade of *carros alegóricos*, including replicas of the 1909 floats. This book republished the original event's sermons and the conclusions of the 1909 National Catholic Congress.

11 See Turner, *Dramas, Fields, and Metaphors* and *From Ritual to Theatre*.

12 Scott, *Domination and the Arts of Resistance*.

13 Hobsbawm, "Introduction." Hobsbawm alludes to modern Catholicism's novel political use of ritual, ceremony, and myth in his concluding essay in this volume without providing details; see Hobsbawm, "Mass-Producing Traditions," 283.

14 Davis, *Parades and Power*.

15 For a discussion of the Cajonos case in terms of Zapotec religion and evangelization, see Tavárez, "Colonial Evangelization and Native Resistance." See also Tavárez, "Autonomy, Honor, and the Ancestors."

16 See Gillow, *Apuntes históricos*. See also Fondo Bustamante Vasconcelos (FBV), Expediente de los Ficales de San Francisco Cajonos, Villa Alta, Oaxaca. Labastida mentioned the book in a personal letter to Gillow; see AHAO, DGC 1890, La Bastida to Gillow, March 9, 1890.

17 AHAO, DGC 1890, Carlos Gracida to Gillow, September 12, 1890. In this letter, the recently ordained priest, who later served as Gillow's and Núñez's vicar general, wrote to his prelate in Europe as the head of the commission to promote the canonization. He revealed that he had prepared a set of documents with the appropriate signatures and sent it on to Gillow.

18 Robles may have been named after one of the martyrs.

19 FBV, Expediente de los Ficales de San Francisco Cajonos, Villa Alta, Oaxaca. A curious omission from stories about the martyrs that the Oaxacan church now employs is that Gillow's forensic testimony claimed that the remains of one of the martyrs showed evidence of mestizo heritage. This suggests that there may have been some interest in promoting their twin martyrdom as symbolically panethnic.

20 In February 1891, archdiocesan secretary Anastacio Santaëlla mentioned the

receipt of documents relevant to the martyrs and instructions from Gillow as to further action on them; see AHAO, DGC 1891, Santaella to Gillow, February 19, 1891. In November 1891, Santaella lamented that the Cajonos case had not been prepared in time for Gillow to present it properly in Rome: AHAO, DGC 1891, Santaella to Gillow, November 20, 1981. In 1905 Father Pedro Rey recalled his personal role in Gillow's miraculous cure in 1889. He was the one who applied the martyr's relics to the prelate's body. He described it as a treasured and moving memory; see AHAO, DGC 1905, caja 2, Rey to Gillow, March 8, 1905.

21 In 2002, the martyrs finally gained beatification during the same visit to Mexico in which the ailing John Paul II canonized Juan Diego; see Bruni and Thomson, "Bolstering the Faith of Indians."

22 FLCG, Eulogio Gillow, Libros de las visitas pastorales del Señor Eulogio Gillow, vol. 5, "Auto de vista de San Francisco Cajonos," March 3, 1910, and "Auto de visita de Yalina," March 5, 1910.

23 Brading, *Mexican Phoenix*, 288–310.

24 Ibid.

25 Mariano Palacios, "Apuntes para la historia," *Boletín Oficial*, March 1, 1909.

26 For detailed coverage of the 1901 Guadalupe pilgrimage from Oaxaca, see the *Boletín Oficial*, March 22, May 9, and May 10, 1901. In May 1910 Gillow was among five hundred Oaxacans who made the trip to Mexico City and the Guadalupe shrine; see *La Voz*, May 22, 1910. Throughout 1910, the centennial of Mexican Independence, *La Voz* covered events at Tepeyac and Oaxacan celebrations in detail, due to the Church's emphasis on Guadalupe as the appropriate symbol of Mexican patriotism.

27 Mariano Palacios, "Apuntes para la historia," *Boletín Oficial*, March 1, 1909.

28 See José Othón Núñez's sermon, *Boletín Oficial*, December 15, 1904. The climax of this eighteen-page homage to Mary Immaculate was a litany of the contemporary heresies and enemies that she would ultimately destroy.

29 *Boletín Oficial*, November 1, 1903.

30 The *Boletín* reported on these events throughout 1904 but provided especially detailed coverage in the last two months of the year; see *Boletín Oficial*, November 15 and December 15, 1904.

31 Examining the records from shrines leads one into the fascinating history of Mexican material culture. The AHAO, DGP yields scores of receipts from Oaxaca's most important pilgrimage devotions. Judging from these documents, the region was awash in images. Although I have yet to find evidence of what they cost at shrine festivals, they were very cheap to purchase in bulk from Oaxaca City printers. In the mid- and late nineteenth century, Libreria y Merceria San German was the main supplier of the various sizes of lithographs. Later, *La Voz* also did considerable image-printing business. A few communities owned their own copper plates and produced prints independently. In 1887, 9,000 prints cost the pastor of Juquila 72 pesos, or eight cents

per sheet; see AHAO, DGP 1885–1887. In 1893, 6,000 prints of the Señor de las Peñas cost 86 pesos; see AHAO, DGP 1893–1894. This may indicate an increase in costs, or inflation, but it also depends on the quantities of the different sizes ordered. Sometimes priests ordered images in different colors, and this was, of course, more expensive. For example, 3,600 half-page and 1,500 quarter-page prints in red ink of the Señor de Tlacolula cost 89.85 pesos in 1891; see AHAO, DGP 1890–1892. Prints were just one of the souvenir items sold at shrines. Often print-shop bills topped 200 pesos. For example, Juquila receipts reveal the purchase of 13,400 prints, 11,000 printed prayers (*alabanzas*), 2 gross of scapulars, and 500 novenas; see AHAO, DGP 1889. To be sure, people independently sold mementos at shrines, but pastors did their best to banish them from the churchyard. Although it is impossible to use this information to determine an estimate of attendance, it does indicate that shrine managers expected large crowds with money to spend.

32 *La Voz*, December 17, 1899.

33 Ruiz y Cervantes, *Memorias de la portentosa imagen de Juquila*.

34 For more recent descriptions of the pilgrimage, see Bradomín, *Oaxaca en la tradición*; and Morales Sánchez, *Romería de Juquila*.

35 AHAO, DGP 1900–1903, Eulogio Gillow, *Decretos y disposiciones del Ilmo. Y Rmo. Sr. Arzobispo Dr. Dn. Eulogio G. Gillow acerca del Santuario de Nuestra Señora de Juquila*, December 8, 1900.

36 In the 1920s, newspapers and Juquila's pastor reported that the festival was suffering from postrevolutionary turmoil, church-state tensions, and banditry. Oaxaca City papers called for increased troop patrols to secure the pilgrimage routes; see *El Mercurio*, December 2 and 13, 1921. During the late 1920s, crowds dwindled further and officials tried to encourage devotees and traders with promises of more troops and the suspension of certain taxes at the festival; *El Mercurio*, November 6 and 24, 1928.

37 Rivera G., *Reminiscencias*, 219–23.

38 FLCG, Las Madres Fundadoras, *Memorias religiosas y ejemplares noticias de la fundación del monasterio de la Soledad* (Oaxaca: Manuel M. Vásquez, 1906).

39 Rivera G., *Reminiscencias*, 219–33. The *Boletín Oficial*, June 1, 1908, reported that the archdiocese sent in its request in January and had received the desired response by February.

40 Gillow, Carta pastoral, *Boletín Oficial*, June 1, 1908.

41 In a sermon concerning the Guadalupe coronation, Antenógenes Silva, then Bishop of Colima, characterized the event as a religious and social plebiscite; see Brading, *Mexican Phoenix*, 299. By 1909 Silva was archbishop of Michoacán, and he led the Mass at Soledad's coronation; "Efemerides Ecclesíasticos," *Boletín Oficial*, June 1, 1909.

42 Rivera G., *Reminicencias*, 219–23.

43 See Viqueira Albán, *Propriety and Permissiveness*. Nineteenth-century lib-

erals were also particularly critical of what they considered the quasipagan religiosity of Catholic festivals and the disorder that accompanied them. They accused the clergy of promoting miracle-obsessed religiosity in order to exploit the financial potential of lower-class ignorance and superstition. Among the best liberal examinations of popular Catholicism are Ignacio Manuel Altamirano's customs and manners sketches; see Altamirano, *Textos costumbristas*. See also my analysis of these texts, "Indian Saints and Nation-States."

44 In reality, these "pilgrimages" were simply organized processions in Oaxaca's city streets, but the archdiocese insisted on calling them pilgrimages.

45 AHAO, *Álbum de la coronación*; and *Boletín Oficial*, December 12, 1908.

46 AHAO, Folletería, Impresos religiosos, 1900–1910, *Estadística del venerable clero de la arquidiócesis de Oaxaca y algunas notas históricas* (Oaxaca: Imprenta La Voz de la Verdad, 1905).

47 This circular's importance is evident in how often one stumbles across it. I have found a draft version in the AHAO, DGP 1904–1909; the pastor of Juquila, Ausencio Canseco, copied it into his parish's Libro de cordilleras, 1898–1922, Archivo Parroquial de Juquila; and in San José Miahuatlán the pastor inserted the circular into his Libro de cordilleras y providencias, 1897–1959, Archivo Parroquial de San José Miahuatlán.

48 *Boletín Oficial*, 1909–1911.

49 AHAO, DGC 1900, Juan E. Quiroz to Anastacio Santaella, June 4, 1900. This letter from the pastor of San Gabriel Chilac represents the best description of a rural mission. Its author described four Josephine missionaries, two priests, and two subdeacons working from 7:45 a.m. to 8:00 p.m. every day from April 25 through May 30, 1900. In addition to a great deal of preaching, this missionary team performed 3,500 confessions, married 102 *amancebados* (couples living out of wedlock), and "fixed" countless *casados descompuestos* (troubled marriages). When discussing missions in their correspondence priests saw them as a means to purify their pueblos or redress local problems. For examples, see AHAO, DGC 1904, caja 1, Onofre Castillo, Tabaa, to Manuel de J. Ochoa, January 2, 1904; and also AHAO, DGC 1905, caja 1, Timoteo Olivera, Putla, to Manuel de J. Ochoa, February 7, 1905. Olivera mentioned the hundred-peso fee for the mission.

50 For a description of missions in Spain, see Christian, *Moving Crucifixes*.

51 Mariano López Ruís, "El Señor de las Vidrieras," *La Voz*, March 19, 1911.

52 On this issue in the colonial period, see Louise Burkhart, *The Slippery Earth*. See also Taylor, *Magistrates*.

53 Pius X's 1903 regulations sought to homogenize and traditionalize liturgical music. They stipulated the banishment of popular instruments from ritual and emphasized the primacy of choral music with organ accompaniment. Churches without organs could use harmoniums, but brass instruments were specifically prohibited. Efforts by Oaxacan clergymen to impose these regula-

tions in indigenous parishes met with resistance. In some cases, parishioners threatened to cease celebrating services if pastors excluded their bands. Some even resisted giving up profane repertoire, such as Italian opera overtures, during services. Other communities simply pleaded poverty and refused to purchase harmoniums. In 1904, correspondence reveals considerable priest-parishioner tension over music. For example, see AHAO, DGC 1904, Bejamín Robles in Yalina to Manuel de J. Ochoa.

54 *La Voz*, February 20, 1910.

THREE THE SPIRIT OF ASSOCIATION

1 O'Dogherty, "El ascenso de una jerarquía eclesial intransigente."

2 Jrade, "Counterrevolution in Mexico"; Meyer, *La cristiada*; and Olivera Sedano, *Aspectos del conflicto religioso.*

3 Adame Goddard, *El pensamiento político,* 17–29 and 153–71. Adame Goddard noted the formation of the separate men's and women's branches of the Sociedad Católica in 1868 and 1869, respectively, and the expansion or emergence of branches of this organization in several other states by 1877, including Oaxaca.

4 Ceballos Ramírez, *El catolicismo social,* 21–26 and 159–74.

5 Traffano, "Indios, curas, y nación," 235–50.

6 Rugeley, *Of Wonders and Wise Men,* 143–67.

7 See AHAO, DGP, 1870–1871, *Reglamento de la Asociación Piadosa de Caridad.* Santo Domingo Ocotlán, February 7, 1870.

8 See AHAO, DGP 1878–1879, María Santaella to Presidenta de la Sociedad Católica de Yanhuitlán, January 20, 1878. See also AHAO, DGP 1878–1879, María Santaella to Presidenta de la Sociedad Católica de Analco, December 16, 1878. Santaella, the sister of Luis Santaella, a locally renowned orator and pastor of Jalatlaco, also published her own religious poetry; see FLCG, Folletería, María Santaella, *Poesías religiosas* (Oaxaca: Imprenta de La Voz de la Verdad, 1900).

9 See AHAO, Impresos Religiosos, 1880–1899, *Breve instrucción aprobada por la Sociedad Católica de esta ciudad: que servirá de reglamento a las señoras de las sociedades foráneas* (Oaxaca: Imprenta de San-German, 1899).

10 For example, see his approval of the Sociedad Católica: FLCG, Libros de las visitas pastorales del Señor Eulogio Gillow, vol. 1, "Auto de visita, Santa Catarina Minas," February 22, 1888.

11 See FLCG, Gillow, Libros de las visitas pastorales del Señor Eulogio Gillow, vol. 1, passim. For a dramatic scolding of a parish and its pastor touching all these issues, see FLCG, Libros de las visitas pastorales del Señor Eulogio Gillow, vol. 6, "Auto de visita, Loxicha," March 9, 1896. Here Gillow criticized the neglect and disorder of all aspects of parish administration and ritual and

threatened to suspend services and transfer the parish seat if these problems were not addressed by Holy Week 1897.

Gillow also revealed that a deep rift between the pastor and parishioners exacerbated the issues. He stressed that the priest had every right to administer the parish as he saw fit, but that did not excuse his slipshod management, disrespectful attitude toward Indians, abuse of their labor service, and his vicious dogs. Parishioners, he maintained, were welcome to voice their complaints and could withdraw services from the priest if he beat them, but they could not avoid their divinely mandated duty to maintain rituals and infrastructure, and treat their pastor with love and respect.

12 FLCG, Libros de las visitas pastorales del Señor Eulogio Gillow, vol. 5, "Auto de visita, Jamiltepec," Februrary 15, 1895. In this particular town the participants in new associations appear to have been primarily women; Gillow spoke exclusively of *socias* in his declaration.

13 See AHAO, Folletería, 1900–1910, Eulogio Gillow, "Tercera instrucción pastoral," *Boletín Oficial*, April 1 and May 1, 1911.

14 *Conclusiones del IV Congreso Católico* (Oaxaca: La Voz de la Verdad, 1909).

15 Gillow frequently used this terminology in reference to Indian groups; see FLCG, Libros de las visitas pastorales del Señor Eulogio Gillow, vol. 1–12, passim. See also AHAO, DGP 1913–1919, Vicente González, *Informe a la Sagrada Mitra,* January 10, 1919. In this document, Father González penned the priest's-eye view of a troubled parish administration history from 1897 through 1919 in the town of San Dionicio Ocotepec. He noted the formation of the Apostolado by one of his predecessors, *"para los de razón,"* amidst a litany of difficulties with the parish's predominantly Indian population. In a nutshell, González and four of his predecessors attempted to alter indigenous Catholicism and faced determined resistance under the local invocation of traditional custom. González came to despise the retort *"no es de costumbre"* (that's not how we do it) in his unsuccessful efforts to shape when and how local Zapotecs celebrated festivals, funerals, and more mundane services. Not surprisingly, he also faced great difficulties in enforcing the fee schedule. Residents opposed clerics openly, and, in a few instances, tensions inspired exchanges of blows.

16 FLCG, Folletería, *Edicto diocesano sobre la erreción de la Asociación Universal de la Sagrada Familia* (Oaxaca: Imprenta San-Germán, 1892).

17 At the other extreme of the association spectrum were groups that had long *reglamientos* stipulating many required liturgical / sacramental obligations, extensive and frequent spiritual exercises, and advanced literacy to read and recite long official prayers. For example, see AHAO, Folletería 1900–1910, *Pequeño manual del tercer orden secular de los siervos de Maria* (Oaxaca: La Voz de la Verdad, 1909). The organization's manual is over one hundred pages long. An example of an intermediate association in terms of commit-

ment was the Cofradía de Nuestra Señora del Perpetuo Socorro, established in 1891 in Oaxaca City's Carmen Alto Church and canonically approved the same year; see AHAO, Folletería, 1900–1910.

18 See Mariano Palacios, "Apuntes para la historia," *Boletín Oficial*, January 1, 1908.

19 For festivities in Oaxaca City prior to Gillow's decree, see AHAO, Impresos Religiosos 1880–1899, *Solemnes cultos al adorable y amantísimo Corazón de Jesús*, June 28, 1888 (this item is a poster). It reveals that the archdiocesan seat already supported a handful of *cofradías* and *sociedades* celebrating the devotion and a popular image of the Sacred Heart at the church of San Felipe Neri. The poster does not mention the Apostolado, suggesting that it had not been established in Oaxaca prior to Gillow's arrival.

20 See *Boletín Oficial*, August 1, 1901.

21 For the devotion's history in Mexico, see Correa Etchegaray, "El rescate de una devoción jesuítica." For a history of the devotion in France, see Jonas, *France and the Cult of the Sacred Heart*.

22 See Meyer, *La cristiada*. Due to his personal participation in Huerta's son's wedding, Gillow was also tarred with *huertismo*. It was ostensibly the cause of his exile; see Esparza, *Gillow*, xxviii.

23 In FLCG, Libros de las visitas pastorales del Señor Eulogio Gillow, vol. 3, "Auto de visita, Zaachila," April 8, 1890, the archbishop used this phrase, revealing his contempt for the famous legislation. *La Voz* became quite shrill about the issue of indigenous social control in its coverage of the Chatino Rebellion of 1896. It maintained that if the nation wanted peace and prosperity, it had to reverse governmental policies toward the church; otherwise, they argued, Mexico was doomed to face the modern world with half its population mired in savagery and cultural inferiority. Indians, they claimed, needed moralization and religious education to purge them of their violent and immoral tendencies. The only means of achieving this goal, they asserted, was through a revived priest-led civilizing apostolate among the region's Indians; see "Plagas sociales: Ignorancia e inmoralidad de los indios," *La Voz*, May 5, 1896.

24 In 1894 Gillow noted with approval that *cofradías* in Juchatengo (a village within the parish of Juquila) had liquidated their last heads of livestock in 1891 and 1892 and transferred remaining funds to their pastor; see FLCG, Libros de las visitas pastorales del Señor Eulogio Gillow, vol. 5, "Auto de visita de Juchatengo," January 30, 1894.

25 See FLCG, Libros de las visitas pastorales del Señor Eulogio Gillow, vol. 6, "Auto de visita, Santa María Huatulco," February 15, 1896. See also Rivera G., *Reminiscencias*, 230–31.

26 See DGP 1870–1900. Bound collections of financial documents from Juquila appear throughout these years, and frequently also those from Cuixtla. Another very important pilgrimage devotion during the period was Etla's Señor

de las Peñas. Father José Epitacio Arrazola provided a minutely detailed account of the devotion's financial activities in an account book encompassing the years 1872–86; see AHAO, DGP 1885–1886. Being close to Oaxaca City, Etla was more easily controlled by the archdiocese, and was considered a model by Gillow. During this time these shrines spent considerable amounts on various building projects, decorations, and aspects of liturgy.

27 Rojas's biography demonstrates that charismatic caciques were fixtures in regional secular politics and local religion. The liberal state government lamented that other district prefects lacked his ability to hold sway over the populations under their jurisdiction; see FBV, *El Regenerador,* March 19 and 22, 1872. Rojas addressed the church as the *mayordomo* of the Lord of Cuixtla; see AHAO, DGP 1876–1877, Cuixtla receipts; and AHAO, DGP 1893–1894, Rojas to Luna, May 30, 1893. For Gillow's views, see FLCG, Libros de las visitas pastorales del Señor Eulogio Gillow, March 8, 1888; and "Auto de visita, Miahuatlán," January 29, 1896, vol. 1 and vol. 3, respectively. On Rojas's management of Cuixtla's sodality, see AHAO, DGP 1890–1892, April 7, 1890, Rojas to Luna. For his inventory of the sodality's document collection, see AHAO, DGP 1890–1892, May 30, 1890. In his obituary *La Voz,* April 19, 1896, lauded him as a great devotee of Cuixtla's Christ. His grandson, Guillermo Rojas, recalled that don Basilio spoke Zapotec fluently and oversaw the Señor's festival for much of his adult life. Don Guillermo mumbled the word "*cacique*" but noted emphatically, "Cuixtla was his town"; Guillermo Rojas, interview with the author, December 3, 2003.

28 See FLCG, Libros de las visitas pastorales del Señor Eulogio Gillow, vol. 1, "Auto de visita, Santuario de Otatitlán," May 8, 1889.

29 This figure is consistent with financial statements remitted to the archdiocese during the period, but it does not include sources of income beyond alms and fees for special Masses. Throughout the AHAO, DGP 1870–1920, receipts reveal how much of this money was spent. Of course, every year the shrine spent on wax (in 1885 the shrine purchased 2,300 pounds of wax), building maintenance and repair, ornaments, linens, laundry, wine, musicians, musical instruments, and fireworks. Receipts also reveal that several clerics participated in the fair and received payments. Parish priests charged fees for the festival liturgies and received a portion of alms outright. Other priests, often three to five of them, received honoraria for hearing several days of confessions, and ten masses (each mass was worth 1 peso) to perform at their convenience. Often Juquila's pastors would remit several hundred mass intentions to the archdiocese. One receipt noted paying José María Méndez 3,200 pesos for the same number of masses said in 1890 and 1891; see AHAO, DGP 1890–1891. This may have been the kind of irregularity that inspired criticism of Juquila's pastor. The archdiocesan missionary leading revival services received upwards of seventy-five pesos in addition to fees for masses. *Mayordomos* and sacristans also were paid stipends. Occasionally Juquila's

Catholic school teacher drew her salary from shrine funds. In addition, the archdiocesan secretary also charged a 50 to 70-peso fee to review and approve receipts from Juquila and other shrines. For particularly extensive collections of Juquila's yearly receipts, see AHAO, DGP 1885–1886 and 1891–1892.

30 FLCG, Libros de las visitas pastorales del Señor Eulogio Gillow, vol. 5, January 23, 31, and February 1–5, 1894. See also AHAO, DGP 1894, Gillow, *Decretos y diposiciones del Ilmo. Y Rmo. Sr. Arzobispo Dr. Dn. Eulogio G. Gillow acerca del Santuario de Nuestra Señora de Juquila*, February 4, 1894. This document also appears in Gillow's pastoral visit diary along with his customary *auto*.

31 For priestly comments on wax holdings, see Huesca, Esparza, and Guzmán, eds., *Cuestionario del Señor Don Antonio Bergoza*; and the 1908 questionnaire responses in AHAO, DGP 1908–1909, caja 1 and 2.

32 AHAO, DGP 1900–1903, Eulogio Gillow, *Decretos y disposiciones del Ilmo. Y Rmo. Sr. Arzobispo Dr. Dn. Eulogio G. Gillow acerca del Santuario de Nuestra Señora de Juquila*, December 8, 1900.

33 See Ruiz y Cervantes, *Memorias de la portentosa imagen de Juquila*, on the church's eighteenth-century move to gain control of the shrine. The author asserts that diocesan action made Juquila a model of colonial pilgrimage management and devotion.

34 See, AHAO, DGP 1884, Hermandad del Señor del Desmayo to Ygnacio Pérez, November 30, 1884.

35 FLCG, Libros de las visitas pastorales del Señor Eulogio Gillow, vol. 3, "Auto de visita, Zimatlán," April 10, 1890. Gillow calls this sodality both a *cofradía* and a *mayordomía*.

36 FLCG, Libros de las visitas pastorales del Señor Eulogio Gillow, vol. 14, "Auto de visita de San Melchor Betaza," March 3, 1910. Gillow reported that the devotion to this image was quite strong and generated large sums managed by a treasurer, civil authorities, and local elders who refused to surrender accounts to their pastor and spent the funds as they saw fit. Allegedly, thousands of pesos were squandered annually, and still the devotion boasted two thousand pesos in reserves.

37 Priests often complained that reports provided by *mayordomías* were of questionable value due to these institutions' propensity toward secretiveness. They often invented data for their pastors. Some priests viewed this as evidence of malice and ignorance. For example, see AHAO, DGP 1884, Informe de Teozacualco.

38 For colonial examples, see Taylor, *Magistrates of the Sacred*; and Eric Van Young, *The Other Rebellion*.

39 Huesca, Esparza, and Castañeda Guzmán, eds., *Cuestionario del Señor Don Antonio Bergoza y Jordán*, 210–30.

40 Rugeley, *Of Wonders and Wisemen*.

41 See Chance and Taylor, "Cofradías and Cargos"; and Chance, "Changes in Twentieth-Century Cargo Systems."

42 AHAO, DGP 1908–1909, caja 1 and 2.

43 This fits Ceballos Ramírez's observation that 1899–1902 witnessed a dramatic surge in Church institutional establishment throughout Mexico; see Ceballos Ramírez, *El catolicismo social*, 159–74.

44 For an example of this process, see AHAO, DGP 1895–1899, Manuel Ramírez to Ignacio Merlin, February 25, 1898. In this particular case, it appears to have been a completely priest-driven process. The back and forth between Ramírez and Merlin contains no evidence of local lay input.

45 For example see AHAO, Folletería 1900–1910, Mariano Palacios, *Informe que el que subscribe, Director Diocesano de la Obra de la Propagación de la Fé* (Oaxaca: Imprenta de la Voz de la Verdad, 1909). In this case, the association enjoyed some successes collecting funds for missionary work and put on attractive celebrations, but nevertheless teetered on the verge of collapse.

46 FLCG, Libros de las visitas pastorales del Señor Eulogio Gillow, vol. 14, "Auto de Tabaá," March 9, 1910.

47 Comments about the lack of official *"erguimiento canónico"* appear in many 1908 parish questionnaires' comments on associations; see AHAO, DGP 1908–1909, caja 1 and 2.

48 For an example, see AHAO, DGP 1900–1903, which contains a copy of the official certificate of the Hijas de María of Zimatlán.

49 Esparza, *Gillow*, 171.

50 See *Boletín Oficial*, March 1, 1901 for the publication of the initial circular on the Congregation of the Catechism. The push to generalize this organization in the archdiocese, however, took shape especially strongly in 1905 and 1906. In pastoral letters, articles, and news the archdiocesan organ tirelessly stressed the crucial nature of indoctrinating the youth before modern perversions turned their heads. In 1905, the *Boletín Oficial* also published a collective pastoral letter from Gillow and all of his subaltern bishops (January 15) underscoring the importance of the Congregation of the Catechism, and another catechism edict (July 1) reiterating the congregation's obligatory status and detailing its structure and establishment protocol. To make sure that the entire clergy understood their obligations in this regard the archdiocese also sent out separate typeset letters to the same effect; see AHAO, DGP 1904–1909.

51 FLCG, Libros de las visitas pastorales del Señor Eulogio Gillow, vol. 12, "Auto de visita de Ojitlán," March 24, 1901.

52 AHAO, DGP 1904–1909, Gillow, Libros de las visitas pastorales del Señor Eulogio Gillow. Although the bulk of Gillow's pastoral visit diaries reside in the private FLCG, two volumes are in the archdiocesan archive. The volume cited here covers Mixteca visits in 1907. The other can be found in AHAO, DGP 1900–1903; it is missing many pages, but provides an account of visits to Tehuacán in 1901 and 1912.

53 FLCG, Gillow, Libros de las visitas pastorales del Señor Eulogio Gillow, vol. 14, "Auto de visita de Yalina," March 5, 1910.

54 FLCG, Gillow, Libros de las visitas pastorales del Señor Eulogio Gillow, vol. 12, "Auto de visita de Zautla," December 7, 1906.

55 At the Fourth National Catholic Conference, held in Oaxaca in 1909, representatives of the Catholic intellectual elite and the national clergy recommended that all of Mexico's parishes establish at least four separate associations to spread virtuous practices and increase the frequency of the sacraments among men, women, boys, and girls. The corresponding organizations that they mentioned, respectively, were the Apostolado, Madres Cristianas, San Luis Gonzaga, and Hijas de María; see Arquidiócesis de Oaxaca, *Conclusiones del IV congreso católico nacional* (Oaxaca: La Voz de la Verdad, 1909).

56 FLCG, Gillow, Libros de las visitas pastorales del Señor Eulogio Gillow, vol. 14, "Auto de visita de Tlacolula," February 25, 1910. Gillow's praise turned out to be somewhat premature. In 1919 the *cofradía* of Tlacolula's miraculous image of Christ and the archdiocese clashed intensely over control of the group's finances, the exclusion of Tlacolula's cleric from oversight, and their management of the image's pilgrimage festival. See AHAO, DGP 1913–1919.

57 FLCG, Gillow, Libros de las visitas pastorales del Señor Eulogio Gillow, vol. 14, "Auto de visita de Mitla," February 26, 1910, and other comments written on the same date.

58 FLCG, Gillow, Libros de las visitas pastorales del Señor Eulogio Gillow, vol. 14, "Auto de visita de San Francisco Cajonos," March 3, 1910, and comments penned on March 2, 1910.

59 Although other documents in the AHAO, testify to the broad expansion of the Apostolado at this time, the archive lacks much evidence of their official bylaws. Perhaps the association's local director, although still subject to Gillow, was part of a separate institutional bureaucracy, and thus these types of documents were sent to the national director in Mexico City. Invariably, the local directors of canonical associations were prominent urban clerics. As demonstrated by Mariano Palacios's report on the Obra de la Propagación de la Fé cited above, they reported periodically to their prelate and the national director of the association.

60 AHAO, DGP 1900–1903, Bases de la Hermandad de Guadalupe, Miahuatlán, January 1, 1903.

61 AHAO, DGP 1904–1909. In the case of the Nieves chapel, a short note mentions the association's founding in February 1904, and its canonical establishment seven months later. The Reglamento de la Cofradía del Santísimo Sacramento at the Soledad sanctuary reveals the contemporary Romanizing thrust of this group, citing Leo XIII's emphasis on the cult of the Blessed Sacrament as its inspiration.

62 AHAO, DGP 1904–1909, Reglamento de la Hermandad del Sr. San José and Reglamento de la Sociedad de la Santísima Virgen de la Luz. This text reveals that it was an all-female organization enjoying official canonical approval and affiliation with a branch of the association in Rome.

63 AHAO, Folletería 1900–1910, Reglamento de la Archicofradía de la Preciosa Sangre de Cristo.

64 Arenas was not alone, other priests attempted to dress up venerable sodalities in the garb of a canonically structured association as well. For example, see AHAO, DGP 1904–1909, Estatutos para la Cofradía de la Preciosa Sangre de Cristo de N. S. Jesucristo. This document purported to establish the requirements for the brothers of Etla's Señor de las Peñas. According to these regulations, the members were required to contribute twenty-five centavos per year, purchase and wear the group's medallion, and take communion during its three principle celebrations during the year. In keeping with other documents of its type, it listed the pastor as the cofradia's director and mentioned that he would be aided by a group of officers. The statutes did not mention specifically the gender of the "brothers," although in listing the officers they used the feminine, *presidenta, tesorera*, etc. This suggests that it was a primarily female sodality. As mentioned earlier, Gillow viewed this devotion as a model for local Lenten pilgrimage celebrations centered on images of Christ and the cross, and sought to duplicate it in at least one instance. Thanks in large part to the revenues generated during the Señor's fifth Friday of Lent festival, Etla's pastors undertook extensive renovations of the colonial church and ex-Dominican Convent in the late nineteenth century. The festival became a kind of yearly religious field trip for Oaxaca City's residents, with the Mexican Southern Railroad providing a special *tren de recreo* (recreational train) to ferry devotees and revelers between the city and nearby shrine; Teresa Pulido, interview with the author, May 27, 2002. Pulido, Etla's reigning local *cronista* and a self-proclaimed lifetime devotee of the Señor de las Peñas, stresses the image's strong following among the state capital's residents throughout the early and mid-twentieth century. She also provided some clues about how different groups "shared" this devotion: the actual feast day of the image, the fifth Friday, attracted Indians from distant towns and the mountains; Oaxaca City residents preferred to make their railroad pilgrimage on the Sunday two days later. See also Lira Vásquez, "La ciudad de Oaxaca," 257.

65 AHAO, DGP 1904–1909, Felipe Arenas, Hermandades de Tlalixtac, 1909. This document resides in the 1909 folder, but some of the documents reveal earlier dates.

66 In addition to AHAO, DGP 1904–1909, Felipe Arenas, Hermandades de Tlalixtac, 1909, see AHAO, DGP 1908–1909, Felipe Arenas, Cuestionario de San Miguel Tlalixtac, January 1, 1909.

67 AHAO, DGP 1904–1909, Felipe Arenas, Hermandad del Santo Cristo y del Santo Rosario. This document provides the date of establishment of the regulations as May 30, 1906, but Arenas signed this copy on May 30, 1907.

68 It was not uncommon in Oaxacan communities for the Virgin of the Rosary to be the primary Marian devotion. This is due to its role as the chief

Marian advocation encouraged by the Dominican missionaries who dominated the region during the colonial period. If this was the case in Huayapan,
it would mean that the new brotherhood represented a marriage of the community's most popular devotions, one to Mary and the other to an image of
Christ.

69 See AHAO, DGP 1908–1909, caja 1, Felipe Arenas, Cuestionario de San Miguel Tlalixtac, January 1, 1909.

70 Arenas at one point seems to have slipped and referred to the "new" group
simply as the Brotherhood of the Santo Cristo, suggesting that the Virgin
of the Rosary aspect of the devotion may have played a secondary role. It is
also possible that since Huayapan's festival to the image took place on Ash
Wednesday, the Rosario feast, held in October, provided a halfway point for a
secondary celebration. It was common for sodalities to celebrate a *sexagésima*
(six-month anniversary of the primary feast), and presumably priests encouraged this for pecuniary as well as religious reasons.

71 AHAO, DGP 1908–1909, caja 2, Ignacio Ortiz, Cuestionario de San Pablo
Mitla, December 19, 1908; Cuestionario de San Pdero Teocoquilco; and
Barolomé Martinez, Cuestionario de San Melcho Betaza, April 26, 1909.

72 AHAO, DGP 1908–1909, caja 1 and 2.

73 AHAO, DGP 1908–1909, caja 1, Antonio Romero, Cuestionario de San Pedro
Atoyac, November 15, 1908.

74 AHAO, DGP 1908–1909, caja 1, Joaquín Salazar, Cuestionario de San Juan
Cacahuatepec, December 8, 1908.

75 See Huesca, Esparza, and Castañeda Guzmán, eds. *Cuestionario del Señor
Don Antonio Bergoza y Jordán.*

76 By invoking mestizaje, I am referring mostly to cultural hybridity rather than
genetics.

77 Incidentally, testimonials of exemplary female piety are not in evidence in the
early-nineteenth-century questionnaires; see ibid.

78 AHAO, DGP 1908–1909, caja 2, Manuel Castellanos, Cuestionario de Santa
Ana Tlapacoyan.

79 AHAO, DGP 1908–1909, caja 1, Manuel Gutiérrez, Cuestionario de San
Pedro Apostol, January 26, 1909.

80 AHAO, DGP 1908–1909, caja 2, Francisco Hernández, Cuestionario de Tehuacán, December 31, 1908.

81 AHAO, DGP 1908–1909, caja 2, Hilario Pérez, Cuestionario de Santo Domingo Teojomulco, December 22, 1908.

82 AHAO, DGP 1908–1909, caja 1, Antonio Romero, Cuestionario de San Pedro
Atoyac, November 15, 1908.

83 Barring the discovery of more documents, it is impossible to establish an exact
figure. If associations in other parishes are any guide, however, there probably
were an especially devout handful of individuals in both organizations.

84 AHAO, DGP 1908–1909, caja 2, Rosendo Romay, Cuestionario de San Miguel Peras, December 1, 1908.

85 AHAO, DGC 1897, Hermandad del Santísimo, Teotitlán del Camino, to Gillow, January 15, 1897.

86 AHAO, DGC 1897, Hermandad de las Ánimas, Teotitlán del Camino to Gillow, Juanary 17, 1897.

FOUR CATHOLICS IN THEIR OWN WAY

1 AHAO, DGP 1908–1909, caja 1 and caja 2, Arquidiócesis de Oaxaca, Cuestionario. Many copies of the questionnaire accompany the responses remitted by the archdiocesan clergy. It was also published in its entirety in the archdiocese's *Boletín Oficial*, October 1, 1908.

2 AHAO, DGP 1908–1909, caja 2, Julian Maria Miramar, Cuestionario de Santa María Coyomeapan, October 26, 1908.

3 AHAO, DGP 1908–1909, caja 1, Nápoles, Cuestionario de San José Miahuatlán, October 31, 1908.

4 See Byers, ed., *The Prehistory of the Tehuacan Valley*; MacNeish, ed., *El orígen de la civilización mesoamericana*; MacNeish, *The Origins of Agriculture*; Winter, Gaxiola, and Hernández, *Comparaciones arqueológicas*. For irrigation and social organization, see Enge and Whiteford, *The Keepers of Water*; and Henao, *Tehuacán*.

5 See Hernández, "Orígen prehistórico."

6 Torres Bautista, "Notas para la microhistoria de Tehuacán." The author emphasizes Tehuacán's historiographical abandonment. The only published historical study on the entire area is still J. Paredes Colín's 1922 book, *El distrito de Tehuacán*.

7 For the classic and complex treatments of this phenomenon, see Gibson, *The Aztecs*; and Lockhart, *The Nahuas*.

8 The parishes of the Archdiocese of Oaxaca were grouped together in outlying subdistricts, called *foráneas*. The pastor of the most prominent town, or at least historically most important town, served as the *vicario foráneo*. In this office he functioned as a kind of head parish priest.

9 See Gómez Sosa, "La region de Tehucán."

10 All of the towns that became separate municipalities had surpassed Coxcatlán in population by 1891: Coxcatlán, 3,472; Ajalpan, 4,313; San José Miahuatlán, 3,686; Chilac, 4,491. See Vélez Pliego, "Tehuacán." The establishment of the Mexico Southern Railroad near these towns in 1892 further fueled these demographic trends.

11 Vélez Pliego, "Tehuacán."

12 Enge and Whiteford, *The Keepers of Water*; and Henao, *Tehuacán*.

13 Tutino, *From Insurrection to Revolution in Mexico*.

14 See Henao, *Tehuacán*, 71–72. Henao cites evidence of the system's existence in Tlacoxcalco in the late colonial period.

15 Tetiaxca or Tetiachca: the chief of chiefs or supreme head of a group or tribe; see Cabrera, *Diccionario de aztequismos*, 135.

16 Henao's discussion of the function and nature of *mayordomías* emerges from his examination of documents produced by an Ajalpan *mayordomía* dedicated to the souls of purgatory in the eighteenth and nineteenth centuries. He drew data on barrio structure from documents in Chilac; see Henao, *Tehuacán*, 80–84 and 100–106.

17 Henao uses the vocabulary of class formation when discussing the prevailing social categories in the valley. I would argue, however, that ethnic identity construction is a more accurate way to describe these markers of difference; see Henao, *Tehuacán*, 87–98.

18 Henao, *Tehuacán*, 32–45.

19 These stimuli include increased investment, a great reduction in marketing costs (i.e., freight), the emergence of new markets with the inauguration of the Mexico Southern Railroad in 1892 (especially Puebla, Orizaba, and Oaxaca), and the growth of the city of Tehuacán, the region's traditional market hub.

20 In Oaxaca's archdiocesan archive the extant responses to the 1908 questionnaire are stored together; see AHAO, DGP 1908–1909, caja 1 and caja 2. The reports relevant to the Tehuacán region are: Nápoles, Cuestionario de San José Miahuatlán, October 31, 1908; Julian María Miramar, Cuestionario de Santa Maria Coxcatlán, October 26, 1908; Julian María Mirmar, Cuestionario de Santa María Coyomeapan; Juan Alonoso, Cuestionario de la vicaría de San Sebastian Zinacatepec; Juan Alfaro, Cuestionario de San Juan Bautista Ajalpan, December 6, 1908; Francisco Hernández, Cuestionario de la Ciudad de Tehuacán, December 31, 1908; Cutberto Ortiz, Inventario de los pocos fondos con que cuentan algunas mayordomías de la parróquia; and Inventario de San Gabriel Chilac.

21 AHAO, Folletería, Impresos religiosos, 1900–1910, *Estadística del venerable clero de la arquidiócesis de Oaxaca y algunas notas históricas* (Oaxaca: Imprenta La Voz de la Verdad, 1905).

22 AHAO, DGP 1908–1909, caja 2, Hernández, Cuestionario de la Ciudad de Tehuacán, December 31, 1908. Probably a handful of Tehuacán residents belonged to more than one canonically structured association, but even if the actual percentage of population participating in these groups was only 20 or 30 percent, it still stands out in comparison to other parishes in the archdiocese, where under 3 percent was the norm.

23 AHAO, DGP 1908–1909, caja 1, Nápoles, Cuestionario de San José Miahuatlán, October 31, 1908. Record of his previous posting appears in *Estadística del venerable clero de la arquidiócesis de Oaxaca y algunas notas históricas*.

24 The pastor noted that the community only enjoyed nineteen days of water from a nearby Spanish-owned hacienda every month, and irrigation rights on these

days belonged to a small number of prominent residents; AHAO, DGP 1908–1909, caja 1, Nápoles, Cuestionario de San José Miahuatlán, October 31, 1908.

25 AHAO, DGP 1908–1909, caja 1, Nápoles, Cuestionario de San José Miahuatlán, October 31, 1908.

26 Aurelio Sánchez Lima, interview with the author, July 19, 2003.

27 Hora Santa is a special prayer performed on Thursdays at midnight in commemoration of Christ's agony and prayers on Holy Thursday. It is also said when worshiping the Blessed Sacrament; Real Academia Española, *Diccionario de lengua española*.

28 AHAO, DGP 1908–1909, caja 1, Nápoles, Cuestionario de San José Miahuatlán, October 31, 1908.

29 Many priests proclaimed ignorance of *mayordomía* resources, but the pastor of Caltepec, a parish on the eastern fringes of the Tehuacán region, described a range of *mayordomía* economic activities. These included maguey planting and alcoholic beverage production, goat herding, cattle raising, maize cultivation, and salt production; the priest estimated that the capital employed in these endeavors exceeded eight thousand pesos. See AHAO, DGP 1908–1909, caja 2, Cutberto Ortiz, Inventario de los pocos fondos con que cuentan algunas mayordomías de la parróquia, January 13, 1909.

30 Here I am referring to the questionnaires from the villages of Coxcatlán, Coyomeapan, and the *vicaría* of Zinacatepec.

31 See AHAO, DGP 1908–1909, caja 1, Juan Alonso, Cuestionario de San Sebastian Zinacatepec; and AHAO, DGP 1908–1909, caja 1, Juan Alfaro, Cuestionario de San Juan Bautista Ajalpan. Since Zinacatepec was a *vicaría* of Coxcatlán, this report was filed along with Coxcatlán's. Incidentally, it is one of the rare separate *vicaría* responses to the 1908 questionnaire. The fact that clerics dealt with the community separately suggests that it maintained an independent religious identity.

32 Alonso listed the *mayordomía* of Jesús Nazareno twice. First he included it among the well-funded Indian sodalities, with approximately one hundred pesos at its disposal. But he also referred to it as one of the "*mayordomías privadas*," and cited the astounding figure of four thousand pesos. In the inventory he appended, he described the presence of an image of Jesús Nazareno of great antiquity; it probably served as the devotional centerpiece of this sodality. See AHAO DGP, 1908–1909, caja 1, Juan Alonso, Cuestionario de San Sebastian Zinacatepec.

33 Alonso listed as brotherhoods some organizations his colleagues in Tehuacán considered canonically structured associations. In Zinacatepec, gender appears to have set brotherhoods and associations apart. In Alonso's responses, associations are listed as having *socias* (female members) and brotherhoods as having *socios* (male or perhaps male and female members).

34 AHAO, DGP 1908–1909, caja 1, Nápoles, Cuestionario de San José Miahuatlán, October 31, 1908.

35 Quite commonly in questionnaires, priests listed a number of *mayordomías* but commented that several were only intermittently celebrated. This might indicate that a particular devotion was losing support.

36 AHAO, DGP 1908–1909, caja 1, Juan Alfaro, Cuestionario de San Juan Bautista Ajalpan.

37 FLCG, Los libros pastorales del Señor Eulogio Gillow, vol. 7.

38 Henao, *Tehuacán*, 100–106.

39 Nápoles also lamented that the previous owner of the Axusco hacienda tithed forty pesos per year, but after his recent death his heirs terminated this family custom; see AHAO, DGP 1908–1909, caja 1, Nápoles, Cuestionario de San José Miahuatlán, October 31, 1908.

40 This pattern appears repeatedly in archdiocesan documentation and represents one of the key ways that the gradual implementation of liberal reforms targeting the church was experienced. Typically, parish seats, through their civil authorities, initiated the termination of their participation in fee and tithe collection, as well as personal services traditionally provided to pastors. Later, subject towns often followed suit. The 1908 questionnaires reveal communities at various stages of this process. Some priests described it taking place prior to their arrival; others, like Nápoles, witnessed these changes during their tenure. Although it did not necessarily entail a loss of faith, priests often ascribed it to a cooling of piety and as a part of the modern era's deplorable anti-Catholic biases. Clearly sensing this, communities petitioning the archdiocese for a priest or for promotion to parish status underscored their love of the faith and "our Holy Mother Church," and also emphasized their eagerness to provide fees, goods, and personal service.

41 The similarities in priest-parishioner relationships between early-twentieth-century communities of the Tehuacán Valley and those described by historians of colonial Mexico are striking. A set of issues—tensions over practice, attitudes among priests concerning Indians, traditions of tolerance and accommodation, and indigenous efforts to assert control over local religion—endured, although new devotions, institutions, and modes of practice had come into being. For comparison, see Carmagnani, *El regreso*; Farriss, *Maya Society*; Taylor, *Magistrates of the Sacred*; and Van Young, *The Other Rebellion*. Van Young describes an early 1800s standoff in San Gabriel Chilac that sounds eerily familiar to the issues aired only a handful of kilometers and a century removed in San José and Tlacoxcalco; see 204–6.

FIVE CHRIST COMES TO TLACOXCALCO

1 AHAO, DGP 1910–1912, Anonymous. This report is filed along with the devotee's petition for official recognition; see AHAO, DGP 1910–1912, La hermandad del Señor de las Llagas, July 8, 1911.

2 Intense, long-running rivalries between neighboring indigenous pueblos have become something of a cliché in Mexican historiography. Conflicting festivals are a time-honored bone of contention between feuding communities. For example, see Monaghan, *The Covenants with the Earth and Rain*, 307–34.

3 Here I draw cautiously on Guha, *Elementary Aspects of Peasant Insurgency*, and "The Prose of Counter-Insurgency." For a discussion of these ideas in Latin American historical scholarship, see Mallon, "The Promise and Dilemma of Subaltern Studies."

4 Catholic legend is full of stories of sacred images that miraculously move or cry; for example, see Christian, *Moving Crucifixes*. Christian describes a rash of "image activations" in the early-twentieth-century Spain. He views them as an outgrowth of the surge in apparitionism and modern shrine pilgrimage in the wake of the Marian apparitions at Lourdes in 1858.

Mexico has its own extensive Catholic folklore concerning peripatetic sacred images. Stories of the patron saint or other image appearing in the morning with muddy feet or briars clinging to their vestments are standards of local legend. Even Mexico City produced similar alleged miracles. On May 1, 1912, an image of Mary in the barrio of Candelaria de los Patos allegedly began moving her eyes, and observers reported the Christ child squirming in her arms. Throngs of the devout and curious converged upon the church, and riots broke out when the city's police tried to bar entry into the sanctuary; see *El Tiempo* (Mexico City), May 8 and 31, 1912, AGN, Hemeroteca. Closer to the Lord of the Wounds, Oaxaca's Señor de las Peñas has done his share of legendary traveling and even left his footprints in stone; Teresita Pulido, interview with the author, San Pedro Etla, May 27, 2002. Similar stories circulate in Yucatán; see Rugeley, *Of Wonders and Wisemen*.

5 Of course, the implication here is that the devotees were trying to disarm their critics by showcasing Bartola's penance.

6 AHAO, DGP 1910–1912, Anonymous.

7 AHAO, DGP 1910–1912, La hermandad del Señor de las Llagas, July 8, 1911.

8 In general, when priests and parishioners referred to the highest level of solemnity they meant a festival with all the possible liturgical extras, such as vespers, matins, sermons, and three priests officiating. According to the parish's *arancel* (fee schedule), this would have cost twenty-five pesos; see AHAO, DGP 1908–1909, caja 1, Nápoles, Cuestionario de San José Miahuatlán, October 31, 1908. The devotees were also planning on providing food, alcohol, music, and fireworks, and hence, they planned to spend much more.

9 AHAO, DGP 1910–1912, La hermandad del Señor de las Llagas, July 8, 1911. Communities frequently promised to fix or build temples and rectories, or sought to explain why they had failed to do so. Pastoral visit reports reveal prelates constantly reminding parishes of past construction and maintenance

promises; see FLCG, Libros de las visitas pastorales del Señor Eulogio Gillow, passim. See also AHAO, DGP 1924, Francisco Campos y Ángeles, Copias de las actas de visitas pastorales.

10 In this regard, the petition is reminiscent of James Scott's conception of how subordinate groups communicate with dominant institutions; see Scott, *Domination and the Arts of Resistance.*

11 Nápoles had used the dramatic tactic of the pulpit denunciation before. As a priest in Chapulco, a village near the city of Tehuacán, he had assailed his opponents within the local civil administration during a sermon; see AHAO, DGC 1905, caja 2, Náploes in Chapulco to Gillow, August 25, 1905.

12 The author of the Miltepec denunciation offered these statistics; see AHAO, DGP 1910–1912, Anonymous.

13 AHAO, DGP 1910–1912, Anonymous.

14 Reflecting Mexico's rich and creative linguistic heritage, *pilhuanejo* combines the Nahuatl *pilhua/n*, referring possessively to children and the Spanish ending *-ejo*. The Nahuatl portion lacks the proper prefix, for example, *nopilhuan* (my children) or *diosipilhuan* (children of God). According to Santamaría and García Icazbalceta, *Diccionario de mejicanismos, pilhuanejo* refers to a domestic servant of a friar or a mindless parasite dependent upon another person. Considering its Nahuatl roots, it seems logical that missionaries chose to label their native servants "my sons." It is not surprising that servants of the evangelizers may have inspired contempt among other residents of colonial Mexico. Ironically, our informant chose an insult rooted in the criticism of the missionary clergy's minions to refer to Bartola and her followers as they challenged church authority. I suspect that by 1912, the term connoted an unseemly combination of convert fervor and ignorance, and also conflated derogatory racial and social class sentiments beneath the invocation of servile indigenous status.

15 The date suggests that this was probably the festival's farewell Mass.

16 AHAO, DGP 1910–1912, Anonymous.

17 Marroquín, *La cruz mesiánica,* 164–75.

18 Barabas, "La aparición de la Virgen en Oaxaca."

19 AHAO, DGP 1910–1912, Anonymous.

20 Blackbourn, *Marpingen*; and Christian, *Visionaries.*

21 See Turner and Turner, *Image and Pilgrimage,* 173–75 and 203–30.

22 Harris, *Lourdes,* 136–68.

23 Ibid.

24 Recent Oaxacan history provides examples of this dynamic; the Devotees of the Virgin of Soledad of Tututepec, interview with the author, March 5, 2002. On September 29, 1987, a young girl saw the Virgin near the village of El Ciruelo. The devotees and caretakers of the private shrine to this recent apparition describe the same kinds of struggles with the contemporary clergy that their counterparts experienced nearly a century before. Above all, the

church accuses them of profiteering, a charge that greatly offends them. For a similar recent example, see Barabas, "La aparición."

25 Christian, *Moving Crucifixes*; Christian, *Visionaries;* Della Cava, *Miracle at Joaseiro*; and Harris, *Lourdes.*

26 AHAO, DGP 1913, "Señor de las Llagas que se venera en el pueblo de San Mateo Tlacoxcalco, Distrito de Tehuacán; el primer viernes de cuaresma."

27 Bolaños and her supporters probably commissioned their prints in Tehuacán, the most dynamic provincial newspaper market in the state of Puebla; see Enrique Cordero, *Historia del periodismo en Puebla*, 409.

28 Pablo Cervantes Bolaños, interview with the author, June 2, 2002. Don Pablo was born in 1917 and claimed to have enjoyed a close relationship with his grandmother until she died in the mid-1930s.

29 Cures are so central to popular religious devotions, pilgrimages, and the careers of folk saints and miraculous apparitions it is hard to exaggerate their importance. Quite simply, health concerns are paramount for groups with limited access to medical care and living in conditions conducive to disease. For a discussion of these issues in early-nineteenth-century southern Mexico, see Rugeley, *Of Wonders and Wisemen*, 1–38. In addition, see Paul Vanderwood's discussion of similar issues in late-nineteenth-century northern Mexico and the healing career of Saint Teresa de Cabora in *The Power of God*. See also Vanderwood, *Juan Soldado*, an analysis of curing relative to Tijuana's twentieth-century devotion to this popular saint. Of course, miraculous cures attributed to the waters emerging from the grotto at Lourdes became the focus of pilgrimage to the famous shrine; see Harris, *Lourdes*, chap. 9.

30 *Boletín Oficial*, November 1, 1912.

31 AHAO, DGC 1917, J. Velasco to Carlos Gracida, April 25 and May 25, 1917.

32 AHAO, DGC 1917, Mauro Rodríguez to Carlos Gracida, July 20, 1917.

33 Pablo Cervantes Bolaños, interview with the author, June 2, 2002. Cervantes Bolaños could not recall the date of this event, so I cannot claim with certainty that he was referring to the same happening. However, since it is the only moment when any source mentioned the presence of troops at the chapel, and both of them note the miraculous stone's role as the bone of contention, they probably represent two different interpretations of the same event. Of course, several decades separate the testimonies of Velasco and Bartola's grandson. Both of their accounts can be challenged in a strict legalistic sense. The former's testimony may have been colored by his attempts to please his superiors, while the latter's may reflect eighty years of mythmaking.

34 Pablo Cervantes Bolaños, interview with the author, June 2, 2002.

35 AHAO, DGC 1919, Cenobio Mendoza to Carlos Gracida, September 4, 1919.

36 AHAO, DGC 1919, Cenobio Mendoza to Carlos Gracida, November 19, 1919.

37 AHAO, DGP 1920–1922, Carlos Gracida to Cenobio Mendoza, January 30, 1920.

38 AHAO, DGC 1921, caja 2, Carlos Gracida to Eulogio Gillow, July 26, 1921.

39 Ibid.

40 AHAO, DGP 1920–1922, Eulogio Gillow, "Auto de la visita pastoral, San José Miahuatlán," August 7, 1921. In keeping with the standard form of his pastoral visit reports, Gillow described his arrival, his reception, and initial sermon before listing his recommendations and decisions regarding issues in the parish. The extant copy in Oaxaca's church archive bears a note that it was copied from the original in San José Miahuatlán on September 13, 1922.

41 AHAO, DGP 1920–1922, Eulogio Gillow, "Auto de la visita pastoral, San José Miahuatlán," August 7, 1921.

42 Esparza, *Gillow*, 185–86; Luis Castañeda Guzmán, interview with the author, January 12, 2002.

43 Paredes Colín, *El distrito de Tehuacán*, 90.

44 AHAO, DGC 1922, caja 2, Everardo Gracida to Agustín Espinoza, September 1, 1922.

45 *Boletín Oficial*, January 15, 1906.

46 José Othón Núñez, "Informe leido," *Boletín Oficial*, January 1, 1908.

47 "Nombramientos ecclesiásticos," *Boletín Oficial*, January 1, 1913.

48 AHAO, DGC 1921, caja 1, Naturales y vecinos de Cacahuatepec, Jamiltepec to Carlos Gracida, July 20, 1921; and AHAO, DGC 1922, caja 2, September 12, 1921 (the second letter is misfiled amidst 1922's correspondence).

49 AHAO, DGC 1922, caja 2, Esther Iglesias to Carlos Gracida, October 10 and October 11, 1921 (these letters are bound to the second letter described above).

50 AHAO, DGC 1922, caja 2, Everardo Gracida to Agustín Espinoza, September 1, 1922.

51 Antonio de P. Valencia enjoyed the hierarchy's confidence throughout his career. He was the first administrator of the archdiocese's Catholic newspaper, *La Voz*, in the mid-1890s, one of Gillow's top priorities. The archdiocese also used this capable priest to lead parishes experiencing problems with civil officials. Valencia noted in one of his letters that he spoke Nahuatl; see AHAO, DGC 1905, caja 2, Valencia in Huehuetlán to Gillow, July 4, 1905. This would have been a definite asset for the church in the Puebla-Oaxaca boarder region. His ability to communicate with the Indians of the Tehuacán Valley in their native language may have influenced Valencia's willingness to accommodate the devotees of the Lord of the Wounds, but none of the documents pertaining to the case comment on this issue.

52 AHAO, DGC 1922, caja 2, Everardo Gracida to Agustín Espinoza, September 1, 1922.

53 AHAO, DGC 1922, caja 2, Everardo Gracida to Estanislao Rodríguez, February 27, 1922.

54 Ibid., emphasis in the original.

55 AHAO, DGC 1922, caja 2, Vecinos de San Sebastián Zinacatepec to José Othón Núñez, September 13, 1922. All of the documents relevant to this case are bound together.

56 AHAO DGC 1922, caja 2, Estanislao Rodríguez, Contestación a un escrito de acusación promovida por tres vecinos de San Sebastian Zinacatepec.

57 AHAO, DGP 1924, Francisco Campos y Ángeles, Copias de las actas de visitas pastorales.

58 In his letter to Estanislao Rodríguez, Everardo Gracida had mentioned the participation of "Isidoro" in the celebration of the Lord of the Wounds, too. If he was referring to Palacios, it would seem to indicate that one of Gracida's friends had replaced Valencia.

59 AHAO, DGP 1924, Francisco Campos y Ángeles, Copias de las actas de visitas pastorales.

60 Pablo Cervantes Bolaños, interview with the author, San Mateo Tlacoxcalco, June 2, 2002.

SIX THE SECOND JUAN DIEGO

1 *El Mercurio*, February 7, 1929. The report was filed on January 27 but did not appear in print until February 7.

2 Sadly, the reporter did not comment further on the content of Sánchez's queries.

3 For Oaxacan examples, see *El Correo del Sur* and *El Mercurio* in 1928, UABJO, hemeroteca.

4 Justina Vásquez, interview with the author, Juquila, Oaxaca, March 11, 2002. In addition, see the report published by a team of seismologists based on 20 days of field work in Oaxaca not long after the earthquake; Barrera, *El tembor del 14 de 1931*.

5 For good coverage of the period, see Martínez Vásquez, ed., *La revolución en Oaxaca*. See also Sánchez Silva, *Crisis política y contrarrevolución*; Garner, *La revolución en la provincia*; and Garner, "Federalism and Caudillism in the Mexican Revolution."

6 Chassen-López, *From Liberal to Revolutionary Oaxaca*; see also Chassen-López, "Los precursores de la revolución en Oaxaca."

7 Sánchez Silva, "Crisis política."

8 Martínez Medina, "Génesis y desarrollo del maderismo en Oaxaca en 1909–1912."

9 Sánchez Silva, "Crisis política."

10 Ruiz Cervantes, "El movimiento de la soberanía en Oaxaca."

11 Meyer, "El conflicto religioso en Oaxaca, 1926–1929," unpublished conference paper presented at Queen's University Belfast, Northern Ireland, October 14 and 15, 2005. In another essay, Meyer explores Oaxaca's more conten-

tious period of church-state conflict in the mid-1930s; Meyer, "Religious Conflict and Catholic Resistance in 1930s Oaxaca." See also Smith, "Cardenismo, Caciquismo, and Catholicism," chap. 6.

12 Martínez Vásquez, "El régimen de García Vigil."

13 Meyer, "El conflicto religioso en Oaxaca."

14 Luis Castañeda Guzmán, interview with the author, January 12, 2002.

15 Ruiz Cervantes, "Carlos Gracida."

16 Luis Castañeda Guzmán, interview with the author, January 12, 2002.

17 Meyer, "Religious Conflict and Catholic Resistance in 1930s Oaxaca."

18 Meyer, "El conflicto religioso en Oaxaca."

19 For example, see AGPEO, Periodo Revolucionario, leg. 143, exp. 36, where a public citizen in Tlalixtac wrote to the state in 1923 to denounce the role of municipal officials in the management of local sodalities and the amount of money spent during religious feasts. This prompted state officials to scold the municipal president and demand that he put an end to such illegal actions. Said official simply wrote back, denying the allegations. In another case from 1923, AGPEO, Periodo Revolucionario, leg. 139, exp. 53, an individual from a village near Nochixtlán sent in a poster advertising the town's pilgrimage festival dedicated to a local image of Christ, including the participation of Archbishop Núñez. This person underlined portions of the scheduled celebration that he felt violated laws against public religious expression. State officials directed local authorities to make sure these events did not take place and ultimately provided an armed escort requested by the local officials charged with this task.

20 Father Jacobo Martínez in Putla wrote that the announcement by the local municipal president that Putla's clergymen were to be "reconcentrated" led to Catholic risings near his parish. He claimed to know who the leaders of these movements were but maintained that he had taken no part in their actions. See AHAO, DGC 1927–1928, Martínez to Gracida, September 15, 1928.

21 See AHAO, DGC 1932, Canseco to Espinoza, November 4, 1932; and AHAO, DGP 1930–1943, Tututepec residents to Canseco, January 5 and 11, 1933. Some present-day older residents of the town recall this event with bitterness and claim the perpetrators were socialists from Oaxaca City. But they report that just as the culprits destroyed the sacred images by fire, they, in turn, died of implacable fevers while in jail in Chilpancingo, Guerrero; Francisco Mata, interview with the author, March 5, 2002.

22 For reports on these bands and efforts to intercept them around Juquila and Tututepec, see El Mercurio, September 12 and 28, November 6, and December 23, 1928. See also February 20, 1929.

23 Meyer, "El conflicto religioso en Oaxaca."

24 El Mercurio, October 6, 1928.

25 El Mercurio, October 27, 1928.

26 El Mercurio, January 11; July 7, 18, and 26; and August 3, 8, and 14, 1929.

27 Guillermo Rojas, interviews with the author, Oaxaca City, December 3, 2001, and January 26, 2002.

28 Meyer, "El conflicto religioso en Oaxaca."

29 Martínez Gracida, *Colección de cuadros sinópticos*, 292. At this time, the municipal seat of Juquila had 1,135 residents.

30 For more demographic information on the Chatino region, see Bartolomé and Barabas, *Tierra de palabra*. The Chatinos had been tributary subjects of the coastal Mixtec kingdom of Tututepec before the arrival of the Spanish. Data indicate a precipitous postconquest demographic collapse. Bartolomé and Barabas suggest that there were 180,000 Chatinos at contact, only 6,858 in 1826, and 9,731 in 1883.

31 Hilario Cortés, "Historia de Juquila," unpublished manuscript, private collection, Juquila.

32 Literally, *devout woman* and *church mouse*, these terms are not invoked as compliments. They are usually used to deprecate people seen as sanctimonious and fawningly devoted to priests. I have not been able to determine when Narváez was born. Father Canseco's testimony indicates that she was a church activist for at least three decades prior to 1928. Oral sources indicate that she died in the early 1940s; Justina Vásquez, interview with the author, Juquila, Oaxaca, March 11, 2002.

33 Rafael León, interview with the author, Juquila, Oaxaca, February 13, 2002; Teresa Narváez, interview with author, Juquila, Oaxaca, March 10, 2002; and Justina Vásquez, interview with the author, Juquila, Oaxaca, March 11, 2002.

34 Guillermo Rojas, interview with the author, Oaxaca City, January 26, 2002. Rojas, the patriarch of one of Juquila's powerful families, married into the Narváez family as a young man and recalled Matilde's devotion to the town's priests. Rojas was a shrewd, no-nonsense entrepreneur and by no means anti-Catholic, but his description of the energetic Catholic lady reveals an enduring gendered construction of church activism and close association with priests as an old lady's activity of lesser importance. He viewed her as a woman, *"como muchas"* (like many women), always involved with the pastor.

35 Rafael León, interview with the author, Juquila, Oaxaca, February 13, 2002. León, Father Canseco's nephew, recalled that the arrival of *carrancista* troops caught the padre, Hilario Cortés, and a young León by surprise. They had been out together administering the sacraments to a sick parishioner, and León had gone to the sacristy to retrieve some altar linens when the shooting began. He described sneaking out of Juquila and rendezvousing with Canseco and Cortés in Ixpantepec, where they took refuge until the revolutionary commander, Jesus Acuña, guaranteed the priest's safety.

36 This history must be pieced together from a variety of sources; see Bartolomé and Barabas, *Tierra de palabra*; Greenberg, *Santiago's Sword*; Greenberg, *Blood Ties*; Hernández-Díaz, *El café amargo*; Piñón Jiménez and Hernández-Díaz, *El café*; Basilio Rojas, *Miahuatlán: un pueblo de México*; Romero, *El*

estado de Oaxaca; and Yescas Martínez, "El sacerdote que desafió la voluntad de Dios."

37 See *La Voz*, April 4, 1896. See also *La Voz*, April 19, 1896, when this archdiocese-sponsored weekly published its reconstruction of the rebellion. The Catholic press provided some of the best coverage of the revolt. *La Voz* claimed to have a source that witnessed the events closely. This was most likely Manuel Ramírez, Juquila's pastor at the time. This revolt has yet to receive exhaustive historical analysis although it has been discussed in Bartolomé and Barabas, *Tierra de la palabra*; Chassen-López, *From Liberal to Revolutionary Oaxaca*; and Greenberg, *Santiago's Sword*. Martínez Medina, "La ley de hacienda y la rebelión de 1896 en el estado de Oaxaca," provides an interesting reinterpretation of the revolt based on newspaper reports in *La libertad*. He argues that the revolt encompassed more groups than just Chatinos, asserting that the first uprisings occurred among Zapotecs from Zimatlán in the Central Valley. Related unrest also occurred in the Sierra Juárez and Mixe areas.

38 Zorrilla remained in the region after he was replaced in Juquila and served as pastor in a few different communities in the region. However his priestly profession took a back seat to his entrepreneurial and family life. He never broke with the church, even though long periods elapsed when he had no formal post. Apparently he still said Mass and occasionally oversaw Juquila when Canseco was away. From time to time, Father Canseco and his predecessor, Manuel Ramírez, commented on his activities. One wonders if Zorrilla's openly economic and quasi-marital relations led to an unofficial arrangement with the church authorities in which he became a sort of auxiliary cleric in the region and if these kinds of arrangements were relatively common. When Zorrilla died in 1931, Canseco wrote to the archdiocese for guidance, since he was in the awkward position of asking the priest's sons to pay funeral fees. He reasoned that they had received their father's coffee plantations and had the money. For commentary on Zorrilla, see FLCG, Eulogio Gillow, Libros de las visitas pastorales del Señor Eulogio Gillow, vol. 5, January 28 and 30, 1894; AHAO, DGC 1897, Manuel Ramírez to Gillow, January 16, 1897 and August 31, 1897; AHAO, DGC 1926, Canseco to Espinoza, January 25, 1926; AHAO, DGC 1930–1931, Canseco to Espinoza, February 4, 1930, December 10, 1930, and November 13, 1931.

39 Rafael León, interview with the author, February 13, 2002.

40 Greenberg, *Blood Ties*. Documentation on local Juquila politics is very difficult to find. I have gained considerable insight into Chatino politics during the early twentieth century thanks to personal contact with anthropologist James Greenberg.

41 The first mention of this quarrel appears in AHAO, DGC 1931, Canseco to Campos, May 14 and May 29, 1931. The padre provided more details several months later in AHAO, DGC 1931, Canseco to Espinoza, August 12, Septem-

ber 28, and November 13, 1931. Matilde Narváez addressed the issue in two; see AHAO, DGC 1931, Narváez to Bishop Francisco Campos, May 17 and May 26, 1931. I do not have concrete proof that the quarrel began in 1926, but Canseco specifically linked the funds to his sanctuary tiling project in his 1931 correspondence. The shrine's floor had been the priest's pet project since 1926; see AHAO, DGC 1926, Canseco to Espinoza, the 28th of unknown month, 1926. He described it as a necessary step in his attempts to secure the Virgin of Juquila's official coronation.

42 AHAO, DGC 1931, Canseco to Espinoza, August 12, 1931.

43 Neither Canseco nor church authorities directly linked Narváez's misuse of funds to her support for Nicha's revelations, although a letter from Bishop Francisco Campos to her brothers in Tututepec in 1931 did mention her *"angustias espirituales"* (spiritual anguishes); see AHAO, DGC 1931, Francisco Campos to Samuel and Efrén Narváez, Tututepec, May 21, 1931. Above all, the clergymen strove to compartmentalize the issues. They exerted themselves in the logistics of collection in hopes of keeping civil authorities in the dark about expropriatable wealth in transaction, while avoiding the apparition issue. Meanwhile Narváez did not contest Canseco's claims, but she stalled for years despite his repeated demands for repayment, reminders of the grave nature of her transgressions, and accusations holding her responsible for the miserable appearance of the half-paved sanctuary floor. Her brothers ultimately agreed to liquidate her debt with thirty head of cattle, but even in the last piece of church documentation mentioning the miracles of Ixpantepec in 1934, neither cattle nor cash had changed hands; see AHAO, DGC 1934–1939, Narváez to Archbishop José Othón Núñez, February 8, 1934.

44 Canseco wrote at least three letters describing the apparitions in January 1929: AHAO, DGC 1928–1929, Canseco to Gracida, January 12, 1929; and AHAO, DGC 1928–1929, Canseco to Rafael Torres, January 16, 1929. He mentions an earlier letter written to Torres on January 9, but I was unable to locate it in the archive. The term *"los interesados"* more or less translates as the interested party. In Spanish it can simply mean those who have a particular interest in something. It is also a legal term referring to those with a legitimate interest in the outcome of a case and a legal role in proceedings. However, Canseco employs the word in line with yet another more pejorative usage of the term to describe a person or group who have given themselves over to a particular goal and hence are moved solely to achieve their ends; see Real Academia Española, *Diccionario*, 1290.

45 AHAO, DGP 1930–1943, Matilde Narváez, Algunos datos proporicionados por la Señorita Matilde Narváez, April 5, 1932.

46 Ixpantepec, interviews by author, February 14, 2002. My efforts to collect oral histories in Ixpantepec were only partially successful, hampered as they were by language barriers and suspicion of outsiders. Most people claimed to have

no knowledge of the apparitions. In general, men were difficult to find as many of them work outside the village or in the United States. Some of the men that I approached declined to talk to me. One of Nicha's sons denied that she was his mother. Most of the information I was able to collect came from one woman, who shared with me what she could remember from her grandfather's account of the events. This source also indicates that there was little lag time between Nicha publicizing the visions and the arrival of Canseco, Narváez, and others from Juquila. Nicha's cure by the informant's grandfather may have included a range of Chatino curing practices. One of Nicha's daughters assured me that, indeed, her mother told her about the apparitions, but she lamented that she was born so long after the events and had heard about them so long ago that she remembered very little. The women I spoke to in Ixpantepec requested that I refrain from using their names.

47 On the earthquakes, see *El Mercurio*, August 8, 1928; September 8 and 23, 1928; March 3, 1929; and April 10, 1929.

48 See Barabas, "El aparicionismo en América Latina," and Barabas, "La aparición de la Virgen en Oaxaca, México." See also Marroquín, *La cruz mesiánica*.

49 AHAO, DGP 1930–1943, Matilde Narváez, Algunos datos proporicionados por la Señorita Matilde Narváez, April 5, 1932.

50 Cortés, "Historia de Juquila."

51 AHAO, DGP 1930–1943, Matilde Narváez, Algunos datos proporicionados por la Señorita Matilde Narváez, April 5, 1932.

52 The bishop in question was probably Francisco Campos. I base my conclusion on the incomplete last sentence of the report, which ends with Narváez's mention of talking to the bishop, "*que iva.*" I believe that the rest of the sentence referred to this bishop's presence in that area, perhaps saying, "*que iva de visita.*" We know from archdiocesan correspondence and Juquila's parish archive that he was indeed in the region in May 1931 and addressed the Narváez debt issue. See AHAO, DGC 1931, Canseco to Campos, May 14 and 29, 1931. Narváez's brothers also corresponded with the visiting bishop, AHAO, DGC 1931, May 17 and 26, 1931. See also APJ, Libro de visitas pastorales, where Campos copied his reports on the state of the parish on October 19, 1923, March 22, 1926, and May 11, 1931. Campos praised Canseco's model administration, personal comportment, and pastoral zeal in each of these reports, despite the "difficult circumstances through which we are passing."

53 See his ordination file, AHAO, DGSM 1893–1894. See also priest biographical sketches in FLCG, Eulogio Gillow, Libros de las visitas pastorales del Señor Eulogio Gillow, vol. 7, although the archbishop erroneously recorded Canseco's date of birth.

54 FLCG, Libros de las visitas pastorales del Señor Eulogio Gillow, vol. 7.

55 See AHAO, DGC 1897, Manuel Ramírez to Secretary General Anastacio San-

taella, October 18, 1897; and AHAO, DGC 1901, Ramírez to Archbishop Gillow, January 29, 1901.

56 See AHAO, DGC 1900–1901.

57 AHAO, DGC 1931, Canseco to Espinoza, July 7, 1931. At the time, he was administering the parish of Tututepec in addition to Juquila.

58 AHAO, DGC 1933, Cornelio Bourget to Espinoza, September 3, 1933. Bourget had briefly been Canseco's vicario, and received praise from the pastor for his work. Bourget had his eye on Juquila, but he was sent to deeply troubled Tututepec instead after Canseco's death. In the 1940s, he finally became the pastor of Juquila and beçame something of a local *cacique* and a magnet for controversy until protests forced him from the parish in the 1980s; see Yescas Martínez, "El sacerdote que desafió la voluntad de Dios."

59 Greenberg, *Blood Ties,* 59–60.

60 Canseco wrote several letters to the ecclesiastical secretary, Agustín Espinoza in 1926 detailing his struggles and frustrations during this period; see AHAO, DGC 1926, letters dated August 31, October 6, October 16th, and one letter written on the 28th of an illegible month.

61 Luis Castañeda Guzmán, interview with the author, January 23, 2002.

62 AHAO, DGC 1926, Canseco to Espinoza, August 31, October 6 and 16, and the 28th of an unknown month, 1926.

63 AHAO, DGC 1927–1928, Canseco to Agustín Espinoza, April 17, 1928.

64 See Jean Meyer, *La cristiada.*

65 See AHAO, DGC 1929, anonymous priest, Santa María Ozolotepec to Gracida, April 8, 1929. See also AHAO, DGC 1927–1928, Father Diego Hernández, Santa Catalina Quieri, to Carlos Gracida, March 5, 1928. Hernández mentions a list circulated of suspected schismatic priests in the Isthmus of Tehuantepec.

66 See AHAO, DGSC, Gracida to Aureo Castellanos, Teotepec, March 31, 1928; and Gracida to Maximiano Amador, Pochultla, March 31, 1928.

67 AHAO, DGP 1925–1927, anonymous, Teotepec to Apolinar Palacios, Oaxaca, November 1, 1929. The copies of the documents show that in July 1927, Castellanos approached municipal authorities and expressed his willingness to abide by the national, state, and local laws relating to religious observance if he could be allowed to resume his ministry in the parish. Teotepec's civil authorities gained the approval of the state government. They also produced a document asserting that Castellanos swore to obey the Reform laws, the federal constitution, and all other national laws on religious matters; see AHAO, DGAC 1928–1931.

68 AHAO, DGC 1927–1928, Canseco to Gracida, January 1, 1928. Castellanos and Canseco may have disliked each other before this encounter, but afterwards they were certainly on bad terms. See also AHAO, DGC 1928: Castellanos to Espinoza, April 4, 1928; and Canseco to Espinoza, April 17, 1928. Castellanos was not removed from his post, but the events must have clouded

his career. A few years later he wrote a wistful letter to his boyhood friend and archdiocesan secretary, Agustín Espinoza, alluding to their divergent trajectories; see AHAO, DGC 1931, Castellanos to Espinoza, March 14, 1931.

69 AHAO, DGC 1928–1929, Canseco to Gracida, January 12, 1929. The translation is mine.

70 See AHAO, DGC 1928–1929: Canseco to Gracida, January 12, 1929; and Canseco to Rafael Torres, January 16, 1929.

71 AHAO, DGC 1928–1929, Canseco to Gracida, January 12, 1929.

72 Ibid.

73 AHAO, DGP 1930–1943, Matilde Narváez, Algunos datos proporicionados por la Señorita Matilde Narváez, April 5, 1932.

74 Canseco's original emphasis. See Canseco to Gracida, AHAO, DGC 1928–1929, January 12, 1929.

75 AHAO, DGC 1928–1929, Canseco to Gracida, January 12, 1929.

76 Justina Vásquez, interview with the author, Juquila, Oaxaca, March 11, 2002.

77 AHAO, DGC 1928–1929, Canseco to Gracida, January 12, 1929. The possiblity of a second girl seer appears in other sources as well. Sánchez Alcántara, in *El Mercurio*, February 7, 1929, referred to the girl that spoke to the Virgin as Antonia instead of Nicha. One informant in Ixpantepec reported that as she was told two girls spoke to the Virgin and the angel at the cave. However, this source could only name Nicha; Ixpantepec interviews, February 14, 2002.

78 Canseco did not name the places in his letter, but his assistant Hilario Cortés claimed several decades later that they were Temaxcaltepec and Nopala; Cortés, "Historia de Juquila."

79 Justina Vásquez, interview with the author, Juquila, Oaxaca, March 11, 2002. Vásquez did not provide a date when Canseco performed this ritual.

80 AHAO, DGC 1928–1929, Canseco to Torres, January 16, 1929.

81 In the Ixpantepec apparitions' case, two key intermediaries between people at the scene and archdiocesan authorities stand out. First, the Oaxaca City priest Rafael Torres appears to have had a good personal relationship with Canseco. The Juquila pastor frequently requested that Torres be sent to Juquila to run the yearly mission coinciding with the pilgrimage festival, asserting that he knew the people and their customs well; for example, see AHAO, DGC 1930, Canseco to Espinoza, August 8, 1930. Canseco also sent letters such as his January 16, 1929 report on the visions to Torres with instructions that he pass it on to Carlos Gracida. It is possible that Torres functioned as Canseco's advocate before Oaxaca's curia. Another likely conduit of official dispositions and rulings was the exiled Tabasco prelate Francisco Campos, who made several pastoral visits to the region in his temporary auxiliary role in the archdiocese. Aside from these two figures, other priests traveled to Juquila frequently, especially around the Virgin's feast on December 8. Archdiocesan correspondence is full of examples of priests serving as

intermediaries and messengers for their colleagues; obviously it was an integral part of institutional culture.

82 AHAO, DGP 1930–1943, Carlos Gracida to Tereso Frías, February 23, 1934.

83 AHAO, DGC 1930, Canseco to Espinoza, May 27, 1930.

84 AHAO, DGC 1934–1939, Narváez to José Othón Núñez y Zárate, February 8, 1934.

85 Ibid.

86 Ibid.

87 AHAO, DGP 1930–1934, Gracida to Frías, Februrary 23, 1934. The copy of Gracida's letter is not signed, but my assertion that he is the author is based upon reading hundreds of pages of his correspondence in the archive, and hence, recognizing his writing style and typing format.

88 Justina Vásquez, interview with the author, Juquila, Oaxaca, March 11, 2002.

89 Rafael León, interview with the author, Juquila, Oaxaca, February 13, 2002.

90 Hilario Cortés, personal diary, private collection.

91 Amparo García, interview with the author, March 10, 2002.

92 Felipe Neri Cuevas, interviews with the author, February 14, 2002 and March 9, 2002.

93 His niece, Amparo García, lamented that Cortés started writing his history when he was quite old and could not seem to manage organizing it for publication; Amparo García, interview with the author, March 10, 2002.

94 Cortés, Historia de Juquila, unpublished manuscript, private collection, Juquila.

SEVEN THE GENDER DYNAMICS OF DEVOTION

1 Ruiz y Cervantes, *Memorias de la portentosa imagen de Juquila.*

2 Ixpantepec, interviews with the author, February 14, 2002. In this case, my informants asked to remain anonymous.

3 AHAO, DGP 1930–1943, Matilde Narváez, Algunos datos proporcionados por la Señorita Matilde Narváez, April 5, 1932.

4 Cortés, "Historia de Juquila."

5 See Carrasco, *Religions of Mesoamerica.*

6 For the emergence of similar concerns in Northern Mexico sparked by drought, see Vanderwood, *The Power of God*, 32–36. For a discussion of late-nineteenth-century millenarian expectation in Michoacán, see González y González, *San José de Gracia,* 75–77. For a discussion of the deep roots of doom and gloom religious ideas, see Norman Cohn, *Cosmos, Chaos, and the World to Come.*

7 For a present-day anthropological study of an apparition movement in Italy that explores these issues in depth, see Apolito, *Apparitions of the Madonna.*

8 Barabas, "El aparicionismo en América Latina"; and "La aparición de la Virgen en Oaxaca." See also Barabas, ed., *Diálogos.*

9 See Bricker, *The Indian Christ*; Gosner, *Soldiers of the Virgin*; and Patch, *Maya Revolt and Revolution*. Bricker's analysis is especially interesting here. She argues that Maya history reveals an enduring yearning for religious revitalization and repeated efforts to make Catholicism more relevant through local revelation. She asserts that certain episodes of political rebellion and ethnocentric indigenous religious militance, such as the Tzeltal revolt of 1712, were sparked by actions of the church, Ladinos, and colonial officials to suppress local devotional movements. Bricker views the set of apparitions and Maya devotions that emerged between 1708 and 1712 as "a series experiments in the Indians' quest for a saint of their own which would be acceptable to Spanish religious authorities." These visions featured notions of the Virgin appearing in the region to "help" Indians and sparked the construction of local shrines. It was the perception among Maya communities that outsiders (i.e., non-Indians) repeatedly and brutally blocked their efforts to fashion a place within the dominant religion of Spanish Catholicism for an indigenous saint or holy figure that pushed them to contemplate the complete rejection of Spanish religion and the colonial political regime. Thus, as Nancy Farris has argued in colonial Yucatán, and I have discussed in the present study, Bricker describes local indigenous efforts to control and/or make Catholicism more meaningful locally rather than describing religious movements as rejections of Christianity and reassertions of pagan practices. To strengthen her point, Bricker points to twentieth-century talking saint cults that are common in Maya communities in the same region and the tendency of the church hierarchy in recent times to see them as a means through which to reach the Indians rather than as threats to their authority. Thus, although these devotions often managed by individuals are occasionally repressed by local Maya authorities, these acts are not seen as ethnically motivated persecution perpetrated by Ladino institutions. To a degree, we could construe the histories of the Virgin of Ixpantepec and the Lord of the Wounds as supporting Bricker's thesis. In both cases, the church's power in indigenous communities was clearly weaker than it had been in the colonial period, and thus it lacked the means to impose its will in these communities at the height of devotional excitement when it hypothetically may have run the risk of inciting notions of external political and religious repression.

10 Greenberg, *Santiago's Sword* and *Blood Ties*.

11 James Greenberg, a scholar of Chatino ethnohistory, maintains that these types of visions have been occurring in the region since the conquest; personal communication, November 5, 2002.

12 For detailed discussions of Chatino religion and culture, see Bartolomé and Barabas, *Tierra de la palabra*; and Greenberg, *Santiago's Sword*. See also Cordero Avedaño de Durand, *Stina Jo'o Kucha*; and Pride and Zorriano, "Jesús, el Diablo, y Herodes." Since there are relatively few studies of Chatino culture, it is crucial to explore the broader realm of Mesoamerican ethno-

graphic studies. For a more general approach to Oaxacan indigenous Catholicism, see Marroquín, *La cruz mesiánica*. For incisive studies that delve into religion in Mesoamerican communities, see also Lipp, *The Mixe of Oaxaca*; Sandstrom, *Corn Is Our Blood*; Watanabe, *Maya Saints and Souls*; and Monaghan, *The Covenants*.

13 Bartolomé and Barabas, *Tierra de palabra*.

14 Greenberg, *Santiago's Sword*, 82–88.

15 Marroquín, *La cruz mesiánica*, 87–92. A Jesuit priest and anthropologist, Marroquín suggests that almost all Oaxacan indigenous communities have a nearby cave that they consider a locus of supernatural power. He describes them as inspiring a conflictive approach-avoidance impulse among Indian Catholics. On the one hand they believe them to be places where the devil lurks, murders take place, and witchcraft is practiced; on the other hand, they are also the sites of saints' apparitions, the homes of *naguales* (animal protecting spirits), repositories of treasure, and a place where traditional practices found refuge.

16 The word *dueño* literally means owner, but in this context it is perhaps better translated as Lord, making these the Holy Lord, Lord of the Mountain, and Lord of the Animals.

17 Greenberg, *Santiago's Sword*.

18 Bartolomé y Barabas, *Tierra de la palabra*.

19 For an interesting discussion of this among Nahuas in Morelos, see Ingham, *Mary, Michael, and Lucifer*, 103–21. Wilfrido Cruz, *Oaxaca recóndita*, includes a Oaxacan legend, *"El caballito blanco,"* on a similar theme.

20 Cortés, "Historia de Juquila."

21 Bancroft Library, University of California, Berkeley, *La doctrina de Madre Matiana*.

22 Bancroft Library, University of California, Berkeley, María Josefa de la Pasión de Jesús, *Profecías de Matiana*; and Duarte, *Profecías de Matiana acerca del triunfo de la iglesia*; and "Las profecías de Matiana," *Boletín Oficial*, April 1, 1910.

23 Sutro Library, California State Library, Series 4: The Mexican Rare Monograph Collection, Microfilm Reel 30, No. 16, *Calendario de las profecías de la Madre Matiana: Arreglado al meridiano de México* (Mexico City: Imprenta de A. Boix, a cargo de M. Zornoza, 1867).

24 Archivo Parroquial de Santa Catarina Juquila, Libro de visitas pastorales.

25 Another source on Matiana's life and prophecies is Josefina Muriel, *Conventos de monjas*. Muriel cites only one source: an anonymous 1858 document in volume 348 of the *"miscelánea"* collection of the National Library of Mexico.

26 De la Pasión de Jesús, *Profecías de Matiana*.

27 Ibid.

28 This is the exact wording used in discussion of Matiana's visions in Oaxaca's

official archdiocesan organ; see "Las profecías de Matiana," *Boletín Oficial,* April 1, 1910.

29 Duarte, *Profecías.*

30 Ibid.

31 *Boletín Oficial,* April 1, 1910.

32 Kselman, *Miracles and Prophecies,* Introduction.

33 AHAO, DGC 1897, Hermandad del Santísimo, Teotitlán del Camino, to Gillow, January 15, 1897.

34 AHAO, DGC 1897, Hermandad de las Ánimas, Teotitlán del Camino to Gillow, Juanary 17, 1897.

35 For a rich source on notions of the devil in New Spain and a discussion of similar concerns among colonial missionaries, see Cervantes, *The Devil in the New World.*

36 Canseco wrote several letters to the ecclesiastical secretary, Agustín Espinoza, detailing his struggles and frustrations during this period. For example, see AHAO, DGC 1926, Canseco to Espinoza, letters dated August 31, October 6, October 16, and one letter written on the 28th of an illegible month.

37 For a detailed discussion of this gender dynamic, see Orsi, *Thank You, St. Jude.*

38 See González y González, *San José de Gracia,* for a late-nineteenth- and early-twentieth-century example of the broad socioeconomic role of priests in a town in Michoacán.

39 For an interesting discussion of the powerful regional role played by Father Canseco's mid-twentieth-century successor in Juquila, see Yescas Martínez, "El sacerdote que desafió la voluntad de Dios."

40 For evidence of women *mayordomas* in colonial Oaxaca, see Starr, "Ideal Models and the Reality."

41 See Chance, "Changes in Twentieth-Century Mesoamerican Cargo Sytems"; and Chance and Taylor, "Cofradías and Cargos." For an example of a popular apparition and the subsequent formation of a new *mayordomía,* see Monaghan, *The Covenants with the Earth and Rain.*

CONCLUSION   PICTURING MEXICAN CATHOLICISM

1 FLCG, Eulogio Gillow, Libros de las visitas pastorales del Señor Eulogio Gillow, passim.

2 For a discussion of Oaxacan bands, see Thompson, "The Ceremonial and Political Role of Village Bands, 1846–1974."

3 FLCG, Eulogio Gillow, Libros de las visitas pastorales del Señor Eulogio Gillow, passim.

4 For example, see AHAO DGC 1904, Bejamín Robles in Yalina to Manuel de J. Ochoa.

5 FLCG, Eulogio Gillow, Libros de las visitas pastorales del Señor Eulogio Gillow, passim.

6 See Mariano Palacios, "Apuntes históricos," *Boletín Oficial*, January 1, 1910.

7 AHAO, DGP 1930–1934, Sacerdotes registrados en la secretaría del estado y capacitados legalmente para el ejercicio del ministerio sacerdotal, junio 1934. A few additional priests may have ministered illicitly in the 1930s, but the numbers of active clergymen still pales compared to a few decades earlier.

8 Cervantes, "Mexico's 'Ritual Constant.'"

9 Butler, "A Revolution in Spirit?"

10 Ibid.

11 See Knight, "Popular Culture"; and "The Mentality and Modus Operandi."

12 Ibid.

13 Bantjes, "The Regional Dynamics of Anticlericalism."

14 Knight, "The Mentality and Modus Operandi."

15 Voekel, *Alone*.

16 Samuel Ruíz García, "The Pursuit of Justice from the Perspective of the Poor," lecture given at the Institute of the Americas, University of California, San Diego, October 28, 2002.

17 See, for example, Boylan, "Gendering the Faith and Altering the Nation"; and Curley, "'The First Encounter.'"

18 See Knight, "The Mentality and Modus Operandi."

ARCHIVAL SOURCES

Archivo General de la Nación (AGN)
Archivo General del Poder Ejecutivo del Estado de Oaxaca
(AGPEO)
Archivo Histórico de la Arquidiósesis de Oaxaca (AHAO)
By Fondo/Sección/Serie:
Diocesano Justicia Asuntos Contenciosos
Diocesano Justicia Provisorato
Diocesano Gobierno Correspondencia (DGC)
Diocesano Gobierno Mandatos
Diocesano Gobierno Parroquias (DGP)
Diocesano Gobierno Sacerdotes (DGSC)
Diocesano Gobierno Seminario (DGSM)
Diocesano Gobierno Informes
Diocesano Gobierno Autoridades Civiles (DGAC)
Other collections within the AHAO:
Folletería
Fotografías
Hemeroteca
Impresos Archivo Parroquial de San Pedro Etla
Archivo Parroquial de Juquila (APJ)
Archivo Parroquial de San José Miahuatlán
Biblioteca Pública del Estado de Oaxaca
Fundación Bustamante Vasconcelos (FBV)
Fondo Luís Castañeda Guzmán (FLCG)
Hemeroteca de la Universidad Autónoma Benito Juárez de Oaxaca
(UABJO)

NEWSPAPERS

Mexico City
El Tiempo
Oaxaca City
Boletín Oficial y Revista Eclesiástica de Antequera
El Correo del Sur
El Mercurio
The Oaxaca Herald
La Victoria
La Voz de la Verdad

ORAL INTERVIEWS

Anonymous residents of Ixpantepec, February 14, 2002.
Cervantes Bolaños, Pablo. Tlacoxcalco, Puebla, June 2, 2002.
García, Amparo. Juquila, Oaxaca, March 10, 2002.
León, Rafael. Juquila, Oaxaca, February 13, 2002.
Narváez, Teresa. Juquila, Oaxaca, March 10, 2002.
Neri Cuevas, Felipe. Juquila, Oaxaca, February 14, 2002, and March 9, 2002.
Pulido, Teresita. San Pedro Etla, May 27, 2002.
Rojas, Guillermo. Oaxaca, Oaxaca, December 3, 2001, and January 26, 2002.
Sanchéz, Aurelio. Tlacoxcalco, Puebla, June 2, 2002, and July 19, 2003.
Vásquez, Justina. Juquila, Oaxaca, March 11, 2002.

PUBLISHED PRIMARY SOURCES

Álbum de la Santísima Virgen de la Soledad que se venera en Oaxaca. Oaxaca: La Voz de la Verdad, 1910.
Barrera, Tomás D. *El temblor del 14 de enero de 1931*. Mexico City: Universidad Nacional de México, Instituto de Geología, 1931.
Conclusiones del IV congreso católico nacional. Oaxaca: La Voz de la Verdad, 1909.
De la Pasión de Jesús, María Josefa. *Profecías de Matiana*. Mexico City: Imprenta de la calle del Cuadrante de Santa Catarina, 1861.
Duarte, Luis G. *Profecías de Matiana acerca del triunfo de la Iglesia*. México: Imprenta del Círculo Católico, 1889.
Gillow, Eulogio. *Apuntes históricos del Ilustrísimo y Reverendísimo Señor Doctor Don Eulogio Gillow, Obispo de Antequera, Diocesis de Oaxaca* (1889). Facsimile edition. Mexico City: Ediciones Toledo, 1990.
Huesca, Irene, Manuel Esparza, and Luis Castañeda Guzmán, eds. *Cuestionario del Señor Don Antonio Bergoza y Jordán Obispo de Antequera a los señores curas de la diócesis*. 2 vols. Oaxaca: Archivo General del Estado de Oaxaca, 1984.

Martínez Gracida, Manuel. *Colección de cuadros sinópticos de los pueblos haciendas y ranchos del estado libre y soberano de Oaxaca*. Oaxaca, 1883.

Oaxaca, Arquidiócesis de. *Estadística del venerable clero de la Arquidiósesis de Oaxaca y algunas notas históricas*. Oaxaca: Imprenta de la Voz de la Verdad, 1905.

———. "Estadística general de la Arquidiócesis de Oaxaca." Oaxaca: Imprenta Económica, 1930.

Pontificia Commissio Pro America Latina. *Actas y decretos del Concilio Plenario de la América Latina*. Facsimile edition. Vatican City: Librería Editrice Vaticana, 1999.

Rivera G., José Antonio. *Reminiscencias del Ilustrísimo y Reverendísimo Señor Doctor Don Eulogio Gillow y Zavalza*. 2nd ed. Puebla: Escuela Linotipográfica Salesiana, 1921.

Romero, Matías. *El estado de Oaxaca*. Barcelona: Tipo-litografía de España y Comp., 1886.

Ruiz y Cervantes, José Manuel. *Memorias de la portentosa imagen de Juquila*. Oaxaca: Imprenta de L. San-German, 1878.

SECONDARY SOURCES

Adame Goddard, Jorge. *El pensamiento político y social de los católicos mexicanos*. Mexico City: Universidad Nacional Autótonoma de México, 1981.

Aguirre Beltrán, Gonzalo. *Regiones de refugio: El desarrollo de la comunidad y el proceso dominical en mestizoamérica*. Mexico City: Instituto Nacional Indigenista, 1967.

Alamán, Lucas. *Historia de México*. 5 vols. 4th ed. Mexico City: Editorial Jus, 1942.

Alonso, Carlos J. *The Burden of Modernity: The Rhetoric of Cultural Discourse in Spanish America*. New York: Oxford University Press, 1998.

Altamirano, Ignacio Manuel. *Textos costumbristas: Obras completas de Ignacio Manuel Altamirano*. Edited by José Joaquín Blanco. Mexico City: Secretaría de Educación Pública, 1986.

Andrés-Gallego, José. "Catolicismo social mexicano: Estudio preliminar." In *Catolicismo social en México: Teoría, fuentes e historiografía*. Edited by Manuel Ceballos Ramírez and Alejandro Garza Rangel, 19–27. Monterrey: Academia de Investigación Humanística, 2000.

Apolito, Paolo. *Apparitions of the Madonna at Oliveto Citra*. Translated by William Christian. University Park: Pennsylvania State University Press, 1998.

Arrom, Silvia Marina. *The Women of Mexico City, 1790–1857*. Stanford: Stanford University Press, 1985.

Austin-Broos, Diane J. *Jamaica Genesis: Religion and the Politics of Moral Orders*. Chicago: University of Chicago Press, 1997.

Bailey, David C. *Viva Cristo Rey: The Cristero Rebellion and the Church and State Conflict in Mexico.* Austin: University of Texas Press, 1974.

Bantjes, Adrian. "Burning Saints, Molding Minds: Iconoclasm, Civic Ritual, and Failed Cultural Revolution." In *Rituals of Rule, Rituals of Resistance: Public Celebrations and Popular Culture in Mexico.* Edited by William H. Beezley, Cheryl English Martin, and William E. French, 261–306. Wilmington, Del.: Scholarly Resources, 1994.

———. *As If Jesus Walked the Earth: Cardenismo, Sonora, and the Mexican Revolution.* Wilmington, Del.: Scholarly Resources, 1998.

———. "The Regional Dynamics of Anticlericalism and Defanaticization in Revolutionary Mexico." In *Faith and Impiety in Revolutionary Mexico.* Edited by Matthew Butler, 111–30. New York: Palgrave Macmillan, 2007.

———. "Religion and the Mexican Revolution: Towards a New Historiography." In *Religious Culture in Modern Mexico.* Edited by Martin A. Nesvig, 223–54. Boulder: Rowman and Littlefield, 2007.

Barabas, Alicia M. "El aparicionismo en América Latina: Religión territorio e identidad." In *La identidad: Imaginación, recuerdos y olvidos.* Edited by Ana Bella Pérez Casto, 29–40. Mexico City: Instituto de Investigaciones Antropológicas, Universidad Nacional Autótonoma de México, 1995.

———. "La aparición de la Virgen en Oaxaca, México. Una interpretación sobre la multivocalidad del milagro." *Thule* 2, no. 3 (1997): 29–48.

———. *Utopías índias: Movimientos socioreligiosos en México.* Quito: Ediciones ABYA-YALA, 2000.

———, ed. *Diálogos con el territorio.* 4 vols. Mexico City: Instituto Nacional de Antropolgía e Historia, 2004.

Bartolomé, Miguel A., and Alicia M. Barabas. *Tierra de la palabra: Historia y etnografía de los Chatinos de Oaxaca.* 2nd ed. Oaxaca: Instituto Oaxaqueño de las Culturas, 1996.

Bastian, Jean Pierre. *Los disidentes: Sociedades protestantes y revolución en México, 1872–1911.* Mexico City: Fondo de Cultura Económica, 1989.

Bazant, Jan. *Alienation of Church Wealth in Mexico: Social and Economic Aspects of the Liberal Revolution, 1856–1875.* Cambridge: Cambridge University Press, 1971.

Beezley, William H. *Judas at the Jockey Club.* Lincoln: University of Nebraska Press, 1987.

Beezley, William H., Cheryl English Martin, and William E. French, eds. *Rituals of Rule, Rituals of Resistance: Public Celebrations and Popular Culture in Mexico.* Wilmington, Del.: Scholarly Resources, 1994.

Berry, Charles. *The Reform in Oaxaca, 1856–1876: A Micro History of Liberal Revolution.* Lincoln: University of Nebraska Press, 1981.

Blackbourn, David. "The Catholic Church in Europe since the French Revolution." *Comparative Studies in Society and History* 33 (1991): 778–90.

———. *Marpingen: Apparitions of the Virgin Mary in Nineteenth-Century Germany*. New York: Alfred A. Knopf, 1994.

Bonfil Batalla, Guillermo. *México profundo*. Austin: University of Texas Press, 1996.

Boylan, Kristina. "Gendering the Faith and Altering the Nation: The Unión Femenina Católica Mexicana and Women's Revolutionary and Religious Experiences (1917–1940)." In *Sex in Revolution: Gender, Politics, and Power in Modern Mexico*. Edited by Gabriela Cano, Jocelyn Olcott, and Mary K. Vaughan, 199–222. Durham: Duke University Press, 2006.

Brading, David A. *The First America*. Cambridge: Cambridge University Press, 1991.

———. *Mexican Phoenix*. Cambridge: Cambridge University Press, 2001.

Bradomín, José María. *Oaxaca en la tradición*. 2nd ed. Mexico City: José María Bradomín, 1968.

Brenner, Anita. *Idols behind Altars*. New York: Payson and Clarke, 1929.

Bricker, Victoria Reifler. *The Indian Christ, the Indian King: The Historical Substrate of Maya Myth and Ritual*. Austin: University of Texas Press, 1981.

Brown, Peter. *The Cult of the Saints: Its Rise and Function in Latin Christianity*. Chicago: University of Chicago Press, 1981.

Burkhart, Louise. *The Slippery Earth: Nahua-Christian Moral Dialogue in Sixteenth-Century Mexico*. Tucson: University of Arizona Press, 1989.

———. *Holy Wednesday: A Nahua Drama from Early Colonial Mexico*. Philadelphia: University of Pennsylvania Press, 1996.

Burridge, Kenelm. *New Heaven, New Earth: A Study of Millenarian Activities*. New York: Schocken Books, 1969.

Butler, Matthew. *Popular Piety and Political Identity in Mexico's Cristero Rebellion: Michoacán, 1927–1929*. New York: Oxford University Press, 2004.

———, ed. *Faith and Impiety in Revolutionary Mexico, 1910–1940*. New York: Palgrave Macmillan, 2007.

———. "A Revolution in Spirit? Mexico, 1910–1940." In *Faith and Impiety in Revolutionary Mexico*. Edited by Matthew Butler, 1–20. New York: Palgrave Macmillan, 2007.

Bruni, Frank, and Ginger Thomson. "Bolstering the Faith of Indians, Pope Gives Mexico a Saint." *New York Times*, August 1, 2002.

Byers, Douglas S., ed. *The Prehistory of the Tehuacan Valley*. Austin: University of Texas Press, 1967.

Cabrera, Luis. *Diccionario de aztequismos*. Mexico City: Ediciones Oasis, 1975.

Cancian, Frank. *Economics and Prestige in a Maya Community: The Religious Cargo System in Zinacantán*. Stanford: Stanford University Press, 1965.

———. "Political and Religious Organizations." In *The Handbook of Middle American Indians*. Vol. 6, *Social Anthropology*. Edited by Manning Nash, 283–98. Austin: University of Texas Press, 1967.

———. *The Decline of Community in Zinacantan: Economy, Public Life, and Social Stratification.* Stanford: Stanford Univeristy Press, 1992.

Carmagnani, Marcello. *El regreso de los dioses: El proceso de reconstrución de la identidad étnica en Oaxaca, siglos XVII y XVIII.* Mexico City: Fondo de Cultura Económica, 1988.

Carrasco, David. *Religions of Mesoamerica: Cosmovision and Ceremonial Centers.* San Francisco: Harper & Row, 1990.

Carrasco, Pedro. "The Civil-Religious Hierarchy in Mesoamerica: Pre-Spanish Background and Colonial Development." *American Ethnologist* 63 (1963): 483–87.

Ceballos Ramírez, Manuel. "La encíclica Rerum Novarum y los trabajadores católicos en la Ciudad de México: 1891–1913." *Historia Mexicana* 33, no. 1 (1983): 3–38.

———. *El catolicismo social: Un tercero en discordia.* Mexico City: El Colegio de México, 1991.

———. "Siglo XIX y guadalupanismo: De la polémica a la coronación y de la devoción a la política." In *Historia de la Iglesia en el siglo XIX.* Edited by Manuel Ramos Medina, 317–32. Mexico City: Centro de Estudios de Historia de México Condumex, 1998.

Ceballos Ramírez, Manuel, and Alejandro Garza Rangel, eds. *Catolicismo social en México: Teoría, fuentes, e historiografía.* Monterrey: Academia de Investigación Humanística, 2000.

Cervantes, Fernando. *The Devil in the New World: The Impact of Diabolism in New Spain.* New Haven: Yale University Press, 1994.

———. "Mexico's 'Ritual Constant': Religion and Liberty from Colony to Post-Revolution." In *Faith and Impiety in Revolutionary Mexico.* Edited by Matthew Butler, 57–74. New York: Palgrave Macmillan, 2007.

Chance, John K. *Race and Class in Colonial Oaxaca.* Stanford: Stanford University Press, 1978.

———. *Conquest of the Sierra: Spaniards and Indians in Colonial Oaxaca.* Norman: University of Oklahoma Press, 1989.

———. "Changes in Twentieth-Century Mesoamerican Cargo Systems." In *Class, Politics, and Popular Religion in Mexico and Central America.* Edited by Lynn Stephen, 27–42. Washington, D.C.: Society for Latin American Anthropology and the American Anthropology Association, 1990.

Chance, John K., and William B. Taylor. "Cofradías and Cargos: An Historical Perspective on the Mesoamerican Civil-Religious Hierarchy." *American Ethnologist* 12, no. 1 (1985): 1–26.

Chassen-López, Francie. "Los precursores de la revolución en Oaxaca." In *La revolución en Oaxaca.* Edited by Víctor Raúl Martínez Vázquez, 35–87. Oaxaca: Instituto de Administración Pública, 1985.

———. *From Liberal to Revolutionary Oaxaca: The View from the South, Mexico 1867–1911.* University Park: Pennsylvania State University Press, 2004.

Christian, William A. *Person and God in a Spanish Valley*. New York: Seminar Press, 1972.

———. *Local Religion in Sixteenth-Century Spain*. Princeton: Princeton University Press, 1981.

———. *Moving Crucifixes in Modern Spain*. Princeton: Princeton University Press, 1992.

———. *Visionaries: The Spanish Republic and the Reign of Christ*. Berkeley: University of California Press, 1996.

Clendinnen, Inga. *Ambivalent Conquests: Maya and Spaniard in Yucatán, 1517–1570*. Cambridge: Cambridge University Press, 1987.

———. "Ways to the Sacred: Reconstructing 'Religion' in Sixteenth Century Mexico." *History and Anthropology* 5 (1990): 105–41.

Cohn, Norman. *The Pursuit of the Millennium: Revolutionary Millenarians and Mystical Anarchists in the Middle Ages*. New York: Oxford University Press, 1970.

———. *Cosmos, Chaos, and the World to Come: The Ancient Roots of Apocalyptic Faith*. New Haven: Yale University Press, 2001.

Comaroff, Jean. *Body of Power, Spirit of Resistance*. Chicago: University of Chicago Press, 1985.

Connaughton, Brian. "La sacralización de lo cívico: La imagen religiosa en el discurso cívico-patriótico del México independiente." In *Estado, Iglesia y sociedad en México, siglo XIX*. Edited by Alvaro Matute, Evelia Trejo, and Brian Connaughton, 223–50. Mexico City: Universidad Nacional Autótonoma de México / Editorial Porrúa, 1995.

Cordero, Enrique. *Historia del periodismo en puebla, 1820–1946*. Puebla: Editorial de Bohemia Poblana, 1946.

Cordero Avendaño de Durand, Carmen. *Stina Jo'o Kucha: El Santo Padre Sol*. Oaxaca: Biblioteca Pública de Oaxaca, 1986.

Correa Etchegaray, Leónora. "El rescate de una devoción jesuítica: El Sagrado Corazón de Jesús en la primera mitad del siglo XIX." In *Historia de la Iglesia en el siglo XIX*. Edited by Manuel Ramos Medina, 369–80. Mexico: Centro de Estudios de Historia de México Condumex, 1998.

Costeloe, Michael P. *Church Wealth in Mexico*. Cambridge: Cambridge University Press, 1971.

———. *Church and State in Independent Mexico: A Study of the Patronage Debate, 1821–1857*. London: Royal Historical Society, 1978.

Curley, Robert. "'The First Encounter': Catholic Politics in Revolutionary Jalisco, 1917–19." In *Faith and Impiety in Revolutionary Mexico*. Edited by Matthew Butler, 131–48. New York: Palgrave Macmillan, 2007.

Crumrine, N. Ross, and Alan Morinis, ed. *Pilgrimage in Latin America*. New York: Greenwood Press, 1991.

Cruz, Wilfrido. *Oaxaca recóndita: Razas, idiomas, costumbres, leyendas, y tradiciones del estado de Oaxaca*. Mexico City: Ediciones del Autór, 1946.

Cuevas, Mariano. *Historia de la Iglesia en México*. 5 vols. Mexico City: Editorial Patria, 1946–1947.

Dalton, Margarita, ed. *Oaxaca, textos de su historia*. Oaxaca: Instituto de Investigaciones Dr. José María Luis Mora / Gobierno del Estado de Oaxaca, 1990.

Davis, Susan G. *Parades and Power: Street Theater in Nineteenth-Century Philadelphia*. Philadelphia: Temple University Press, 1986.

Dawson, Alexander S. "From Models for the Nation to Model Citizens: 'Indigensimo' and the 'Revindication' of the Mexican Indian, 1920–1940." *Journal of Latin American Studies* 30, no. 2 (1998): 279–99.

Dean, Carolyn, and Dana Leibsohn. "Hybridity and Its Discontents: Considering Visual Culture in Colonial Spanish America." *Colonial Latin American Review* 12, no. 1 (2003): 5–35.

de la Lama, Eréndida, ed. *Simposium internacional Tehuacán y su entorno: Balance y perspectivas*. Mexico City: Instituto Nacional de Antropolgía e Historia, 1997.

Della Cava, Ralph. "Brazilian Messianism and National Institutions: A Reappraisal of Canudos and Jaoseiro." *Hispanic American Historical Review* 48, no. 3 (1968): 402–20.

——. *Miracle at Joaseiro*. New York: Columbia University Press, 1970.

——. "Catholicism and Society in Twentieth-Century Brazil." In *The Roman Catholic Church in Latin America*. Edited by Jorge I. Domínguez, 109–52. New York: Garland Publishing, 1994.

Delvin, Judith. *The Superstitious Mind: French Peasants and the Supernatural in the Nineteenth Century*. New Haven: Yale University Press, 1987.

Diacon, Todd A. *Millenarian Vision, Capitalist Reality: Brazil's Contestado Rebellion, 1912–1916*. Durham: Duke University Press, 1991.

Dow, James. *Santos y supervivencias: Funciones de la religión en una comunidad otomí*. Mexico City: Instituto Nacional Indigenista, 1975.

Edmonson, Munro S. "The Mayan Faith." In *South and Meso-American Native Spirituality*. Edited by Gary Gossen, 65–85. New York: Crossroads, 1993.

Edwards, Lisa Marie. "In Science and Virtue: The Education of the Latin American Clergy, 1858–1967." PhD diss., Tulane University, 2002.

Enge, Kjell I., and Scott Whiteford. *The Keepers of Water and Earth: Mexican Rural Social Organization and Irrigation*. Austin: University of Texas Press, 1989.

Esparza, Manuel. *Gillow durante el porfiriato y la revolución en Oaxaca, 1887–1922*. Tlaxcala: Taller Gráfico de Tlaxcala, 1985.

Farriss, Nancy M. *Maya Society under Colonial Rule: The Collective Enterprise of Survival*. Princeton: Princeton University Press, 1984.

Fields, Karen E. *Revival and Rebellion in Colonial Central Africa*. Princeton: Princeton University Press, 1985.

Florence Starr, Jean Elizabeth. "Ideal Models and the Reality: From Cofradia to

Mayordomia in the Valles Centrales of Oaxaca, Mexico." PhD diss., Glasgow
University, 1993.

Gaonkar, Dilip Parameshwar. "On Alternative Modernities." In *Alter / Native
Modernities*. Edited by Dilip Parameshwar Gaonkar, 1–23. Durham: Duke
University Press, 1999.

Garner, Paul H. "Federalism and Caudillismo in the Mexican Revolution: The
Genesis of the Oaxaca Sovereignty Movement (1915–20)." *Journal of Latin
American Studies* 17, no. 1 (1985): 111–33.

———. *La revolución en la provincia: Soberanía estatal y caudillismo en las
montañas de Oaxaca (1910–1920)*. Mexico City: Fondo de Cultura
Económica, 1988.

Gibson, Charles. *The Aztecs under Spanish Rule: A History of the Indians of the
Valley of Mexico, 1519–1810*. Stanford: Stanford University Press, 1964.

Gibson, Ralph. *A Social History of French Catholicism, 1789–1914*. New York:
Routledge, 1989.

Gómez Sosa, Rosa María. "La Region De Tehucán." In *Simposium internacional
Tehuacán y su entorno: Balance y perspectivas*. Edited by Eréndida de Lama,
387–99. Mexico City: Instituto Nacional de Antropolgía e Historia, 1997.

González, María del Refugio. "El pensamiento de los conservadores mexicanos."
In *Mexican and Mexican American Experience in the Nineteenth Century*.
Edited by Jaime E. Rodríguez O, 55–67. Tempe: Arizona Bilingual Press,
1989.

González Navarro, Moisés. *Sociedad y cultura en el porfiriato*. Mexico City:
Consejo Nacional para la Cultura y las Artes, 1994.

González y González, Luis. *San José de Gracia: Mexican Village in Transition*.
Translated by John Upton. Austin: University of Texas Press, 1972.

Gosner, Kevin. *Soldiers of the Virgin: The Moral Economy of Colonial Maya
Rebellion*. Tucson: University of Arizona Press, 1992.

Gossen, Gary. "Mesoamerican Ideas as a Foundation for Regional Synthesis." In
*Symbol and Meaning beyond the Closed Community: Essays in Mesoamerican
Ideas*. Edited by Gary Gossen, 1–8. Albany: Institute for Mesoamerican
Studies, 1986.

Graham, Richard, ed. *The Idea of Race in Latin America, 1870–1940*. Austin:
University of Texas Press, 1990.

Greenberg, James. *Santiago's Sword: Chatino Peasant Religion and Economics*.
Berkeley: University of California Press, 1981.

———. *Blood Ties: Life and Violence in Rural Mexico*. Tucson: University of
Arizona Press, 1989.

Griffiths, Nicholas. *The Cross and the Serpent: Religious Repression and
Resurgence in Colonial Peru*. Norman: University of Oklahoma Press, 1995.

Gruzinski, Serge. *The Conquest of Mexico: The Incorporation of Indian Societies
into the Western World, 16th–18th Centuries*. Translated by Eileen Corrigan.
Cambridge: Polity Press, 1993.

Guardino, Peter. *Peasants, Politics, and the Formation of Mexico's National State: Guerrero, 1800–1857*. Stanford: Stanford University Press, 1996.

———. *The Time of Liberty: Popular Political Culture in Oaxaca, 1750–1850*. Durham: Duke University Press, 2005.

Guerra, Francois-Xavier. *México: Del antiguo régimen a la revolución.* Translated by Sergio Fernández Bravo. 2 vols. Mexico City: Fondo de Cultura Económica, 1985.

Guha, Ranajit. *Elementary Aspects of Peasant Insurgency in Colonial India.* Delhi: Oxford University Press, 1983.

———. "The Prose of Counter-Insurgency." In *Selected Subaltern Studies*. Edited by Ranajit Guha and Gayatri Chakravorty Spivak, 45–88. Oxford: Oxford University Press, 1988.

Gutiérrez Casillas, José. *Historia de la Iglesia en México*. Mexico City: Editorial Porrúa, 1984.

Hale, Charles. *Mexican Liberalism in the Age of Mora, 1821–1853*. New Haven: Yale University Press, 1968.

———. *The Transformation of Mexican Liberalism in Late Nineteenth-Century Mexico*. Princeton: Princeton University Press, 1989.

Hall, Stuart, ed. *Modernity: An Introduction to Modern Societies*. Cambridge: Blackwell, 1996.

Hamnett, Brian. *Politics and Trade in Southern Mexico, 1750–1821*. New York: Cambridge University Press, 1971.

Harris, Ruth. *Lourdes: Body and Spirit in a Secular Age*. New York: Viking, 1999.

Harrington, Joel F. *A Cloud of Witnesses: Readings in the History of Western Christianity*. Boston: Houghton Mifflin, 2001.

Henao, Luis Emilio. *Tehuacán: Campesinado e irrigación*. 1st ed. Colección Ciencias Sociales. Mexico City: Edicol, 1980.

Hernández, Raul. "Orígen prehistórico de la agricultura de riego en México." In *Simposium internacional Tehuacán y su entorno: Balance y perspectivas*. Edited by Eréndida de la Lama, 79–93. Mexico City: Instituto Nacional de Antropolgía e Historia, 1997.

Hernández-Díaz, Jorge. *El café amargo: Diferenciación y cambio social entre los chatinos*. Oaxaca: Universidad Autónoma Denito Juárez de Oaxaca, Instituto de Investigaciones Sociologicas, 1987.

Hewitt de Alcántara, Cynthia. *Anthropological Perspectives on Rural Mexico*. London: Routledge and Kegan Paul, 1984.

Hobsbawm, Eric. *Primitive Rebels: Studies in Archaic Forms of Social Movement in the 19th and 20th Centuries*. 2nd ed. New York: Praeger, 1963.

———. "Peasants and Politics." *Journal of Peasant Studies* 1, no. 1 (1973): 3–23.

———. "Introduction: Inventing Traditions." In *The Invention of Tradition*. Edited by Eric Hobsbawm and Terence Ranger, 1–14. Cambridge: Cambridge University Press, 1982.

———. "Mass-Producing Traditions: Europe, 1870–1914." In *The Invention of Tradition*. Edited by Eric Hobsbawm and Terance Ranger, 263–308. Cambridge: Cambridge University Press, 1982.

Holston, James. "Alternative Modernities: Statecraft and Religious Imagination in the Valley of the Dawn." *American Ethnologist* 26, no. 3 (1999): 605–31.

Ingham, John M. *Mary, Michael, and Lucifer: Folk Catholicism in Central Mexico*. Austin: University of Texas Press, 1986.

Iturribaría, Jorge Fernando. "La política de conciliación del General Díaz y el Arzobispo Gillow." *Historia Mexicana* 14, no. 1 (1964): 81–101.

Ivereigh, Austen, ed. *The Politics of Religion in an Age of Revolution: Studies in Nineteenth-Century Europe and Latin America*. London: Institute of Latin American Studies, 2000.

Jonas, Raymond Anthony. *France and the Cult of the Sacred Heart: An Epic Tale for Modern Times*. Berkeley: University of California Press, 2000.

Joseph, Gilbert. "On the Trail of Latin American Bandits." *Latin American Research Review* 25, no. 3 (1990): 7–54.

Joseph, Gilbert M., and Daniel Nugent, eds. *Everyday Forms of State Formation: Revolution and Negotiation of Rule in Modern Mexico*. Durham: Duke University Press, 1994.

Jrade, Ramón. "Counterrevolution in Mexico: The Cristero Movement in Sociological and Historical Perspective." PhD diss. Brown University, 1980.

———. "Inquiries into the Cristero Rebellion against the Mexican Revolution." *Latin American Research Review* 20, no. 2 (1985): 53–69.

Katz, Freidrich, ed. *Riot, Rebellion, and Revolution: Rural Social Conflict in Mexico*. Princeton: Princeton University Press, 1988.

Kaufman, Suzanne. *Consuming Visions: Mass Culture and the Lourdes Shrine*. Ithaca: Cornell University Press, 2004.

———. "Selling Lourdes: Pilgrimage, Tourism and the Mass-Marketing of the Sacred in Nineteenth-Century France." In *Being Elsewhere: Tourism, Consumer Culture and Identity in Modern Europe and North America*. Edited by Shelly Baranowski and Ellen Furlough, 63–88. Ann Arbor: University of Michigan Press, 2001.

Klor de Alva, J. Jorge. "Spiritual Conflict and Accommodation in New Spain: Toward a Typology of Aztec Responses to Christianity." In *The Inca and Aztec States, 1400–1800: Anthropology and History*. Edited by George A. Collier, Renato Rosaldo, and John D. Wirth, 345–66. New York: Academic Press, 1982.

———. "Language, Politics, and Translation: Colonial Discourse and Classical Nahuatl in New Spain." In *The Art of Translation: Voices from the Field*. Edited by Rosanna Warren, 143–59. Boston: Northeastern University Press, 1989.

———. "Colonizing Souls: The Failure of the Indian Inquisition and the Rise of Penitential Discipline." In *Cultural Encounters: The Impact of the Inquisition in Spain and the New World*. Edited by Mary Elizabeth Perry and Anne J. Cruz, 3–22. Berkeley: University of California Press, 1991.

———. "Religious Rationalization and the Conversions of the Nahuas: Social Organization and Colonial Epistemology." In *To Change Place: Aztec Ceremonial Landscapes*. Edited by David Carrasco, 233–45. Bolder: University of Colorado Press, 1991.

———. "Aztec Spirituality and Nahuatized Christianity." In *South American and Meso-American Native Spirituality*. Edited by Garry Gossen, 173–97. New York: Crossroads, 1993.

Knight, Alan. "El liberalismo mexicano desde la Reforma hasta la revolución (una interpretación)." *Historia mexicana* 35, no. 1 (1985): 59–91.

———. *The Mexican Revolution*. 2 vols. Lincoln: University of Nebraska Press, 1986.

———. "Popular Culture and the Revolutionary State in Mexico, 1910–1940." *Hispanic American Historical Review* 74, no. 3 (1994): 393–444.

———. "Weapons and Arches in the Mexican Revolution." In *Everyday Forms of State Formation: Revolution and Negotiation of Rule in Modern Mexico*. Edited by Gilbert Joseph and Daniel Nugent, 24–68. Durham: Duke University Press, 1994.

———. "The Mentality and Modus Operandi of Revolutionary Anticlericalism." In *Faith and Impiety in Revolutionary Mexico*. Edited by Matthew Butler, 21–56. New York: Palgrave Macmillan, 2007.

Knowlton, Robert J. "Expropriation of Church Property in Nineteenth Century Mexico and Columbia." *The Americas* 25, no. 1 (1968): 387–401.

———. *Church Property and the Mexican Reform, 1856–1910*. DeKalb: Northern Illinois Press, 1976.

Kselman, Thomas. *Miracles and Prophecies in Nineteenth-Century France*. New Brunswick: Rutgers University Press, 1983.

———. "Introduction." In *Belief in History: Innovative Approaches to European and American Religion*. Edited by Thomas Kselman, 1–18. Notre Dame: University of Notre Dame Press, 1991.

Lannon, Frances. *Privilege, Persecution, and Prophecy: The Catholic Church in Spain, 1875–1975*. Oxford: Clarendon Press, 1987.

Larraín, Jorge. *Identity and Modernity in Latin America*. Cambridge: Polity Press, 2000.

Lavrin, Asunción. "Mexican Nunneries from 1835 to 1860: Their Administrative Policies and Relations with the State." *The Americas* 28, no. 3 (1972): 288–310.

Lee, James H. "Church and State in Mexican Higher Education, 1821–1861." *Journal of Church and State* 20, no. 1 (1978): 57–72.

———. "Clerical Education in Nineteenth-Century Mexico: The Conciliar Seminaries of Mexico City and Guadalajara, 1821–1910." *The Americas* 36, no. 4 (1980): 456–77.

León-Portilla, Miguel. *Native Mesoamerican Spirituality*. New York: Paulist Press, 1980.

——. *The Aztec Image of Self and Society: An Introduction to Nahua Culture.* Norman: University of Oklahoma Press, 1992.

——. "Those Made Worthy by Divine Sacrifice: The Faith of Ancient Mexico." In *South and Meso-American Native Spirituality.* Edited by Gary Gossen, 42–60. New York: Crossroads, 1993.

Levine, Robert. *Vale of Tears: Revisiting the Canudos Massacre in Northeastern Brazil, 1893–1897.* Berkeley: University of California Press, 1992.

Lipp, Frank. *The Mixe of Oaxaca: Religion, Ritual and Healing.* Austin: University of Texas Press, 1991.

Lira Vásquez, Carlos Antonio de Jesús. "La ciudad de Oaxaca: Una aproximación a su evolución urbana decimonónica y al desarrollo aquitectónico porfiriano." Master's thesis, Universidad Nacional Autónoma de México, 1997.

Lockhart, James. *The Nahuas after the Conquest: A Social and Cultural History of the Indians of Central Mexico, Sixteenth through Eighteenth Centuries.* Stanford: Stanford University Press, 1992.

Lomnitz, Claudio. *Deep Mexico, Silent Mexico: An Anthropology of Nationalism.* Minneapolis: University of Minnesota Press, 2001.

Mabry, Donald J. "Mexican Anticlerics, Bishops, Cristeros, and the Devout During the 1920s: A Scholarly Debate." *Journal of Church and State* 20, no. 1 (1978): 81–92.

MacCormack, Sabine. *Religion in the Andes: Vision and Imagination in Early Colonial Peru.* Princeton: Princeton University Press, 1991.

MacNeish, Richard S., ed. *El orígen de la civilización mesoamericana visto desde Tehuacán.* Mexico City: Instituto Nacional de Antropolgía e Historia, 1964.

——. *The Origins of Agriculture and Settled Life.* Norman: University of Oklahoma Press, 1992.

Madsen, William. *Christo-Paganism: A Study of Mexican Religious Syncretism.* New Orleans: Middle American Research Institute, 1957.

——. *The Virgin's Children: Life in an Aztec Village Today.* Austin: University of Texas Press, 1960.

Mallon, Florencia. "The Promise and Dilemma of Subaltern Studies: Perspectives from Latin American History." *American Historical Review* 99, no. 5 (1994): 1491–1515.

——. *Peasant and Nation: The Making of Postcolonial Mexico and Peru.* Berkeley: University of California Press, 1995.

Marroquín, Enrique. *La cruz mesiánica: Una aproximación al sincretismo católico.* 2nd ed. Mexico City: Palabra Ediciones, 1999.

Martínez Assad, Carlos, ed. *Religiosidad y política en México.* Mexico City: Universidad Iberoamericana, 1992.

——, ed. *A Dios lo que es de Dios.* Mexico City: Aguilar, 1995.

Martínez Medina, Héctor Gerardo. "La ley de hacienda y la rebelión de 1896 en el estado de Oaxaca." *Guachachi' Reza* 43 (1994): 22–31.

Martínez Vásquez, Víctor Raul, ed. *La revolución en Oaxaca*. Oaxaca: Instituto de Administración Pública, 1985.

Matson, Robert W. "Church Wealth in Nineteenth-Century Mexico: A Review of Literature." *Catholic Historical Review* 65, no. 4 (1979): 600–609.

Matute, Alvaro, Evelia Trejo, and Brian Connaughton, eds. *Estado, Iglesia y sociedad en México, siglo XIX*. Mexico City: Universidad Nacional Autótonoma de México / Editorial Porrúa, 1995.

Mecham, John Lloyd. *Church and State in Latin America: A History of Politico-Ecclesiastical Relations*, 1934. Revised edition, Chapel Hill: University of North Carolina Press, 1966.

Medina Villegas, Humberto. *Monografía de Nuestra Señora de la Soledad y álbum de cincuentenario de su coronación*. Oaxaca: Editorial Progreso, 1971.

Meyer, Jean. *La cristiada*. 3 vols. Mexico City: Siglo Veintiuno, 1973.

———. *The Cristero Rebellion: The Mexican People between Church and State, 1926–1929*. Translated by Richard Southern. Cambridge: Cambridge University Press, 1976.

———. *El catolicismo social en México hasta el 1913*. 2nd ed. Mexico City: Instituto Mexicano de Doctrina Social Cristiana, 1992.

———. "Religious Conflict and Catholic Resistance in 1930s Oaxaca." In *Faith and Impiety in Revolutionary Mexico*. Edited by Matthew Butler, 185–202. New York: Palgrave Macmillan, 2007.

Mills, Kenneth. *Idolatry and Its Enemies: Colonial Andean Religion and Extirpation, 1640–1750*. Princeton: Princeton University Press, 1997.

Misner, Paul. *Social Catholicism in Europe: From the Onset of Industrialization to the First World War*. New York: Crossroad, 1991.

Monaghan, John. *The Covenants with the Earth and Rain: Exchange, Sacrifice and Revelation in Mixtec Sociality*. Norman: University of Oklahoma Press, 1995.

———. "Theology and History in the Study of Mesoamerican Religion." In *Supplement to the Handbook of Middle American Indians*, vol. 6. Edited by John Monaghan, 24–49. Austin: University of Texas Press, 2000.

Morales Sánchez, Antonio. *Romería de Juquila*. Oaxaca: Sedetur, 1997.

Mulhare, Eileen. "Mesoamerican Social Organization and Community after 1960." In *Supplement to the Handbook of Middle American Indians*, vol. 6. Edited by John Monaghan, 9–23. Austin: University of Texas Press, 2000.

Muriel, Josefina. *Conventos de monjas en la Nueva España*. Mexico City: Editorial Santiago, 1946.

Nash, Manning. "Political Relations in Guatemala." *Social and Economic Studies* 7, no. 65–75 (1958).

———, ed. *Handbook of Middle American Indians*. Vol. 6, *Social Anthropology*. Edited by Robert Wauchope. Austin: University of Texas Press, 1967.

Nolan, Mary Lee, and Sidney Nolan. *Christian Pilgrimage in Modern Western Europe*. Chapel Hill: University of North Carolina Press, 1989.

O'Dogherty, Laura. "El ascenso de una jerarquía eclesial intransigente, 1890–1914." In *Historia de la Iglesia en el siglo XIX*. Edited by Manuel Ramos Medina, 179–98. Mexico City: Centro de Estudios de Historia de México Condumex, 1998.

——. *De urnas y sotanas: El Partido Católico Nacional en Jalisco*. Mexico City: Consejo Nacional para la Cultura y las Artes, 2001.

Olivera Sedano, Alicia. *Aspectos del conflicto religioso de 1926 a 1929: Sus antecedentes y consecuencias*. Mexico: Instituto Nacional de Antropolgía e Historia, 1966.

Orsi, Robert. *The Madonna of 115th Street: Faith and Community in Italian Harlem, 1880–1950*. New Haven: Yale University Press, 1985.

——. *Thank You, St. Jude: Women's Devotion to the Patron Saint of Hopeless Causes*. New Haven: Yale University Press, 1996.

Overmyer-Velázquez, Mark. "Visions of the Emerald City: Politics, Culture and Alternative Modernities in Oaxaca City, Mexico, 1877–1920." PhD diss., Yale University, 2002.

Paredes Colín, J. *El distrito de Tehuacán: Breve relación de su historia, censo, monumentos aqueológicos, datos estadísticos, geológicos, etnográficos y otros*. Tehuacán: Tipografía "El Refugio," 1921.

Patch, Robert. *Maya Revolt and Revolution in the Eighteenth Century*. Armonk, New York: M. E. Sharpe, 2002.

Pessar, Patricia. "Three Moments in Brazilian Millenarianism: The Inter-relationship between Politics and Religion." *Luso-Brazilian Review* 28, no. 1 (1991): 95–116.

——. *From Fanatics to Folk: Brazil Millenarianism and Popular Culture*. Durham: Duke University Press, 2004.

Piccato, Pablo. *City of Suspects: Crime in Mexico City, 1900–1931*. Durham: Duke University Press, 2001.

Piehl, Mel. "A Wealth of Notions: Rerum Novarum and Its Offspring in America." *Commonweal* 118, no. 9 (1991): 283–88.

Piñon Jiménez, Gonzalo, and Jorge Hernández-Díaz. *El café: Crisis y organización. Los pequeños productores en Oaxaca*. Oaxaca: Instituto de Investigaciones Sociológicas, Universidad Antónoma Benito Juárez de Oaxaca, 1998.

Poole, Deborah. *Vision, Race, and Modernity: A Visual Economy of the Andean Image World*. Princeton: Princeton University Press, 1997.

Pride, Leslie, and Cristino Zorriano. "Jesús, el Diablo y Herodes: Cuento chantino de Panixtlahuaca." *Tlalocán* 10 (1985): 325–36.

Purnell, Jennie. *Popular Movements and State Formation in Revolutionary Mexico: The Agraristas and Cristeros of Michoacán*. Durham: Duke University Press, 1999.

Quirk, Robert E. *The Mexican Revolution and the Catholic Church*. Bloomington: Indiana University Press, 1973.

Real Academia Española. *Diccionario de la lengua española.* 22nd ed., 2 vols. Madrid: Espasa Calpe, 2001.

Redinger, Matthew. *American Catholics and the Mexican Revolution, 1924–1936.* Notre Dame: Notre Dame University Press, 2005.

Restall, Matthew. *The Maya World: Yucatec Culture and Society, 1550–1850.* Stanford: Stanford University Press, 1997.

Ricard, Robert. *The Spiritual Conquest of Mexico.* Berkeley: University of California Press, 1966.

Rodríguez O., Jaime E. "The Conflict between Church and State in Early Republican Mexico." *New World* 2, no. 1 and 2 (1987): 93–112.

Rojas, Basilio. *Miahuatlán: Un pueblo de México.* 3 vols. Mexico City: Editorial Luz, 1958.

Romero Frizzi, María de los Ángeles, ed. *Lecturas históricas del estado de Oaxaca, 1877–1930.* Vol. 4. Mexico City: Instituto Nacional de Antropolgía e Historia, 1990.

Roseberry, William. *Anthropologies and Histories: Essays in Culture, History, and Political Economy.* New Brunswick: Rutgers University Press, 1989.

Rugeley, Terry. *Of Wonders and Wise Men: Religion and Popular Cultures in Southeast Mexico, 1800–1876.* Austin: University of Texas Press, 2001.

Ruiz Cervantes, Francisco José. "Carlos Gracida: Los primeros años difíciles (1914–1919)." In *A Dios lo que es de Dios.* Edited by Carlos Martínez Assad, 99–110. México: Aguilar, 1994.

Sánchez Silva, Carlos. *Crisis política y contrarrevolución en Oaxaca, 1912–1915.* Mexico City: Instituto Nacional de Estudios Históricos de las Revolución de México, 1991.

———. *Indios, comerciantes, y burocracia en la Oaxaca poscolonial, 1760–1860.* Oaxaca: Instituto Oaxaqueño de las Culturas / Fondo Estatal para la Cultura y las Artes / Universidad Autónoma Benito Juárez de Oaxaca, 1998.

Sandstrom, Alan. *Corn Is Our Blood: Culture and Ethnic Identity in a Contemporary Aztec Village.* Norman: University of Oklahoma Press, 1991.

Santamaría, Francisco Javier, and Joaquín García Icazbalceta. *Diccionario de mejicanismos.* Mexico City: Porrúa, 1959.

Schmitt, Karl. "The Díaz Conciliation Policy on State and Local Levels, 1876–1911." *Hispanic American Historical Review* 40, no. 4 (1960): 289–312.

———. "Church and State in Mexico: A Corporatist Relationship." *The Americas* 40, no. 3 (1984): 349–76.

Scott, James. *Domination and the Arts of Resistance: Hidden Transcripts.* New Haven: Yale University Press, 1990.

———. *Seeing Like a State: How Certain Schemes to Improve the Human Condition Have Failed.* New Haven: Yale University Press, 1998.

Sierra, Justo. *Evolución política del pueblo mexicano: Obras completas.* Tomo XII. Mexico City: Universidad Nacional Autónoma de México, 1977.

Sinkin, Richard N. *The Mexican Reform, 1855–1876: A Study in Liberal Nation Building.* Austin: University of Texas Press, 1979.

Smith, Benjamin T. "Cardenismo, Caciques and Catholicism: The Political Process of State Formation in Oaxaca, Mexico, 1928–1947." PhD diss., Cambridge University, 2005.

Stepan, Alfred. *The State and Society: Peru in Comparative Perspective.* Princeton: Princeton University Press, 1978.

Stephen, Lynn, and James Dow, eds. *Class, Politics and Popular Religion in Mexico and Central America.* Washington D.C.: The Society for Latin American Anthropology and the American Anthropology Association, 1990.

Stern, Steve J. *The Secret History of Gender: Women, Men, and Power in Late Colonial Mexico.* Chapel Hill: University of North Carolina Press, 1995.

Tavárez, David. "Colonial Evangelization and Native Resistance: The Interplay of Native Political Autonomy and Ritual Practices in Villa Alta, 1700–1704." In *Interpreting Colonialism.* Edited by Byron Wells and Philip Stewart, 209–30. Oxford: The Voltaire Foundation, 2004.

———. "Autonomy, Honor, and the Ancestors: Native Local Religion in Seventeenth-Century Oaxaca." In *Local Religion in Colonial Mexico.* Edited by Martin Nesvig, 119–54. Albuquerque: University of New Mexico Press, 2006.

Taylor, William B. *Landlord and Peasant in Colonial Oaxaca.* Stanford: Stanford University Press, 1972.

———. *Magistrates of the Sacred: Priests and Parishioners in Eighteenth-Century Mexico.* Stanford: Stanford University Press, 1996.

Tenorio-Trillo, Mauricio. *Mexico at the World's Fairs: Crafting a Modern Nation.* Berkeley: University of California Press, 1996.

Thompson, Guy. "Popular Aspects of Liberalism in Mexico, 1848–1888." *Bulletin of Latin American Research* 10, no. 3 (1991): 265–92.

———. "The Ceremonial and Political Role of Village Bands, 1846–1974." In *Rituals of Rule, Rituals of Resistance: Public Celebrations and Popular Culture in Mexico.* Edited by William H. Beezley, Cheryl English Martin, William E. French, 307–42. Wilmington, Del.: Scholarly Resources, 1994.

Thompson, Guy, and David LaFrance. *Patriotism, Politics and Popular Liberalism in Nineteenth-Century Mexico.* Wilmington, Del.: Scholarly Resources, 1999.

Toro, Alfonso. *La Iglesia y el Estado en México.* Mexico City: Talleres Gráficos de la Nación, 1927.

Torres Bautista, Marianno E. "Notas para la microhistoria de Tehuacán." In *Simposium internacional Tehuacán y su entorno: Balance y perspectivas.* Edited by Eréndida de la Lama, 291–98. Mexico City: Instituto Nacional de Antropolgía e Historia, 1997.

Toulmin, Stephen. *Cosmopolis: The Hidden Agenda of Modernity.* New York: Free Press, 1990.

Traffano, Daniela. "Indios, curas, y nación: La sociedad indígena frente un proceso de secularización: Oaxaca, siglo XIX." PhD diss., El Colegio de México, 2000.

Turner, Victor. *Dramas, Fields, and Metaphors: Symbolic Action in Human Society*. Ithaca: Cornell University Press, 1974.

———. *From Ritual to Theatre: The Human Seriousness of Play*. New York: Performing Arts Journal Publications, 1982.

———. *The Ritual Process: Structure and Anti-Structure*. New York: Aldine De Gruyter, 1969.

Turner, Victor, and Edith Turner. *Image and Pilgrimage in Christian Culture: Anthropological Perspectives*. New York: Columbia University Press, 1978.

Tutino, John. *From Insurrection to Revolution in Mexico: Social Bases of Agrarian Violence, 1750–1940*. Princeton: Princeton University Press, 1986.

Van Young, Eric. "Millennium on the Northern Marches: The Mad Messiah of Durango and Popular Rebellion in Mexico, 1800–1815." *Comparative Studies in Society and History* 28, no. 3 (1986): 385–413.

———. "The Raw and the Cooked: Elite and Popular Ideology in Mexico, 1800–1821." In *The Middle Period in Latin America*. Edited by Mark D. Szuchman, 75–102. Boulder: Lynne Rienner Publishers, 1989.

———. "The Cuautla Lazarus: Double Subjectives in Reading Texts on Popular Collective Action." *Colonial Latin American Review* 2 (1993): 3–26.

———. "The Messiah and the Masked Man: Popular Ideology in Mexico, 1810–21." In *Indigenous Responses to Western Christianity*. Edited by Steven Kaplan, 144–74. New York: New York University Press, 1995.

———. *The Other Rebellion: Popular Violence, Ideology, and the Mexican Struggle for Independence, 1810–1921*. Stanford: Stanford University Press, 2001.

Vanderwood, Paul. "Using the Present to Study the Past: Religious Movements in Mexico and Uganda a Century Apart." *Mexican Studies* 10, no. 1 (1994): 99–134.

———. *The Power of God against the Guns of Government: Religious Upheaval in Mexico at the Turn of the Century*. Stanford: Stanford University Press, 1998.

———. *Juan Soldado: Rapist, Murderer, Martyr, Saint*. Durham: Duke University Press, 2004.

Vélez Pliego, Roberto. "Tehuacán: Caso disímil en la estructura agraria poblana, 1905." In *Simposium internacional Tehuacán y su entorno: Balance y perspectivas*. Edited by Eréndida de la Lama, 299–311. Mexico City: Instituto Nacional de Antropolgía e Historia, 1997.

Viqueira Albán, Juan Pedro. *Propriety and Permissiveness in Bourbon Mexico*. Translated by Sonya Lipsett-Rivera and Sergio Rivera Ayala. Wilmington, Del.: Scholarly Resources, 1999.

Voekel, Pamela. *Alone before God: The Religious Origins of Modernity in Mexico*. Durham: Duke University Press, 2002.

Watanabe, John. *Maya Saints and Souls in a Changing World*. Austin: University of Texas Press, 1980.

Winter, Marcus, Margarita Gaxiola and Gilberto Hernández, *Comparaciones arqueolóicas de la Cañada, la Mixteca Alta, el Valle de Oaxaca y el Valle de Tehuacan*. Estudios de antropología e historia, no. 1. Oaxaca: Centro Regional de Oaxaca Instituto Nacional de Antropología e Historia, 1977.

Wolf, Eric R. "Types of Latin-American Peasantry: A Preliminary Discussion." *American Ethnologist* 57 (1955): 452–71.

——. "Closed Corporate Peasant Communities in Mesoamerica and Java." *Southwestern Journal of Anthropology* 13 (1957): 1–18.

Worsley, Peter. *The Trumpet Shall Sound: A Study of "Cargo" Cults in Melanesia*. New York: Schocken Books, 1968.

Wright-Rios, Edward. "Indian Saints and Nation-States: Ignacio Manuel Altamirano's Landscapes and Legends." *Mexican Studies/Estudios Mexicanos* 20, no. 1 (2004): 47–68.

Yescas Martínez, Isidoro. "El sacerdote que desafió la voluntad de Dios: El caciquismo de Cornelio Bourget en Oaxaca." In *A Dios lo que es de Dios*. Carlos Martínez Assad, 183–94. México: Aguilar, 1994.

Bolaños, Bartola (*continued*)
messenger, 165; as a healer, 164,
186, 203, 277; legacy of, 203–5,
285–87; Miltepec denunciation
and, 165–67, 170, 175, 180; miracles
and, 167–69

*Boletín Oficial y Revista Ecclesiástica
de Antequera*, 50, 67, 94, 100–101,
120

Bourbon reforms, 24

Bourget, Cornelio, 327 n. 58

Bricker, Victoria Reifler, 330 n. 9

Caciques, 307 n. 27

Calles, Plutarco Elías, 20, 208

Camacho, Manuel Ávila, 20

Campos y Ángeles, Francisco, 200–
202, 204, 275, 328 n. 81

Canseco, Ausencio, 211, 216, 219–39,
245–48, 253–56, 261–69, 280;
background, 226–28; biases of,
248, 264–65; dispute between Narváez and, 220–21, 224–26, 237–
38, 267–68; Nicha and, 230–36,
248, 265–69; Virgin of Ixpantepec
and, 222, 224–26, 230–37, 246–
48

Canseco, Francisco Diez, 117–18

Capitalism, 8, 10,16, 24

Cargo system, 22, 60, 101, 147, 268

Carranza, Venustiano, 20, 213–14

Castellanos, Aureo, 229, 264

Catholic church, 2, 7, 9–10, 14–15,
33; European transformation, 8, 10,
11. *See also* Mexican Catholicism

Catholic Workers' Circle (Oaxaca),
66–67, 74, 86, 120

Cervantes, Fernando, 278

Cervantes Bolaños, Pablo, 186, 189–
90, 202

Chatino Revolt (1986), 219–20, 227,
306 n. 23

Christian, William, 29, 35, 57

Christianity, 11–13. *See also* Catholic
church; Mexican Catholicism

Christ of Etla. *See* Señor de las Peñas
(Etla)

Christ of Tlacoxcalco. *See* Lord of the
Wounds (Tlacoxcalco)

Church-state relations, 9, 13–14, 32–
33, 35, 208, 254, 258, 267, 275; Chatinos and, 220; Díaz and, 18–19, 50

Class and Catholic identity, 8

Clergy: clerical fees, 15; influence of, 9;
parishioners and, 18–19, 21, 41,
57–58, 194, 277–78, 316 n 41;
women and, 267–68

Colegio Pío Latinoamericano (CPL),
65–66

Congregación del Catequismo (Con-
gregacion of the Catechism), 120–
22, 173

Conservatism, 16, 60, 78

Constitution of 1857, 16, 18, 213, 258

Constitution of 1917, 19–20, 209,
285

Conversion, 11, 13

Coronations, 36

Cortés, Hilario, 211, 216–19, 221,
239–41, 244–48, 255

CPL. *See* Colegio Pío Latinoamericano
(CPL)

Cristiada/Cristero Revolt (1926–29),
20–21, 208–9, 211–17, 261

Cures, 37, 141, 186, 233–34, 287, 319
n. 29, 326 n. 46

Davies, Susan, 80

Dávila, José Inés, 213–14

Devotions, 31, 47, 82, 159, 162, 308
n. 36, 330 n. 9; gender dynamics of,
260–69; promotion of, 113, 311
n. 64. *See also* specific Virgins

Díaz, Félix, 213

Díaz, Porfirio, 18–19, 50–51, 53, 56,
63, 102, 213

Dionisia. *See* Nicha
Duarte, Luis, 255–56, 259–63

Echeverría, Agustín, 95–96
Education. *See* Religious education
Espinoza, Agustín, 194, 215
Ethnography, 21–23
Etla Christ. *See* Señor de las Peñas
(Etla)
Excommunication, 59

Feasts, 19, 57, 332 n. 19
Fiesta costs, 297 n. 24

Galíndez, José Mariano, 53
Gijón, Octavio, 115
Gillow, Eulogio y Zavalza (Archbishop), *46*, 101, *107*, 226–27, 272–
79, *273*; background, 61–62; biography of, 50; exile of, 71; indigenous
people and, 49–51, 78, 91–94, 108–
9, 297 n. 30; indigenous practices
and, 113–17, 165; lay associations
and, 107–13, 117–29, 304–5 n. 11;
legacy of, 48, 51, 63–65, 71–72,
275–77, 284; Lord of the Wounds
and, 165, 188, 191–93; on Oaxacan
martyrs, 49, 82–85, 300 n. 19; as a
politician, 50, 62, 65, 114–15; questionnaires and, 4, 117–18, 130–35,
141–42, 149–51; reform program
of, 44, 63–64, 68–69, 72, 98–137,
282–85; religious message of, 64;
shrines and, 115–17, 308 n. 36; Vatican ties of, 49–50, 62–63, 65, 84,
98–100, 120, 275; Virgin of Guadalupe and, 85–87; Virgin of Juquila
and, 89–90; Virgin of Solitude and,
45–48, 75–82, 91–93; writings of,
49, 68–70, 106, 121–22, 274, 304
n. 11, 306 n. 23
González, Vincente, 109
Good Press Society. *See* Sociedad de la
Buena Prensa

Grace, visions as, 32
Gracida, Carlos, 165, 188, 190–93,
214–15, 229, 275, 300 n. 17
Gracida, Everardo, 195–201
Greenberg, James, 249, 330 n. 11
Guerra, Madre, 256–57

Hernández, Francisco, 150–51, 161
Hispanization, 13
Hobsbawm, Eric, 80
Holston, James, 28
Huerta, Victoriano, 19, 112, 214
Hybridity, 12

Identity: Catholic, 8; of indigenous
community, 148, 275; social, 80
Idolatry, 49–50, 55, 83–84, 107, 197,
209, 230
Iglesias, Esther, 195
Images, 184–85, 301–2 n. 31, 317 n. 4
Indigenous community, 148, 275, 294
n. 47; Gillow and, 49–51, 64, 78,
91–94, 108–9, 113–17, 165, 297
n. 30; indoctrination of, 78, 306
n. 23; Marian devotion and, 78–79;
Mexican Catholicism and, 7, 22, 306
n. 23; pilgrimages and, 93–97
Individual autonomy, 24
Institutionalism, 101–9

Jesuits, 61–62
Jesús, Felipe de, 62
John Paul II (Pope), 84
Juárez, Benito, 51, 53, 55–56

Knight, Alan, 280
Kselman, Thomas, 33, 261

Labastida y Dávalos (Archbishop),
62–63, 68, 83, 85
Lady of Lourdes. *See* Virgin of Lourdes
Languages, 12, 318 n. 14
Larraín, Jorge, 24
Latin American Pious College. *See*
Colegio Pío Latinoamericano (CPL)

Miramar, Julián María, 141
Modernity: apparition movements and, 23–24, 32; Catholic church and, 9–10; fight against, 9; influence of, 24–27; Mexican Catholicism and, 25–27, 45; secular, 259
Muriel, Josefina, 331 n. 25

Napoleon III, 17
Nápoles, Luis, 141–43, 151–56, *152*, 160, 276, 278; Lord of the Wounds and, 169–70, 172, 176–81, 186–87, 191
Narváez, Matilde, 2, 274–76; background, 211, 218–19, 220–26; dispute with Canseco, 220–21, 224–26, 237–38, 267–68; legacy of, 285, 287–88; Madre Matiana and, 256, 261–64; Nicha and, 218, 221–26, 231, 234, 246–48, 263; Virgin of Ixpantepec and, 221–25, 231, 237–39, 245–47, 254
National Catholic Congresses, 67, 73, 92, 109, 298 n. 41, 310 n. 55
National Catholic Party. *See* Partido Católico Nacional (PCN)
Nationalism: ascendancy of, 8; Creole, 78; Mexican Catholicism and, 26, 78
Nation-states, 7–8
Nicha, 207–11, 218–20, 238–40, 261–64, 276; Canseco and, 230–36, 248, 265–69; early visions of, 243–45, 252–54; legacy of, 243, 287–88; Narváez and, 218, 221–26, 231, 234, 246–48, 263; as second Juan Diego, 209–11, 240, 243, 269; visionary tradition and, 249–52
Núñez y Zárate, José Othón, 66–67, 86, 299 n. 1; Lord of the Wounds and, 195, 197, 200–202

Oaxaca, *54*: Catholic institutionalism in, 102–9; Cristiada and, 211–17; economy of, 52–53, 212; foundations of Mexican Catholicism and, 6, 43, 52–60; laity in, 58, 283; lay associations in, 98–137; martyr narrative in, 82–83; Mexican Revolution and, 211–17; model church and, 60–72; pilgrimages in, 86–87, 301 n. 31; reforms, 44, 55–58, 63–64, 68–69, 72, 98–137, 282–85; seminary, 68–69, *69*; spirit loci, 331 n. 15
Obregón, Álvaro, 20, 208, 214
Ortiz, Ignacio, 122
Osorio, Rafael, 137
Our Lady of Lourdes. *See* Virgin of Lourdes

Pagan resistance school, 11
Palacios, Isidoro, 200
Papal infallibility, 9
Paredes Colín, Joaquín, 193–94
Partido Católico Nacional (PCN), 70, 298–99 n. 52
Pentecostalism, Jamaican, 29
Pía Unión, 111
Piety: continuum of, 149–63; modeling, 60–72
Pilgrimages, 30; Oaxacan, 86–87, 93–97. *See also* specific Virgins
Pious Union. *See* Pía Unión
Pius IX (Pope), 9, 33, 61–62, 65, 110
Pius X (Pope), 78, 87, 303 n. 53
Plancarte y Labastida, José Antonio, 85
Populations: growth, 8; nation-states and, 7
Press, Catholic, 50, 66, 70, 94–97, 102, 120, 309 n. 50. *See also Voz de la Verdad, La*
Priests. *See* Clergy
Privatization of church properties, 17, 56
Public worship, banned, 20, 322 n. 19
Pulido, Teresita, 317 n. 4
Puros. See under Liberalism

Valencia, Antonio de P., 194–99, 202, 320 n. 51

Vásquez, Genaro V., 215

Vásquez, Justina, 235–36, 266, 269, 323 n. 32

Velasco, J., 188–89

Vatican: directives, 47–48, 98–100; First Council (1869–70), 9; Gillow ties to, 49–50, 62–63, 65, 84, 98–100, 120, 275; on Mexican sovereignty, 14–15

Violence: liberal-conservative, 258; in Oaxaca, 55–56

Virgin of Guadalupe, 36, 48, 82, 85–87, 91, 123–24, 151, 210

Virgin of Ixpantepec (Virgen de Ixpantepec), 6, 7, 26, 210–11, 242–69; Chatino culture and, 249–53, 267; devotions, 221, 224, 225–26, 263; evidence, 223, 235, 271–76, 288; grotto experiences, 232–33; Narváez on, 221–22; pilgrimages, 224; wrath of God and, 257. *See also* Nicha

Virgin of Juquila, 87–90, *89,* 242–43

Virgin of Lourdes, 31, 33, 62–63, 82, 85, 157, 179, 182–83

Virgin of Ocotlán, 90

Virgin of Solitude (Virgen de la Sol-edad): coronation of, 73–97, *81;* coronation parade and, 75–76, *77;* crown of, 78, 82; Gillow and, 45–48, *46,* 75–82, 91–93; as Oaxaca's patroness, 44–45; pilgrimages, 74, 93–97; purpose of coronation, 79–82

Visions. *See* Apparitions

Voz de la Verdad, La, 67; on Chatino Rebellion, 306 n. 23; emergence of; on Juquila's *feria,* 88; on PCN, 298–99 n. 52; on pilgrimages, 94–97

War of the Pants (1896). *See* Chatino Revolt (1896)

War of the Reform (1858-61), 17

Wars of Independence (1810-21), 21

Women: Catholic activism, 261–64, 267, 285; Catholic church on, 284; in lay associations, 104, 106, 133, 134–37; preferred agents, 263; public sphere agency, 26, 33–35; religious orders as suppressed, 17; visions of, 264–69

Workers' syndicates, Catholic, 66–67, 103

Zorrilla, Federico, 74

Zorrilla, Francisco, 220, 324 n. 38

EDWARD WRIGHT-RIOS is an Assistant Professor in the Department of History at Vanderbilt University.

Library of Congress Cataloging-in-Publication Data

Wright-Rios, Edward N. (Edward Newport), 1965–
Revolutions in Mexican Catholicism : reform and revelation
in Oaxaca, 1887–1934 / Edward Wright-Rios.
p. cm.
Includes bibliographical references and index.
ISBN 978-0-8223-4357-8 (cloth : alk. paper) —
ISBN 978-0-8223-4379-0 (pbk. : alk. paper)
1. Catholic Church—Mexico—Oaxaca (State)—
   History—19th century.
2. Catholic Church—Mexico—Oaxaca (State)—
   History—20th century.
3. Catholic Church—Mexico—History—19th century.
4. Catholic Church—Mexico—History—20th century.
I. Title.
BX1429.O2W75 2009
282'.727409034—dc22
2008052619